# Visualizing Landscape Architecture

ELKE MERTENS

# Visualizing Landscape Architecture

FUNCTIONS | CONCEPTS | STRATEGIES

BASEL • BOSTON • BERLIN

BIRKHÄUSER

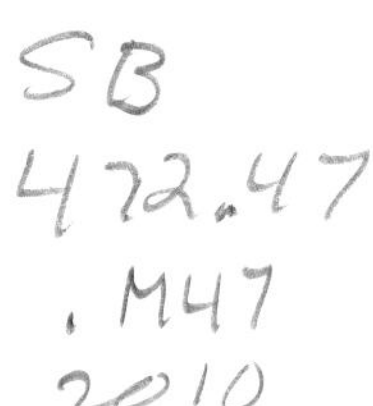

# CONTENTS

## Editorial Note

The illustrations used as examples were numbered to correspond with the three parts of the book. The illustration numbers are quoted in the text where explanations refer to individual figures specifically. Short explanations were integrated into the picture captions. The practices who provided the illustrations are identified in the captions; if several illustrations attached to the same project from the same practice follow each other in sequence, they are identified in the caption for the first illustration.

In the extensive chapters in the Functions section, the introductory passages are accompanied by small emblematic sketches, which refer to particular statements in the text. They were kindly supplied by Jan and Jens Steinberg, Berlin, and are to be interpreted as follows:

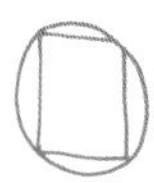
Plane

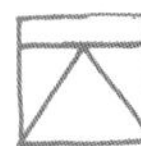
Space

Time

Hand drawing

Vegetation

Key statement

Man

# PREFACE

"We are not selling a garden or a park. We are selling the image of a garden or a park. The image has to have an impact." (plancontext, April 2007)

Images of any kind are the primary language used by landscape architects to represent ideas and persuade people. They show us the future of open spaces and the environment – part of the future of our society. The ability of landscape architects to express themselves in plans, pictures and visualizations is understandably envied by those working in other disciplines. The basis for this book was a desire for a compilation, overview, description and analysis of visualizations (in the broad sense of the word) used to represent and communicate ideas and solutions for landscape architecture projects.

This desire grew out of my own design work and many years spent teaching in Berlin and in Neubrandenburg, Germany. Numerous conversations with colleagues revealed a broad base of support for the idea, which ultimately came to fruition. The plans and perspectives, models and schematic drawings, simulations and films used both as a basis for work and as examples have aesthetic power as well as communicative ability, with the result that working on this book has given great pleasure, which will hopefully be shared by the reader. This may take time; many pictures will become more interesting the more they are studied, and some details only become apparant gradually.

In this description and analysis of plans and pictures as visual communication tools, the emphasis is not on individual projects and firms (as it so often is in landscape architecture publications), but on the great diversity allowed by the available techniques. This is a demonstration of how different and highly individual a design can be, and also of how personal and individual its representation can be. Of course, the images are not completely isolated from the projects and their authors, and this is why they are mentioned in the captions to each illustration. After the basic functions of presentations in two, three and four dimensions have been introduced, the second part of the book shows their specific use in competitions and the planning and design process. A landscape architect has to work with people in mind, and influence nature and the environment in a forward-looking, sustainable way. Images can communicate the wide perspective, both in terms of space and time, in a compelling way, and visual presentation of alternatives can also support an open and democratic planning process – as their use for specific strategic planning goals in the preceding section of this book impressively demonstrates.

This book presents representation techniques in common use today, in a broad cross-section. How these will develop in future and which techniques will come to be used more frequently, remains to be seen. It is safe to say that films (examples of which are included in this book) will play a greater role in future, but we can only wait in anticipation to see which approaches will dominate.

I would like to thank all my colleagues and all firms involved for their willingness to make their own work available to me. I was able to conduct extensive conversations with many of them, thereby gaining insights which have influenced the text of this book, as well as valuable advice on arranging and structuring the contents. I cannot stress the effort involved for all the firms and individuals represented here too much. In particular, they had to deal with many questions and requests from me during the book's genesis. As they are not represented by visual examples, I would like to thank Professor Erich Buhmann and Thies Schröder at this point for their valuable advice, as well as Dr. Gabriele Holst for her works on creative design.

Regarding the transformation of my ideas into the final concept for the book, I would like to thank Andreas Müller for his long and patient work as an editor and partner in detailed discussions. I would also like to thank Oliver Kleinschmidt for his commitment to making the idea of this book – a book about visual presentation in which the visual material is suitably presented – a reality. Last not least I would like to thank Michael Robinson and Alison Kirkland for the congenial translation.

# INTRODUCTION

Landscape architects develop ideas for changing places and landscapes with the intention of improving their design, making them better to use and more able to meet ecological requirements. Their work includes comprehensive and sustainable planning of the environment as it is lived in, and reconciling the different demands for creating open spaces capable of facing the future. The design process as an essential part of landscape architects' activities includes both finding ideas and also presenting them visually. Landscape design is first and foremost a problem-solving strategy for open areas and open spaces. Images, sketches, plans and other drawings as well as models are produced, using a variety of techniques, with the aim to convey concrete planning intentions or possible consequences of developments that can occur under certain conditions. A written explanation is usually provided to support the strategies presented, but this could never be an adequate substitute for a visual presentation. As visual presentations are universally understood, their significance and statements largely make sense without words, a great advantage in a globalized world.

Plans and images also remain – and this is perhaps particularly true today because so many possibilities are available – unique objects, each with its own justification. Even though they are prepared in large numbers for any planning process, each one has its own statement to make, and is potentially interesting, exciting, harmonious, aesthetic or simply beautiful to look at. Even though the large numbers of visual presentations might suggest something different, landscape architects work economically: images are not prepared for their own sake, but because of the statement that each one makes.

Gabriele Holst, Vertical Rhythm III.

# Conveying ideas and planning aims in plans and images

Great demands are made on images intended to convey ideas that occur in planners' minds. They have to be precise, to a certain extent, in presenting the elements of the concept; they have to be comprehensible, sometimes for laymen as well; and at the same time they have to convey the planners' professional expertise. Also, such presentations give an idea of the creative designers' attitude to the social use of open spaces, to the development of nature and the environment and thus to the discipline's current state of mind. Landscape architecture is essentially a practice-oriented discipline in which theoretical considerations traditionally play a subordinate role in looking back at past achievements and the conditions under which they came into being. It is only in recent times that the general conditions for each planning process have been more carefully analysed, but this hardly produces a theory on concrete procedures in the sense of instructions about an approach, either for the planning itself or how it is presented visually. It is much more that a clearer understanding is created about how the planning measures fit in with prevailing social conditions and meet particular challenges. The planning itself and the way it is presented seem to be affected by these reflections to an astonishingly limited extent.

Conventions exist for presenting plans and images, but there is also a great deal of freedom, which means that the way they are presented develops constantly, adapting to the technical possibilities, and also determined to a certain extent by current trends. The creative approach has to be subjective to a certain extent, as design also expresses the author's individual views of solutions and creative ideas. Therefore, visual presentations are always a personal expression of the people involved in relation to the planning commission.

Just as the design itself has to be up to date, the graphic devices used to express it must be, too. They may even need to be so far ahead of their times as to use the very latest resources, which may be available only to some designers. The range of possibilities is greater than ever, today. Two-dimensional drawings are still used, and so are the familiar ways of drawing three-dimensional images. And thanks to what modern computers have to offer, it has become easier to present time as the forth dimension more powerfully in visual form: for example in terms of changing seasons, by showing the plants getting older, or in the form of walks, drives or flights through or over the planned terrain.

Using computers has largely taken over from the hand drawings that used to be found exclusively. Critical voices say that all plans tend to look the same. However, the presentations are very diverse and different, because computer programs offer so many possibilities, hand drawings are still used, and also because there is more competition within the discipline. Plans are revised much more frequently at ever shorter intervals, and conveying material comprehensibly and clearly is increasingly emphasized.

This book analyses plans and a wide range of presentation modes currently used in terms of their expressiveness and ability to convince. The point of departure are the types of images used to make statements about the future development of places. This makes it possible to discern trends and anticipated developments. Illustrations are also used to guide and direct people's behaviour towards ideas of sustainable development, as shall be shown in the last sections of this book.

After a short look at the historical development of presentation methods, "Finding ideas and forms", gives examples of how visual presentations emerge in the context of the creative process. These are changed and reassessed a great deal in-house before they point to a solution that finally sums up the ideas and presents all the requirements in a balanced fashion. In contrast with these, the pictures and plans shown in the other parts of the book are intended to present the proposed design or planning solution, and as a rule outsiders are shown and discuss only these. Almost all the illustrations used here were made available by landscape architects from their ongoing projects, so that they have to be considered in the context and as part of the current planning processes. It should be noted that they are usually shown here in reduced form, so that their expressive values may not always be fully appreciated.

Every visual presentation, whether it is drawn up as a plan, view, simulation or as part of a film has its own particular part to play within a planning process. In the first part, "Functions", they are considered in three groups as representations of the second, third and forth dimension. Here the illustrations are analysed and interrogated individually about their potentials, while the second part introduces "Concepts" relating to how they work together in various planning processes. The last part focuses on "Strategies" that do not simply address concrete planning for specific locations, but also contribute to facing society in future with the resources of landscape architecture, both its professional expertise and also its presentational methods. This is about a holistic approach to living conditions and the future of landscape, and about suitable methods for implementing democratic understanding of planning. In this context, visual presentations serve to stimulate planning decisions, they can draw attention to conditions and dangers, and show how the world we live in can be developed.

# Presentation methods in the past

Plans have been drawn ever since gardens went beyond growing fruit and vegetable to serve as representative places. The surviving depictions are usually of the situations as found or completed, rather than design plans for future developments. The fundamental modes of representation used in contemporary landscape architecture have essentially been in use since the first plans were drawn, though materials and the technology supporting them have developed enormously. Here we intend to show some basic presentation types for different gardens and other projects from earlier centuries, focusing on the techniques they use.

The oldest known garden images come from Egypt. Typical drawings have come down to us, some of them copied only recently in a known older style. As well as general views showing work in gardens that are not part of a design process, some actual plans have survived. They show the site, its boundaries and the precise positioning of the individual elements in two-dimensional presentations. In contrast with the way we look at things today, a plan like the one shown here seems difficult to understand, as the trees are not presented as a top view of the crown from above, but in their elevation. This special feature, whose proportionality is particularly striking in comparison with plans from later eras in which this kind of presentation was also used, makes it possible to provide information about the trees which would not be possible in a top view, such as their species, for example. The planting arrangements are very easy to understand, and so is the positioning of the pools of water needed for irrigation. The scale, an essential feature of ground plans today, is not given on known Egyptian plans. The buildings are often drawn much too small, which can underline the importance of a garden.

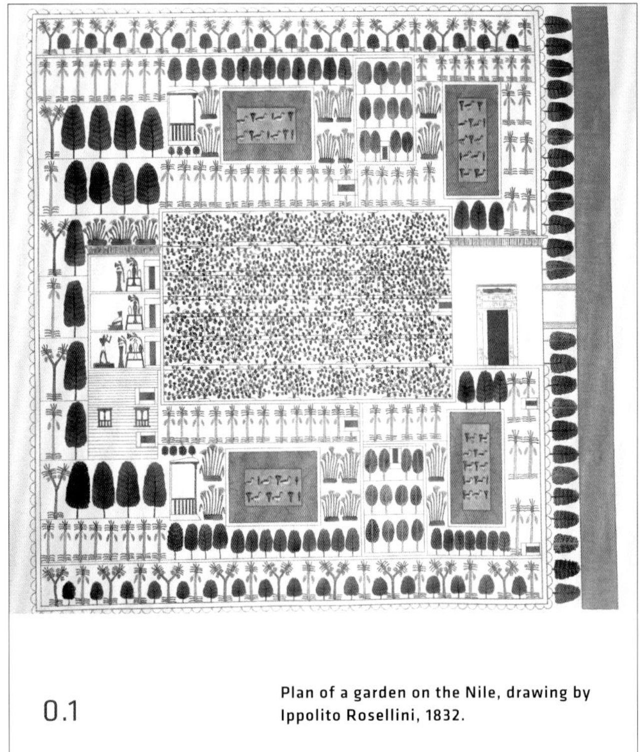

0.1 Plan of a garden on the Nile, drawing by Ippolito Rosellini, 1832.

0.2 Axonometric view of Schloss Uranienbaum on the island of Hveen, where Tycho Brahe lived and worked for twenty years. Copperplate engraving, coloured by Joan Blaeu, 1663.

This drawing of a garden on the Nile (Ill. 0.1) was not produced until 1832, but it does show the garden in the ancient Egyptian way. The trees are drawn individually in frontal view in rows, above and next to each other in the ground plan of this almost square garden. This presentation method, unusual for the modern eye, means that different kinds of trees and their different sizes can be distinguished. Certainly the colouring is freely invented, but it does tend towards the usual colours of nature, which correspond with common ideas: green for the crowns, brown for the tree trunks, blue for the water, red for the buildings and a white background for the ground surface covering. The garden is enclosed by a wall and arranged symmetrically, and the plants are largely placed symmetrically as well. Most of the trees are shown from the viewers' angle, only the row on the right by the river is drawn sideways. It is to be assumed that the bottoms of the tree trunks mark the tree positions, and that the trees are then "tilted" to fit the image so that the elements do not overlap. Overall, the plan conveys a lucid and precise impression of the garden.

A coloured copperplate engraving by Joan Blaeu, a Dutch engraver, of Tycho Brahe's observatory at the Uranienbaum palace and its garden, dating from 1663 (Ill. 0.2), is an example of axonometry, a drawing method that is still used frequently today. Working on the basis of the ground plan, the enclosing walls, including the towers and gates; the trees and the pavilions in the garden; and the observatory in the middle of the picture are all tilted in the same direc-

0.3

**Bassin d'Apollon, park of the Palace of Versailles, copperplate engraving by Gabriel Perelle, c. 1670.**

tion and presented as oblique images. As the ground plan of the whole area is square, this kind of drawing achieves a spatial effect if the drawing is positioned so that one corner points in each direction. Like all axonometries, the image is drawn without perspective distortion. All visible vertical elements cast a shadow to the right, which further enhances the three-dimensional effect. Because they are so precise in detail, copperplate engravings can also reproduce individual elements.

A scene from the park in the Palace of Versailles (Ill. 0.3) presents the idea of the Baroque garden in ideal form. This is also a copperplate engraving, but executed as a bird's-eye view in central perspective. The eye is drawn along the central axis from the first terrace, on which a series of people and horses, and indeed coaches, are moving around, drawn in some detail, over the first pool of water, the second terrace and the canal with the three-masted ship and other boats to the horizon. The dramaturgy of the image reflects the self-perception of the absolute monarch. Power over tamed nature and human affluence is presented on an immeasurable scale. This is not a plan, not a design idea, but an idealized representation of the garden after it had been laid out. No plans survive for many gardens of the past, they were often of little interest once the project was completed.

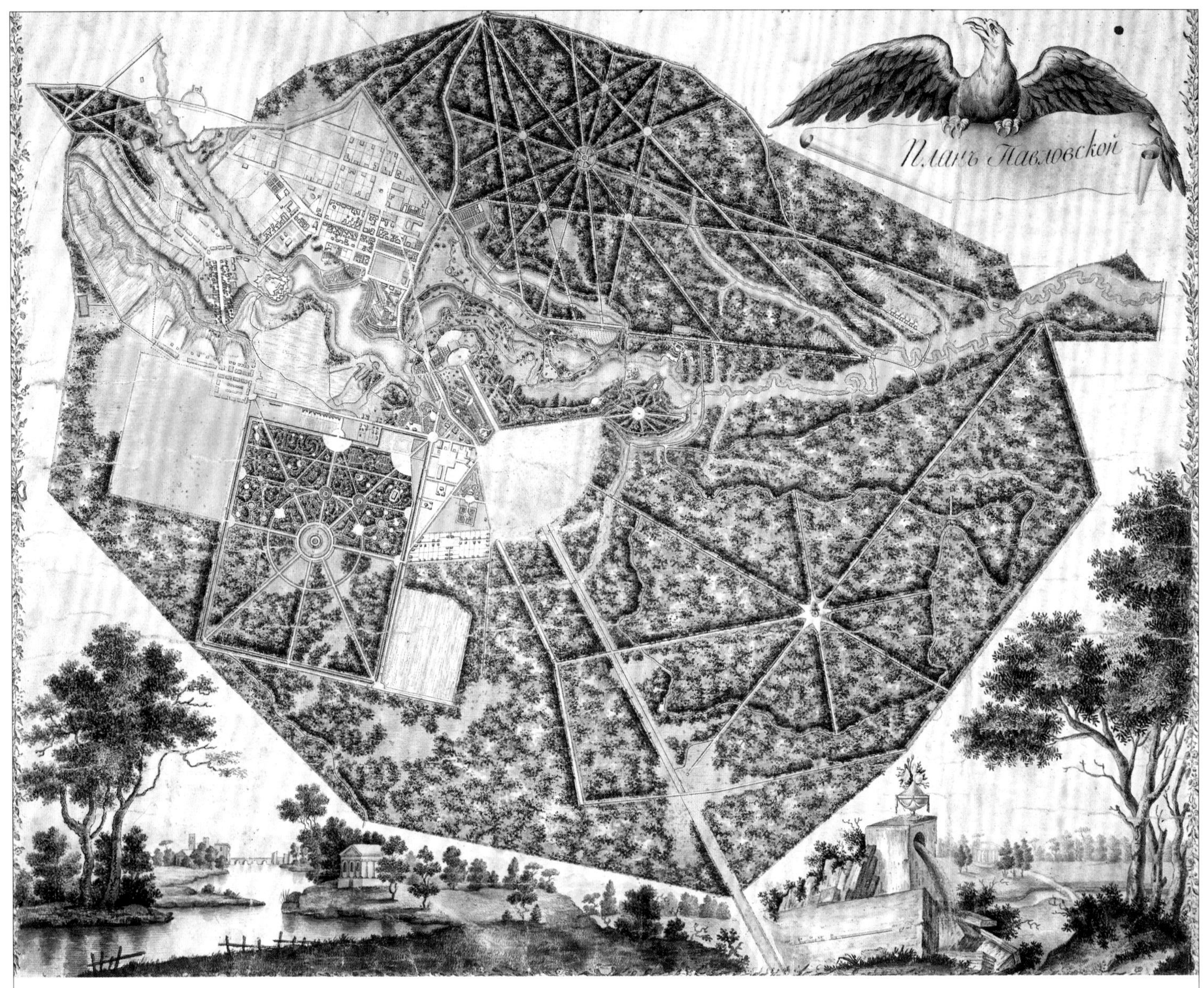


0.4

Pavlovsk Palace park near St. Petersburg, design by Charles Cameron, water-colour and ink on paper, c. 1780.

0.5

**Adam fountain in the Peterhof Palace park near St. Petersburg, water colour by Vasily Ivanovich Bajenov, 1796.**

This example by Charles Cameron for the Pavlovsk Palace park (Ill. 0.4) dating from 1780 is a hand drawing in ink and water-colour. The central garden plan is in the form of a two-dimensional drawing, while below individual details from the garden are drawn in perspective. The elements of the plan are executed in great detail, and the plan is given an overall three-dimensional quality by a light shading of the timber structures; however, no cast shadows are shown, which could have unduly shaded the ground area. The perspective drawings add the missing third dimension and convey an impression of the place's atmosphere. But even so they seem to have been added to fill the sheet; this could even be their main *raison d'être*, as their size has been adapted to fit the edges of the sheet outside the ground plan. The decorations of the sheet on the left- and right-hand side also support this assumption, as they are irrelevant to the planning.

This drawing of the Adam fountain in Pavlovsk (Ill. 0.5) by Vasily Ivanovich Bajenov dating from 1796 combines the three-dimensional ground plan drawing with a two-dimensional view in order to convey a complete impression of the design. The sectional view reveals that the intersection line runs through the centre of the fountain and across the square. Only the sectional view can show how the fountain is framed. The two drawings are contingent upon each other, on their own they present only partial views. The irregular quality of the water-colour and the sky as a background for the sectional view make this drawing look almost three-dimensional, despite precision in all its individual parts. The vertical division of the image, measuring 69 x 52 cm in the original, approximates to the proportions of the golden mean, with the ground plan as the larger area below and the sectional view as a smaller area above. Sectional views often accompany ground plans today, but usually as independent illustrations and not, as in this example, placed together to form a single image.

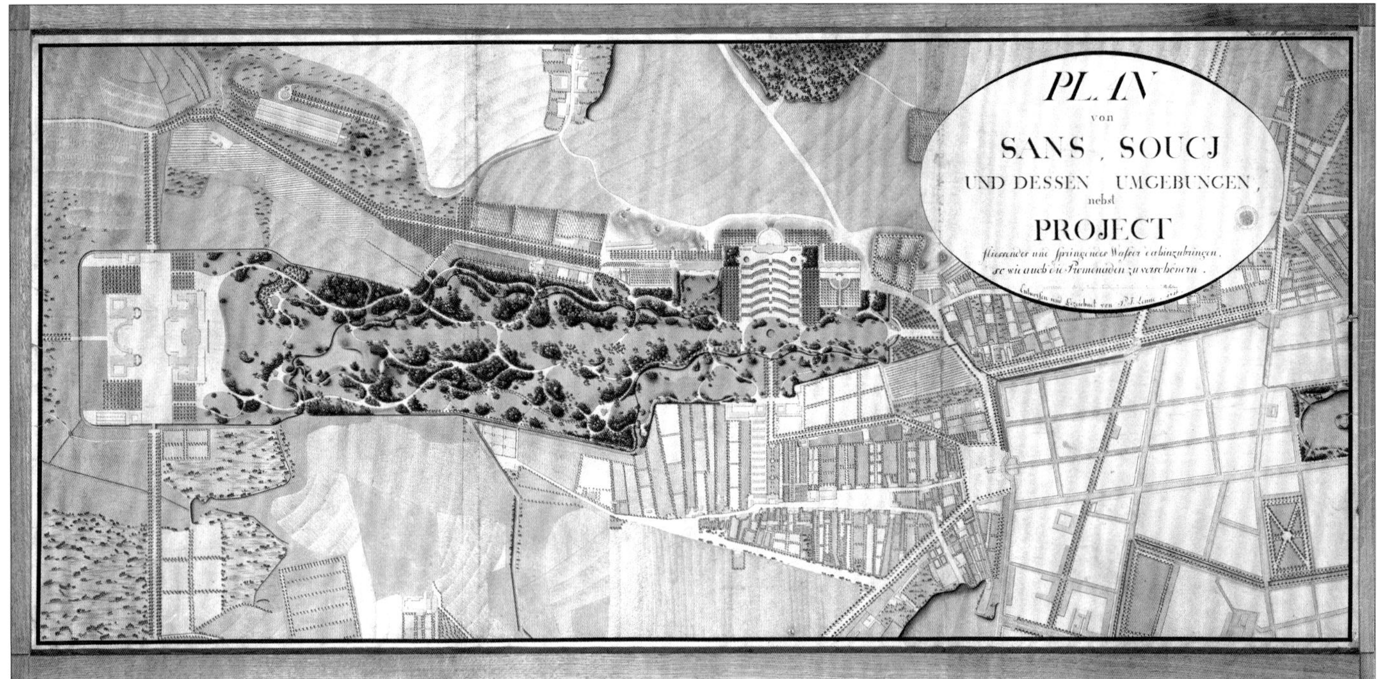


0.6

**Plan of Sanssouci and surroundings including the project of introducing flowing waters and fountains and of embellishing the promenade ways, Peter Joseph Lenné, 1816.**

This plan of Potsdam-Sanssouci and its environs (Ill. 0.6) by Peter Joseph Lenné dating from 1816 shows the design of the park and its surroundings, including the developed area of the town and the area scheduled for development. The landscape is lent coherence by the similar shades of colour. The park is not, as in the previous examples, a plot of land that is made to stand out from the surrounding landscape and presented in its own right, but corresponds with it and is linked to it. In this ground plan the trees and shrubs are again drawn in view, and this and the shadows cast give the plan a three-dimensional look. This is also supported by emphasizing the north-facing edges of banks and paths. In later periods, the plants are not usually drawn in view, but shown in horizontal projection like all other plan elements.

This plan of Charlottenhof or Siam (Ill. 0.7), also by Peter Joseph Lenné and dating from 1839, consists of the ground plan drawing and two detailed drawings, on a scale twice as large, in the two bottom corners. The plan itself is restricted to the site, it does not show the surrounding area. The drawing method is the same as in the first plan by Lenné shown here, but it is more precise and sharper because of the scale of the drawing; the colours are clearer and less mellow in character. The relief of the ground is shown both for the land and for the areas of water. The two detail drawings, executed in the same way as the plan, identify important areas of the site. A similar proposal today would include far more detailed drawings, with each one probably showing essential aspects on a much larger scale and in even more detail.

The general plan of the Tiergarten park (Ill. 0.8) by Peter Joseph Lenné dates from 1840, when the Tiergarten, now in the city centre, was still outside Berlin. It is a lithograph on paper. The streets and paths, the planted and grassy areas, and other facilities with the adjacent river and urban area are presented in great detail, and make a three-dimensional impression. The original sheet measures 90 x 61.4 cm.

The two plans (Ills.0.9-10) dating from April 1835 by Gotthilf Ludwig (Louis) Runge and Ernst Steudener were created in the context of monthly competitions run by the Architektenverein in Berlin from 1827 and open to members of the association. At this time landscape architecture was not a discipline in its own right, and very often the same person designed both building and gardens, which created a sense of unity among the solutions for these tasks, which are dealt with separately today. The difference between these two designs is remarkable, given that they were created at the same period, used similar draw-

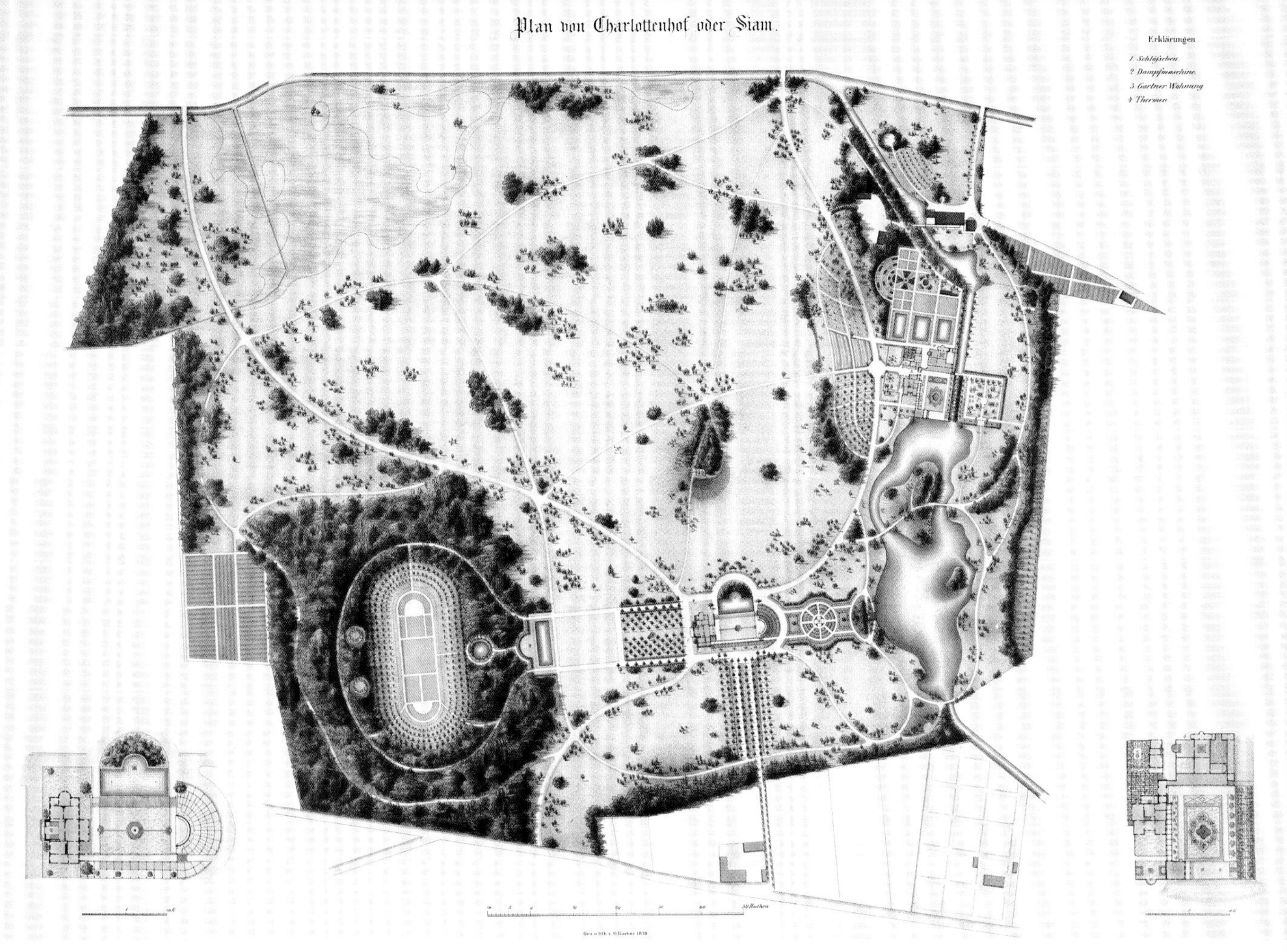

Plan von Charlottenhof oder Siam.
Erklärungen
1 Schlößchen
2 Dampfmaschine
3 Gartner Wahnung
4 Thermen

0.7

Plan of Charlottenhof or Siam, Peter Joseph Lenné, 1839.

0.8

Der Thiergarten bei Berlin
im Jahre 1840.

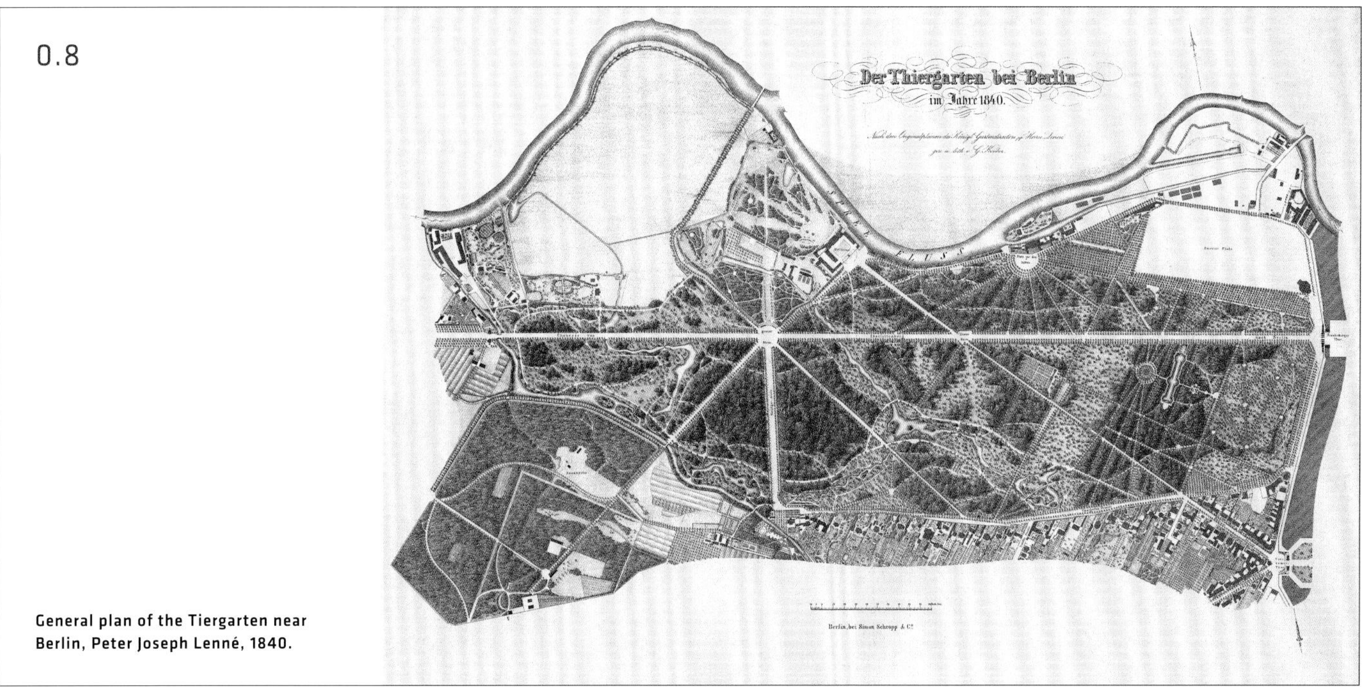

General plan of the Tiergarten near Berlin, Peter Joseph Lenné, 1840.

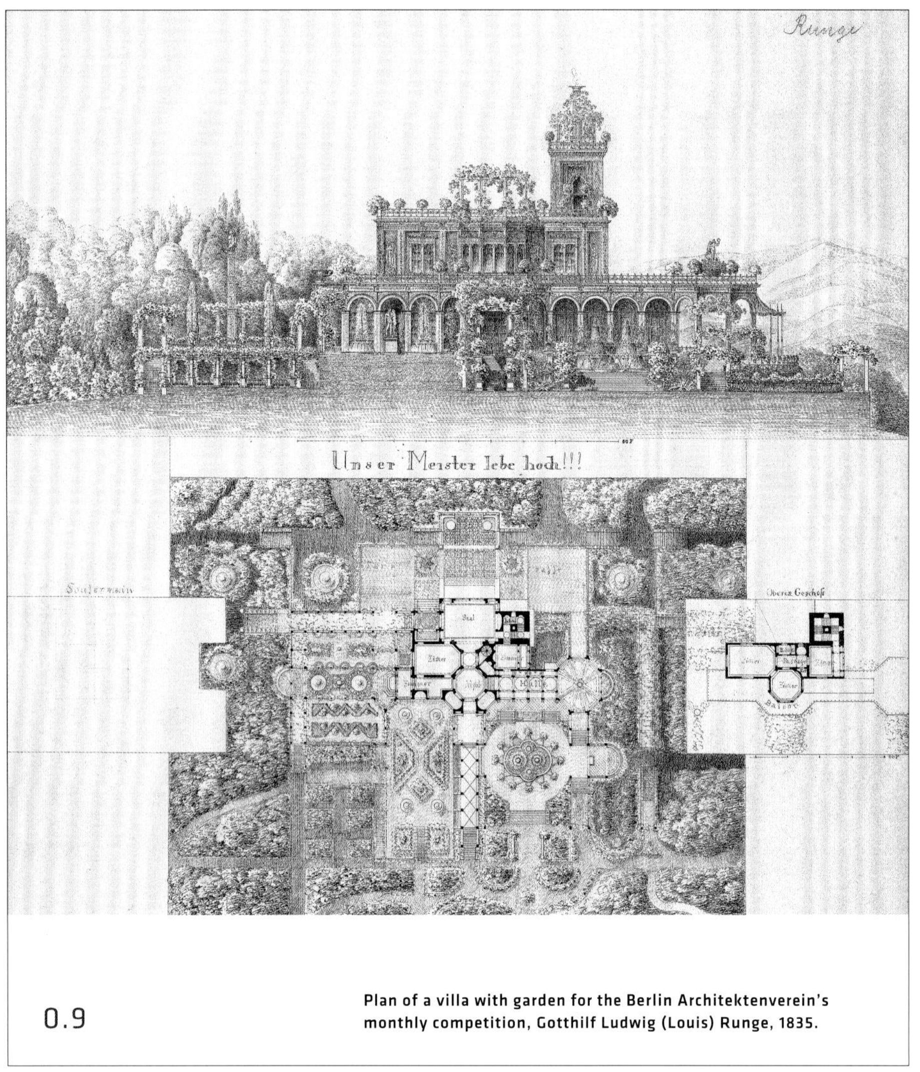


0.9 Plan of a villa with garden for the Berlin Architektenverein's monthly competition, Gotthilf Ludwig (Louis) Runge, 1835.

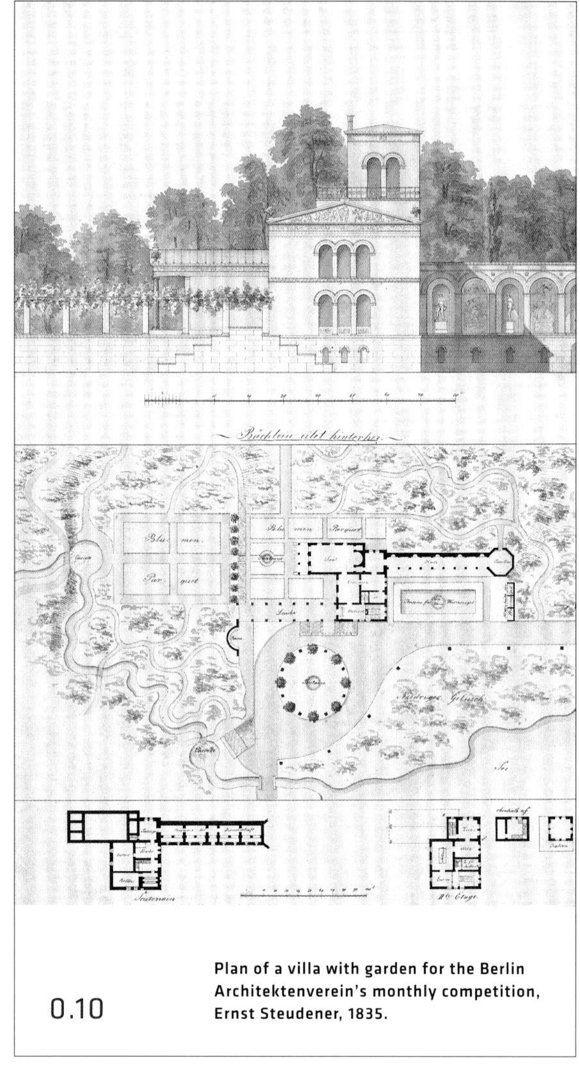

0.10 Plan of a villa with garden for the Berlin Architektenverein's monthly competition, Ernst Steudener, 1835.

ing tools, and the two architects were based in the same region. Runge draws a very formal layout in ink with pencil additions, and also a front view of the building, as well as ground plans of the first and second floor. The original size of the design measures 40.6 x 41.4 cm. Steudener's drawing is significantly smaller at 34.1 x 24.1 cm and executed as a water-coloured ink drawing, with a garden more in the free-form landscape style.

Edwin Barth's 1901 garden plan for a villa in Potsdam (Ill. 0.11) is a drawing in Indian ink, pencil, and ink, water-coloured on transparent paper on a scale of 1:400, and contains the contours of the site in ground plan. The presentation essentially focuses on the site and the trees in the road on the south side, and the sheet is completed with an indication of the subject of the drawing. The shadows added to the vegetation underline the landscape style of the planning.

These two hand drawings (Ills. 0.12-13) in Indian ink on transparent paper by Herta Hammerbacher and Hermann Mattern for the National Horticultural Show in Kassel in 1955 show the general plan, in an original size of 90 x 189 cm, and also a bird's-eye view, in an original size of 42 x 109 cm. These large drawings took a great deal of time and effort to prepare, and could be corrected only to a limited extent. The bird's-eye view shows the design for the overall site, but not in great detail.

0.11

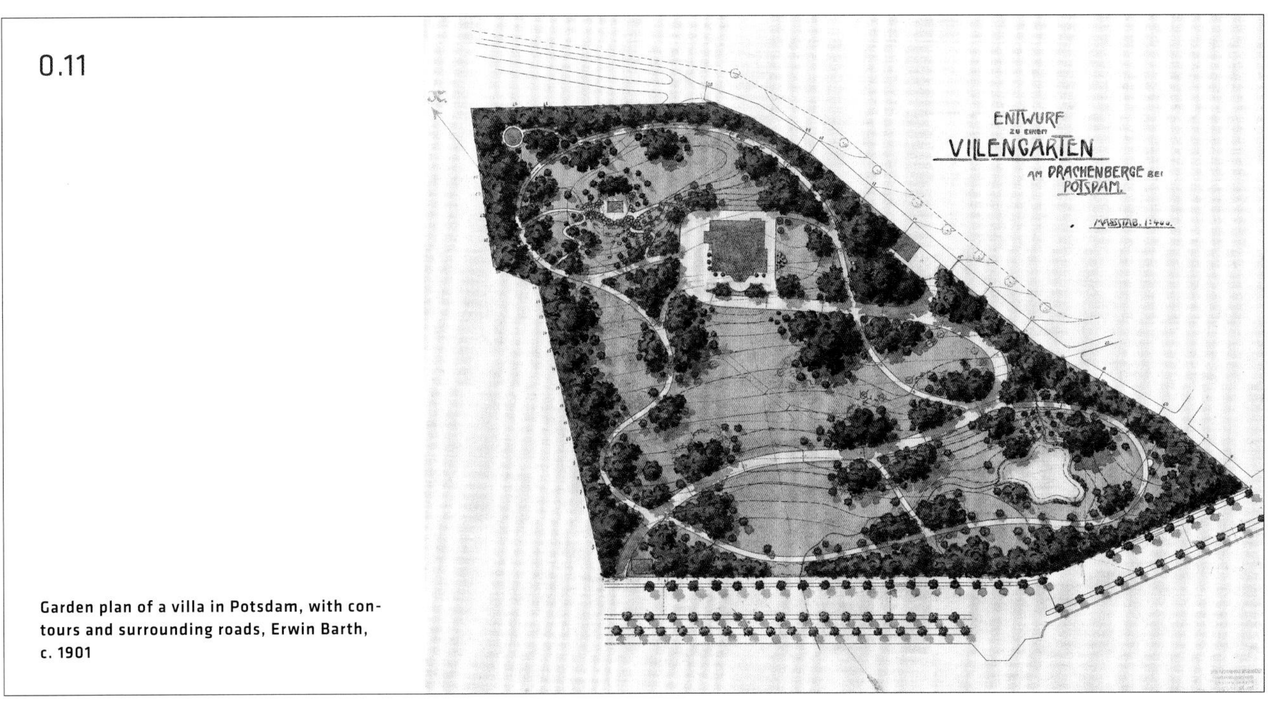


Garden plan of a villa in Potsdam, with contours and surrounding roads, Erwin Barth, c. 1901

0.12

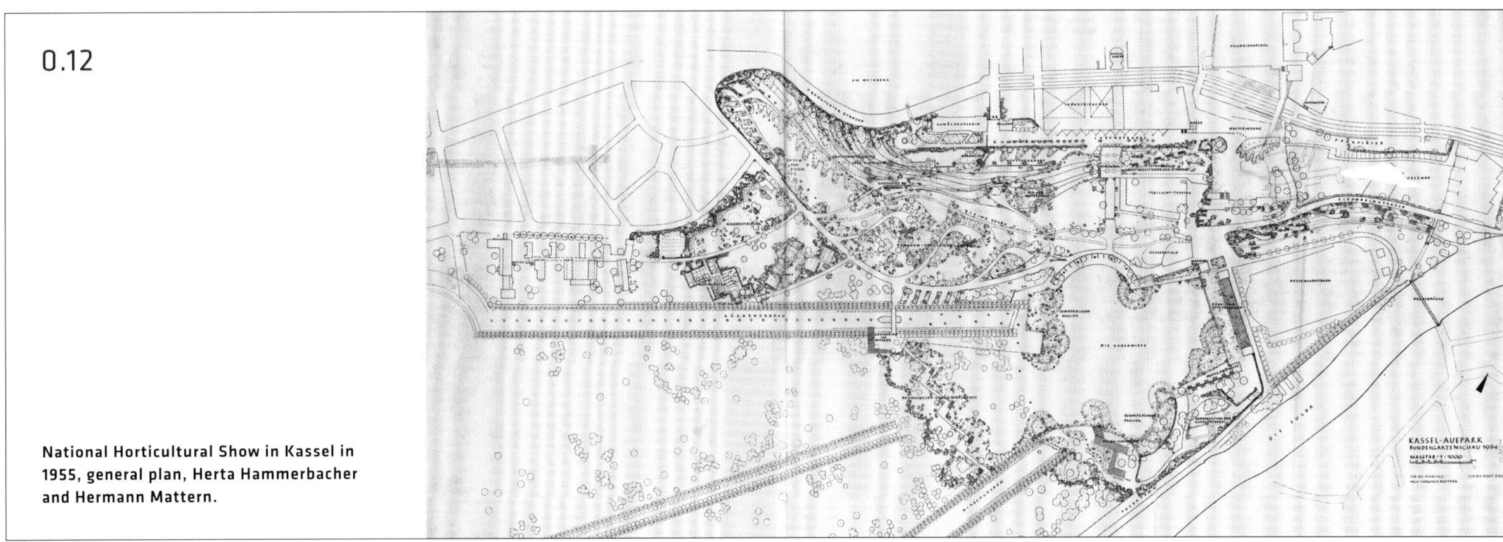


National Horticultural Show in Kassel in 1955, general plan, Herta Hammerbacher and Hermann Mattern.

0.13

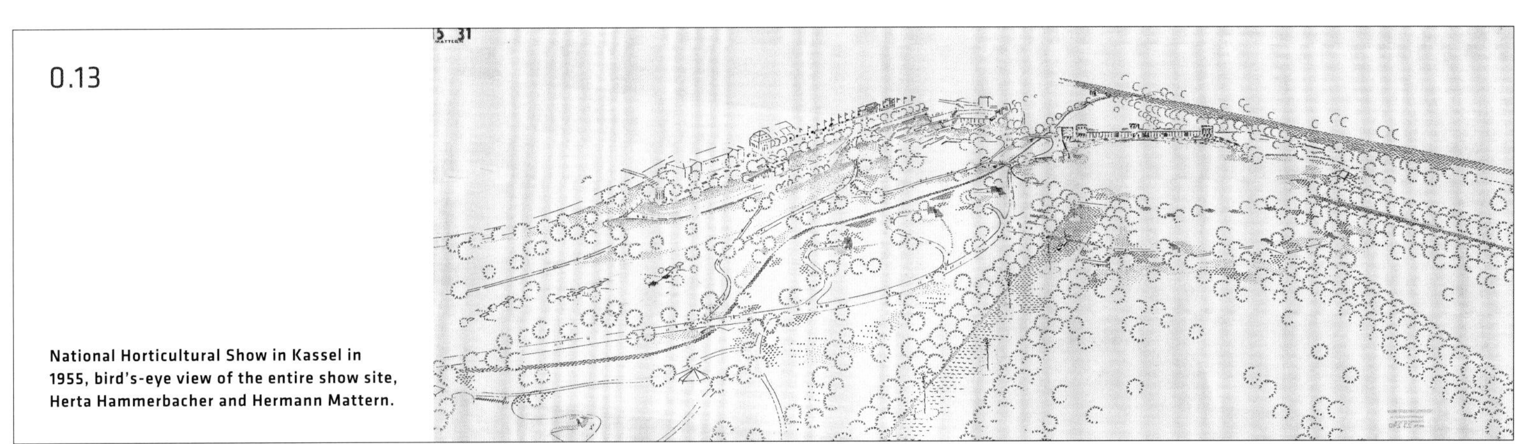

National Horticultural Show in Kassel in 1955, bird's-eye view of the entire show site, Herta Hammerbacher and Hermann Mattern.

# Finding ideas and forms

In landscape architecture, assignments are always tied to a specific location, and are therefore affected by that location's spatial, functional, ecological and cultural properties. Landscape architects have to create solutions to specific problems of the time when the assignment is defined, while remaining aware of the prospect of future changes. Whether the commission is to redesign a garden, to plan a town development or to manage social challenges in terms of local needs and the management of space, it will always set the conditions for possible solutions. The reference to space as an immediate human experience will always be an important part of the planning process.

Visual presentations are key to the process of elaborating concepts, evaluating them and finally determining the forms and other aspects of design. The process often begins with sketches or similar drawings, which are gradually refined and developed further. Models may be built for haptic perception of the design, or alternatively as digital models to be viewed on-screen or as plots.

The process of finding an idea, a shape and a form has two different stages that intersect with each other closely. The deficits of the existing site and the future demands are analyzed and dealt with at a rational, technical and knowledge-based design level. The best possible form and the appropriate ways of representing and communicating it are developed at the creative, intuitive and subjective design level. This level of design cannot be made objective. It is also the seat of something very important to landscape architecture: the perception of space as a bodily experience. If intuitions cannot be communicated objectively, they can be expressed intersubjectively. Due to the way human beings think and experience the world, these two levels of thinking cannot simultaneously contribute to the same result. Instead, each tries to arrive at its own result.

The first, rational step is to record and analyze the site's existing infrastructure. Designers should always investigate whether the existing site has any exceptional properties – such as ecologically valuable areas - that should be protected and developed, and whether it has any historical significance that should be taken into account (not only when the site is listed). They should assess the position occupied by the project area within its surroundings – including, for instance, the existing access routes and barriers that will need to be taken into account. This also means evaluating the profiles of future users. These and other aspects are investigated individually for each specific planning assignment depending on its particular demands, with visual presentations of these different aspects serving as a basis for design. These presentations give the first indications of possible ways of improving the existing situation, but a design cannot be evolved solely from this function-oriented data.

It is only with the inclusion of intuition and creativity, which follow their own rules, that a design becomes individual, harmonious and suited to its location. It is the creative potential that ultimately enables open spaces to be perceived and used as spaces for sensory experience, as a unified whole. Any evaluation of the design must be based on these two aspects of function and form. Although certain theories and approaches to design emphasize one or the other of these two aspects, a viewpoint based on only one aspect will ultimately be insufficient.

The creative part of the planning process is very personal in nature, varying according to the landscape architects' personalities as well as the location. Typically there is no predetermined end result for this process, which follows few hard and fast rules or formulas. As a consequence, it produces highly individual solutions. The creative part of the planning process makes the process as a whole more difficult to map out. At the initial state, during the idea-finding phase, an awareness of how a design would be experienced at the subjective level is particularly important.

Creative methods are more varied than the rational methods. Abandoning normal and familiar elements can help in finding new and better solutions. Systems can be subverted and re-imagined. Designers will always draw on their own knowledge and experiences; trends from other areas of life, ways of working from other professions and methods drawn from other disciplines can be called on, especially at the beginning of a design process.

The process of finding ideas and forms is lengthy and sometimes tedious. It is characterized by cyclical repetitions, which ideally represent an upward spiral of ideas being refined, compared, discussed, modified, detailed and repeatedly discarded. As it is unpredictable and has no definable goal, it may be unsettling for a time. It is a good idea to begin by posing questions rather than by formulating answers.

Rather than taking place on vague terrain, the idea-finding process is often affected by the object and its attendant conditions. The requirements placed on open spaces are often contradictory and impossible to reconcile. In other cases, the area's spatial proportions prevent certain requirements from being implemented. The conflicting goals often encountered in planning processes can and must be resolved differently for each location; since open space design deals with limited sites, which cannot be expanded to accommodate different requirements, decisions must be made, weighing up all the options and then developing the best possible solution. This deliberation process is another area where drawings have a central role.

The images created at the beginning of the individual idea-finding process do not have to be generally comprehensible, as they are rarely published. Instead, they are used as a basis for internal revision and further development, which often involves representing and communicating ideas in the form of drafts and other drawings. Sketching, shaping and modeling ideas helps to make them feasible and executable; anything that can be represented, drawn or shaped can also be discussed, compared, checked and built. By drawing and building models as a means of designing and of checking the feasibility of designs, and by bringing ideas together in drawings, new possibilities are created for taking ideas further.

Often a motto is developed as the central theme and further developed in its relevance to the design: is an idea or a theme sufficient for the whole of the project or only for a part of it? Is it workable at all? A workable idea drawn in a graphically reduced way may turn into a symbolic icon. A simple but effective sketch helps people to recognize and identify the conceptual approach to the overall project (Ill. 0.14). Most sketches of this kind appear as if they were dashed off quickly; they reproduce the particular characteristics of the location and the new view that is the basis for the design with a certain lightness.

The decisions landscape architects make on the design, the uses, etc. give them a major role in shaping modern societies. Every open space expresses an attitude to a society's possible path and development, including its creative development. Conversely, citizens of democratic societies (and not merely decision-makers and disseminators) are increasingly becoming involved in the shaping of open spaces, as they are the ones who will experience the social, ecological and economic consequences of planning and construction measures most directly. Laypeople can provide suggestions for

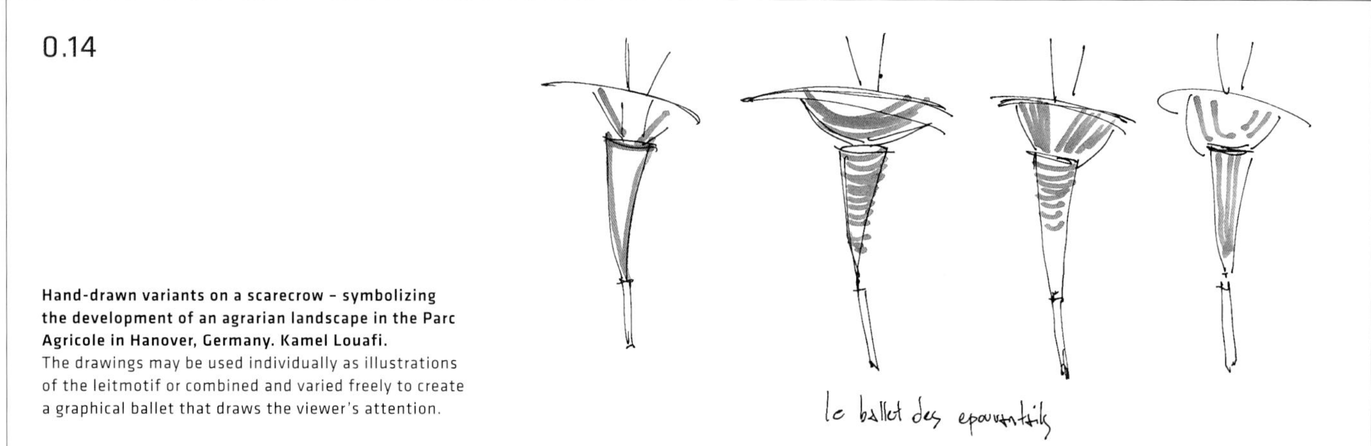


0.14

**Hand-drawn variants on a scarecrow – symbolizing the development of an agrarian landscape in the Parc Agricole in Hanover, Germany. Kamel Louafi.**
The drawings may be used individually as illustrations of the leitmotif or combined and varied freely to create a graphical ballet that draws the viewer's attention.

sensible functional use of open spaces, while landscape architects, who are able to bring expertise to bear on these rational requirements, retain responsibility for the creative part of design development.

One important part of a project, which is also crucial to the acceptance of the proposal, is the involvement of the community. Suitable participation processes such as user consultations or charettes have been developed for this purpose. These are prepared and moderated by landscape architects, and the results are incorporated into the overall process. Participatory methods are usually based largely on photos and drawings, some of which are developed during the collective meetings. In this situation, one clear advantage of working visually is that design and discussion can take place as the plans are being drawn. Not only does participation promote acceptance of the design, it also promotes use of the planned open space. This can be important – in the case of open spaces attached to schools, for instance.

The techniques employed to create visual representations in the idea and form-finding process are many and varied. Often the traditional pencil sketch will be used for the first approximation, but there is no limit to the materials that can be used. In contrast to later phases of the workflow process, diversity may actually be at its greatest at this stage.

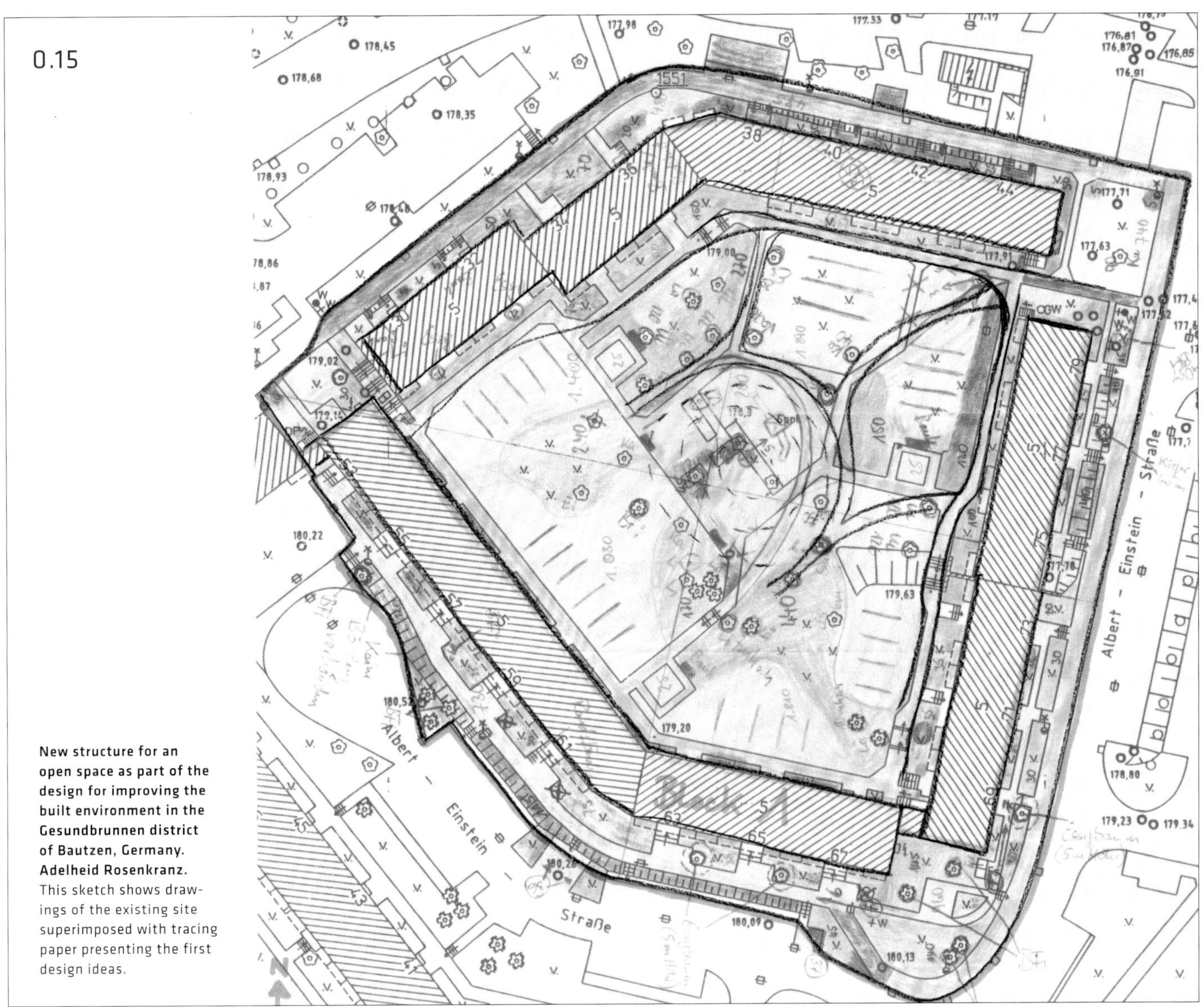


**New structure for an open space as part of the design for improving the built environment in the Gesundbrunnen district of Bautzen, Germany. Adelheid Rosenkranz.** This sketch shows drawings of the existing site superimposed with tracing paper presenting the first design ideas.

## Finding ideas and forms by drawing

Along with the models discussed later, drawings are the most significant tool for the creative form-finding process. The examples reproduced here demonstrate that this process cannot be separated from the conditions on the site, and that it involves the constant checking, improvement and further development of the planning stages already undertaken. Accordingly, the drawings are part of a process, and are not the results of completed working stages, as with the visualisations in the following parts.

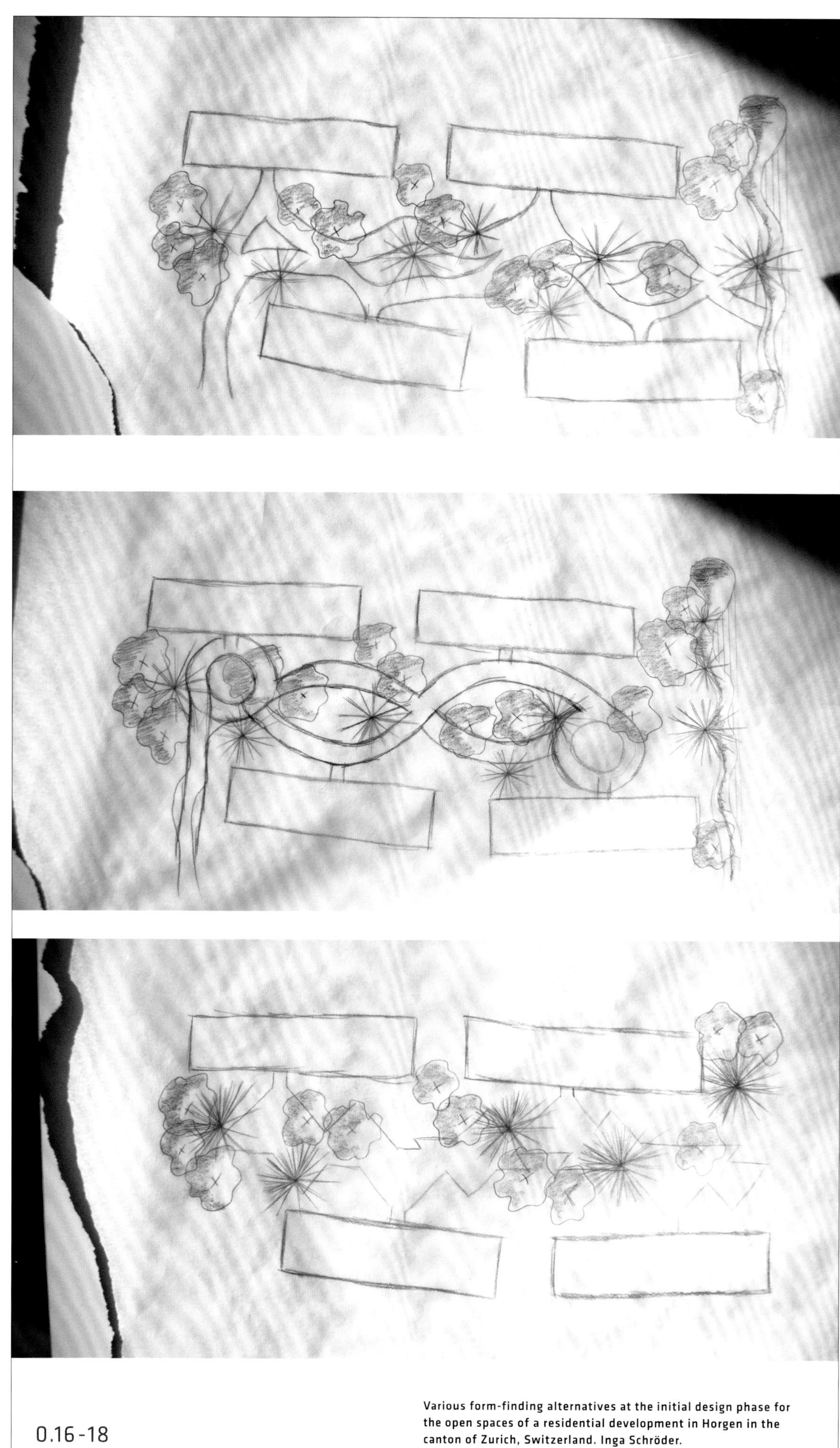

0.16-18

Various form-finding alternatives at the initial design phase for the open spaces of a residential development in Horgen in the canton of Zurich, Switzerland. Inga Schröder.

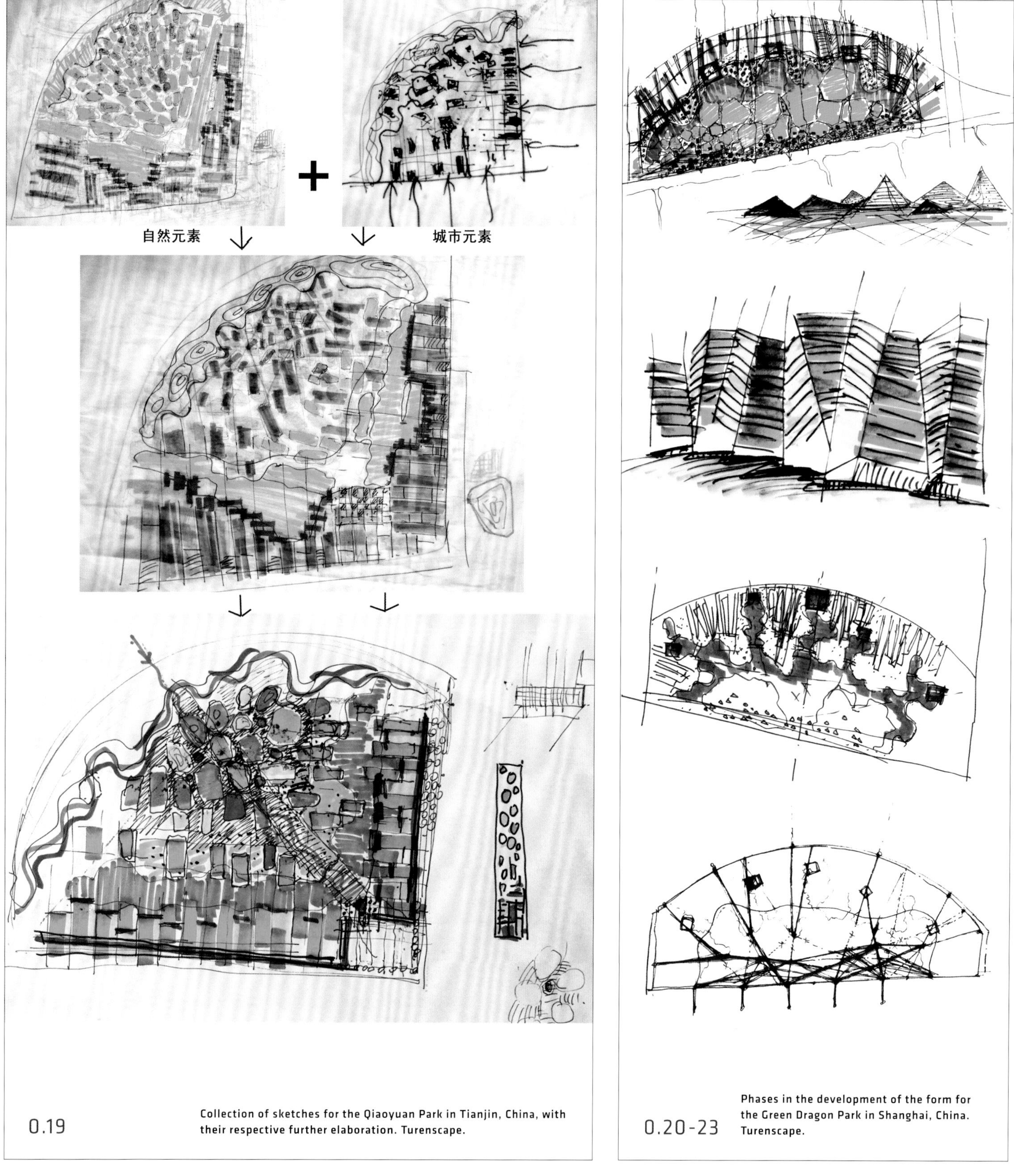


0.19 Collection of sketches for the Qiaoyuan Park in Tianjin, China, with their respective further elaboration. Turenscape.

0.20-23 Phases in the development of the form for the Green Dragon Park in Shanghai, China. Turenscape.

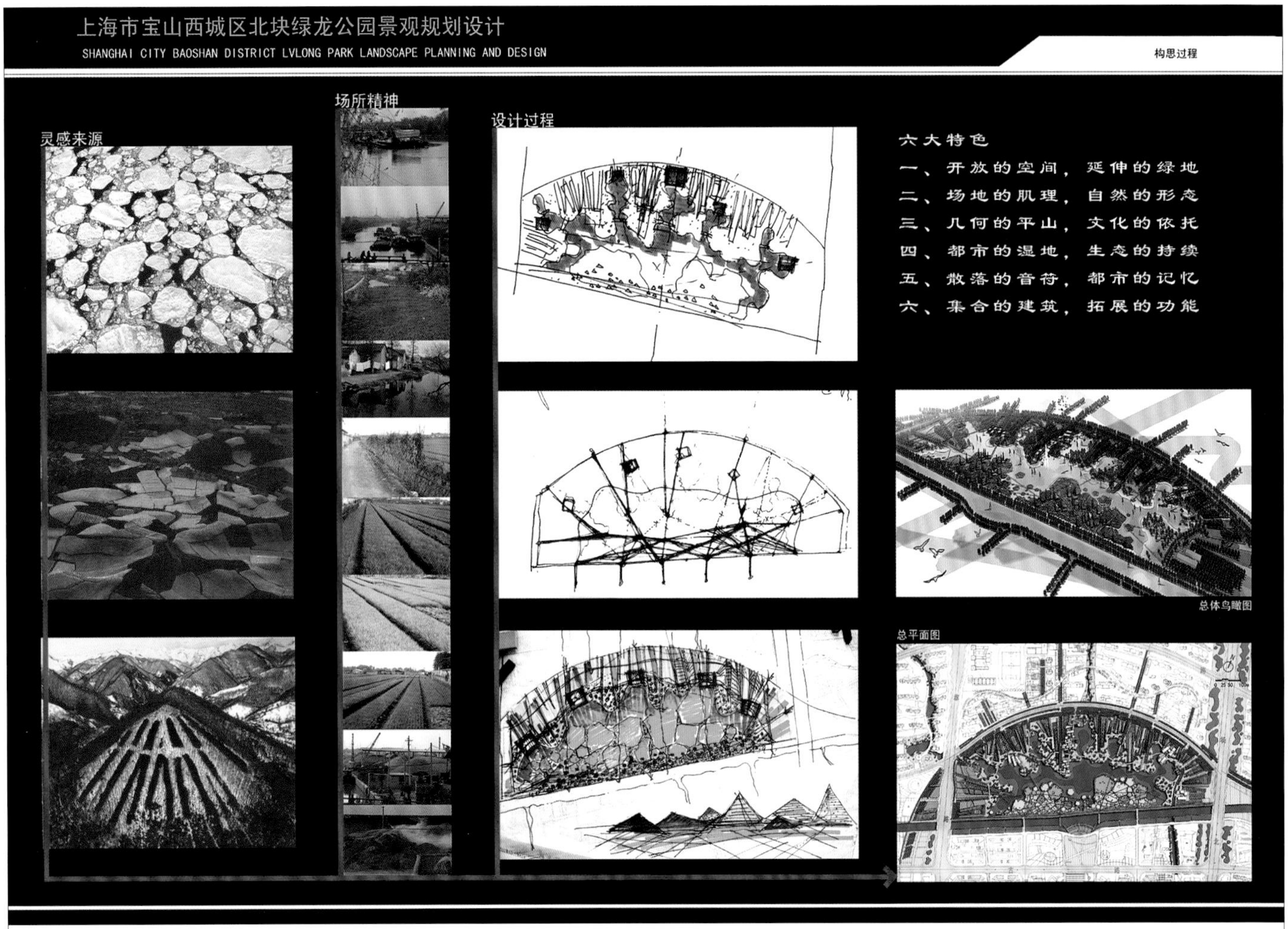

上海市宝山西城区北块绿龙公园景观规划设计
SHANGHAI CITY BAOSHAN DISTRICT LVLONG PARK LANDSCAPE PLANNING AND DESIGN

构思过程

灵感来源

场所精神

设计过程

六大特色
一、开放的空间，延伸的绿地
二、场地的肌理，自然的形态
三、几何的平山，文化的依托
四、都市的湿地，生态的持续
五、散落的音符，都市的记忆
六、集合的建筑，拓展的功能

总体鸟瞰图

总平面图

0.24

Overview and collection of individual drawings from the form-finding process for the Green Dragon Park.

0.25

Checking the design for the new city Khalifa City C, Abu Dhabi, United Arab Emirates, and its integration into the existing landscape. Hand drawing overlaid on an aerial picture. Neumann Gusenburger.

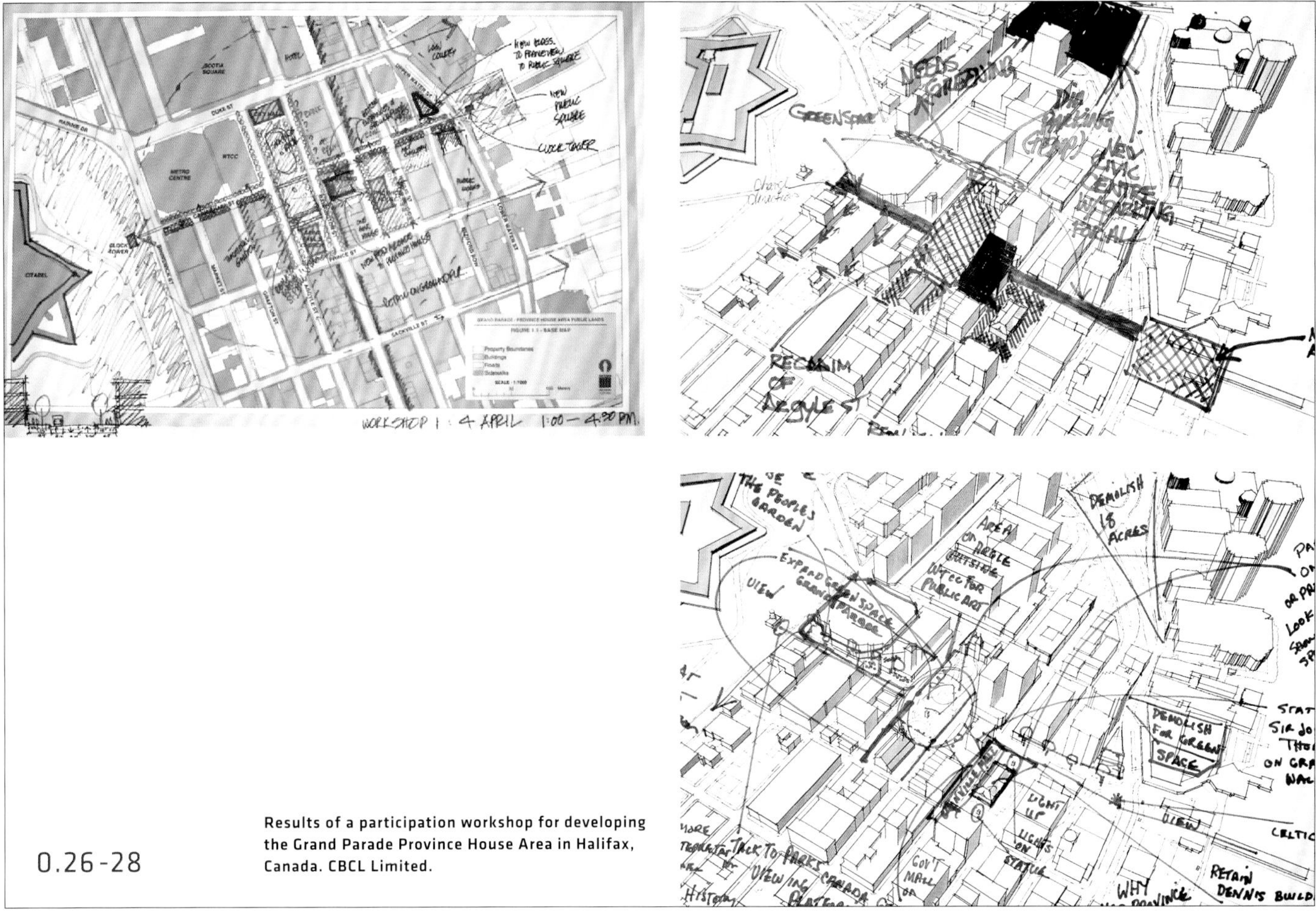


0.26-28

**Results of a participation workshop for developing the Grand Parade Province House Area in Halifax, Canada. CBCL Limited.**

In a democratic model for developing public spaces (Ills. 0.26-28), the results of discussions with and suggestions from citizens, planning offices, designers and politicians provide important information on how to shape functions and amenities for the future. Marking visual presentations on a prepared map makes them more easily comprehensible than any amount of text could do. The image is an important way of placing needs and functions in context, a first step in establishing the intentions and how the different key points relate to each other. People can participate through charettes, workshops, moderated discussions, exhibitions or via the internet.

0.29

Model for the Diana, Princess of Wales Memorial Fountain in London, Great Britain. Gustafson Porter.

## Finding ideas and forms by modelmaking

The design for the Princess Diana memorial fountain emerged from a complex process based on an analogue model, which later became the basis for a digital model. The first step involved creating a model (Ill. 0.29) in clay representing the fountain and the surrounding area of Hyde Park. From this a rubber form was taken, which was then scanned and transformed into a three-dimensional digital form with the aid of an automobile-development computer program. This digital model was used to create sections, which were used as the basis for the detailed design of individual areas. In the course of further digital reworkings, the precise form and arrangement of all 545 granite blocks were calculated. Like the motto "Reaching Out – Letting In", which expresses the design's central concept, the elaborate combination of modern and traditional methods in the design, detailing and implementation of the memorial was intended to reflect the personality of the individual it commemorates.

Finding ideas and forms is a complex process indispensable to the subsequent project. The effort expended generally creates few visible results, and the visual presentations created during this phase are not usually seen by anyone outside the design practice; they are only presented to clients (and sometimes to the public) after being refined in the later design stages. The following chapters deal with visual representations created specifically for an audience.

0.30-31

**Details of the models for a park on a bank. Abigail Feldman.**

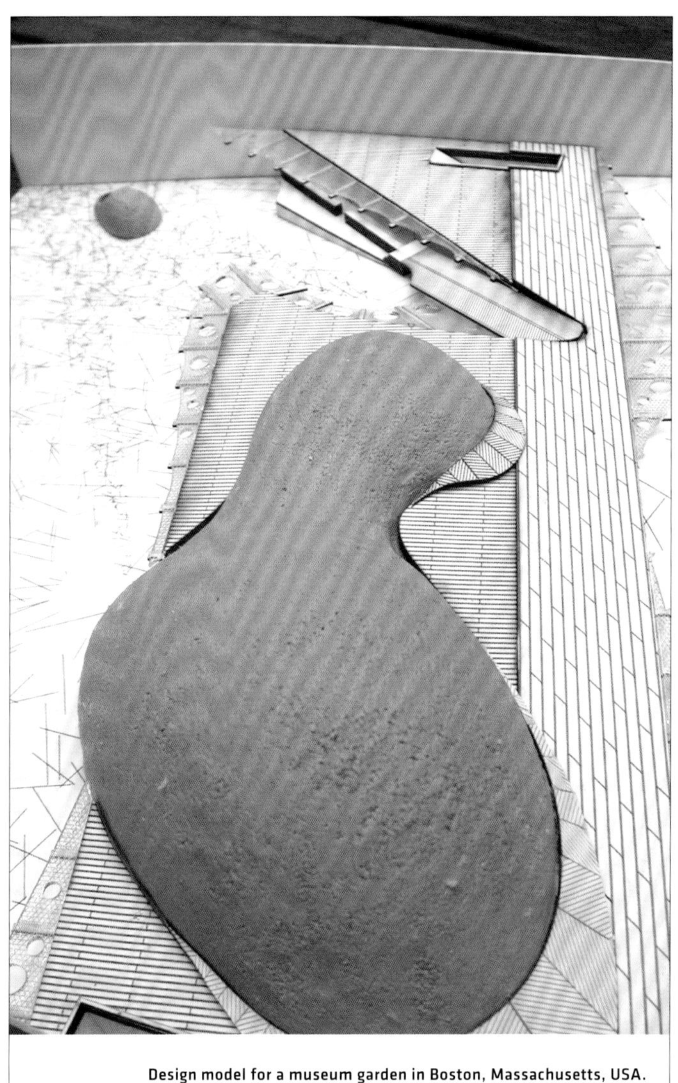

0.32

**Design model for a museum garden in Boston, Massachusetts, USA. Abigail Feldman.**
The organic forms were created by molding clay over styropore, and the final surfaces were cut in cardboard using lasers.

0.33-34

**Working models for the design for the 1001 Trees public park in northwest Copenhagen, Denmark. SLA.**

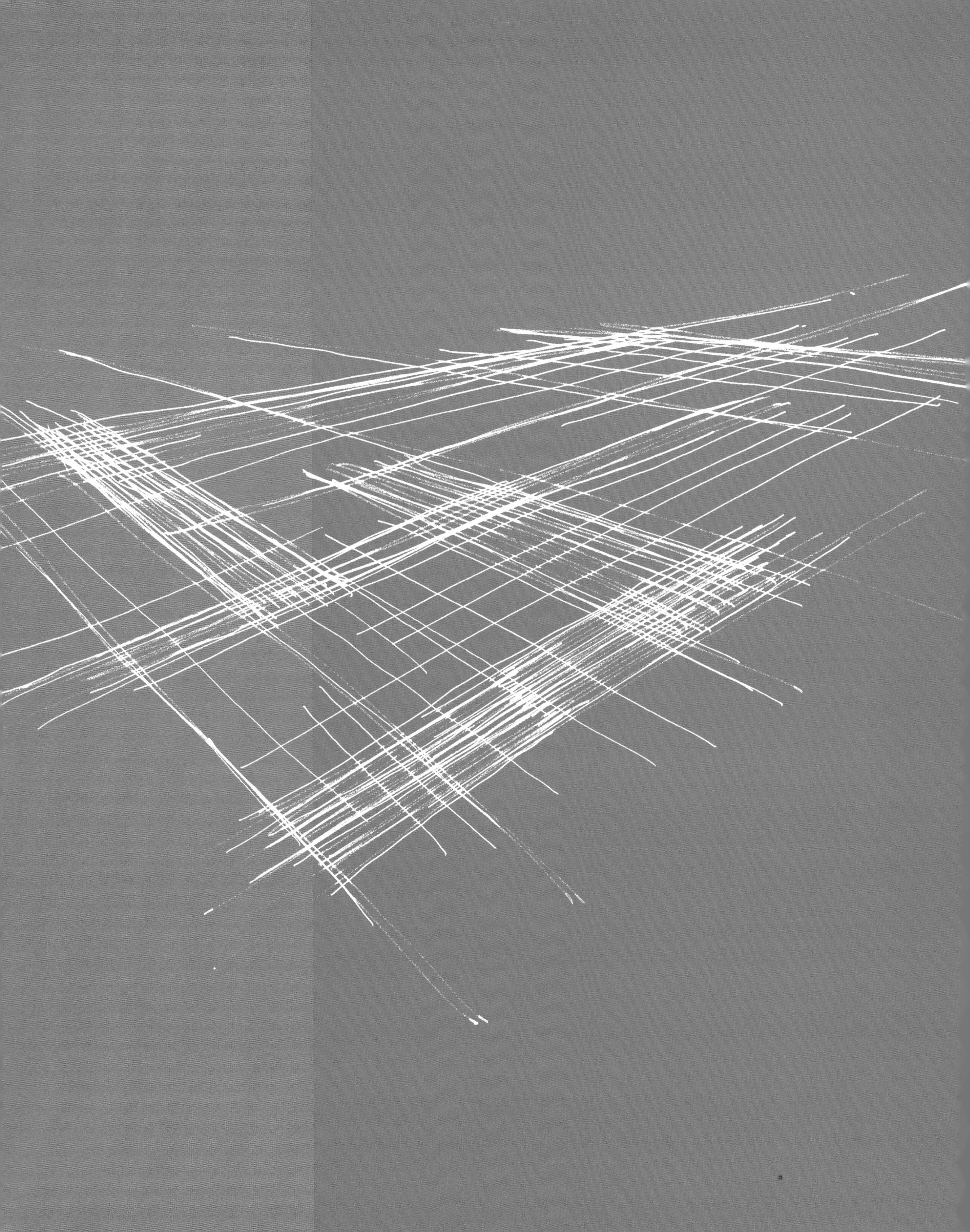

# PART 1 FUNCTIONS

For all planning processes in landscape architecture, pictures, plans and visualizations in general are the most important tools for communicating necessary information. In the following pages, they are presented according to their dimensionality. The two-dimensional representations on a flat plane are dealt with first, followed by the three-dimensional, spatial representations. The third chapter of this part discusses ways of visualizing the fourth dimension of time, always important in landscape architecture. This includes visualizing the development of open spaces and how they are experienced over the course of time. For the purposes of this book, the emphasis in all descriptions is not on the design content of the images but on their visual features.

Every technical method or representation has its own communicative potential, and also its specific limitations. Given the complexity of planning today, no image can fulfill all requirements on its own. Despite this, the first part of the book mainly contains individual drawings, simulations and models. These were created for specific design purposes but are shown here without their context, focusing instead on their own particular communicative strategies. Looking at individual representations separated from their project context demonstrates the diversity of visualizations used to convey design: similar representation techniques used for similar design tasks may produce entirely different images.

A visual representation is an expression both of the design tasks involved and of the approach of its creator. It also expresses a social vision and the landscape designer's applied ability to think of the future both in a global and in a space-related way, and to convey these thoughts to the public.

As well as presenting design ideas, visual material also helps to convince financial investors and present or future users. Today, illustrations are also checked very carefully for practicability, making it important to present the rational functionality of a plan as well as how it will improve open spaces technically, ecologically and aesthetically. The first sign of a good plan is an effective visual representation.

Gabriele Holst, Diagonal, spatial I.

# FUNCTIONS
# **PLANE**

## Two-dimensional presentations: possibilities and limitations

When landscape architects are designing and transforming areas of the Earth's surface it is treated as a two-dimensional plane in the first place, even though it is actually a landscape with lively topography, open to experience only in individual parts at any given moment. The height aspect is not dealt with looking at a surface as a plane. A globe has a smooth surface, just as atlases and maps are usually printed on flat paper. Topography is generally shown on maps by drawing in contours and colouring. Road maps and other orientation plans are presented as vertical projections. For this reason, most people are used to understanding this method of representation, and they have no trouble in reading plans. Google Earth is widely used as a way of looking at all kinds of places by computer. The resolution deployed there is of little use for planning purposes, but if the lighting conditions are right, these shots can be used to convey an aerial impression of a terrain. This program offers other possibilities such as representing journeys through time and calculating the position of the sun. Landscape architects do not as a rule use these at present, but may well do so in future.

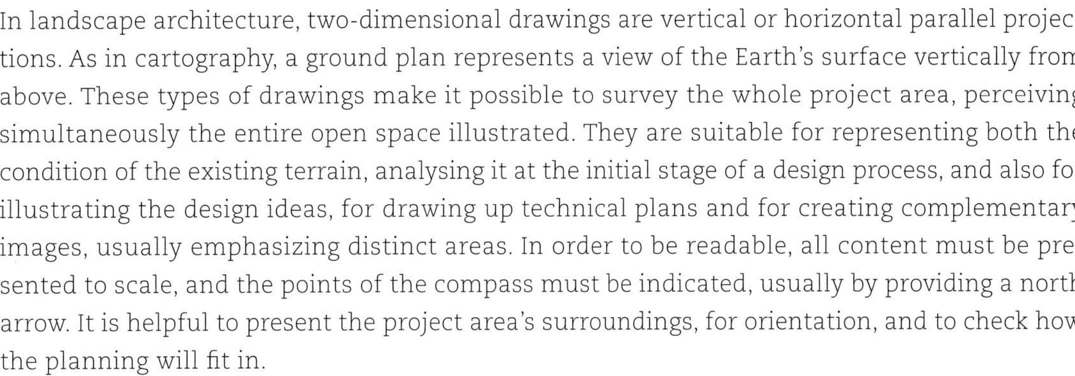

In landscape architecture, two-dimensional drawings are vertical or horizontal parallel projections. As in cartography, a ground plan represents a view of the Earth's surface vertically from above. These types of drawings make it possible to survey the whole project area, perceiving simultaneously the entire open space illustrated. They are suitable for representing both the condition of the existing terrain, analysing it at the initial stage of a design process, and also for illustrating the design ideas, for drawing up technical plans and for creating complementary images, usually emphasizing distinct areas. In order to be readable, all content must be presented to scale, and the points of the compass must be indicated, usually by providing a north arrow. It is helpful to present the project area's surroundings, for orientation, and to check how the planning will fit in.

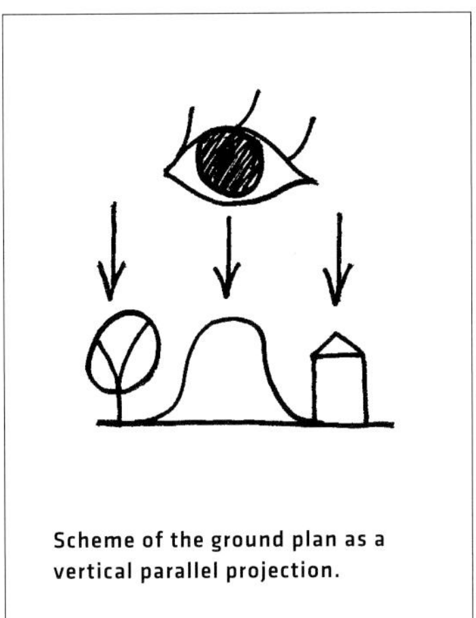

Scheme of the ground plan as a vertical parallel projection.

Unlike maps, which illustrate the situation as it currently is, plans represent a condition that will emerge in the future. They are used for orientation purposes, but to an even greater extent as means of communication between their authors and those who look at them, the users and decision-makers about the future development and design of a place. A two-dimensional representation of an area conveys a view that cannot be experienced in reality in that form. Therefore, laymen – despite an offer of orientation that seems simple at a first glance – often find it difficult to understand what plans are saying and to imagine them realized. They not only have to get their bearings in the project area and its environs, they also have to get to grips with the plans and add the third dimension in their own imagination, for example by fitting several drawings together virtually to arrive at an overall picture. For this reason, authors of two-dimensional plans must present three-dimensional qualities in such a way that they can be understood without ambiguity. Designers have a wide range of possibilities open to them for doing this.

The two-dimensional drawing is to be seen in this process as coding for objects, floor coverings, vegetation, access points, connections and boundaries. It can reproduce only one element of three-dimensional reality – and thus also of planning. Written notes can be added to the ground plan, as well as drawings as other visual information, for example complementary two-dimensional illustrations. A ground plan, for example, is often complemented by sections or sectional elevations, reproducing the run of the relief contours and showing plants and buildings to scale.

Ground plans or sectional views can never be experienced in reality as they are presented, because the effect of three-dimensional vision – all objects seem to taper with increasing distance – cannot be conveyed in two-dimensional representations. But even so, there is a large repertoire of two-dimensional illustrations, serving mainly to communicate the project and make it comprehensible. There are very few rules. Ultimately the criterion for judging illustrations is whether they make the planning, the ideas and implementation possibilities unambiguously comprehensible. If this is achieved, ground plans in particular are superior to text, not just because they are clearly comprehensible, but also because they make it possible to understand the project all over the world regardless of language.

## The ground plan as the basis for design

In most cases, ground plans provide a basis for all further representation of the design ideas. They can be used for implementation in built form and as point of reference for further explanatory drawings. They define the ideas, links, details, uses, spatial allocations and the terrain division. They must be comprehensible, unambiguous in their message, expressive and of course open to actual implementation. As the required tasks are very different in their character and purpose and dependent on the conditions at the specific site, each piece of graphic representation will address the given conditions and requirements, while the authors' design approach and attitude will be expressed here as well.

Ground plans are limited in their ability to convey three-dimensional plan content, but to a certain extent this can be indicated by the use of graphic means such as drawn shading, applied to elements of the plan such as buildings or woodland that make a height impact, or shades of colour and gradations of grey, depicting the elements closer to the eye in darker shades than the distant ones, or also by using lines of differing thicknesses, contrasts or other techniques.

The ground plan also acquires its particular significance because it clearly demonstrates the proportions of all parts in relation to each other and shows organization and spatial formation, along with what seem to be the focal points, connections and boundaries of the individual areas. These functions are supported by appropriate graphic design and emphasized in the work as a whole.

When comparing two-dimensional drawings by landscape architects from various countries and different cultures, plan contents and messages tend to agree in essentials. Differences tend to arise mainly from the individual approaches of the designers, not from certain regional conventions. They can also be caused by different legal requirements in individual countries, or by different availability of maps as a basis for planning.

Ground plans as base drawings for planning are complemented in the design process by detail, section and elevation drawings, perspective views and other representations in order to define all dimensions of the intended solution. These complementary drawings all relate to the two-dimensional ground plan and are derived from it. For this reason it still occupies a central position in the design process, despite the limitations cited. Ground plans are used to present design ideas in the context of competitions and other strategic processes, in documenting and analysing the existing situation, at all preliminary design and design stages, implementation planning and also in large-scale landscape planning. Other intentions are also conveyed via the ground plan. They allow, for example, a comparison of approaches to potential users or options for dividing up and allocating terrain, as part of a competition process.

A plan of the present state of the site as built is usually drawn up at the beginning of the project, identifying information about the present situation that is important for the following interventions. This can include the existing topography, existing buildings, roads or pathways, and frequently also show how the project area is located within its relevant surroundings. Subsequent preliminary design and design drawings will form the basis for the actual implementation of the ideas, so they are not necessarily intended for show, and often already contain technical information such as heights and materials to be used. Plans of the existing terrain and of the design are often on the same scale, so that the planned changes are clearly discernible. The working plans then mainly present clearly marked areas and contain dimensions with other details for the actual building process, often including concise written explanations as well. In landscape planning the detailing is usually less precise, as the areas are usually larger and so the scale is smaller. Several ground plans of an area are often needed to present the necessary information, as levels of information would overlap too much in a single plan and become unmanageable.

Individual, reduced two-dimensional structural plans are often drawn up for different project phases. These emphasize particular aspects of the existing and the planned situation, for example how an area is tied into its surroundings, indicating internal and external access routes, or functions and uses. Structural plans are also in two dimensions, and usually on a smaller scale. They serve as drawn explanations of the particular project phase and make the complex messages of the planning intelligible. The design plans themselves may be used for the presentation of the design intentions, or else special presentation plans can be drawn up, emphasizing the core ideas more strongly and allowing other aspects of the design planning to fade into the background. Presentation plans are often drawn up for competitions or used in discussions as a basis for community participation.

## Height as a second dimension: sections and elevations

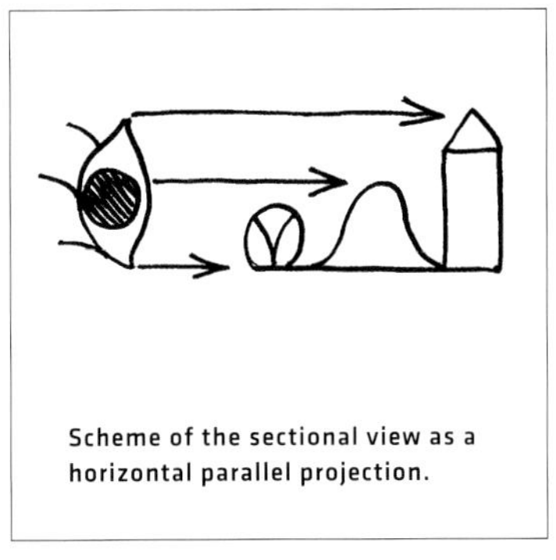

Scheme of the sectional view as a horizontal parallel projection.

Sectional drawings show a vertical cut through terrain. This is a particularly appropriate way of illustrating the relief of the ground as well as height and length ratios in open spaces. Together with the ground plan, the different types of two-dimensional drawings make it possible to illustrate all three dimensions in which our surroundings are experienced. As a sectional drawing can only show the conditions along one sectional line, numerous sections may be needed to give a complete impression of a project area.

If the sections indicated in the ground plan are complemented with planning content situated behind the section line, this produces a sectional elevation, a combination of section and elevation or view. The sectional elevation is a device commonly used to introduce the vertical elements of a design in combination with other open space elements beyond the section line. It offers the advantage of reducing what could become a greater number of sectional drawings, and is also more expressive, as both the elevation at a certain point and the depth of the emerging image can be conveyed. Although a sectional elevation does not correspond with normal human sight, as a complement to plain sections it can contribute much to the understanding of a design.

It is possible to convey the height of the terrain and of trees, buildings and all other design elements involving height effectively in sectional elevations. Yet as they are two-dimensional representations, viewers must still create the three-dimensional impression for and by themselves, on the basis of a number of drawings.

Sectional elevations serve mainly to explain the ground plan; they relate to it directly and use the same or similar modes of representation. However, they possess their own message and aesthetic. They are used both at the design phase and also in the process of drawing up working plans, details and construction drawings for implementation. As technical drawings, they are created on an often larger scale of detail.

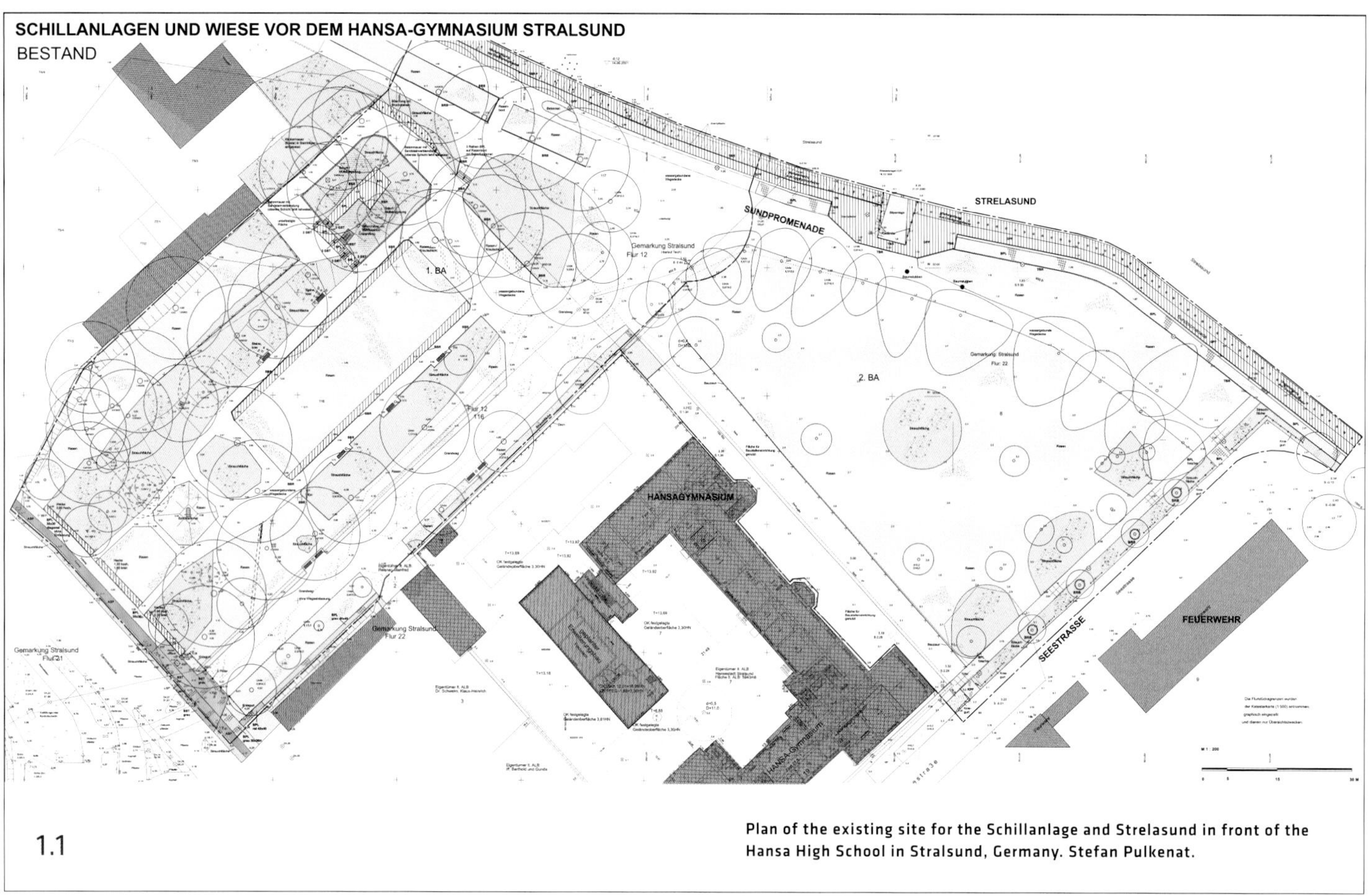


1.1

**Plan of the existing site for the Schillanlage and Strelasund in front of the Hansa High School in Stralsund, Germany. Stefan Pulkenat.**

## Plans and analyses of the existing fabric

Prior to the actual process of design, a plan is often made of the terrain in its existing condition, or showing important features of the area. It is often not possible to identify planning requirements in detail at this stage. As part of their task, landscape architects then have to present the site not just in its present condition, but also to indicate the area's strengths and weaknesses. In this way these plans are also used to better define the planning requirements, and to elaborate first indications of planning necessities. Their scale will be dependent on the degree of detail required; usually it will be the same as that subsequently used during design. This makes it possible to compare the existing conditions and the design planning directly. The input and content of plans showing the area as built depend on the site, its location and size, and also on whether the terrain might be polluted, for example by soil contamination.

Graphic statements must be made particularly clear here, as plans of the existing terrain rarely include written explanations, although the legend usually conveys additional information. Plans of the existing site tend to differ from the subsequent design plans at a first glance in their choice of colour: they are often less colourful, and contain less detail.

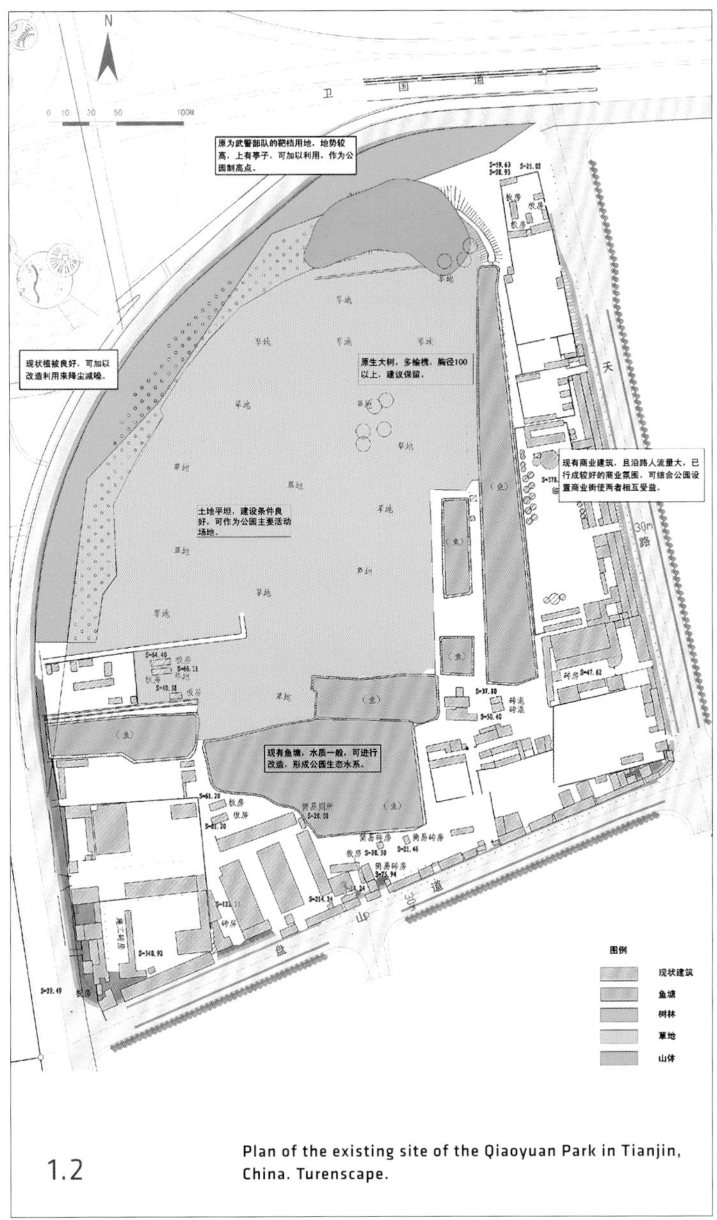

1.2 Plan of the existing site of the Qiaoyuan Park in Tianjin, China. Turenscape.

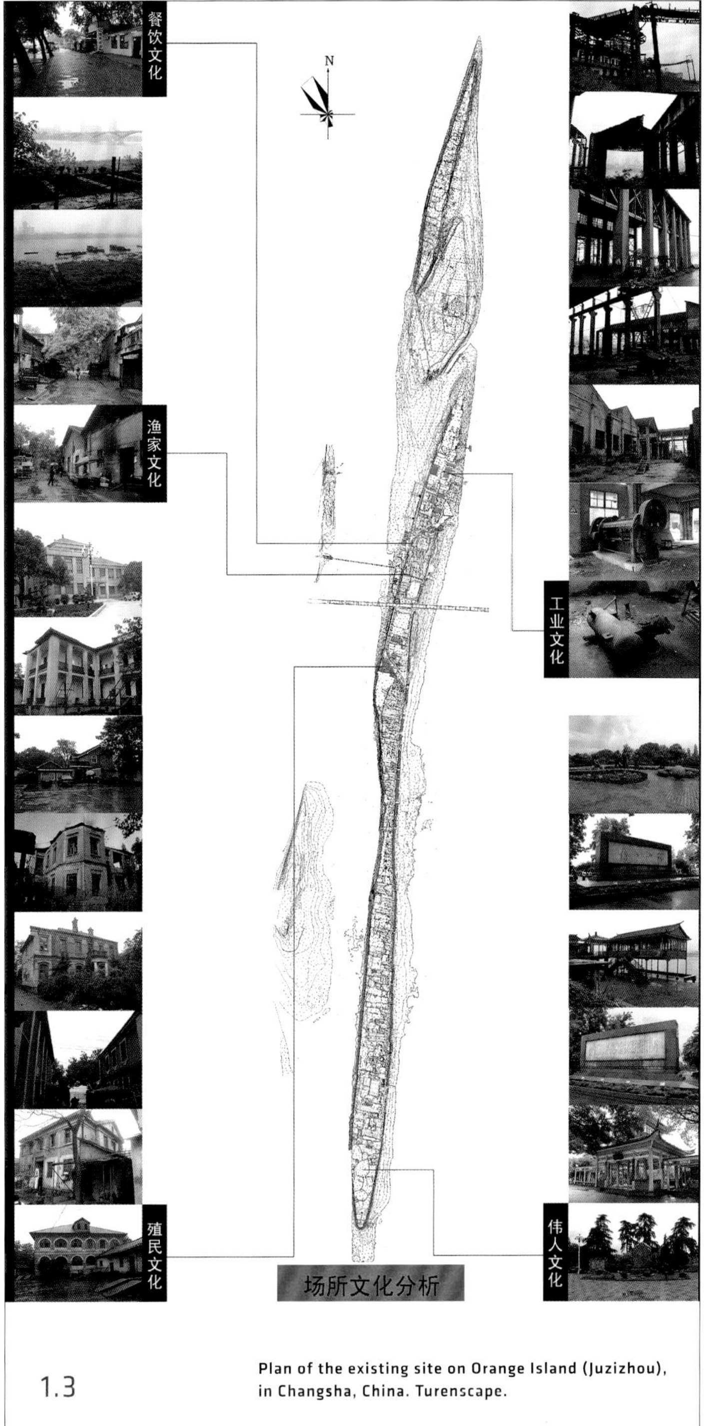


1.3 Plan of the existing site on Orange Island (Juzizhou), in Changsha, China. Turenscape.

This example of a plan of the existing site (Ill. 1.1) is in black and white and shades of grey only. It is based on a survey plan, details from which are included in the drawing. The boundary between the project area and its environs is clearly identified by a line, and yet the adjacent area is shown for orientation purposes, complete with roads and buildings. In the right-hand section of the plan, the second building phase, the trees are drawn as oval or egg-shaped, as they actually have grown and extended at the time the survey was made. The locations of the trees are drawn in precisely, and their crowns shown according to the reality of the individual trees. This could indicate necessary changes, for example, if trees should turn out to be unstable because of their slanting growth and lopsided crown formation. Street names are given on the plan, as well as public facilities, as an orientation aid. The plan provided the basis for the design, and for agreement between the practice and its clients.

The two-dimensional plan for Qiaoyuan Park (Ill. 1.2) has coloured areas. There were ponds and wet areas on the site before planning. These are drawn in colour, and identified by text in the areas concerned. The buildings around the open space, which are part of the site, are also shown in colour. Few colour shades are used overall, and their significance is explained in a short legend. The site as drawn is surrounded by roads forming its borders: these are coloured grey, and are not part of the project area.

Another plan of an existing state of Orange Island (Ill. 1.3) is accompanied by photographs of selected buildings and open spaces, some with lines indicating their locations. Photographs are a current means of documenting the original state of a project area, so that an eye can be kept on the terrain throughout the process while reducing the number of visits to the site. The photographs convey impressions and views that are then presented and analysed in the plan; they help to make it more comprehensible, and can form the record of the first step of a planning sequence.

A village renewal plan (Ill. 1.4) shows details of all the open spaces, the existing vegetation and the buildings including their date, type and roof covering. It also presents vegetation that is important for the apperance of a townscape and a landscape, and evaluates the buildings in terms of town planning and monument preservation. The plan includes the strongly coloured village area and the street patterns, as well as the vegetation and topography of its surroundings, the latter shown in black and white. An extensive explanatory legend is added to cover the copious amount of detailed information. The design can then be prepared in the same way as this drawing, on the same scale, with similar colouring and analogous detailing, so that the original state of the site and the planned project can be compared.

The history of the former mining activities in this town is important for the design of this garden for the Louvre collection museum in Lens (Ill. 1.5), therefore the site of the former pits, extraction areas and former rail connections were included, as well as the topography and soil conditions. The man-made landscape is shown as it was before the new design, so that it could be taken into account in the further design process.

1.4

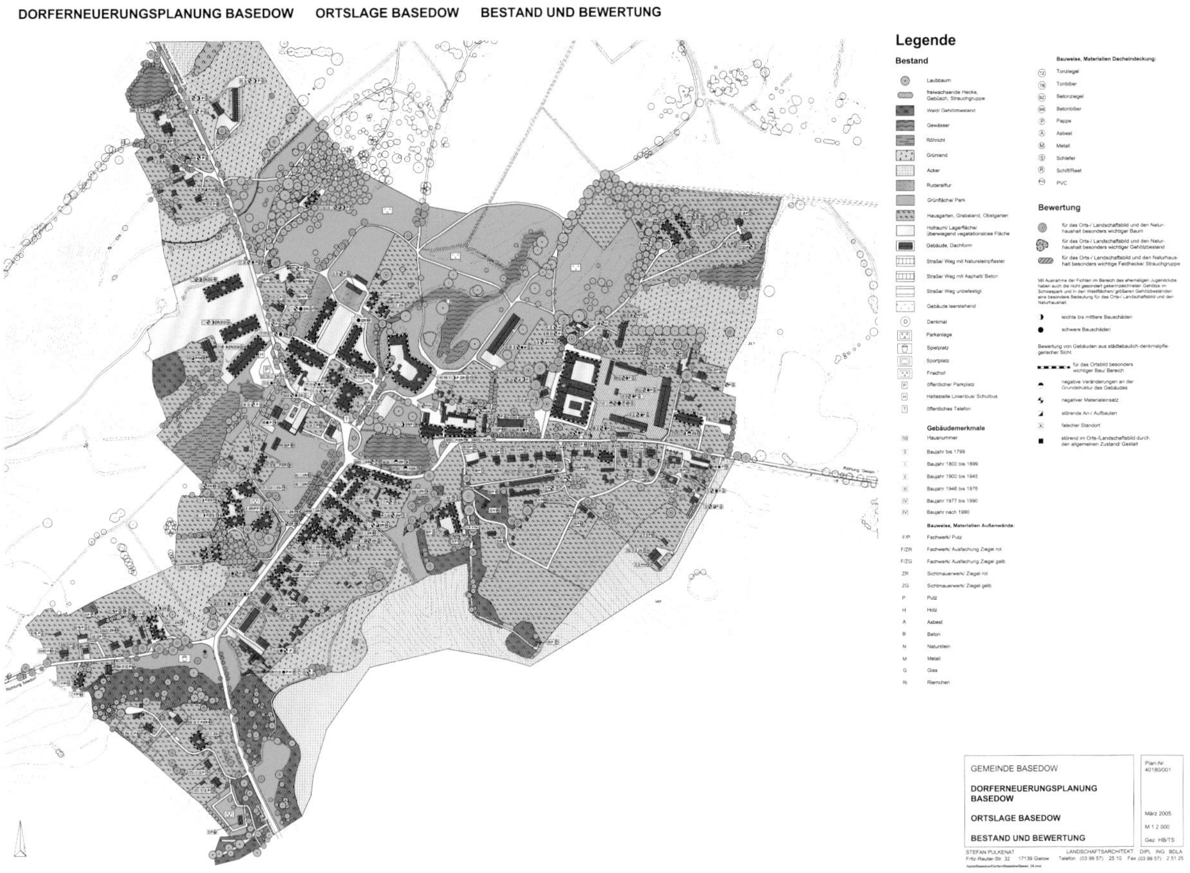

DORFERNEUERUNGSPLANUNG BASEDOW ORTSLAGE BASEDOW BESTAND UND BEWERTUNG

Plan of the existing site as a basis for planning a village renewal in Basedow, Germany. Stefan Pulkenat.

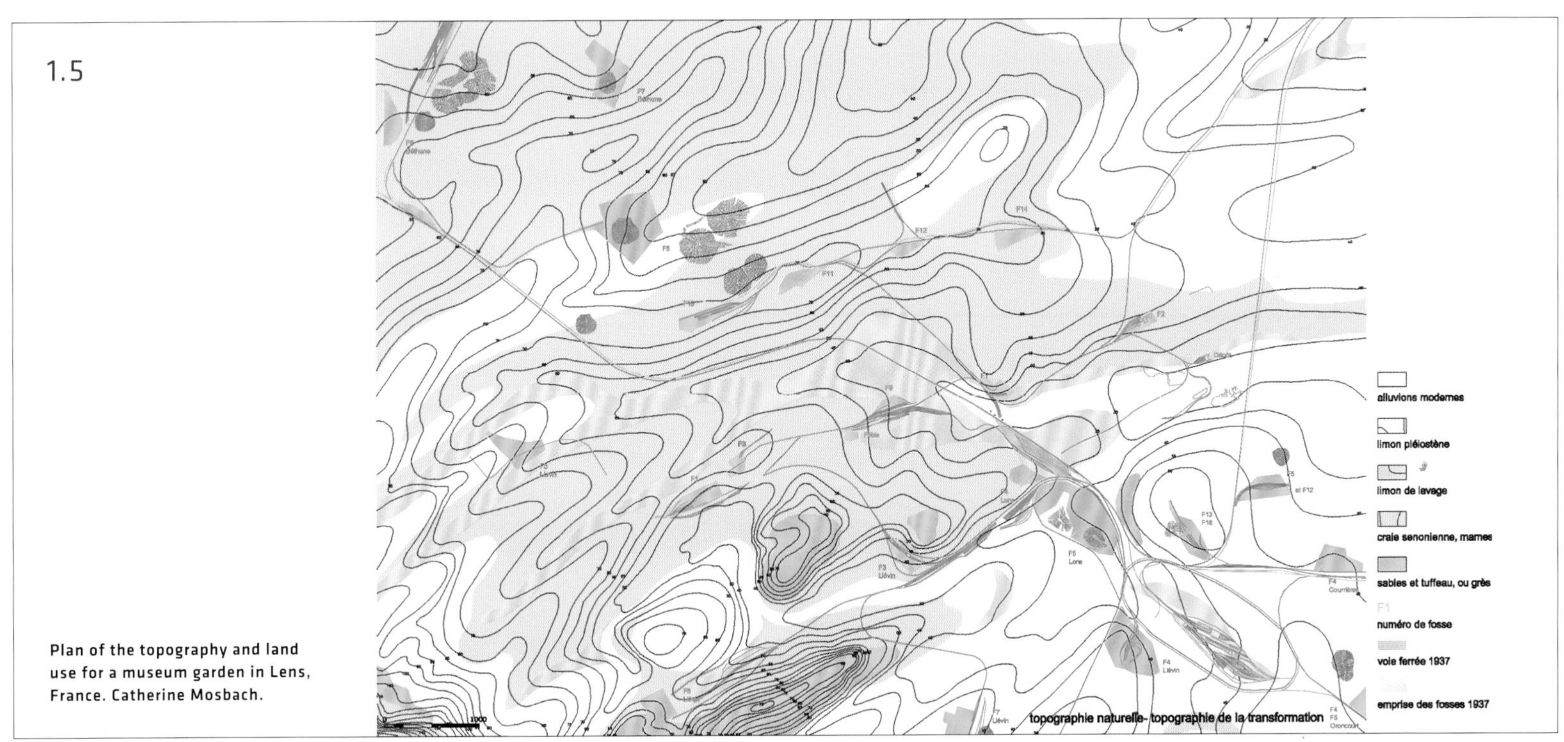


1.5

Plan of the topography and land use for a museum garden in Lens, France. Catherine Mosbach.

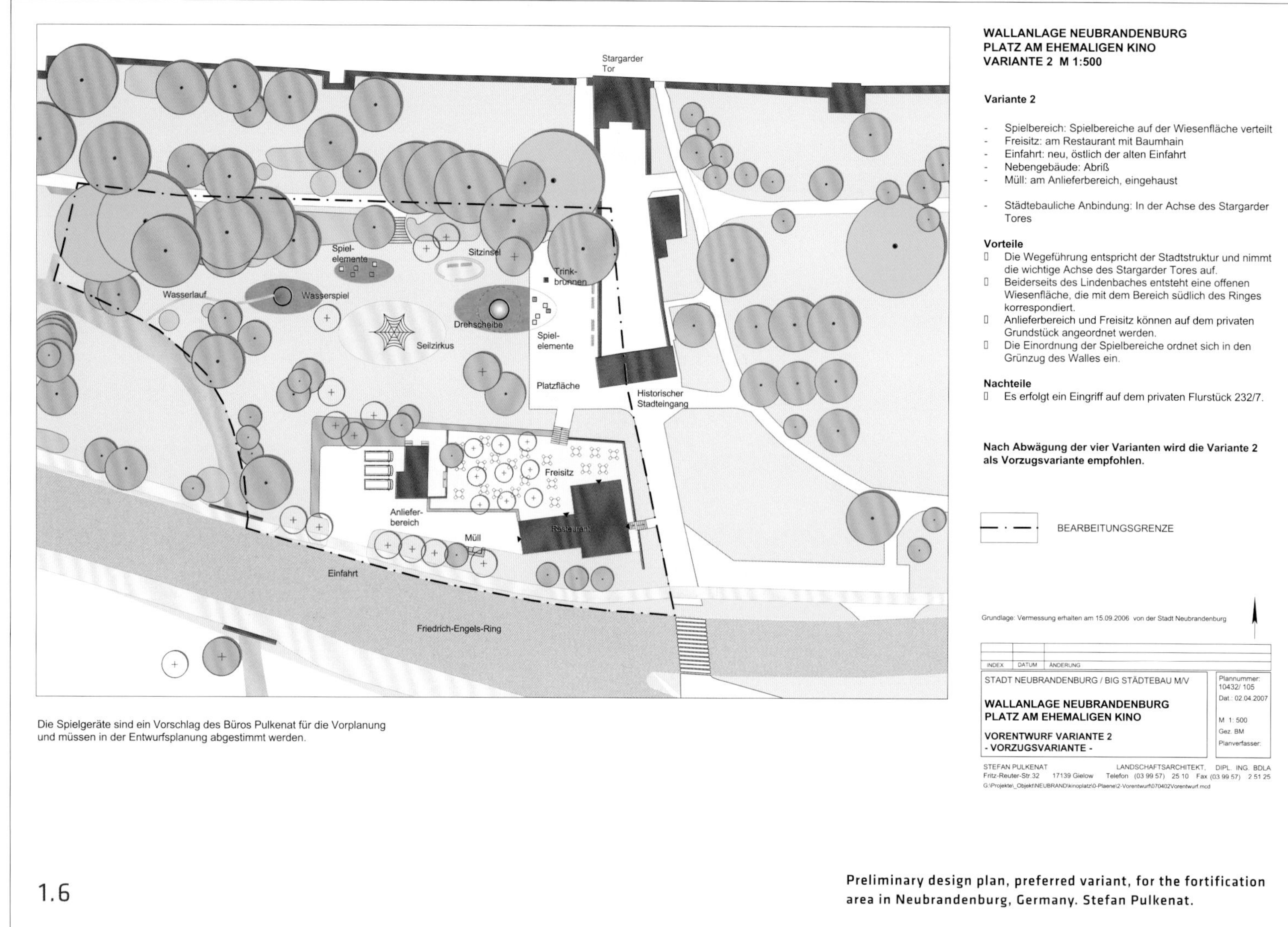


1.6

**Preliminary design plan, preferred variant, for the fortification area in Neubrandenburg, Germany. Stefan Pulkenat.**

## Preliminary design and design plans

Preliminary designs as part of the design process present a planning concept, examine possible alternative solutions and evaluate them according to given requirements. A preliminary design is typically drawn in a clearly structured form, so that the alternatives can be quickly discerned, in order to identify solutions among the variants that ultimately lead to the best development for the project area. Preliminary design plans are usually ground plans, the variants are often underlaid in colour, and descriptions and evaluations of the alternatives are often appended as text or incorporated into a legend.

This preliminary design for a fortification area (Ill. 1.6) shows one of several planning options. It is expressly marked as the preferred option, so that here the planners are presenting the result of their deliberations and demonstrating their ability not just to explore options but also to assess them and put forward the best plan. Here notes describing the preliminary design are built into the drawing, listing the advantages of this solution and also clearly identifying one disadvantage, namely that the proposal would require intervention on a private plot of land. Unlike other as-built and design plans, here the entire area is in colour, and the project area is marked with a line. Often only the project area is coloured, and the surroundings sketched as a black-and-white drawing.

1.7 Preliminary design plan for the floral hall at the Internationale Grüne Woche trade fair in Berlin, Germany. Neumann Gusenburger.

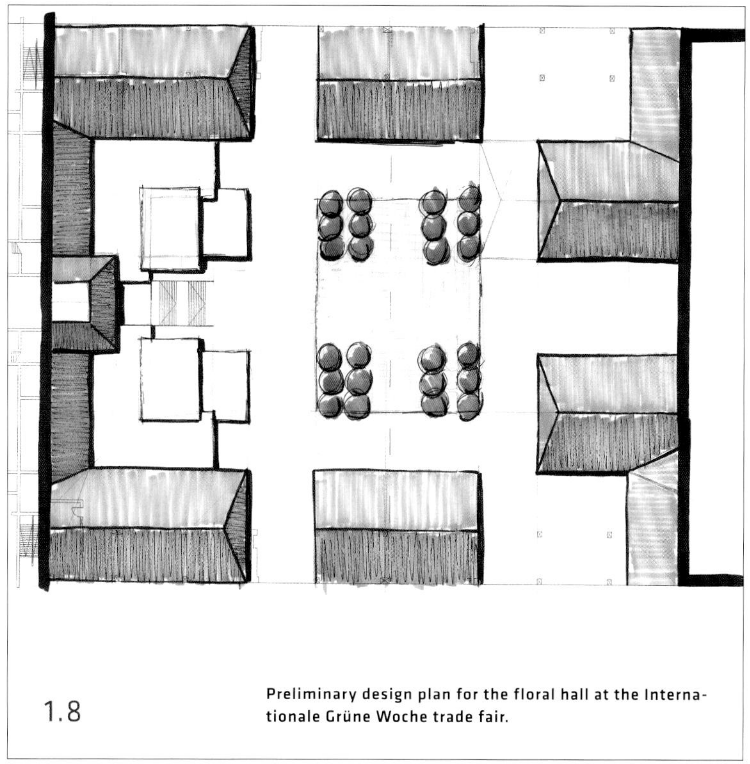

1.8 Preliminary design plan for the floral hall at the Internationale Grüne Woche trade fair.

Two sheets (Ills. 1.7-8) show alternative designs for the floral hall at the Internationale Grüne Woche trade fair in Berlin, where the flower show is traditionally staged with a motto. The hand-coloured drawings first develop a similar framework for the same theme, then put forward various possible designs for the covered space.

The next section presents design drawings, following preliminary planning in the workflow and showing the best solution, typically as a basis for implementation. This plan type represents the best combination of the various aspects involved: users' requirements, ecological development of the location, formal design quality in terms of aesthetics and style, urban development, technical requirements and economic conditions. Sections, sectional elevations or other illustrations usually complement the ground plans in order to represent the third dimension of the design.

There is considerable diversity in planning for open spaces of all kinds and uses. The following section uses examples of classical garden and park design, from domestic gardens via cemetery design to public gardens and parks. The first examples are adequately represented by ground plans, while the subsequent examples show the combination of ground plans with sections.

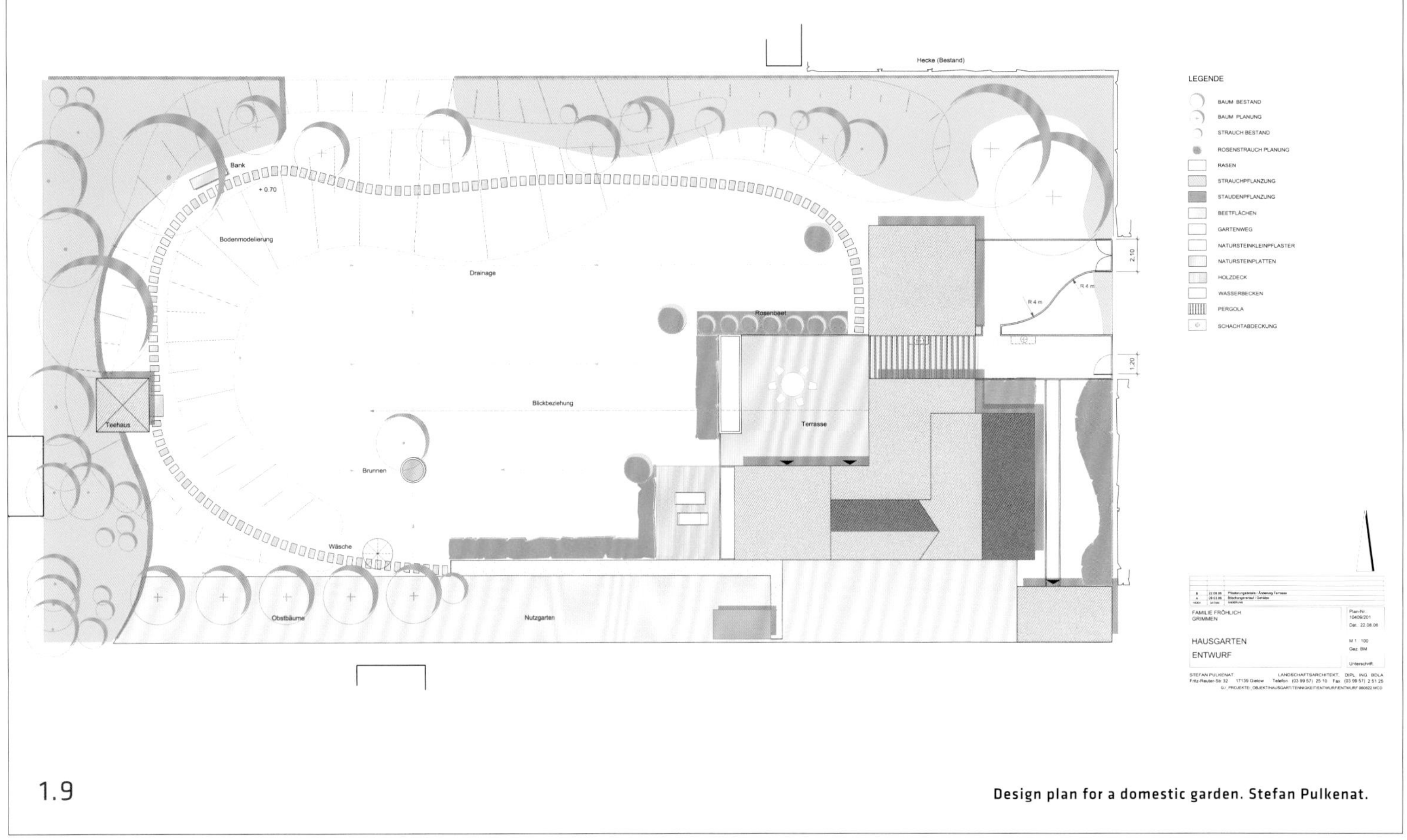


1.9

**Design plan for a domestic garden. Stefan Pulkenat.**

This design for a domestic garden (Ill. 1.9) is presented in areas of colour and provided with a classical legend. The choice of colours is immediately comprehensible according to their conventional meanings: they are clearly distinguished from each other and their significance is easy to understand. The surrounding area is almost completely omitted. The buildings and trees, as three-dimensional components making an impact through height, are given a shadow edge, a device that helps to suggest the third dimension already in this two-dimensional representation. The shadow edge is not drawn to look natural, but kept in a darker shade of grey for the buildings and a darker shade of green for the trees. In reality, the surface covering would appear darker in shaded areas. For the purposes of graphic presentation, the shadow was attached to the elements casting the shadow, usually in a size appropriate to plan graphics, and this deviates from shadows as actually cast, which also change their size and position constantly. This kind of shading is used mainly to make the planned spatial situation more readily readable.

The fine and lucid structures for this domestic garden design make it possible to build additional content into the drawing. It identifies the existing vegetation that is to be taken over for the further development of the garden, and also the new vegetation to complement it. In addition, technical details of radii, drainage placement and path widths are included: typically, these are worked out at later design stages, in the working plans.

1.10

**Design plan for the Japanese Garden of Confluent Water in the Marzahn district recreation park in Berlin, Germany. Practice of Shunmyo Masuno.**

This hand-drawn plan for a closed Japanese garden (Ill. 1.10) shows the vegetation as an important element in different colour shades. The plan identifies the key areas of the Japanese garden: the front, back and central gardens, and contains main technical information such as contour lines. The plants are particularly emphasized, with the shadows they cast lightly marked. Other important areas such as the dry waterfall, the functioning waterfall and the dry garden are also identified, while emphasis is given to individual rocks and the surface structures of the paths. The lucid plan already contains the full range of the future garden spaces.

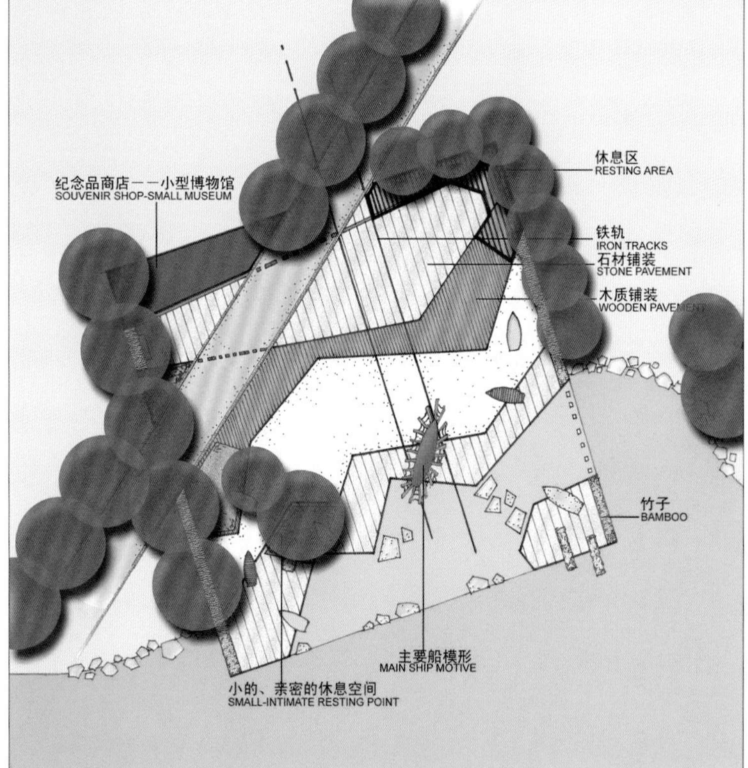


DESIGN IDEA IS BASED ON SHIPYARD INDUSTRY PRESENT IN THIS AREA FOR A LONG TIME. THROUGH THIS TOPIC AND DESIGN PEOPLE SHOULD EXPERIENCE THE CULTURE OF SHIPYARD INDUSTRY AND THE PEOPLE WHO WORK THERE. MAIN DESIGN ELEMENTS ARE SHIPS WHICH HAVE DIFFERENT FUNCTIONS SUCH AS RESTING POINTS , REPRESENTATION AND CHILDREN PLAY. WHOLE PLAZA REPRESENTS SHIPYARD TRANSFORMED INTO A URBAN SPACE ADJUSTED TO PEOPLE'S NEEDS.

设计灵感来源于这个区域有较长历史的造船工业。根据这一主题，通过设计，让人们体验船舶工业的文化并了解工作在那里的人的情况。主要设计元素是船，在这里船提供了各种各样的功能，诸如：休息场所、标志物和儿童游戏场所等。整个广场表达了造船工厂已演绎为适应现代人们需要的城市空间这一设计思想。

1.11 **Detail of the design for the Green Dragon Park in Shanghai, China. Turenscape.**

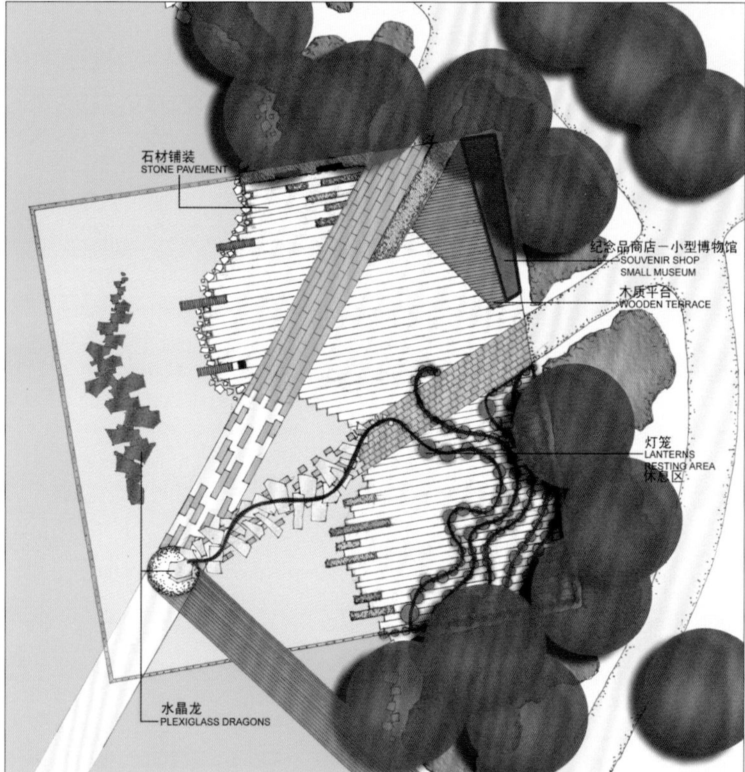


LOCAL CULTURE PLAZA REPRESENTS LOCAL CUSTOMS AND BELIEFS AND DESIGN ELEMENTS ARE SUPPORTING STRONGLY THAT TOPIC. THIS PLAZA IS BY DESIGN IMAGINED AS PEOPLE'S PLAZA, FOR ALL THE USERS AND PEOPLE'S GATHERING. THE PLAZA IS SOME KIND OF REMINDER OF CHINESE CULTURE AND TRADITION. MAIN DESIGN ELEMENTS ARE TWO DRAGONS PLAYING WITH A BALL AND LANTERNS WHICH ARE MOST COMMON AND VERY RECOGNIZABLE PART OF CHINESE CULTURE. THEY ARE ALSO MULTIFUNCTIONAL: REPRESENTATION, CHILDREN PLAY, RESTING POINT AND PASSAGE.

民俗文化主题园应代表当地的习俗和信仰，设计元素应强烈表达这一主题思想。这个广场设计定位为人民广场，为所有使用者和人们聚会使用，表达了宝山区传统的彩灯和龙船文化民俗。主要设计思想是以二龙戏珠和彩灯展示为主题，这些都是宝山区最公认的传统文化组成部分。在这里飞舞的水晶龙，路上、水中，晶莹剔透；红灯笼好似摇曳的大风铃，吸引大人小孩驻足休憩，人们沉浸在一片欢乐祥和之中。

1.12 **Detail of the design for the Green Dragon Park.**

The design drawings for the Green Dragon Park in Shanghai (Ills. 1.11 - 12) present ideas for core areas, very detailed and accompanied by short explanatory texts. The similar graphic approach, the matching colours and the same layouts emphasize their coherence. The aim of this project is to restore the former link between the local population and the water features in their surroundings. All the elements of the square, like the shading in the form of a sail or the curved fountain with seats for relaxing, are intended as reminders of this background. The water features also symbolize the river than runs through Shanghai. Chinese culture and tradition are addressed in the design by two dragons playing ball and the use of typical lanterns.

The plan for refurbishing the old cemetery in Dargun (Ill. 1.13) contains both changes to the existing design, like the felling of trees, and also new arrangements for graves, paths and other facilities. Here attention is paid to continuing tradition while at the same time taking the necessary steps towards the intended modernization. In addition to the design concept, the plan also contains instructions for technical implementation.

In the design for the Westergasfabriek in Amsterdam (Ill. 1.14), vertical modulations in the main open spaces were shown using colour scales. The different areas are separated from each other mainly by the colours – as with a painting – rather than by the black contour lines. In addition to green spaces and water spaces, the culture park for the former industrial site includes monuments to industry. These are integrated into the overall concept and their connections with the green spaces and water spaces are shown.

1.13

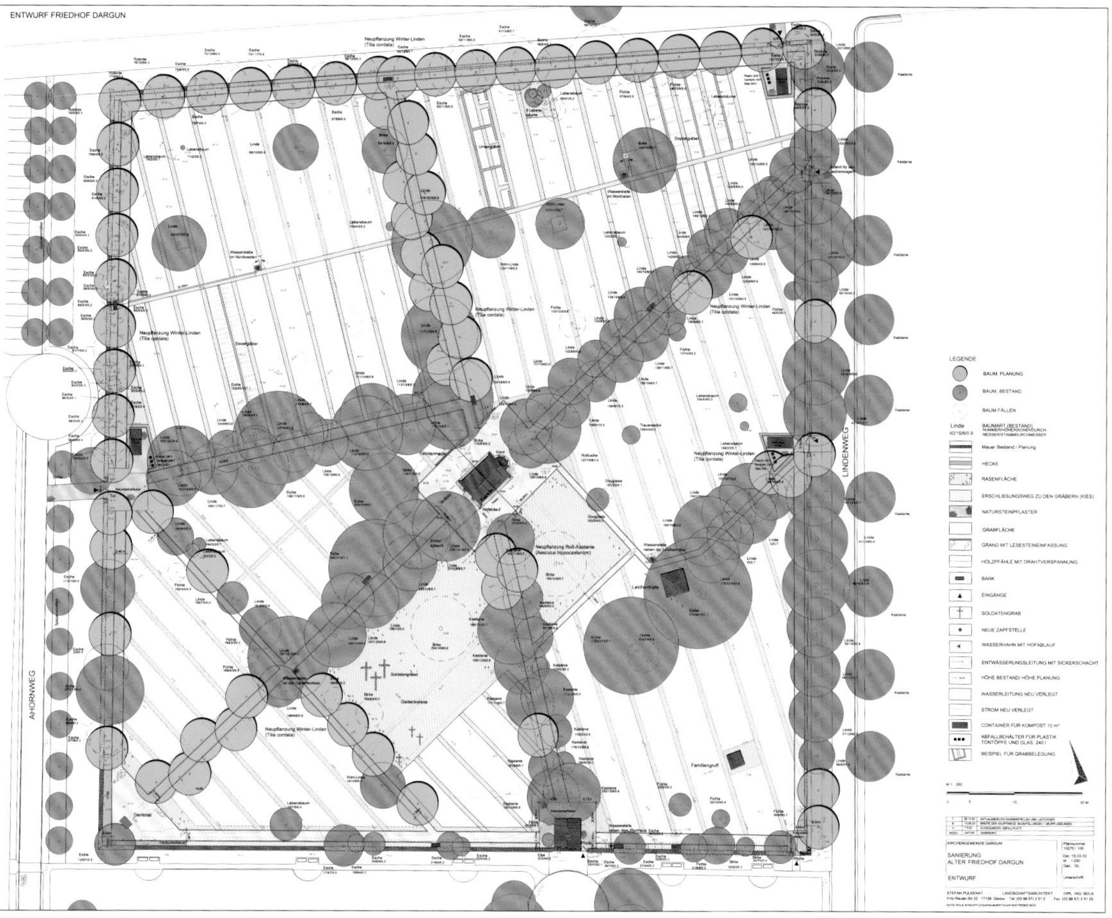

Design plan for refurbishing the old cemetery in Dargun, Germany. Stefan Pulkenat.

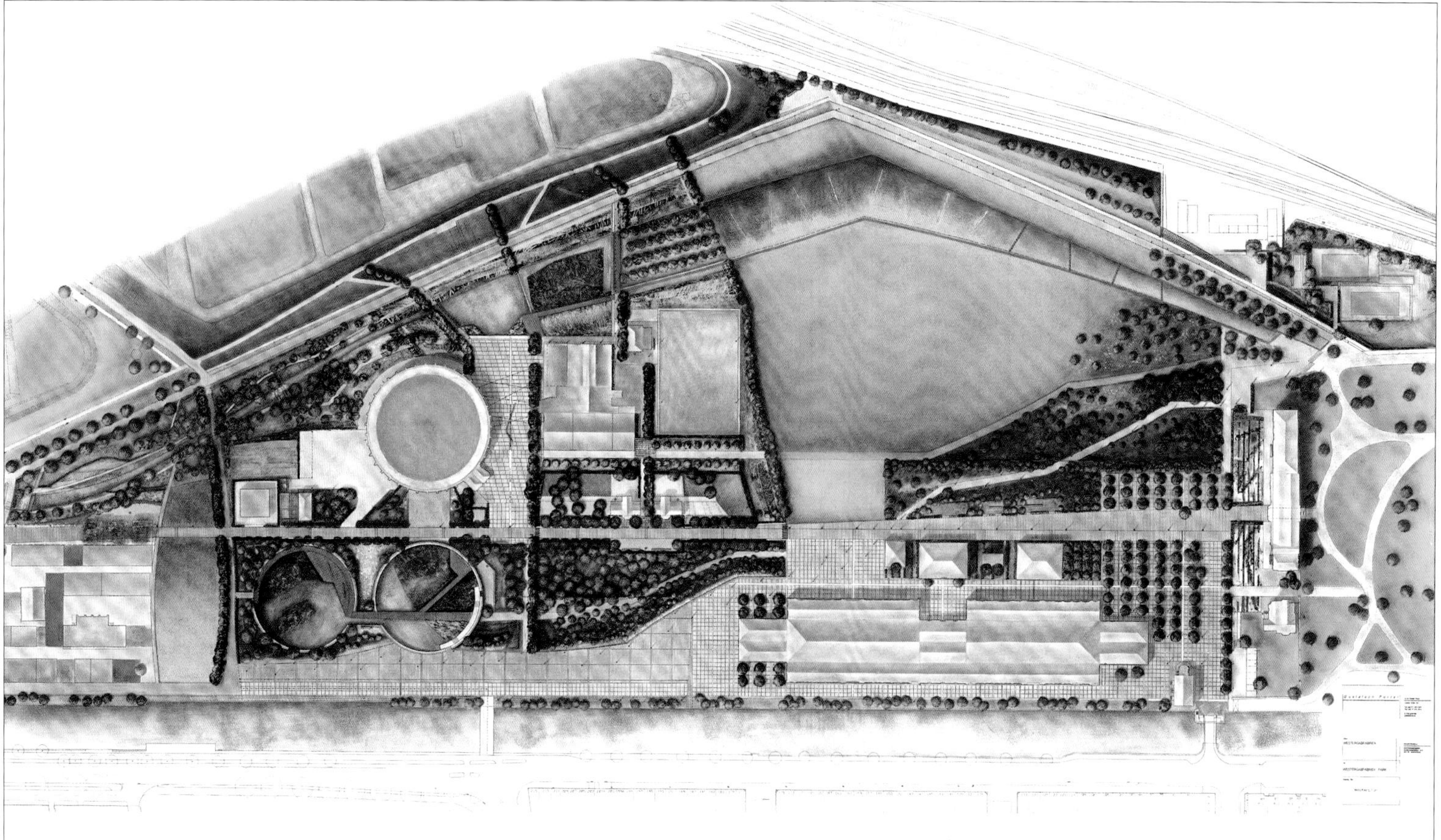

1.14

Design plan for the Westergasfabriek Park in Amsterdam, Netherlands. Gustafson Porter.

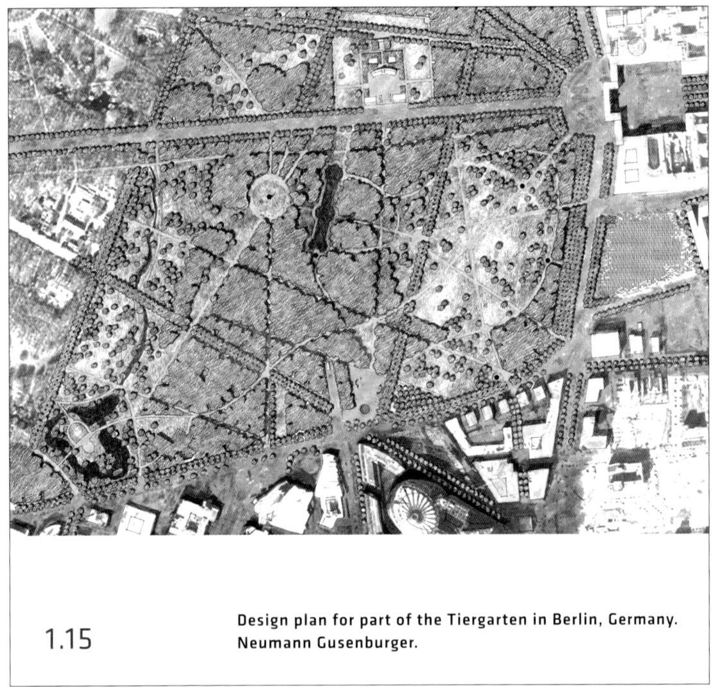

1.15 **Design plan for part of the Tiergarten in Berlin, Germany. Neumann Gusenburger.**

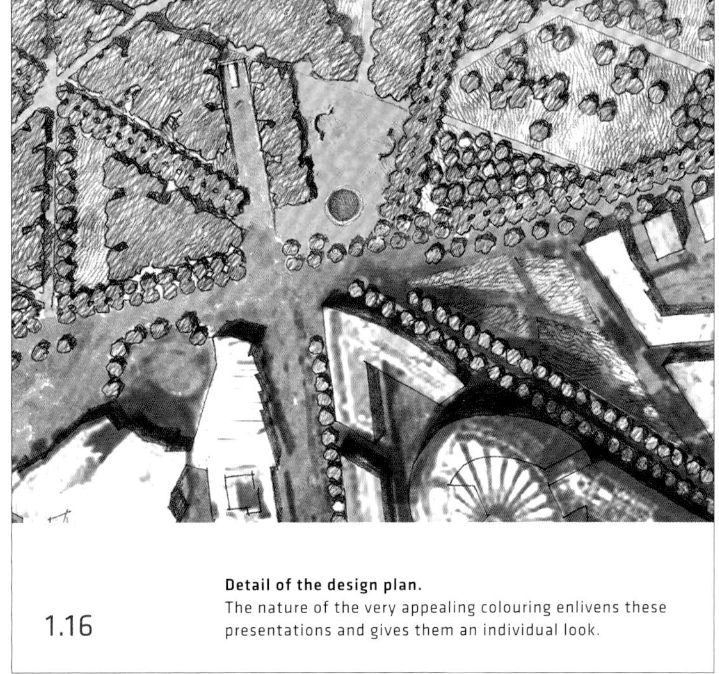

1.16 **Detail of the design plan.**
The nature of the very appealing colouring enlivens these presentations and gives them an individual look.

1.17

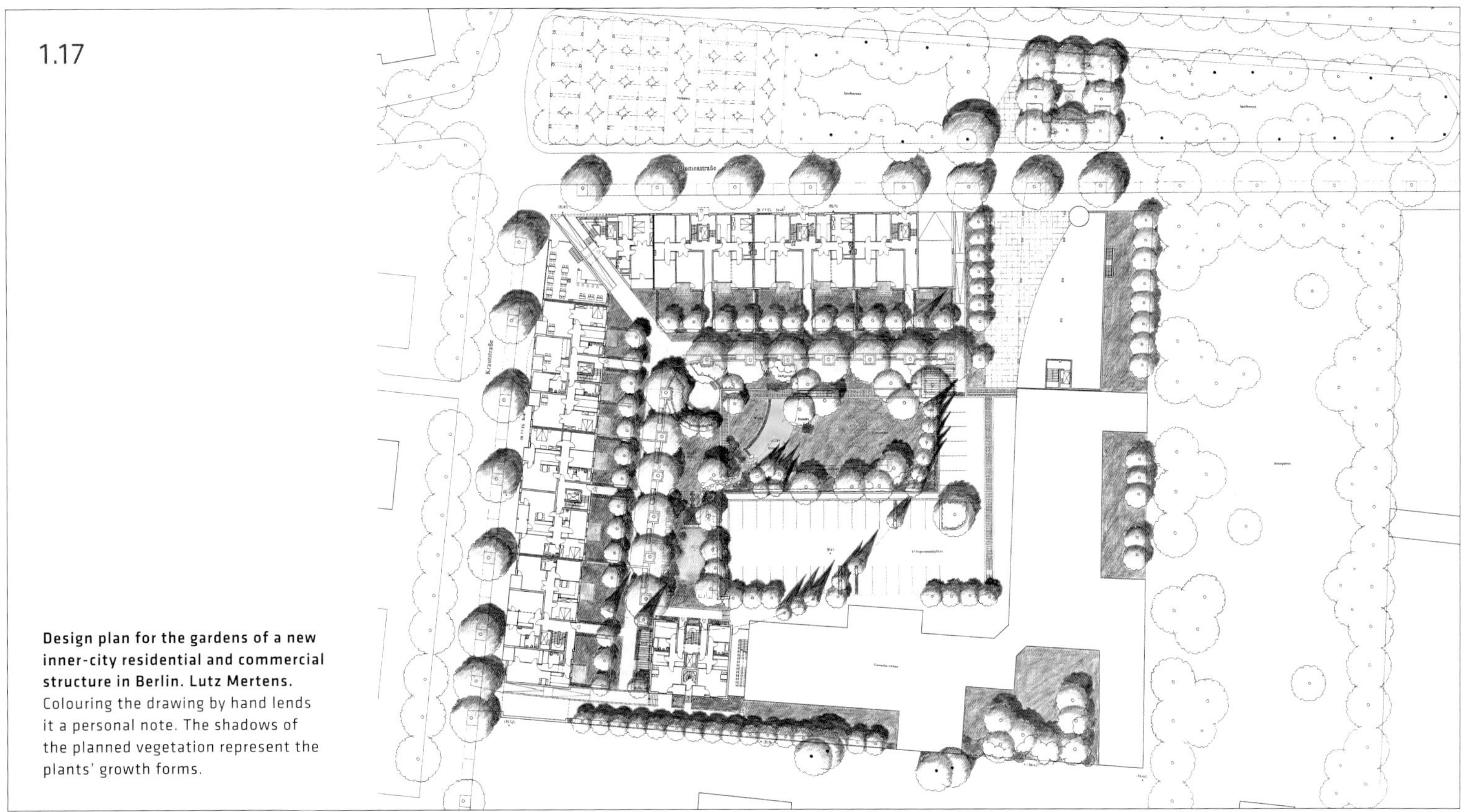

**Design plan for the gardens of a new inner-city residential and commercial structure in Berlin. Lutz Mertens.**
Colouring the drawing by hand lends it a personal note. The shadows of the planned vegetation represent the plants' growth forms.

1.18 **Design plan for the Qiaoyuan Park in Tianjin, China. Turenscape.**
This design for an urban park is strikingly presented with a clear choice of colour areas and a high degree of legibility.

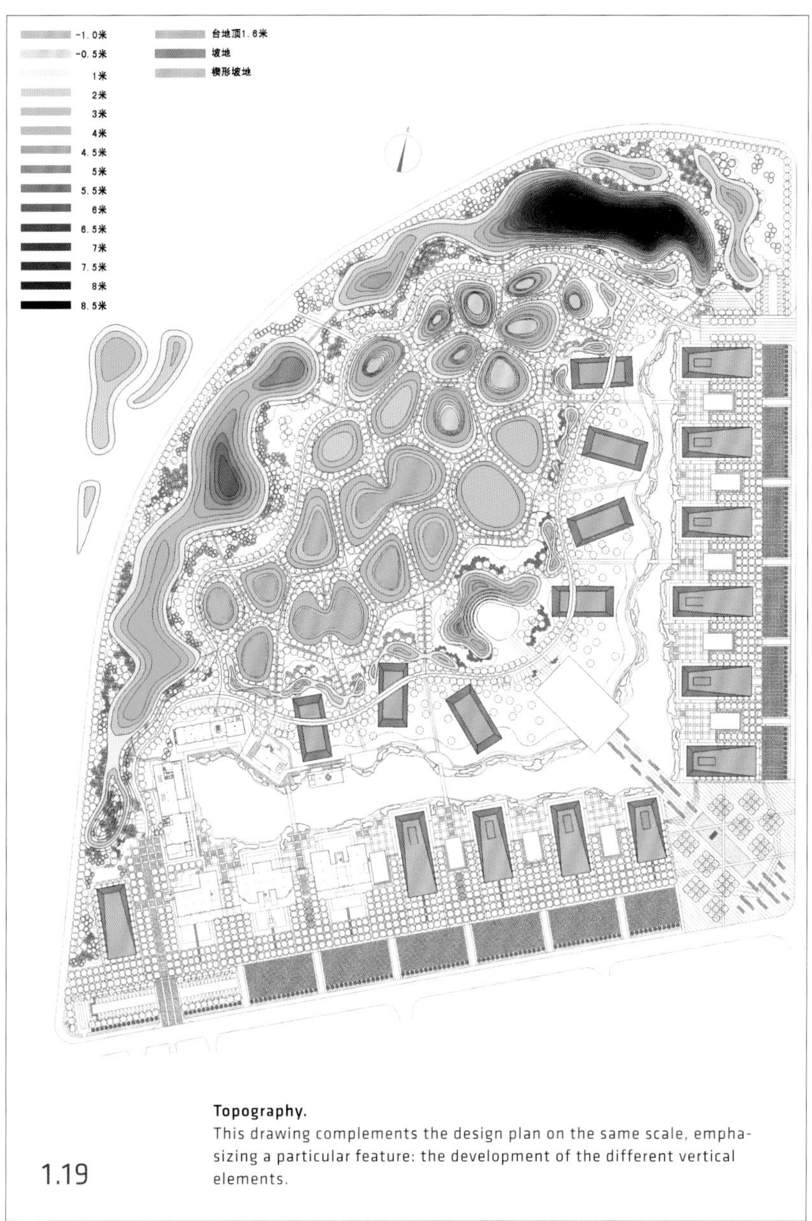


1.19 **Topography.**
This drawing complements the design plan on the same scale, emphasizing a particular feature: the development of the different vertical elements.

Most design plans are coloured, as their information can be much more clearly conveyed in this way than in black-and-white drawings. The choice of colour is frequently based on the natural colour of the planned objects, but tends to be rather stronger than the natural or built environment is in reality. The drawings are intended to evoke important positive associations: a site looks perfect on plans, a pleasant atmosphere seems to dominate, and the problems are solved by the proposed design. As nature displays a large number of shades of green and this colour is said to be calming, having positive associations in most cultures, for example, being equated with hope, several shades of green are typically to be found in design plans. A gradation of brightness values can give an impression of a topography that cannot be conveyed in two-dimensional drawings otherwise.

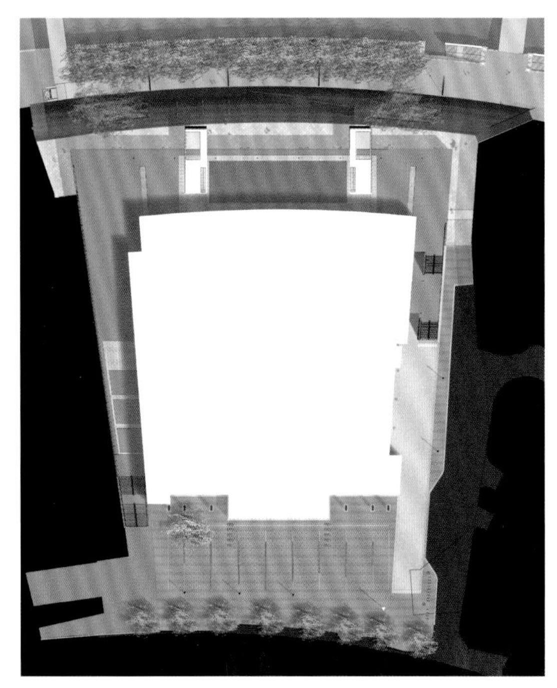

1.20

**Design plan for the environs of the Royal Festival Hall in London, Great Britain. GROSS.MAX.**
This important concert hall, shown in white in the centre of the plan, acquires an appropriate open space that can be used in many ways. Its prestigious reputation is underlined by clear structures and details.

1.21

**Design plan for the market square in Nottingham, Great Britain. Gustafson Porter.**
Nottingham's second-largest square is redesigned as a place for everyday activities and also for special events and markets; key areas are mentioned separately in the legend.

1.22

A CAJICA

A CHIA

**Design plan for a park in Chia, Colombia. Grupo Verde Ltda.**

1.23 **Design plan for the park at Gleisdreieck, Berlin, Germany. SLA.**

1.24 **Design plan for Potters Fields Park in London, Great Britain. GROSS.MAX.**
This clearly structured presentation emphasizes the significance of the herbaceous planting in the entrance area through striking colour schemes.

1.25 **Design plans for gardens on Singapore Bay. Gustafson Porter.**
The design for the shore area is distinguished from its environs by the colouring, with the special colour quality for the areas emphasizing an intricate and varied design even on this rough scale.

1.26

Section for the design for an area at the regional horticultural show in Bad Wildungen, Germany. Plancontext.

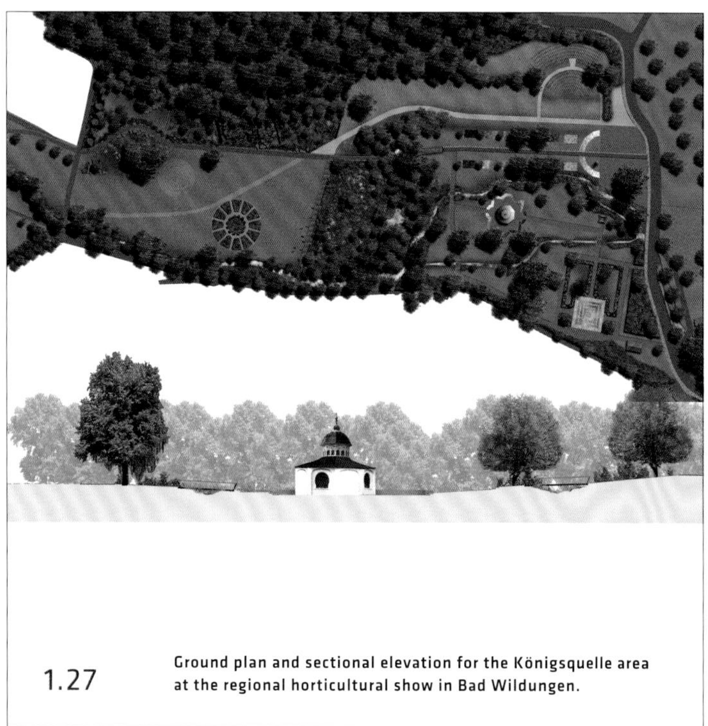

1.27

Ground plan and sectional elevation for the Königsquelle area at the regional horticultural show in Bad Wildungen.

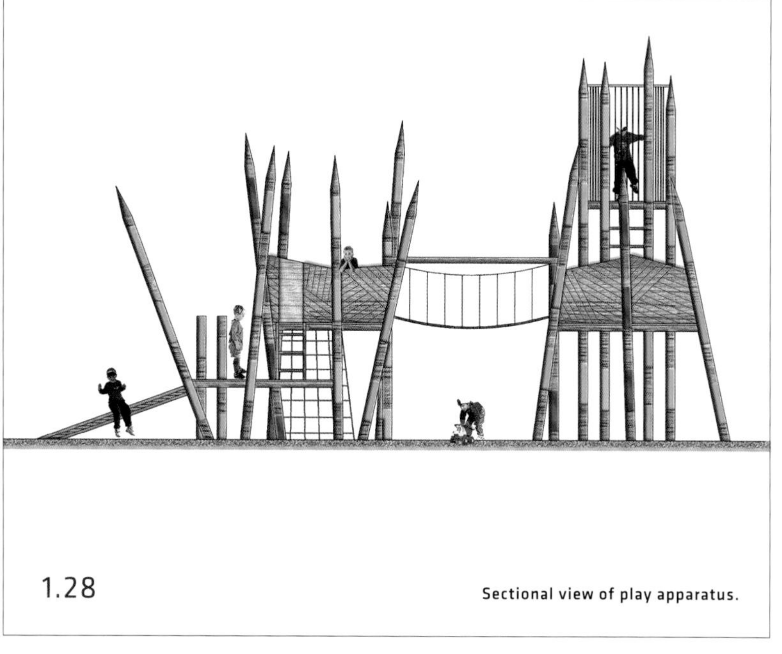

1.28

Sectional view of play apparatus.

## Sections and elevations

Sectional drawings complement the ground plans as design drawings, giving information about the shape of terrain heights and indicating how buildings and vegetation create space. Sectional elevations are sometimes placed on the same sheet as the ground plan (Ill. 1.27), while sections are often presented on an additional sheet (Ills. 1.26 and 1.29). Larger, more detailed scales were chosen for the sectional elevations as shown here, in order to illustrate both the terrain heights and also how the building and tree heights relate to each other. The representation of the vegetation and the colouring are close to reality in all drawings used, so that their interrelations are evident on first sight. The play area is shown in a sectional elevation of its own (Ill. 1.28), on a larger scale, and without the context.

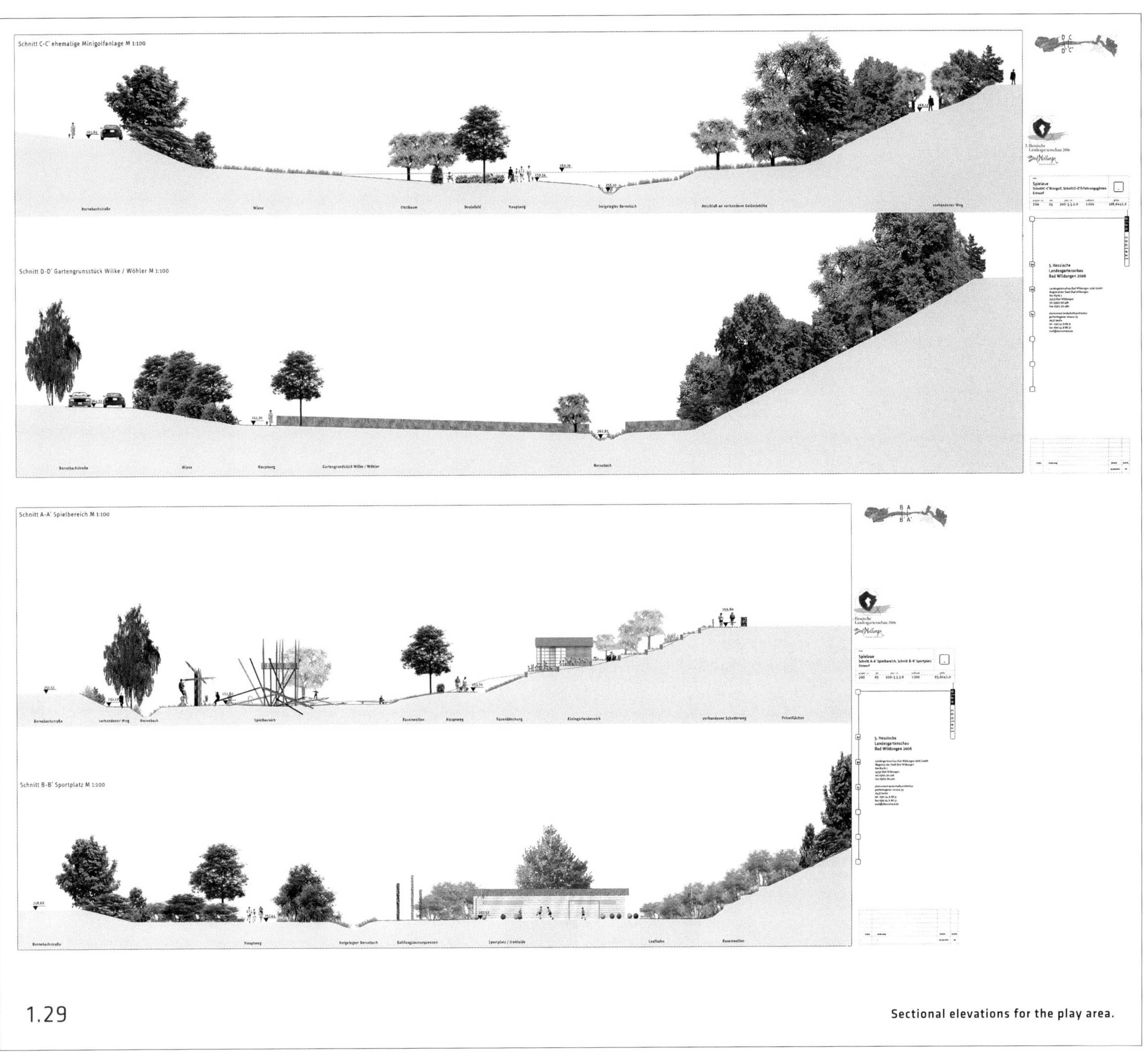


1.29

**Sectional elevations for the play area.**

Recognizing the dimensions and proportions is particularly important for understanding the design drawings. Here, as in most sectional elevations, it is not just the vegetation that permits familiar size comparisons, but above all the human figures. The children and adults shown with their suggested activities can also indicate the planned uses for the open spaces and play apparatus.

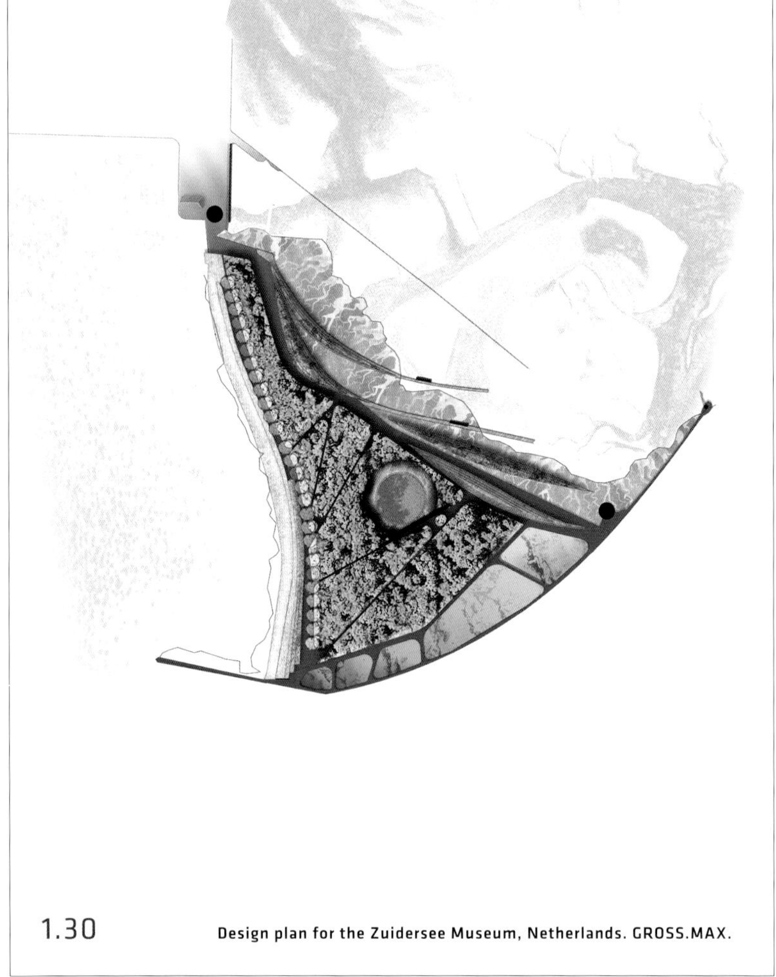

1.30 Design plan for the Zuidersee Museum, Netherlands. GROSS.MAX.

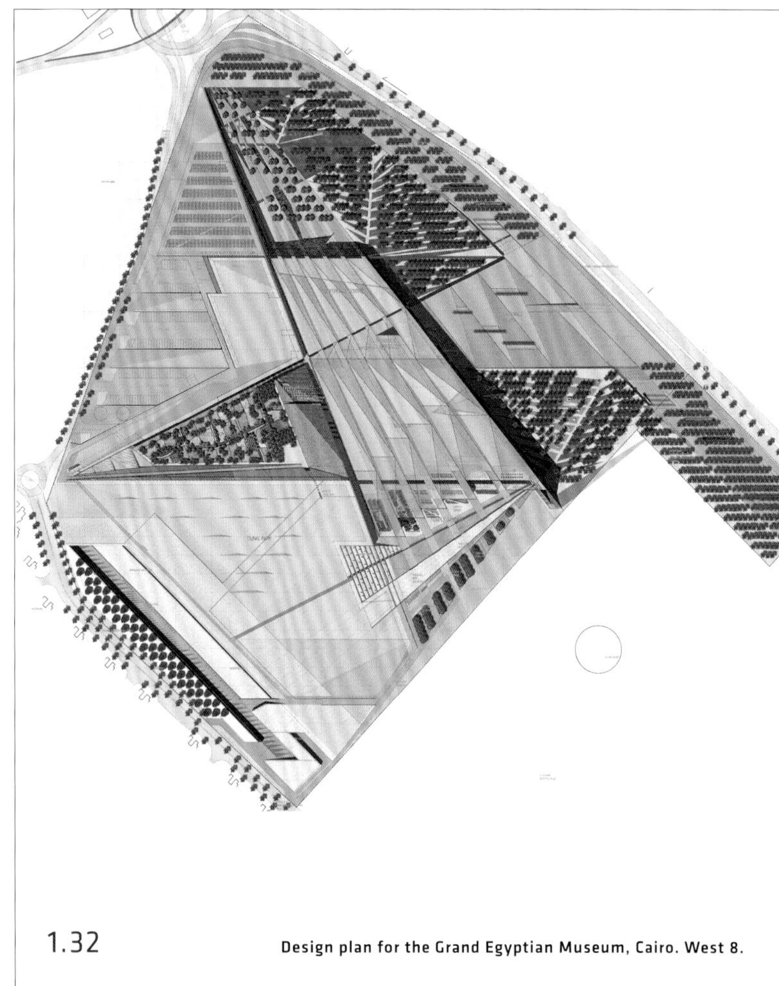

1.32 Design plan for the Grand Egyptian Museum, Cairo. West 8.

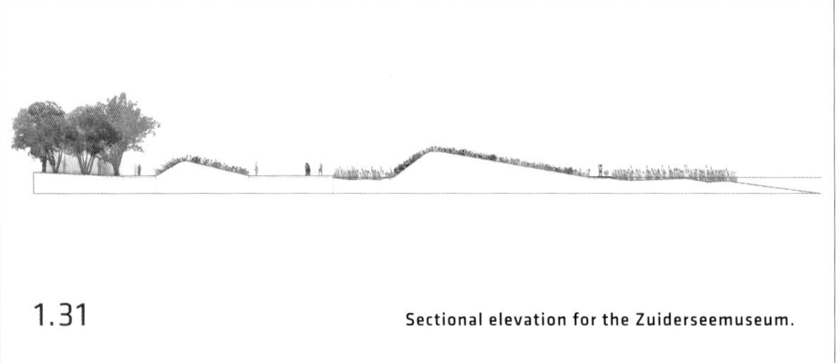

1.31 Sectional elevation for the Zuiderseemuseum.

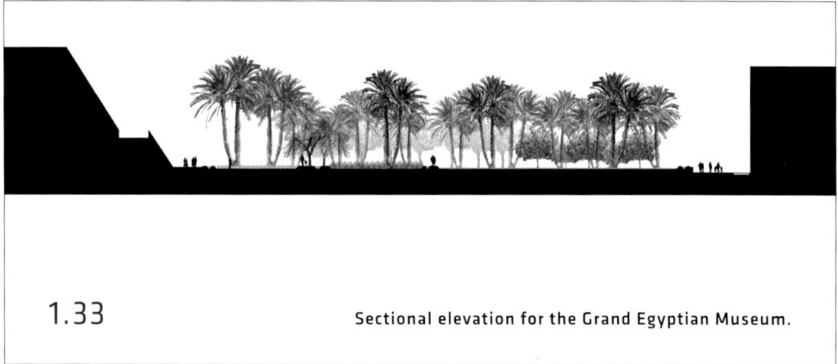

1.33 Sectional elevation for the Grand Egyptian Museum.

The ground plans for the Zuiderzee Museum (Ills. 1.30-1.31) and the Grand Egyptian Museum (Ills. 1.32-1.33) are complemented by sectional elevations. Both examples are effective through their graphics alone; no explanatory texts, legends or technical details are added in. This also applies to the sectional elevations: they are not marked on the ground plans, so the section line on which the drawing is based can be found only by comparing the images. The drawings are intended principally to represent heights, and both use images of people and small trees or palms as relative sizes for purposes of comparison. The example of the Zuidermeer Museum shows the key aspect of the dune formations and their varying heights, while the Grand Egyptian Museum picks out the dimension of architecture, presented as a black frame, and the size of the vegetation inside of it.

1.34

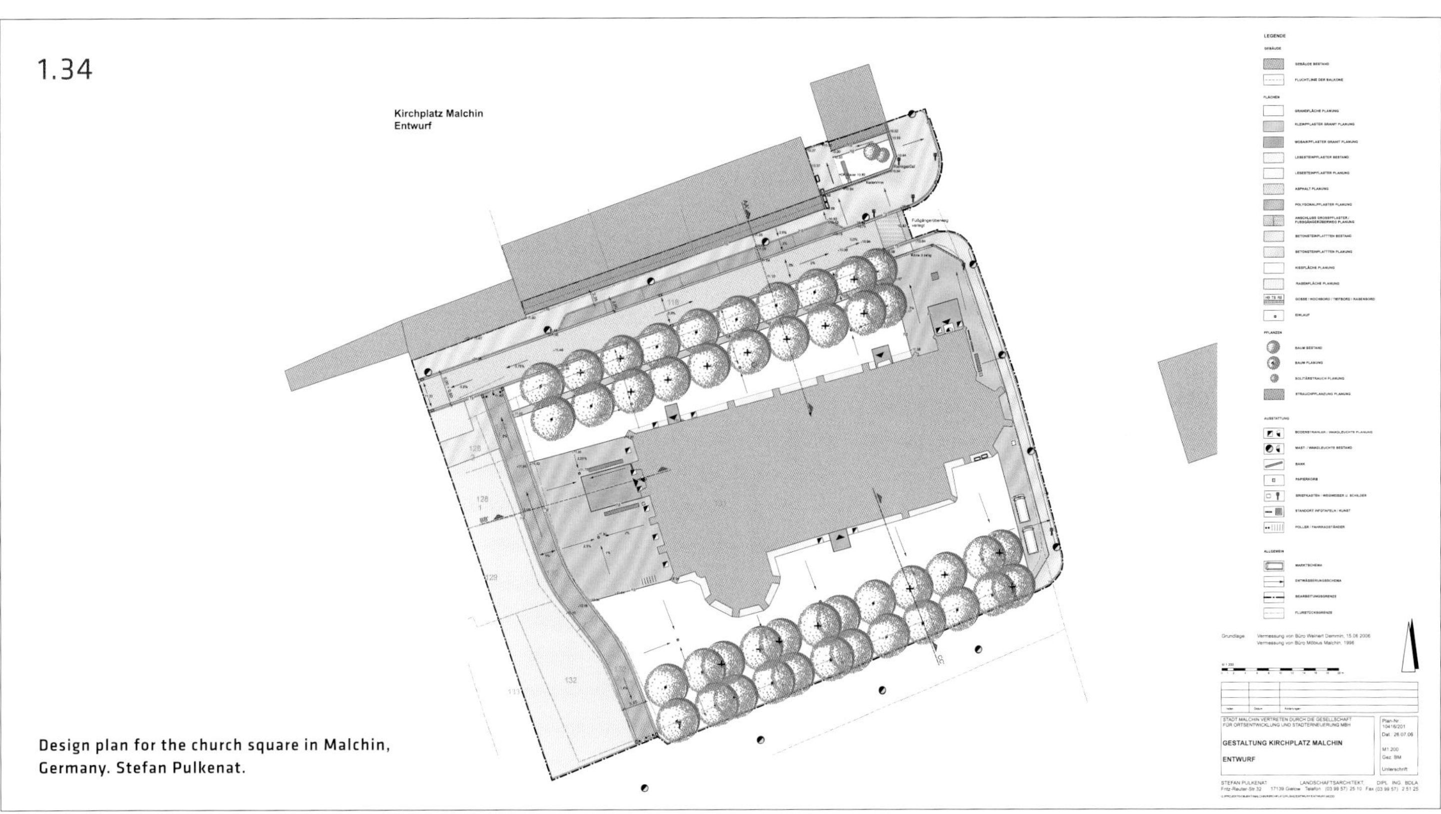


Design plan for the church square in Malchin, Germany. Stefan Pulkenat.

1.35

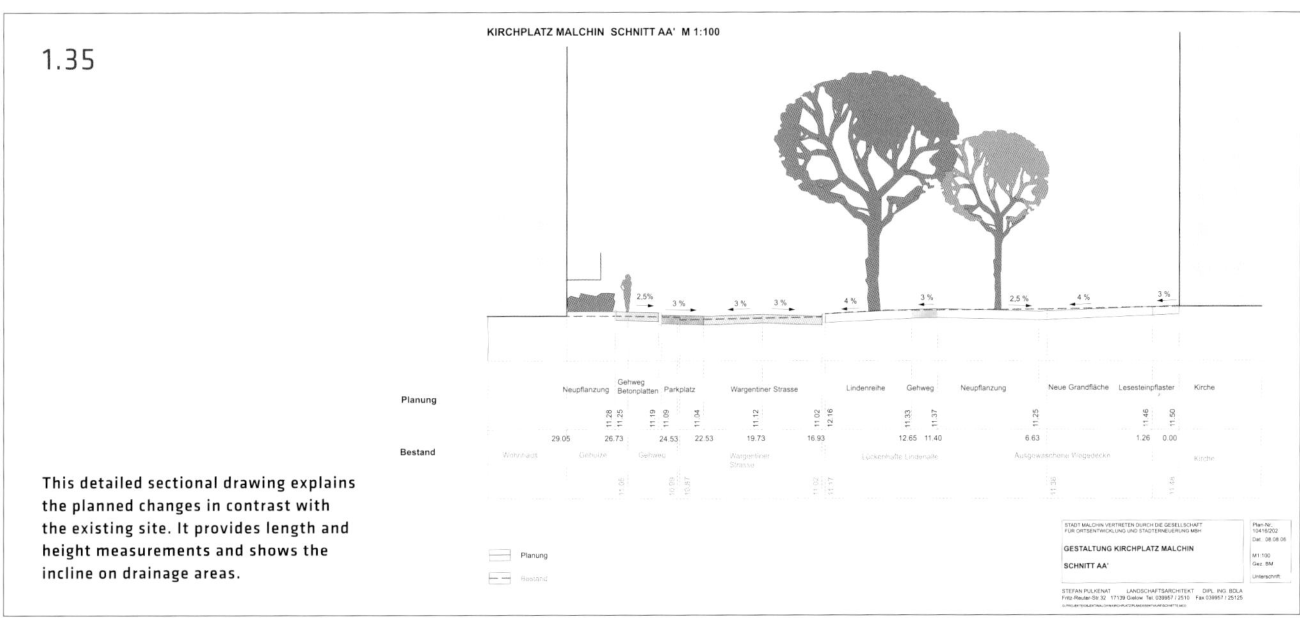


This detailed sectional drawing explains the planned changes in contrast with the existing site. It provides length and height measurements and shows the incline on drainage areas.

Important squares in most cities are the market and the town hall square, as well as squares relating to churches, which often double as market places. As central squares, they are used for trade, socializing, for purveying food and as celebration areas. Any creative intervention in these areas kindles a great deal of interest among residents, as identification with the place where they live can depend on central open spaces. Hence the design and its presentation is seen as very important, and design planning is often discussed intensively between residents and with those who are responsible politically. Far-reaching changes can exercise considerable influence over possible uses and whether these places are accepted or rejected. For this reason the plans and the way in which the planning suggestions are conveyed also serve the purpose to encourage public acceptance.

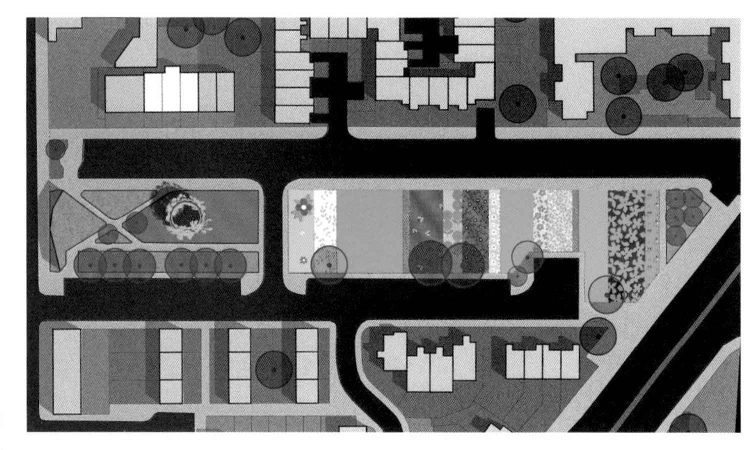

1.36

Design plan for rotunda and community gardens in Liverpool, Great Britain. GROSS.MAX.

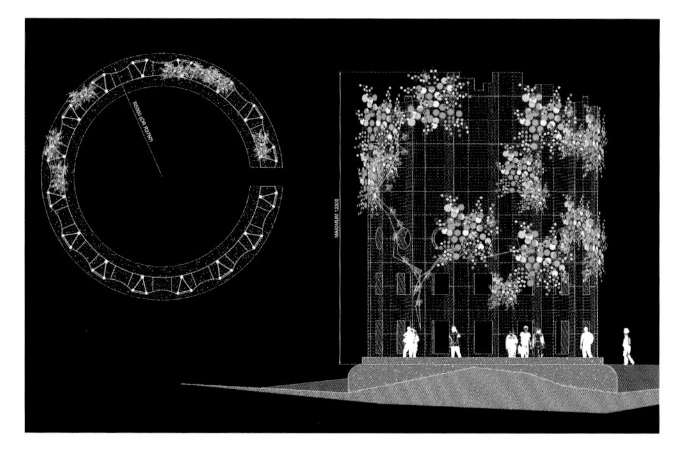

1.37

**Ground plan and section.**
The radius and maximum height are given, other dimensions can be established from the figures depicted. The rotunda makes a light, filigree impression, particularly because of the black background, which makes the foreground seem to glow.

1.38

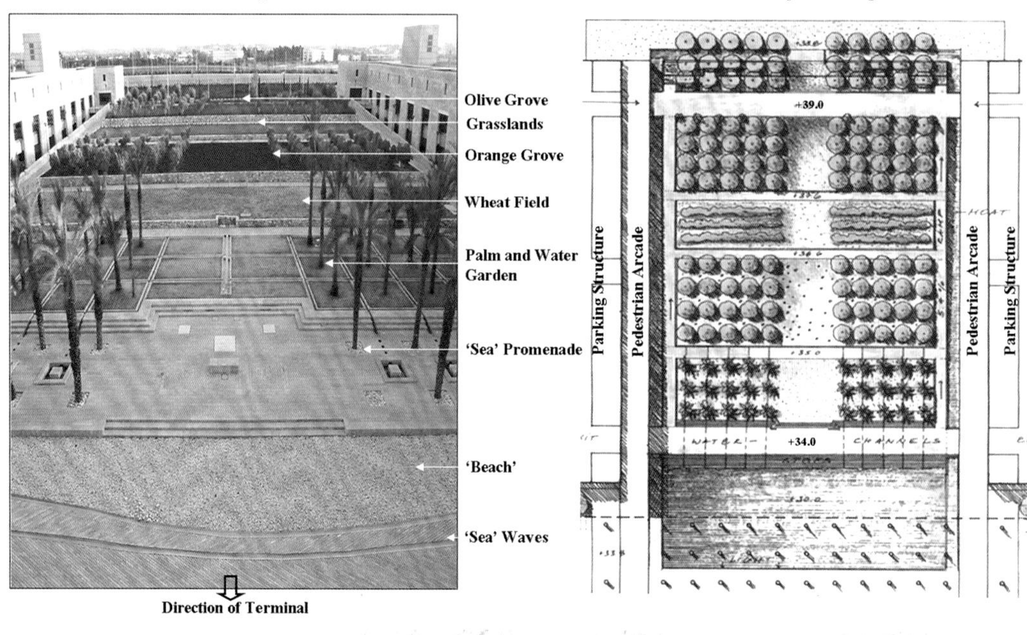


Ground plan (right) with section, complemented by a photograph of the built complex at Ben Gurion International Airport in Tel Aviv, Israel. Shlomo Aronson.

1.39 **Sectional elevation for the street design with accompanying planting in Khalifa City, Abu Dhabi, United Arab Emirates. Neumann Gusenburger.**
Shading in open spaces becomes particularly important in a new, rapidly growing city in a hot climate.

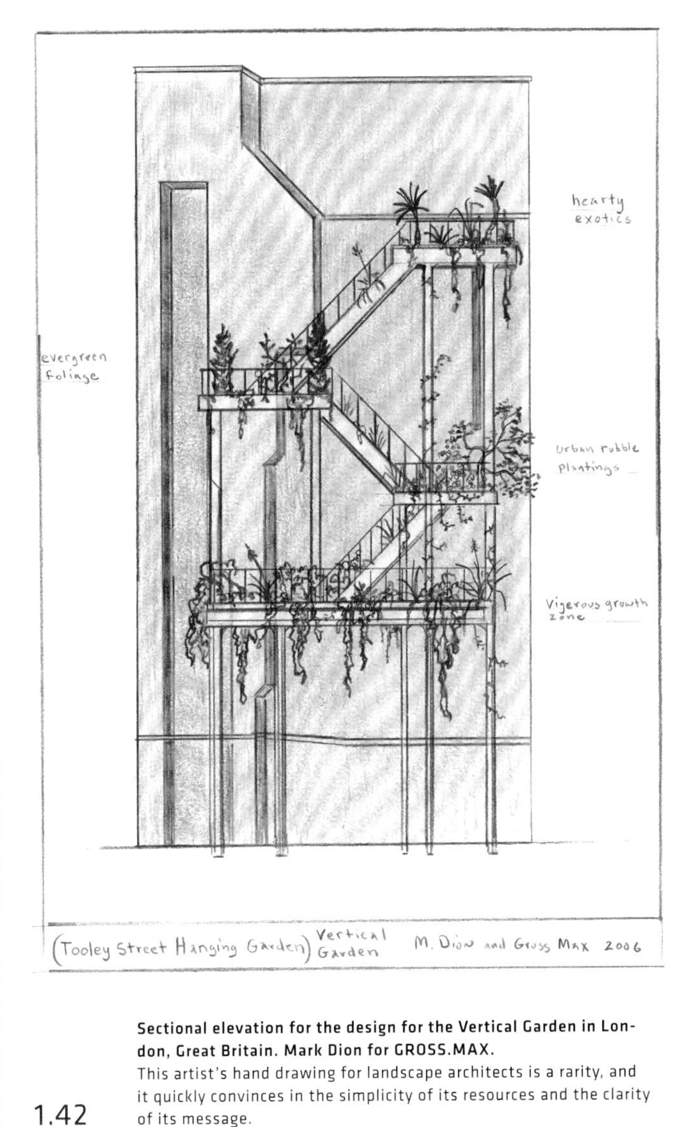


1.42 **Sectional elevation for the design for the Vertical Garden in London, Great Britain. Mark Dion for GROSS.MAX.**
This artist's hand drawing for landscape architects is a rarity, and it quickly convinces in the simplicity of its resources and the clarity of its message.

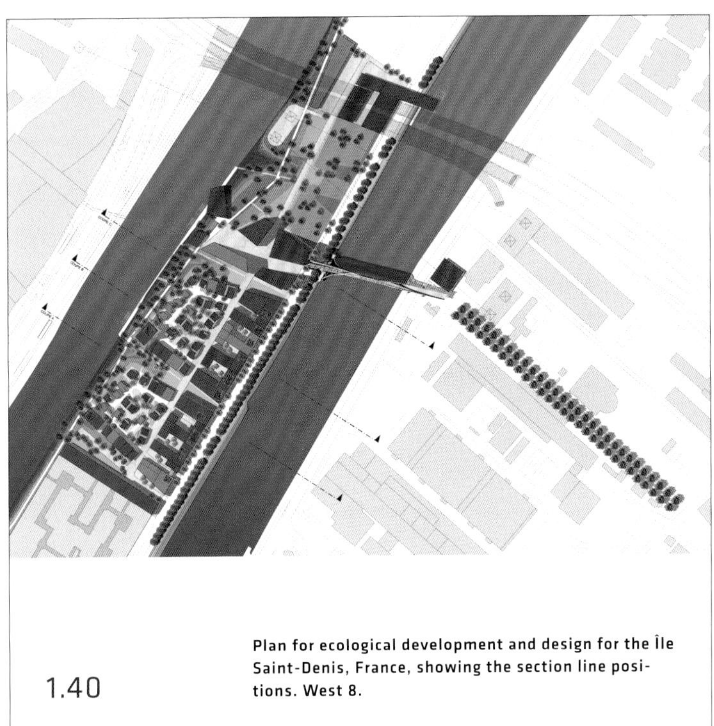

1.40 **Plan for ecological development and design for the Île Saint-Denis, France, showing the section line positions. West 8.**

1.41 **Sections for the Île Saint-Denis.**
These sectional drawings, cutting through buildings in this case, show terrain heights as well as the planned buildings and vegetation, providing important information for the ecological development of this narrow island.

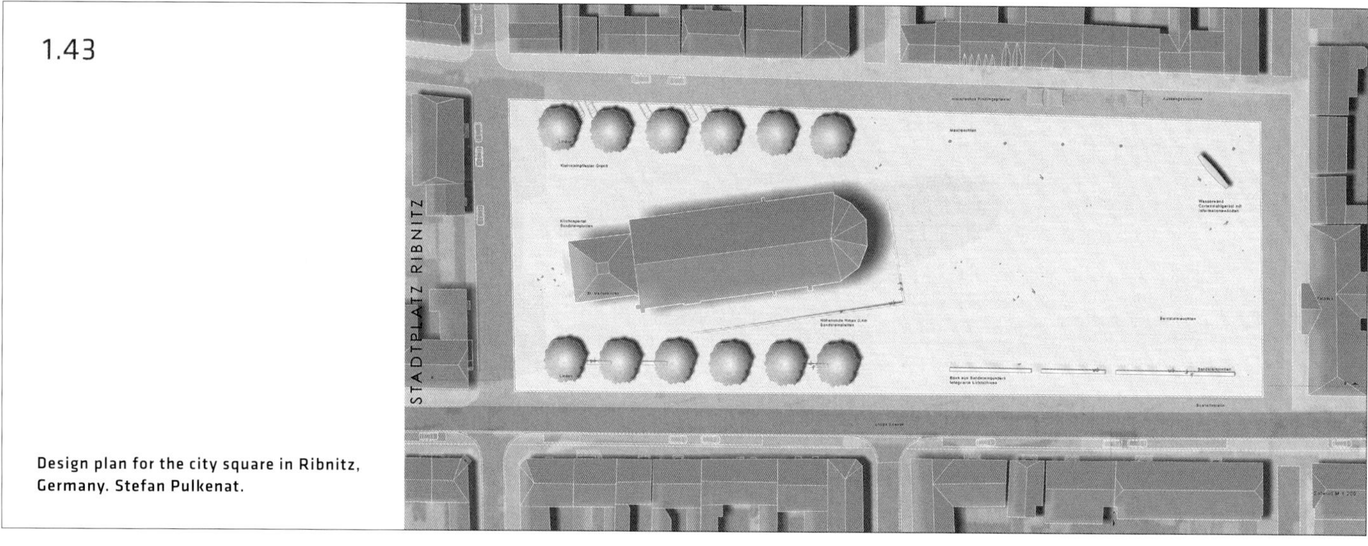


1.43

**Design plan for the city square in Ribnitz, Germany. Stefan Pulkenat.**

1.44

**Sectional elevations.**

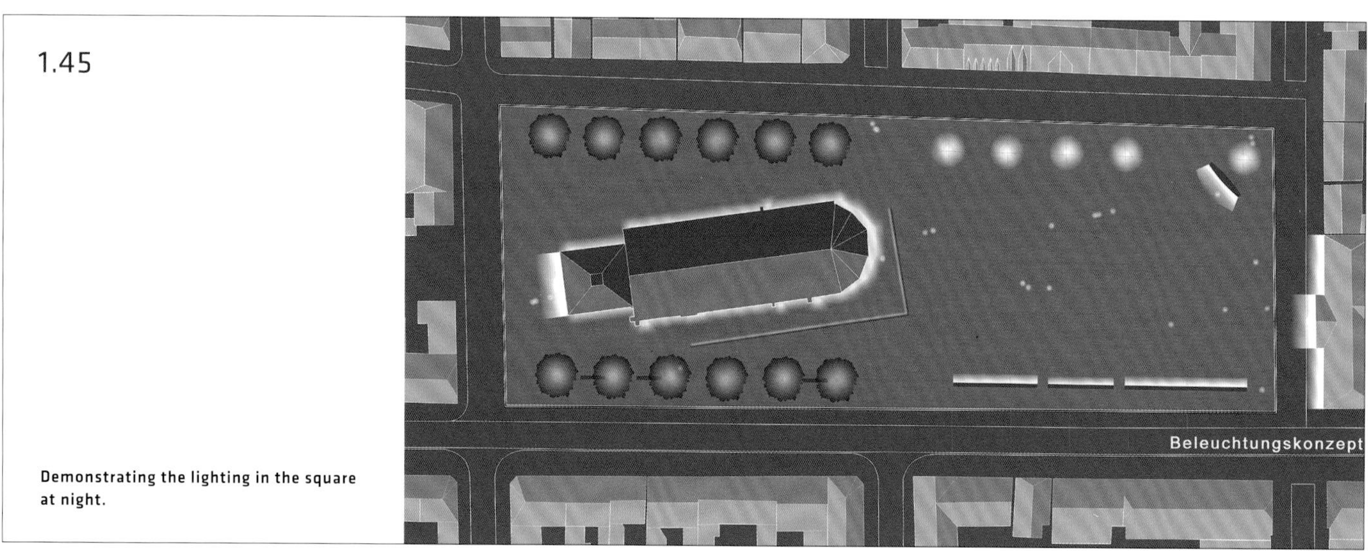


1.45

**Demonstrating the lighting in the square at night.**

Lighting allows open spaces to be used longer, and is essential for safety and orientation in open urban spaces. Lighting planning always starts from a design for the situation in daylight. As open spaces can present themselves differently when it is dark rather than daytime, creating a special atmosphere at night is an important task, and a challenge.

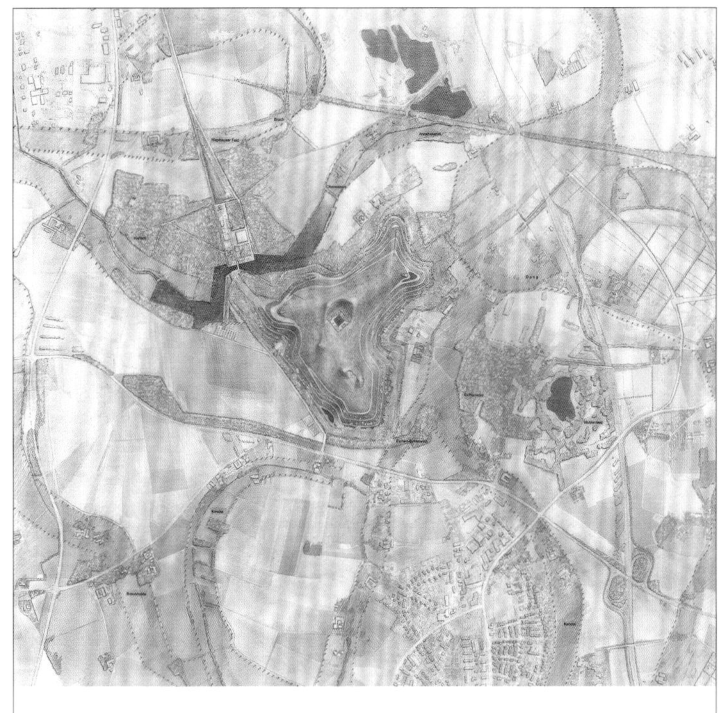

1.46 **Design plan for the slagheap in Moers, Germany. WES & Partner.** The former North-Germany slagheap is the largest in the Ruhr area. About 80 million tons of slag cover 91 hectares and rise about 80 metres into the sky. Their centre forms a crater-like high plain. This design makes the slagheap into a "mountain of silence"; a small number of calculated interventions turn the slagheap into an art landmark, a point of reference for the identity of the Lower Rhine region.

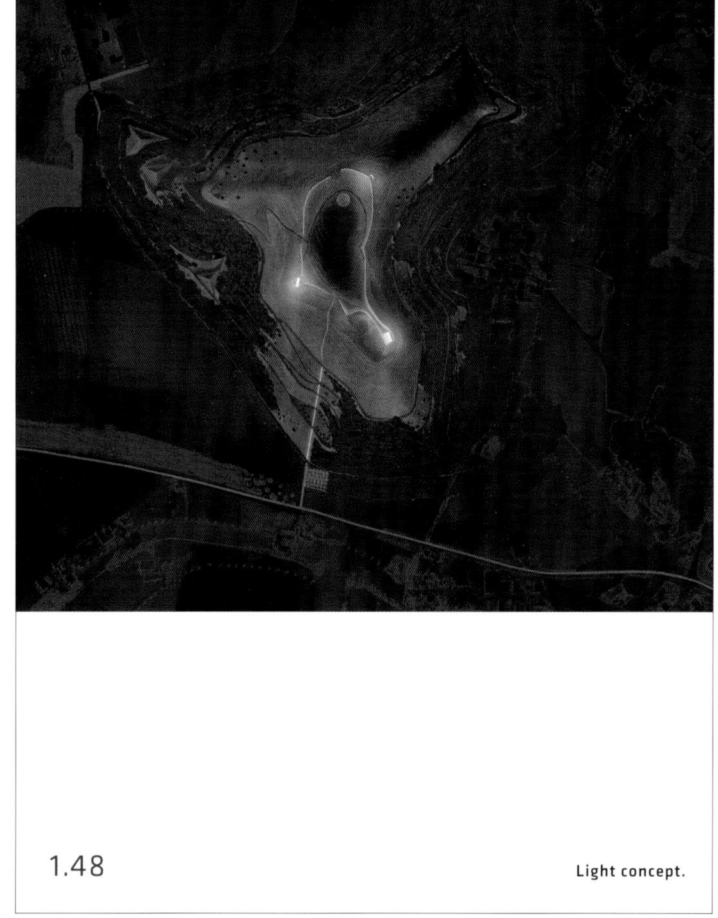

1.48 **Light concept.**

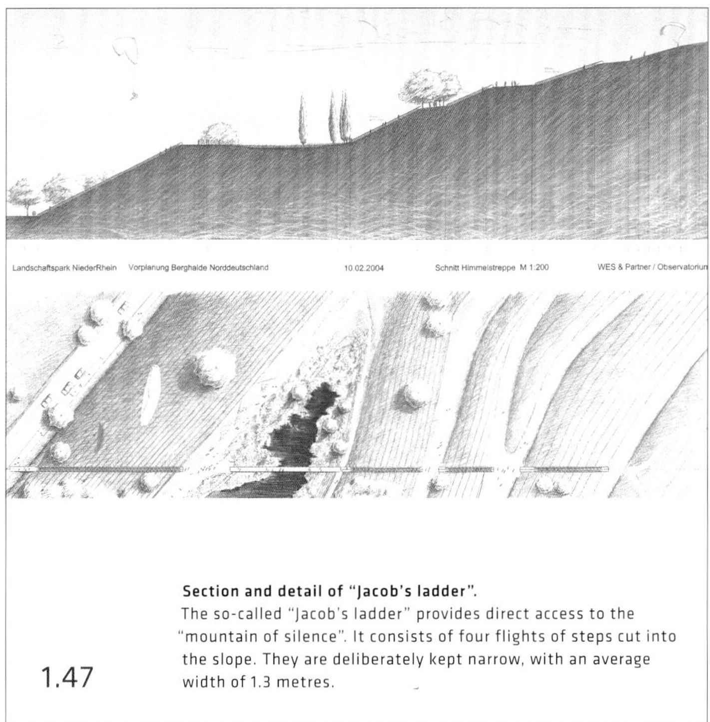


1.47 **Section and detail of "Jacob's ladder".** The so-called "Jacob's ladder" provides direct access to the "mountain of silence". It consists of four flights of steps cut into the slope. They are deliberately kept narrow, with an average width of 1.3 metres.

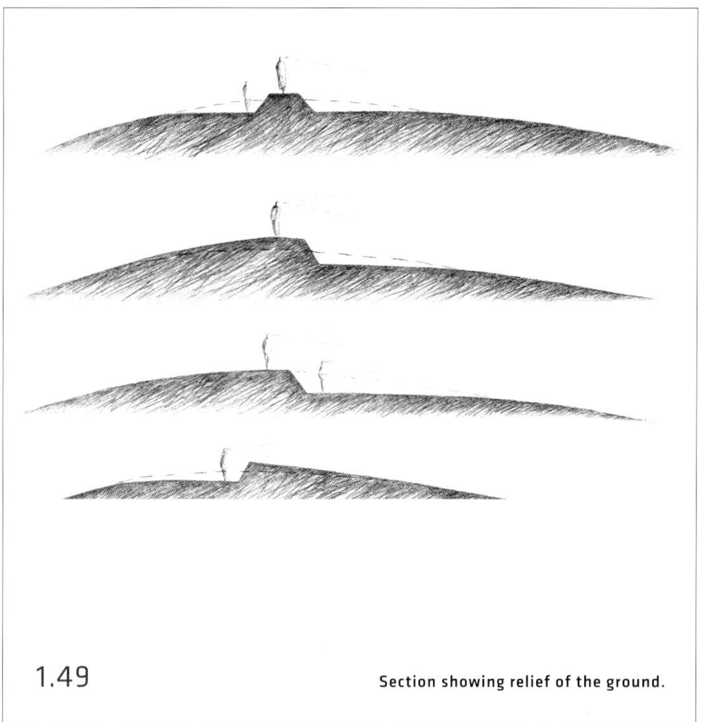

1.49 **Section showing relief of the ground.**

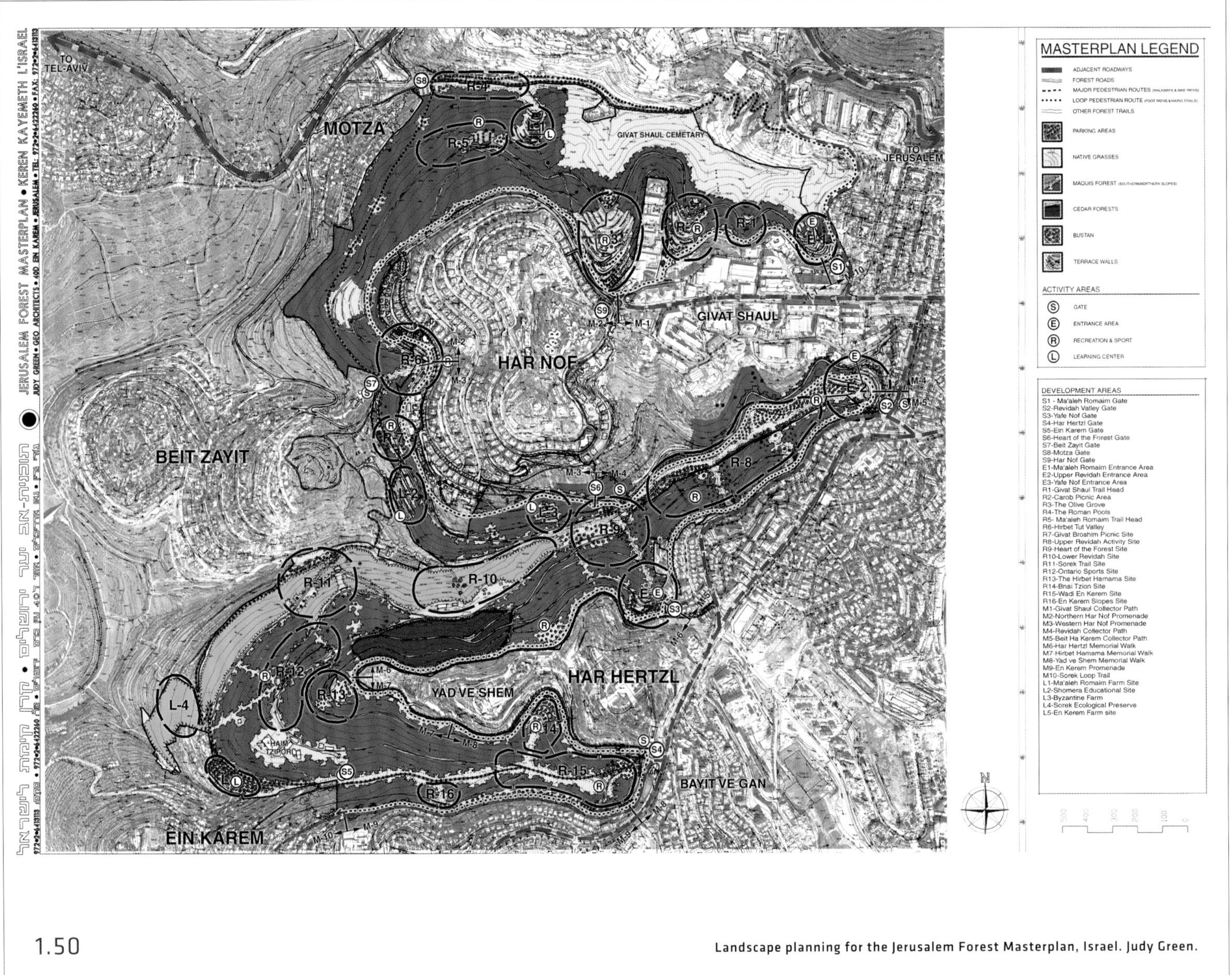


1.50

**Landscape planning for the Jerusalem Forest Masterplan, Israel. Judy Green.**

## Landscape planning

Because they are dealing with much larger areas, landscape planning projects are presented on smaller scales and, unlike plans for urban spaces, in a lesser degree of detail. The format of regional landscape plans and land use plans is often very large, because of the size of the area and the amount of content to be conveyed, so that reproducing them in a considerably reduced form can easily lead to loss of detail.

In the aerial photograph for this project in Jerusalem (Ill. 1.50), the planning aims are marked in colour and distinguished by means of letters and numbers. An aerial photograph was used as a basis: it is actually three-dimensional, yet looks two-dimensional because it was taken from very far away. Thus the development areas can be clearly drawn in, in two dimensions. Superimpositions on the aerial photograph provide orientation and scale. However, the order and layout of the areas for vegetation and use become clear only via designation and legend; they cannot be conveyed by this type of presentation alone. The legend explains the colours and structures as well as the letters and figures.

1.51

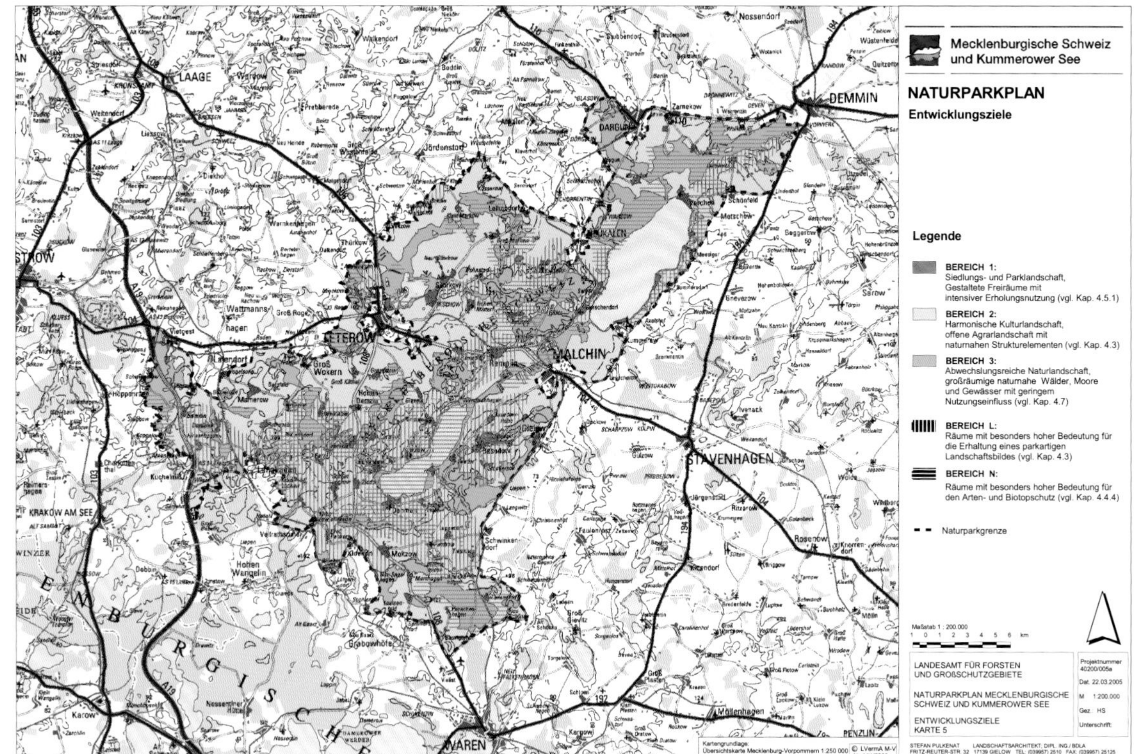


**Development goals for the Mecklenburgische Schweiz and Kummerower See nature park development plan, Germany, on a scale of 1:200.000. Stefan Pulkenat.**
This plan, one of several, presents the nature park on the basis of a map. The legend explains the aims, which are marked in colour.

1.52

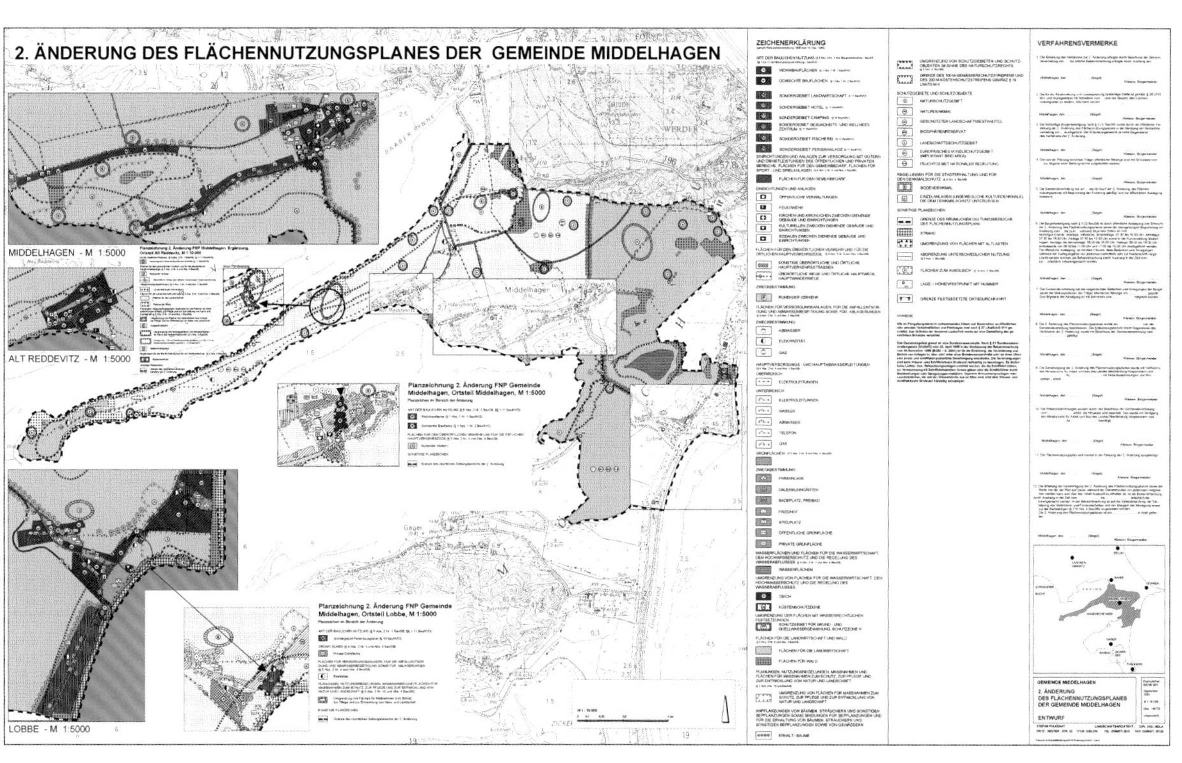


**Proposal for changing the land use plan for the Middelhagen community, Germany. Stefan Pulkenat.**
The proposal comprises several drawings and explanations of the changes in relation to the existing situation for individual parts of the town. An extensive legend explains the design ideas.

1.53 **Green links in the park planning for Jeddah, Saudi Arabia. Gustafson Porter.**
The planned park is 12.5 kilometres long and creates a linking element in the city. Its position is shown as a red line crossed by three green lines: the three planned green links running through the city area from the mountains to the sea.

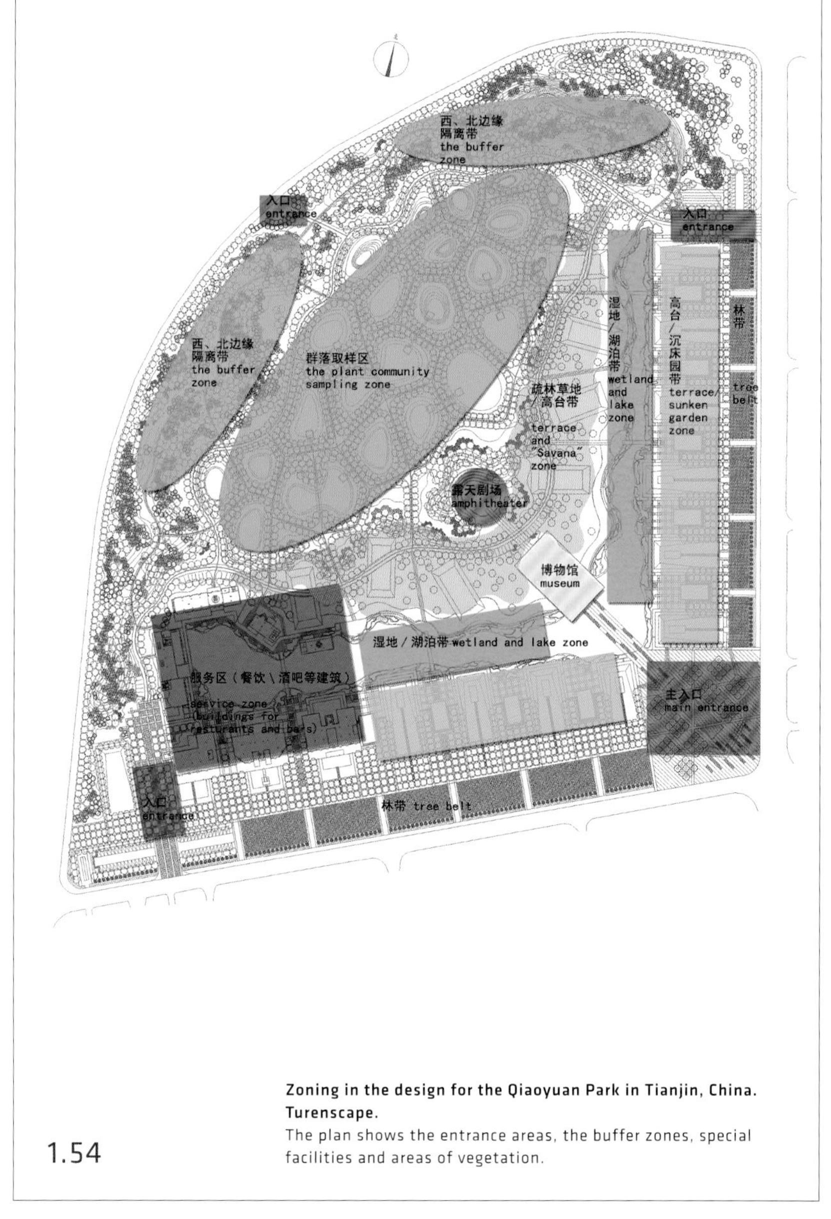


1.54 **Zoning in the design for the Qiaoyuan Park in Tianjin, China. Turenscape.**
The plan shows the entrance areas, the buffer zones, special facilities and areas of vegetation.

## Explanatory structural plans

Explanatory depictions complementing design plans can help to understand the drawings. For example, items of plan content can be individually selected and presented in drawings emphasizing structures relevant to the design, or showing sequences of events that further explain the ground plan. The examples shown here would not convey much without the design drawing, but they have an aesthetic quality of their own and an explanatory function that make them an important element within the design process..

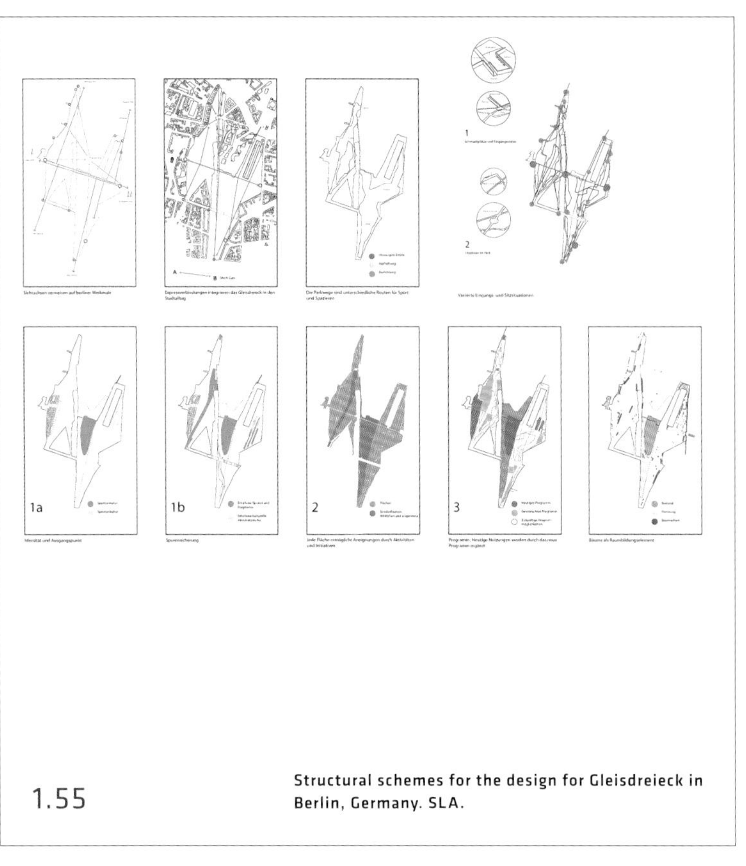


1.55

**Structural schemes for the design for Gleisdreieck in Berlin, Germany. SLA.**

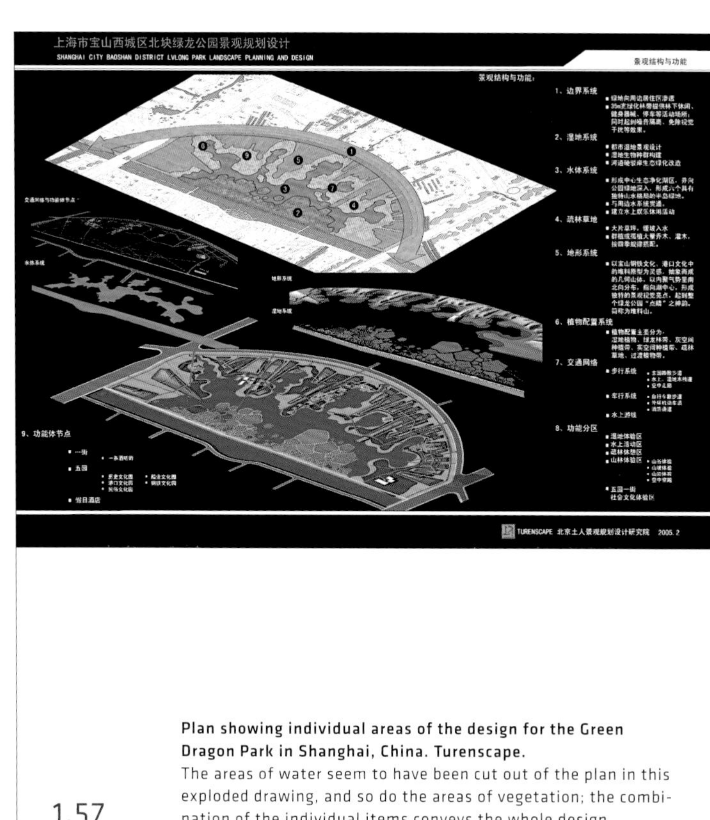


1.57

**Plan showing individual areas of the design for the Green Dragon Park in Shanghai, China. Turenscape.**
The areas of water seem to have been cut out of the plan in this exploded drawing, and so do the areas of vegetation; the combination of the individual items conveys the whole design.

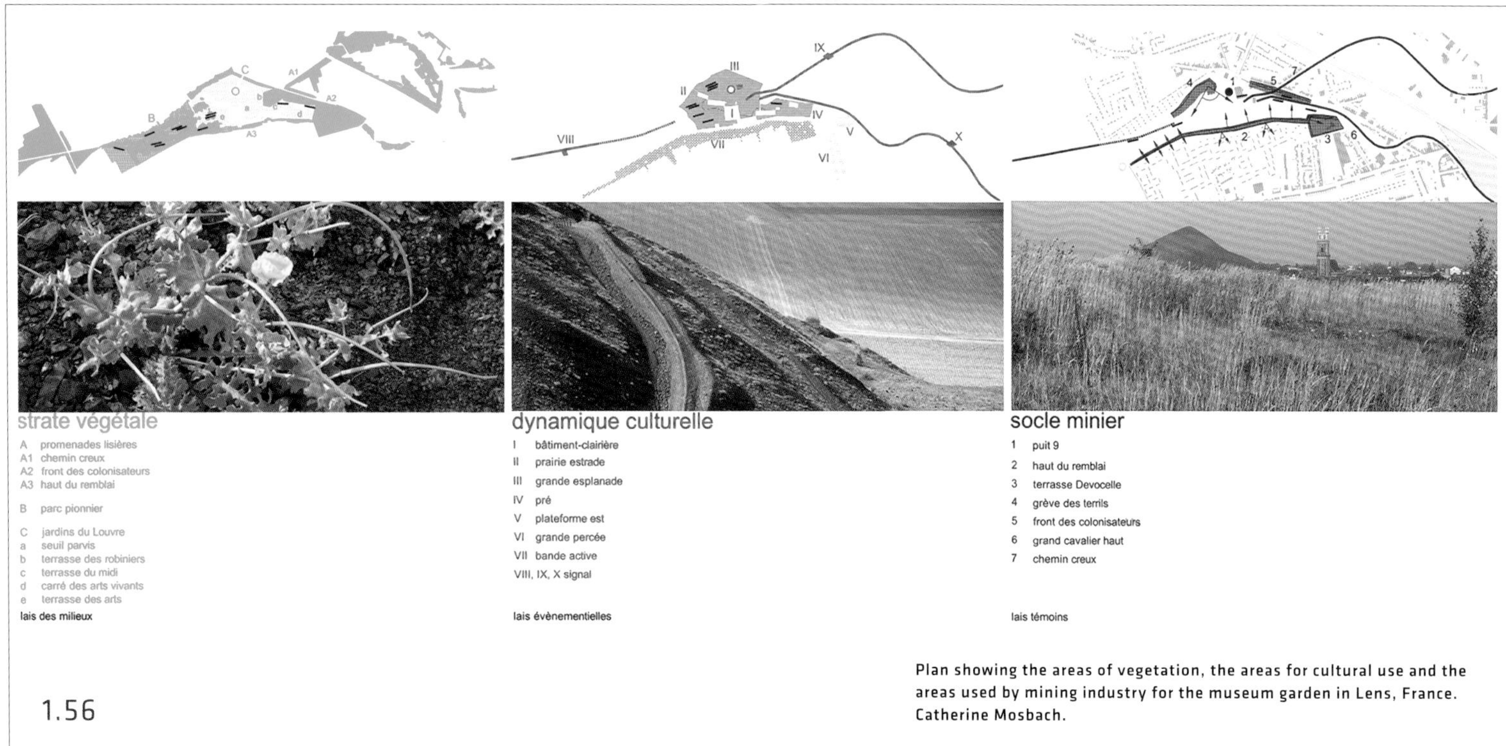


1.56

**Plan showing the areas of vegetation, the areas for cultural use and the areas used by mining industry for the museum garden in Lens, France. Catherine Mosbach.**

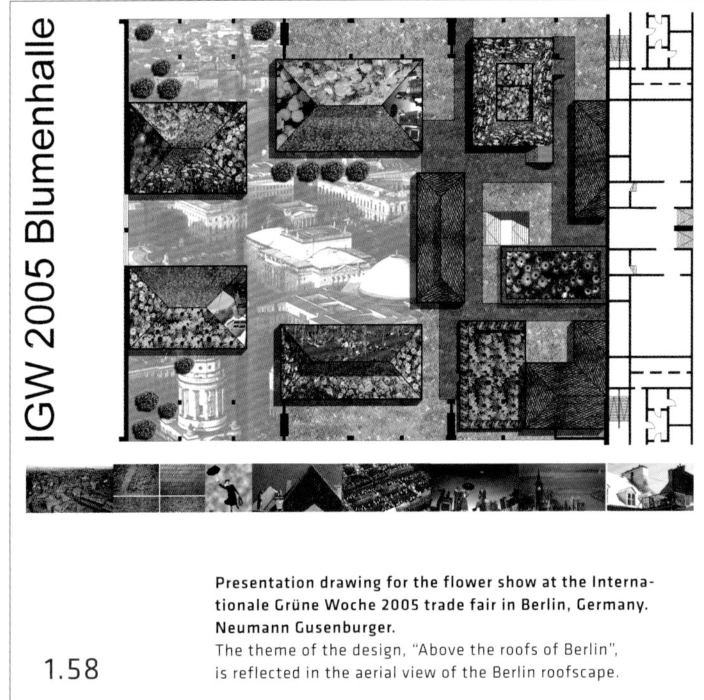


1.58

**Presentation drawing for the flower show at the Internationale Grüne Woche 2005 trade fair in Berlin, Germany. Neumann Gusenburger.**
The theme of the design, "Above the roofs of Berlin", is reflected in the aerial view of the Berlin roofscape.

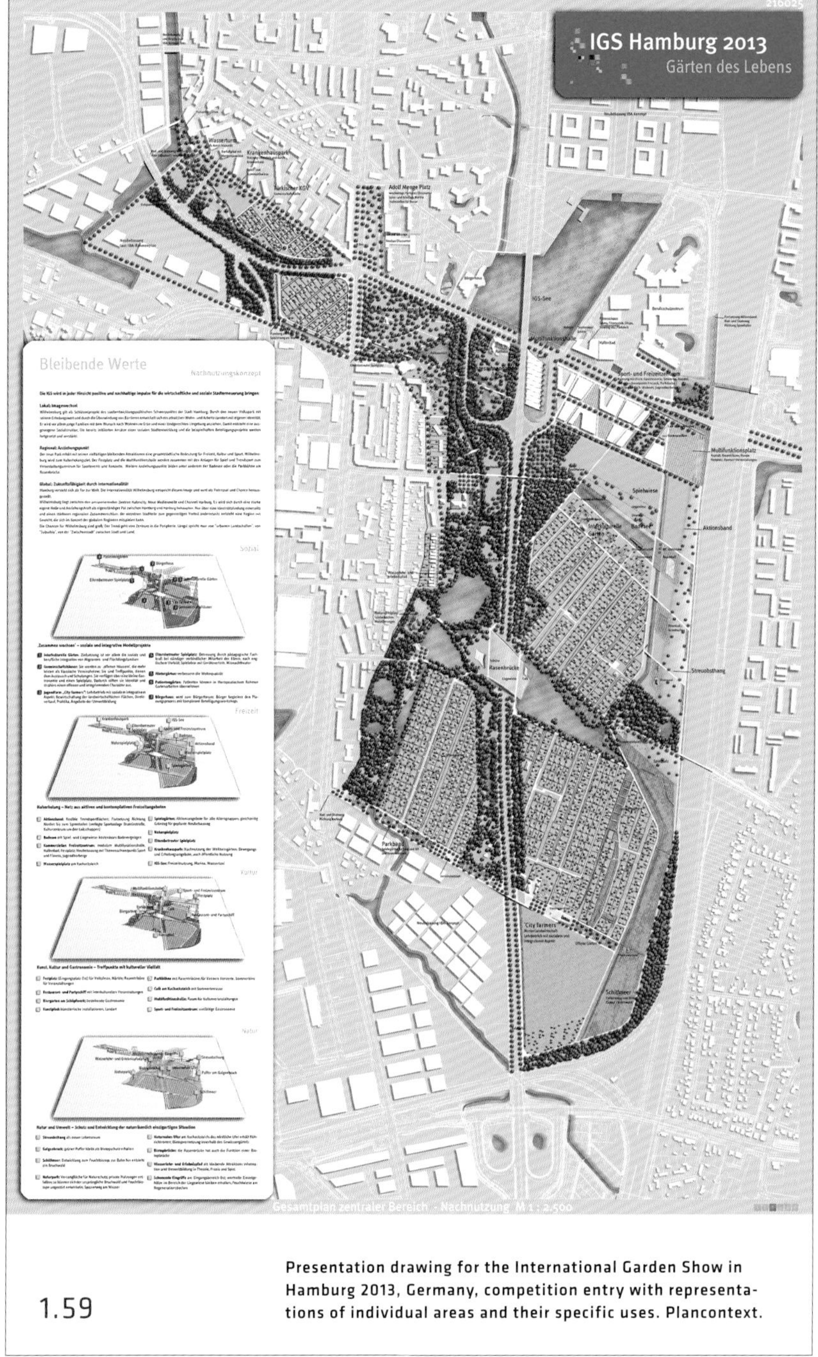


1.59

**Presentation drawing for the International Garden Show in Hamburg 2013, Germany, competition entry with representations of individual areas and their specific uses. Plancontext.**

## Presentation drawings

Two-dimensional representations of designs can be used as presentation drawings. In competitions in particular, ground plans, complemented to some extent by further drawings, two-dimensional in the examples shown, are used for presentation purposes. Here the design idea and the integration of the project in its local context may be emphasized, or the design is complemented by further content to explain the conceptual idea. Presentation drawings have to demonstrate the design ideas particularly impressively. They should also help viewers to get their bearings, as they will often be discussed by laymen, politicians and residents.

1.60

**Proposal for a playground; ground plan with additional images to explain the use of individual areas. Plancontext.**

1.61

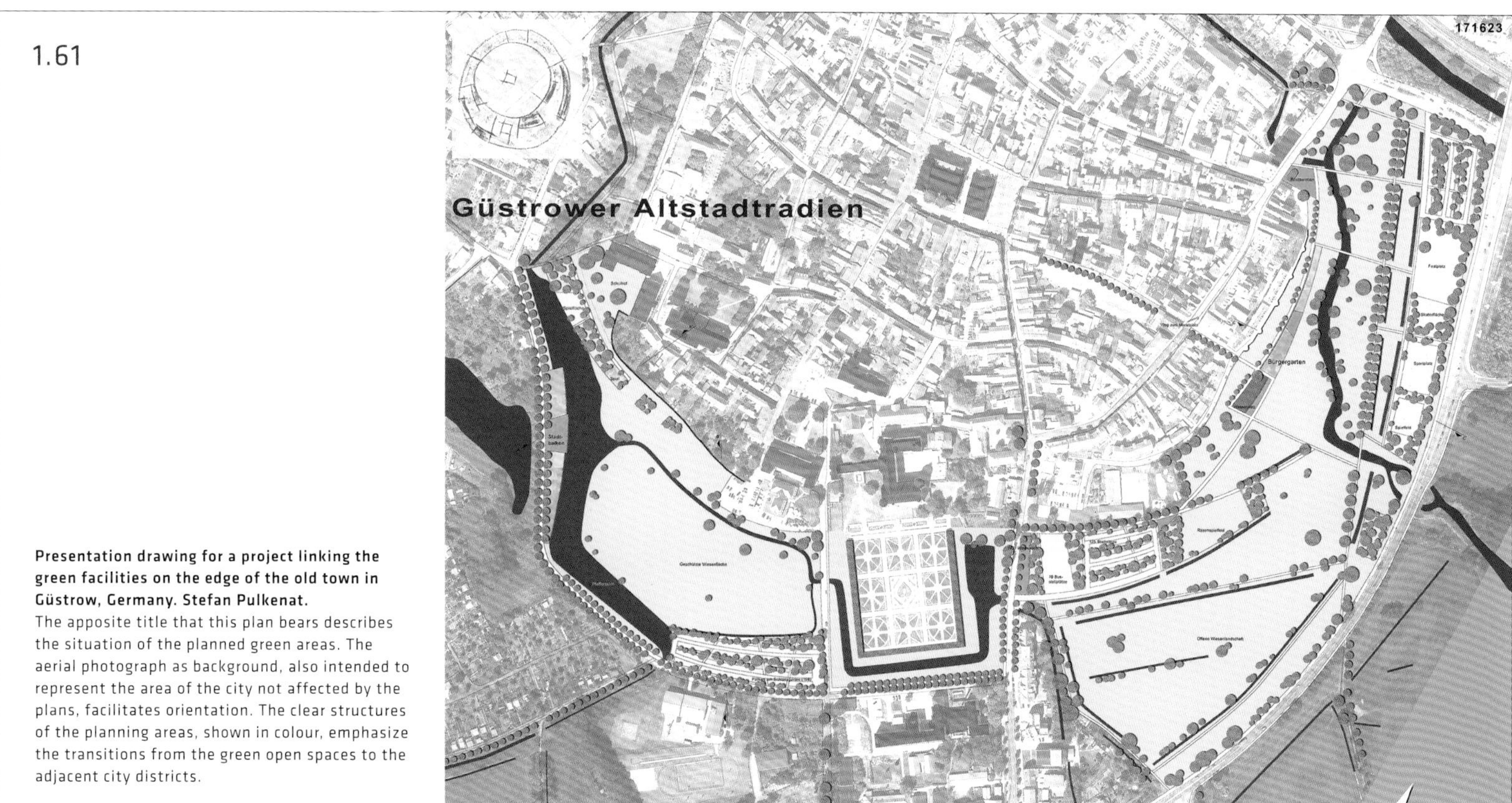


**Presentation drawing for a project linking the green facilities on the edge of the old town in Güstrow, Germany. Stefan Pulkenat.**
The apposite title that this plan bears describes the situation of the planned green areas. The aerial photograph as background, also intended to represent the area of the city not affected by the plans, facilitates orientation. The clear structures of the planning areas, shown in colour, emphasize the transitions from the green open spaces to the adjacent city districts.

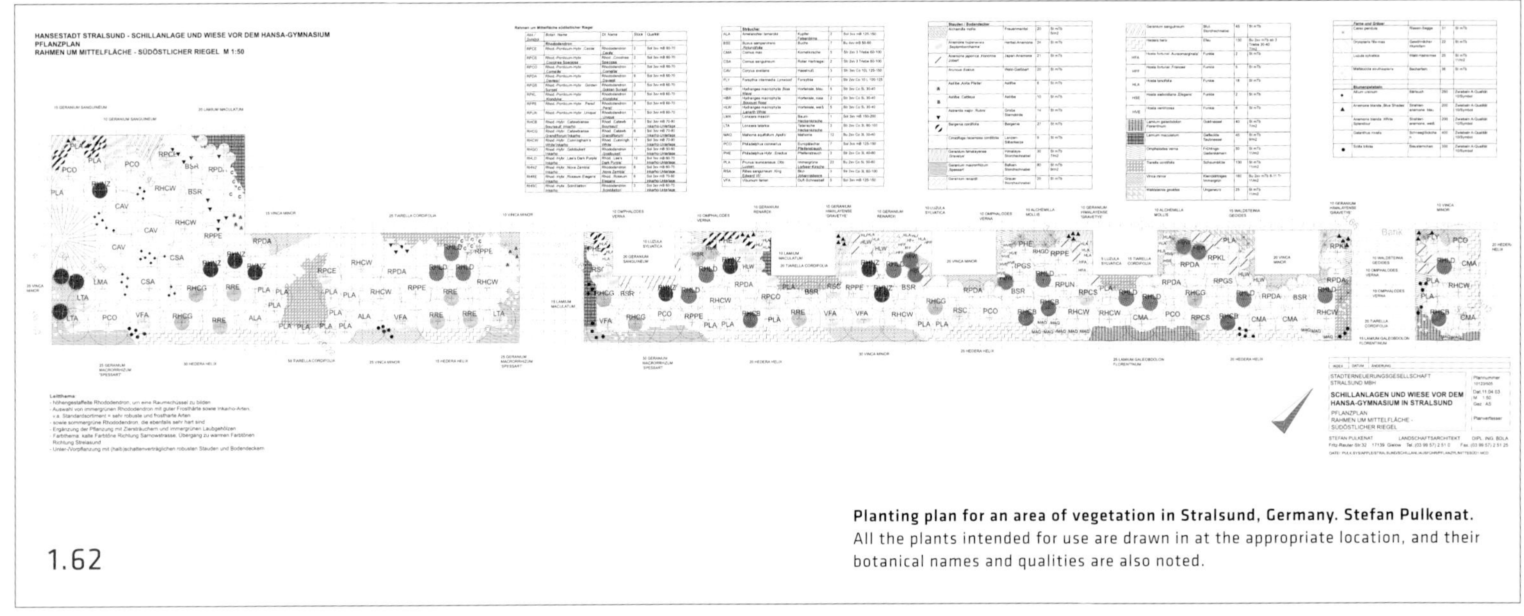

1.62

**Planting plan for an area of vegetation in Stralsund, Germany. Stefan Pulkenat.**
All the plants intended for use are drawn in at the appropriate location, and their botanical names and qualities are also noted.

1.63

**Selection of plants for the Potters Fields Park in London, Great Britain. Piet Oudolf for GROSS.MAX.**
This collection of photographs of the plants intended for the realized project serves essentially to support the design idea. Botanical names are supplied, but there is no information about arrangements or quantities.

## Working plans

For the implementation of a proposal, additional material is needed to explain how the ideas presented in the design are to be built. This visual material is known as working plans, representing an object with all the information needed for realizing it. Working plans include information about sizes and materials, and also planting plans. As a rule, working plans take the form of two-dimensional drawings. Some examples of technical details are also shown here, because a design process usually produces a large number of detailed plans of this kind.

Retrofit Boxcar
Contaminated Soil 14' deep
Gravel 1' deep
Water Catchment
Concrete Runnel
N. C. O. 688

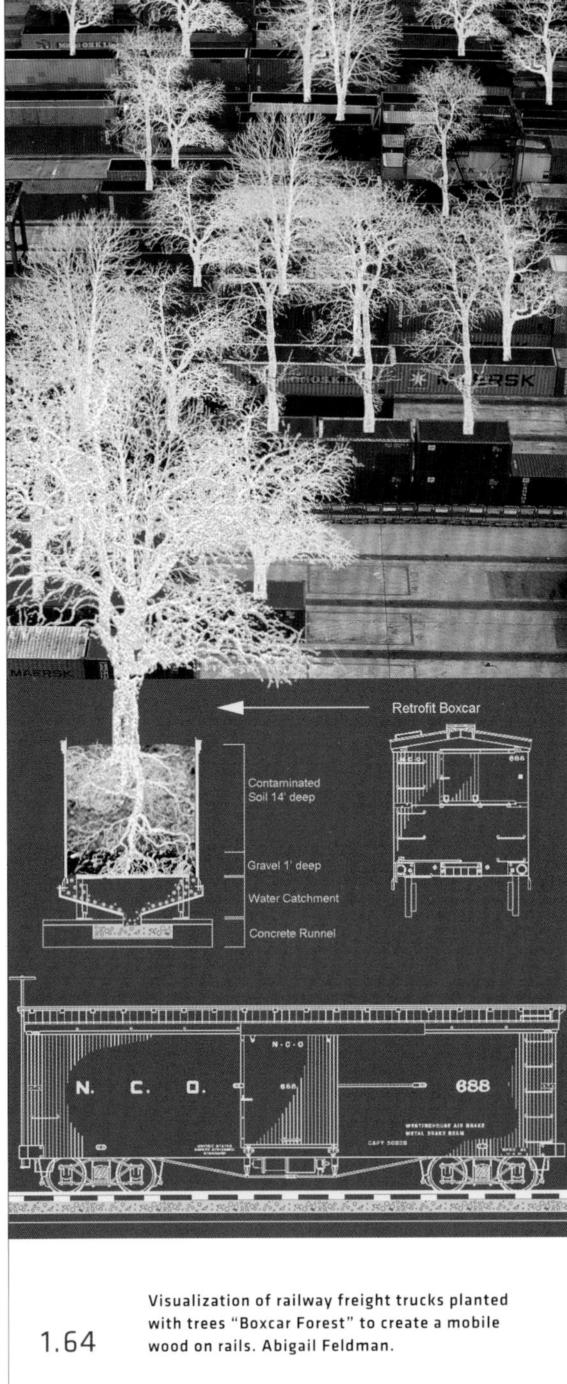

1.64 Visualization of railway freight trucks planted with trees "Boxcar Forest" to create a mobile wood on rails. Abigail Feldman.

Construction detail of tree planting in a high groundwater table
-> Trench construction for a tree.
Important is to have a separate irrigation guiding sytem for the trees in order to prevent waterlogging!

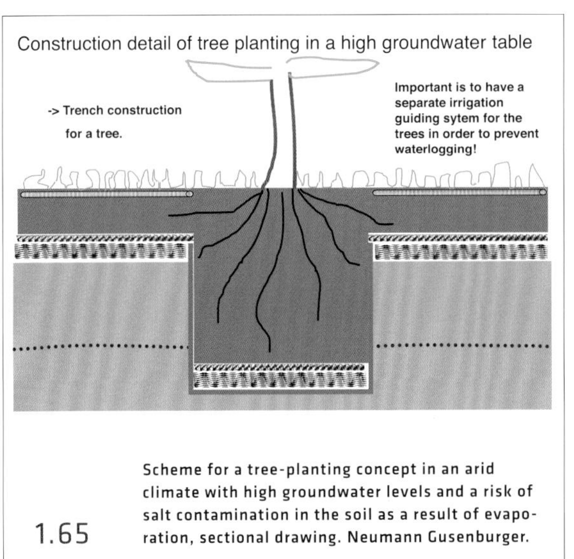

1.65 Scheme for a tree-planting concept in an arid climate with high groundwater levels and a risk of salt contamination in the soil as a result of evaporation, sectional drawing. Neumann Gusenburger.

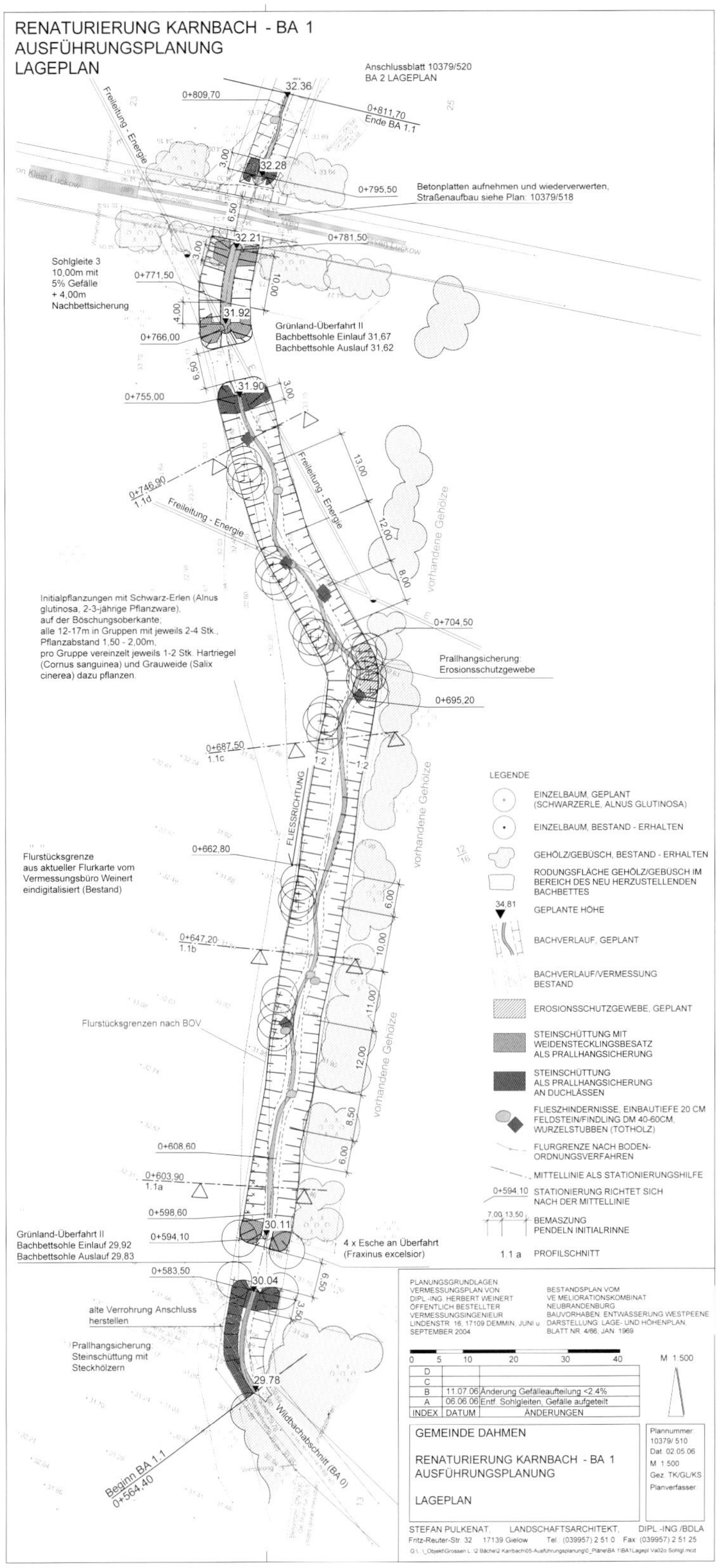

RENATURIERUNG KARNBACH - BA 1
AUSFÜHRUNGSPLANUNG
LAGEPLAN
Anschlussblatt 10379/520
BA 2 LAGEPLAN
Betonplatten aufnehmen und wiederverwerten,
Straßenaufbau siehe Plan: 10379/518
Sohlgleite 3
10,00m mit
5% Gefälle
+ 4,00m
Nachbettsicherung
Grünland-Überfahrt II
Bachbettsohle Einlauf 31,67
Bachbettsohle Auslauf 31,62
Freileitung - Energie
Initialpflanzungen mit Schwarz-Erlen (Alnus glutinosa, 2-3-jährige Pflanzware),
auf der Böschungsoberkante;
alle 12-17m in Gruppen mit jeweils 2-4 Stk.,
Pflanzabstand 1,50 - 2,00m,
pro Gruppe vereinzelt jeweils 1-2 Stk. Hartriegel (Cornus sanguinea) und Grauweide (Salix cinerea) dazu pflanzen.
Prallhangsicherung:
Erosionsschutzgewebe
vorhandene Gehölze
FLIESSRICHTUNG
Flurstücksgrenze
aus aktueller Flurkarte vom
Vermessungsbüro Weinert
eindigitalisiert (Bestand)
Flurstücksgrenzen nach BOV
LEGENDE
EINZELBAUM, GEPLANT (SCHWARZERLE, ALNUS GLUTINOSA)
EINZELBAUM, BESTAND - ERHALTEN
GEHÖLZ/GEBÜSCH, BESTAND - ERHALTEN
RODUNGSFLÄCHE GEHÖLZ/GEBÜSCH IM BEREICH DES NEU HERZUSTELLENDEN BACHBETTES
GEPLANTE HÖHE
BACHVERLAUF, GEPLANT
BACHVERLAUF/VERMESSUNG BESTAND
EROSIONSSCHUTZGEWEBE, GEPLANT
STEINSCHÜTTUNG MIT WEIDENSTECKLINGSBESATZ ALS PRALLHANGSICHERUNG
STEINSCHÜTTUNG ALS PRALLHANGSICHERUNG AN DUCHLÄSSEN
FLIESZHINDERNISSE, EINBAUTIEFE 20 CM FELDSTEIN/FINDLING DM 40-60CM, WURZELSTUBBEN (TOTHOLZ)
FLURGRENZE NACH BODENORDNUNGSVERFAHREN
MITTELLINIE ALS STATIONIERUNGSHILFE
STATIONIERUNG RICHTET SICH NACH DER MITTELLINIE
BEMASZUNG PENDELN INITIALRINNE
PROFILSCHNITT
Grünland-Überfahrt II
Bachbettsohle Einlauf 29,92
Bachbettsohle Auslauf 29,83
4 x Esche an Überfahrt
(Fraxinus excelsior)
alte Verrohrung Anschluss herstellen
Prallhangsicherung:
Steinschüttung mit
Steckhölzern
Beginn BA 1.1
0+564,40
GEMEINDE DAHMEN
RENATURIERUNG KARNBACH - BA 1
AUSFÜHRUNGSPLANUNG
LAGEPLAN
STEFAN PULKENAT, LANDSCHAFTSARCHITEKT, DIPL.-ING./BDLA

1.66 Working plan for renaturalising a brook. Stefan Pulkenat.

# FUNCTIONS
# SPACE

## Presentation of living spaces

Landscape architecture does not only address the two-dimensional surface of the Earth; it also considers and plans human and ecological living spaces, the three-dimensional environment. One of its technical terms, used alongside with "open area", and sometimes synonymously, is "open space", understood as usable space in the open air without building in the conventional sense of the term. This means that landscape design refers to human perception of space, especially that of the future users, as an important planning criterion. People experience their environment spatially, both outdoors and indoors. Obviously, open spaces are not perceived as being as clearly limited as rooms in houses; the dimensions are greater and the spatial boundaries are not as clearly defined, and often the sky serves as the upper distant boundary that can be seen but not touched. Open space is bordered laterally by buildings or other structures, or by vegetation, and the boundaries affect the attractiveness and the usefulness of the space, the extent to which it can be experienced, just as much as its dimensions, sub-divisions and content. Forming and defining units that can be perceived spatially in this way is an important element of open space planning.

Complementing ground plans and other two-dimensional drawings, the visualizations discussed here achieve their three-dimensional effects by depicting spatial depth. Beyond the overall spatial effect, three-dimensional illustrations can represent individual scenarios anticipating the perception of the built result and also corresponding with a photographic documentation. Although the situation of an open space project within the larger spatial context is often very important, the context is typically shown in two-dimensional, rather than three-dimensional presentations.

Open space is experienced through several senses: along with sight, hearing, smelling and to an extent touch as well are involved. Images can per se reach only the sense of sight, and yet the aim must be for the sounds and smells expressed in the images to be appreciated in order to convey the desired mood convincingly. Visual perception includes processing stimuli, acquiring relevant information and interpreting it by comparison with memories. This process and the role of the other senses in it are highly individual and differ according to previous experiences, desires and needs. Frequently images are produced that correspond with the accepted social mainstream or current fashion, in an attempt to trigger the desired positive responses in the addressees, often with images being borrowed from other disciplines such as product design or architectural design. Even though the plan, book or screen as media of representation are flat surfaces in two dimensions, the impression is sought of a three-dimensional space, one aim being to make the inherent design ideas more attractive by bringing them as close as possible to everyday perceptions. Visualizing a place particularly realistically, conveying an impression similar to photography makes implementing the planning seem realistic in turn, perhaps even necessary. Realistic simulations of this kind are frequently and entirely justifiably used to illustrate design ideas; they are produced exclusively as digital drawings, and many practices today have the necessary technical facilities at their disposal. Typically photographs of human figures involved in the desired activities, of plants and animals are fitted together to create an image of the newly designed open space, with the desired atmosphere. In principle, students can do this work in their first year, but in fact the images deployed by the profession are mostly very mature illustrations by trained graphic design specialists. However, only the landscape architect as the originator of ideas and experts in open space planning can define and control the relation of the images to reality and to the design ideas.

Visualizations can take the opposite approach and aim to make a planning scheme look unclear, irrational, almost surreal, calling for more time and attention to be invested in dealing with them. There is a wide repertoire of technical means and aesthetic options available for this approach, from choosing an unusual viewing angle or representing figures as shadowy or out of focus, to working with eccentric motifs. Given the daily abundance of images in our everyday world, it can be vital to stand out from the mass, for example in competitions. Yet it remains important that the conceptual ideas provide the guideline for the visual representations. It is rarely possible to predict whether any special effect will fulfil its purpose. Anyway, and despite the large amounts of time, money and effort involved, highly expressive images are quite common today. They considerably contribute to the development of visual presentations, which seems to have no set limitations. This is not the place for an in-depth assessment of how much visual representations themselves influence conceptual design ideas, but obviously, as images emerge in the course of design processes, and beyond illustrating ideas also serve to solve problems, they will certainly contribute to the development of design.

As three-dimensional images can potentially motivate a high degree of identification with projects, more easily than ground plans or sections can serve this purpose, they tend to become created as trade marks. Their main objective then is no longer the actual contents of the design, instead they often serve to put citizens into the picture, as it were, to boost their identification with the project, and sometimes they are used for advertising purposes. Planning practices are then expected to produce images of a similar type and in unchanging quality at regular, even short intervals. This may be intended to convey the sheer impression that the design process keeps evolving, but it can, of course, also record real planning progress.

Three-dimensional images are able to show how people will use a planned open space, or how they are supposed to use it. It is easier to follow active human beings presented figuratively rather than a two-dimensional presentation, as the intentions and meaning of a project are shown more clearly by activities than by signatures, hatching or colours. Atmosphere can also be evoked by depicting weather, often cloudless sunshine or with a summer sky partially covered with expressive clouds, typically in the daytime. Night uses, however, are often different, and also the security aspect becomes more significant by night in particular. Lighting makes a major contribution to keeping an open space usable at darker times of day and also in darker seasons. Considering this aspect during the design stage and expressing it visually can be very important for the acceptance of the project.

Each time the question arises yet again of how "correctly" a visualization should reproduce the – anticipated – reality or when and by what means viewers should be made to feel positive emotions. This is one of the fields where the artistic aspect of landscape architecture becomes particularly clear: artistic freedom and freedom of resources are greater here than in two-dimensional depictions. The wide variety of technical and creative possibilities for three-dimensional representation are constantly being extended, not least because demand is very high. Thus the designer's approach can be expressed ever more clearly.

Ecological planning aspects are rarely recorded in three-dimensional images. Plant species and varieties are usually not clearly identified, and at the time of writing two-dimensional plans tend to be used in advanced ecological contexts. The possibilities for including plants extend from showing their spatial extent in length, width and height, recorded neutrally and abstractly, to true-to-life images. The strawberry plant shown here (Ill. 1.67) is one example of what is possible: a digitally produced image with a viewing angle close to the ground, extremely far from human scale, and scarcely used in open space planning. The unconventional viewpoint, meticulous detail and sensual motif are the attractive features of this image, while a correctly scaled design cannot certainly be visualized in this degree of detail.

The effect of surrounding buildings is usually more powerful than that of plants. It often determines the use and the spatial structure that provide the necessary framework and scale for the open space planning.

1.67

Picture of a strawberry field as a realistic computer visualization. Lenné3D.

Three-dimensional images can be either oblique parallel projections or perspectives, corresponding with normal vision with one or two seeing eyes or a photograph. Perspectives are drawn up with precise dimensions or with reference to the project area's surroundings, in an approximation of the proportions. Built or digitally produced models can also be used. Another possibility, though not (yet) a very common one at present, is creating two slightly different images to achieve a three-dimensional vision using viewing aids. Examples of this are the lenticular screen technology and the anaglyph process. In the latter case, two offset stereoscopic images in complementary colours are superimposed. Special anaglyph spectacles with appropriately coloured lenses or foil are then used to see the images separately and thus as a three-dimensional scene. In lenticular screen technology, computer-generated images are viewed through a lenticular screen (Ill. 1.68), producing a three-dimensional image without any other apparatus. This method is still at the research stage at the time of writing. Early results shows that it is a very good presentation method and can produce livelier impressions, especially when addressing laymen, than traditional images. The technique is not yet suitable for reproduction in a book (like this one).

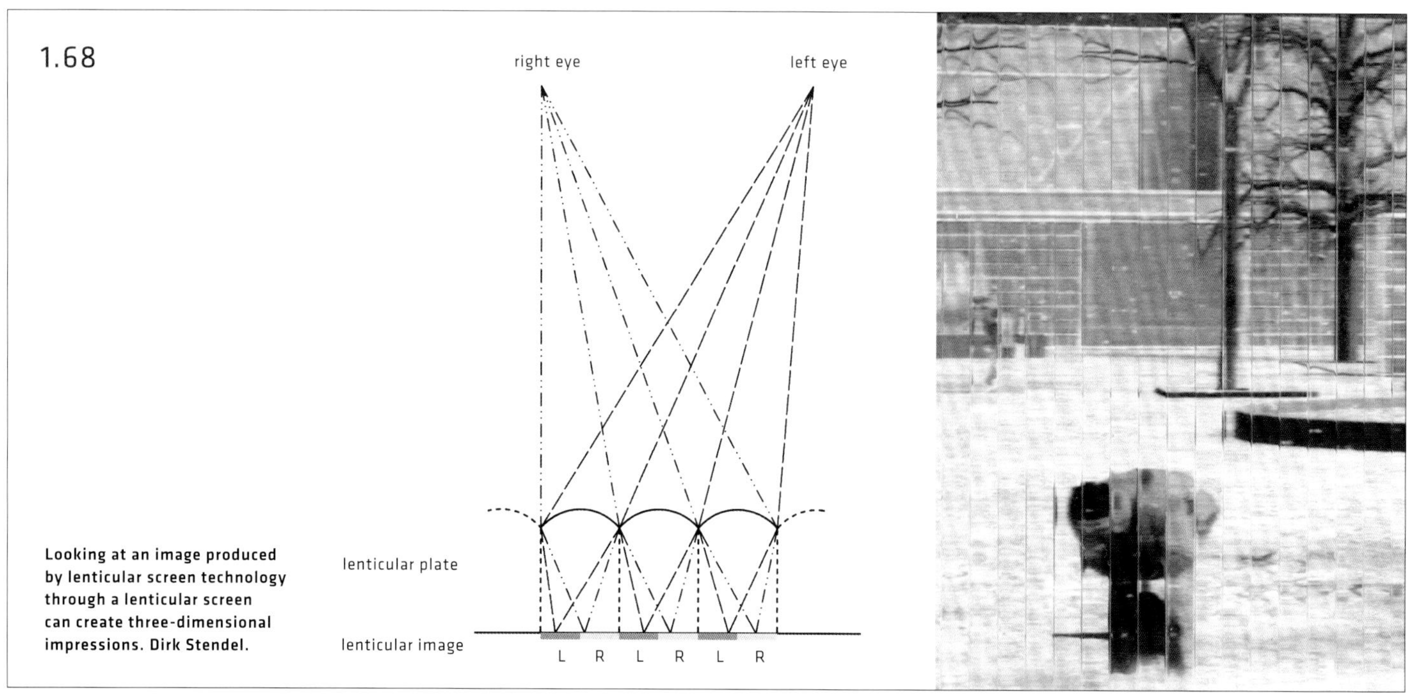


1.68

**Looking at an image produced by lenticular screen technology through a lenticular screen can create three-dimensional impressions. Dirk Stendel.**

## Three-dimensional projections

Techniques commonly used in landscape architecture to represent three-dimensional features in a two-dimensional format depend essentially either on parallel projection, typically in the form of axonometric projection, and vanishing point perspective as central or diagonal perspective.

### Axonometric projection

A type of parallel projection called axonometric projection can be used to depict an entire project area and possibly the surrounding area as well. It gives the effect of looking at a place from an infinite height, or is comparable with the sun's rays, which travel over such distances and create shadows in such a way that it seems as though the rays are parallel with each other. If asked to draw a brick, most people will intuitively come up with a three-dimensional parallelogram, resulting from the process of an axonometric projection. Here lines of sight run parallel, and the scale is retained both in the ground plan and the added vertical elements. The focus is on the ability to see in three dimensions. In the case of the brick, which is a cuboid, both the upper and lower surfaces can be perceived as the front: most viewers can "tip" the image mentally. Spatial impression imposes itself strongly because of this ability of human perception: most people recognize parallelograms as three-dimensional arrangements.

Axonometric projections force viewers to adopt an imagined viewpoint well outside the plane of the drawing. As in the case of the ground plan, the whole project area can be seen at a glance. Drawing in heights to scale makes the plans easier to understand. But at the same time parts of the project area are concealed by the vertical components of the three-dimensional drawing, so this form of visualization can be used only to complement a ground plan, not to replace it. Despite the impressive overview and better three-dimensional understanding, it is true of both parallel projection and ground plan representation that a plot of land can never be fully experienced and explored in this way.

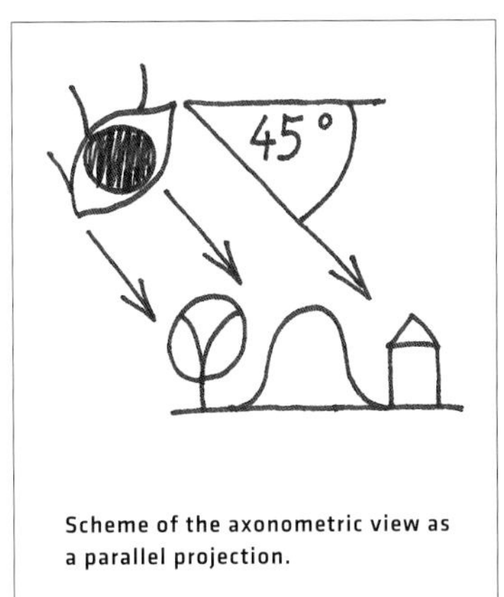


Scheme of the axonometric view as a parallel projection.

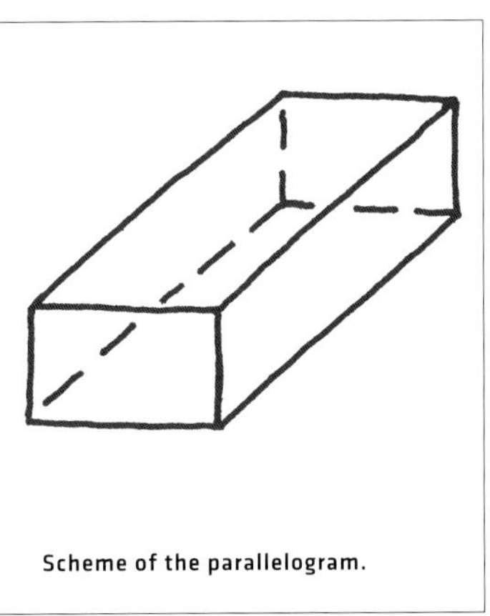

Scheme of the parallelogram.

## Vanishing point perspective

In addition to the other depth characteristics of orthogonal drawings, the perspective depiction demonstrates convergence: bodies, plants and buildings reduce in size as the eye moves increasingly further away. For this reason, the vanishing point perspective is the expressive form that comes closest to human perception. This feature makes it superior to all other forms of graphic representation, even though only sectors of the overall planning can be shown in each drawing. A perspective is a particularly expressive form both for sketching and for presenting design ideas. The free choice of a viewpoint on the surface or above allows free forms of representation; for instance, the viewpoint can be positioned at the viewer's eye level or slightly above, approximately 1.5 m to 5 m above ground level, or at great heights in a bird's-eye view.

In central perspective, parallel straight lines running perpendicular to the picture plane are shown receding from the foreground to intersect at a single point, the vanishing point. In normal or diagonal perspectives the lines intersect at several vanishing points.

Images in central perspective are often used in landscape architecture to present details of an overall design so that people can familiarize themselves with situations that they will encounter later. Bird's-eye perspectives convey an overall impression of the newly designed site. The further the viewpoint of a bird's-eve perspective is away, the more it will become similar to an axonometric projection. A perspective view from the regular eye level gives the best impression of how the planned space will look and be experienced.

Perspective views can be created as hand drawings or by computer, or in a combination of both. Collages, i.e. composite images made up of different elements, are mostly generated digitally. Hand drawing conveys a sense of personal handwriting and commitment that goes beyond the planning information, and also the draughtsman's or –woman's professional competence. In hand drawings, planning can be presented realistically or in rather more abstract form. If the images are concrete and readily recognizable, viewers quickly feel "I have been here before", even though they are looking at a planned, future space. If the perspective views are rather more abstract, requiring more time to understand them, the image appears more as a piece of artistic creation stating a specific position.

One important aspect that contributes to understanding open space planning is establishing a scale by using elements such as buildings, plants and most importantly human figures to convey a sense of height. Both the planned use and the scale can be indicated by figures and their activities. The dimensions of human figures are closest to those of the viewers themselves.

Hierarchic scaling, a method that shows important elements as larger, darker, or emphasized in some other way, runs counter to the required sense of scale in illustrations, and is scarcely used any more. Today various perspective approaches go beyond design and working planning, creating moods and illustrating the desired sense of life intended to be created by the project.

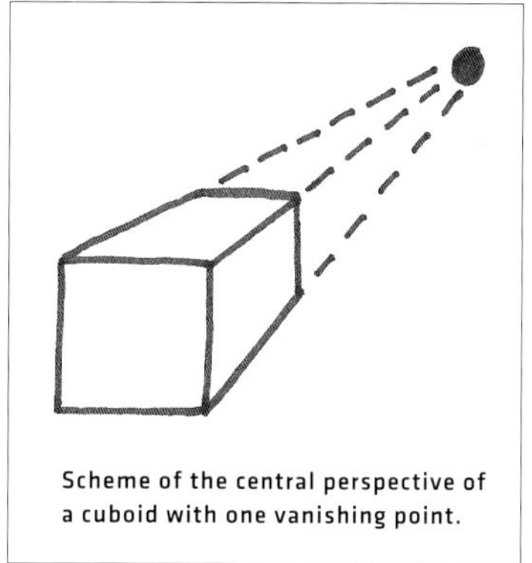

Scheme of the central perspective of a cuboid with one vanishing point.

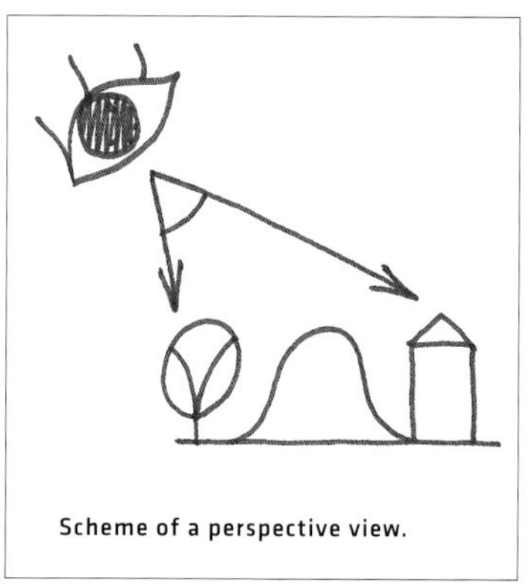

Scheme of a perspective view.

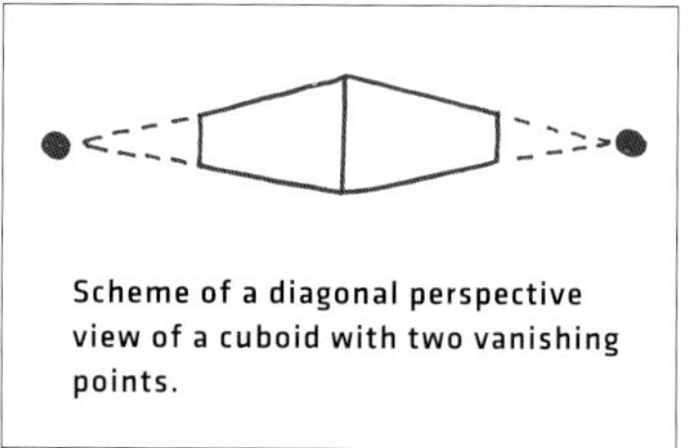

Scheme of a diagonal perspective view of a cuboid with two vanishing points.

## Spatial representation by models

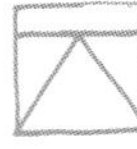

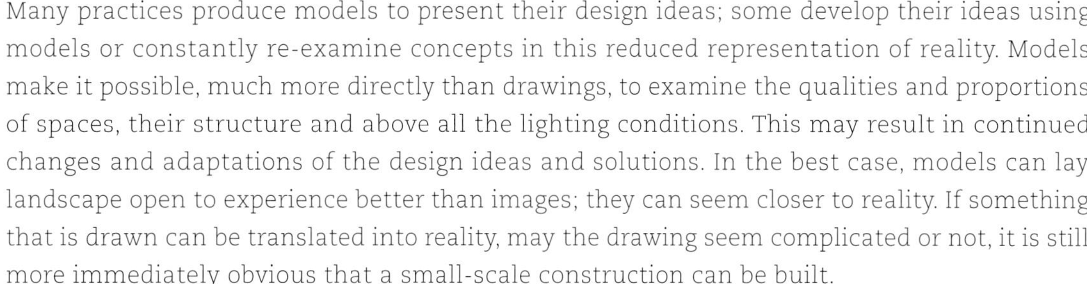

Many practices produce models to present their design ideas; some develop their ideas using models or constantly re-examine concepts in this reduced representation of reality. Models make it possible, much more directly than drawings, to examine the qualities and proportions of spaces, their structure and above all the lighting conditions. This may result in continued changes and adaptations of the design ideas and solutions. In the best case, models can lay landscape open to experience better than images; they can seem closer to reality. If something that is drawn can be translated into reality, may the drawing seem complicated or not, it is still more immediately obvious that a small-scale construction can be built.

Models can be made of various materials or generated by the computer. Building scale models allow viewers to look at them from all angles and from different heights, and also from a distance or close up. The reduction in scale makes it possible to gain a sense of the entire project and also to make statements about details, with the scale setting the limits for what can be represented. Models can be made as simple working models as part of the design process, or constructed by specialists either by hand or mechanically by implementing digital drawings. The materials can be natural or artificial, and here again the question is raised of whether a natural approach is called for, for vegetation in particular, or whether a more abstract and neutral approach could be employed. As a rule, laymen can soon get their bearings with built models, but these are individual objects, often difficult to transport and as a rule expensive in terms of both time and money. Computer-generated virtual models can also be looked at from all sides and from different heights, though only on the screen. Printouts then provide views of individual aspects of the project.

1.69

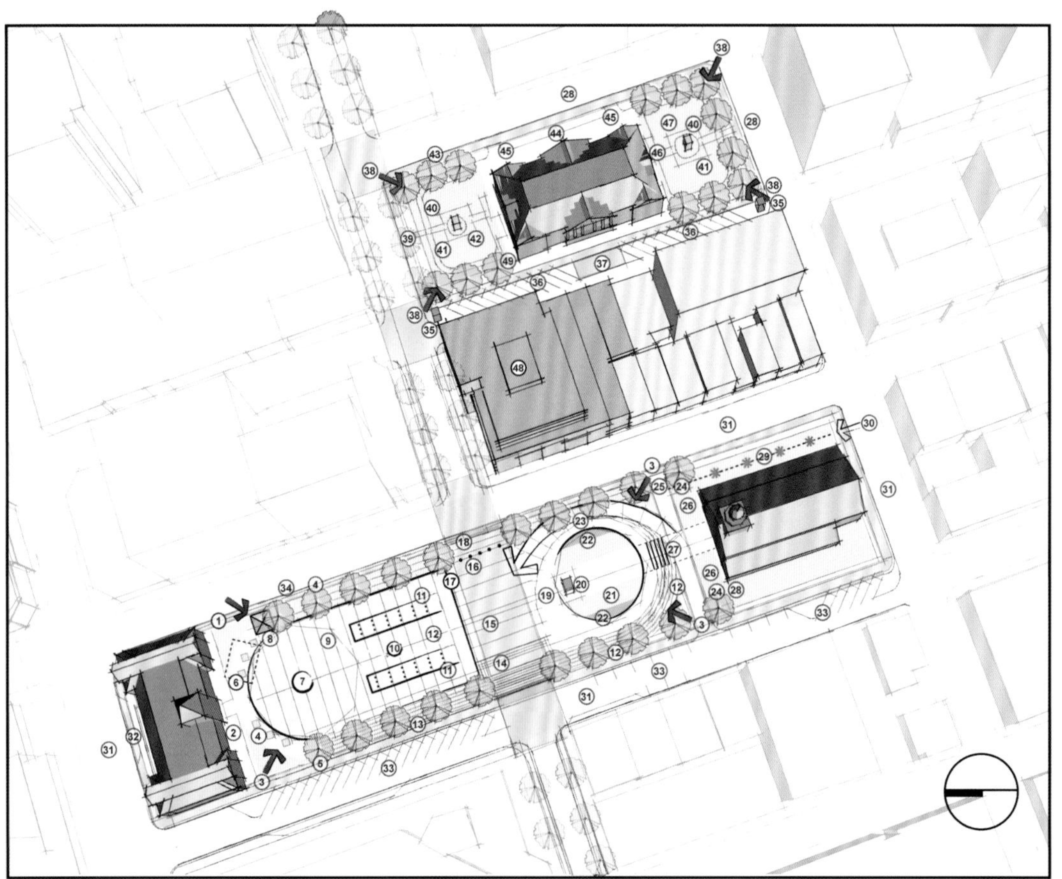

Axonometric projection of the quintessencial features of the design for the Grand Parade Province House Area, Halifax, Canada. CBCL Limited.

## Parallel projections and perspectives

Schematic representations of the links between a site and its surroundings, including the essential aspects of the design, are usually produced as two-dimensional drawings. In this example, a project for an urban area in Halifax (1.69), two- and three-dimensional means are combined: the buildings are shown as axonometric projections, while the open areas are depicted in two dimensions, as a ground plan. Using two different techniques allows the creation of a three-dimensional impression while at the same time specifying details of the planning area. Ill. 1.71 shows details of a park design as parallel projections.

## Perspective views

When functioning as views, perspectives can be arranged so that the viewing angle runs horizontally to ground level, and the eye level adopted is the same as the viewer's. This produces images that correspond most closely with normal human experience. In order to be able to create a larger area for the picture, the viewing or eye level is frequently placed somewhat higher than human eye level, up to about 5 m above ground level. The vanishing point or points at which the lines leading into the depths of the space seem to intersect are always on the line of the horizon, and only the surfaces and elements turned towards the viewer remain parallel within the image.

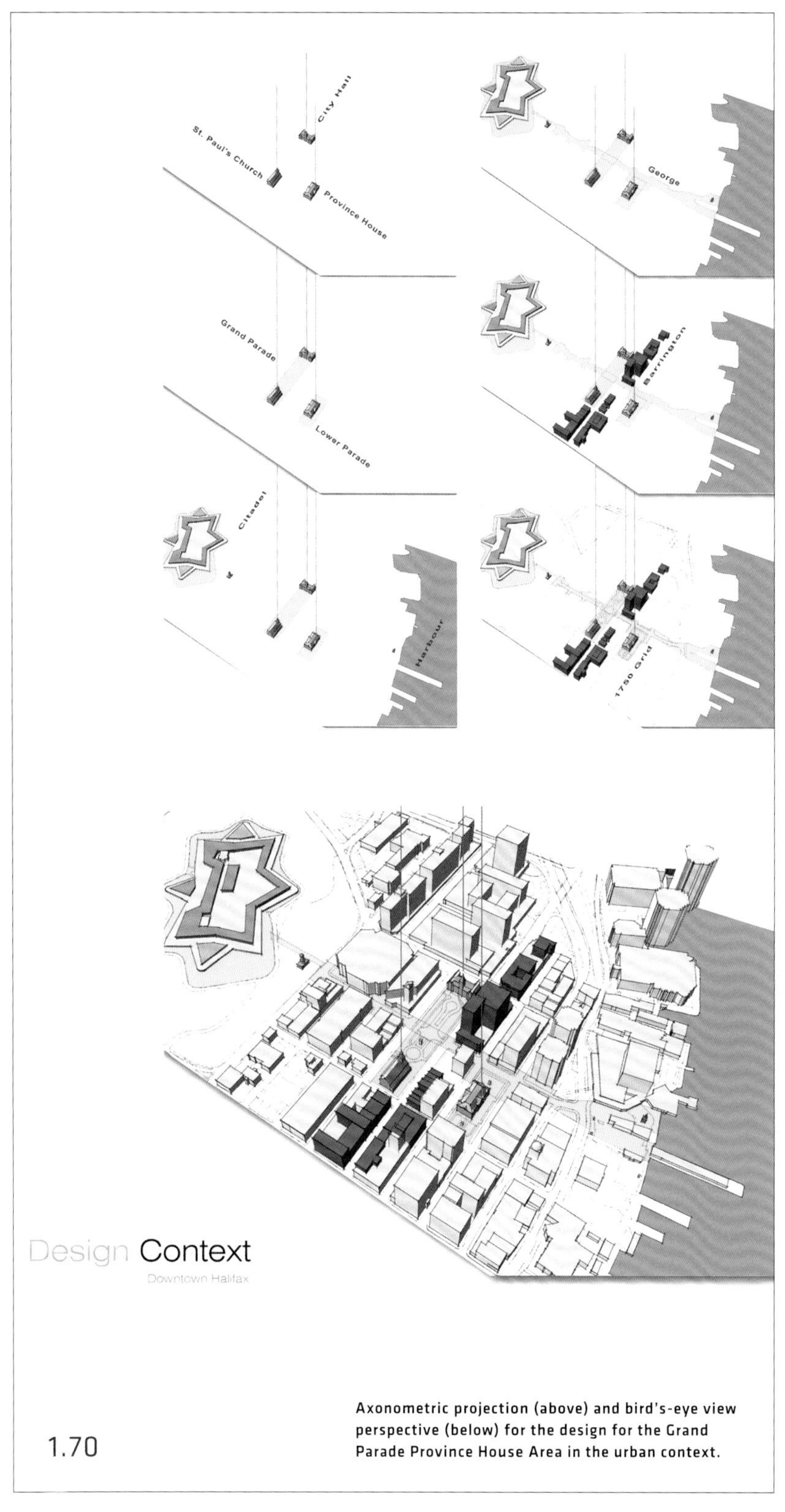


1.70 Axonometric projection (above) and bird's-eye view perspective (below) for the design for the Grand Parade Province House Area in the urban context.

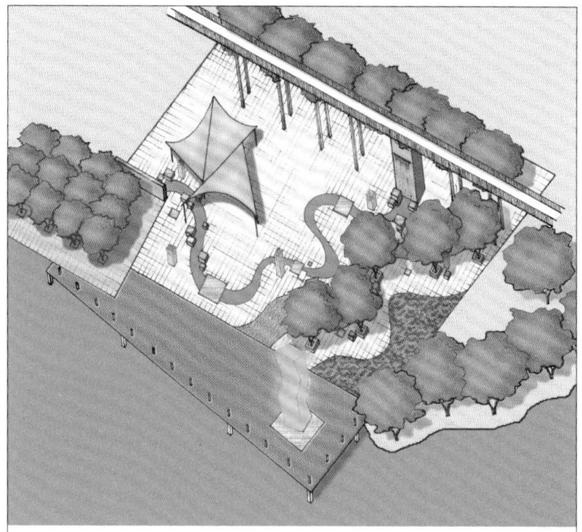

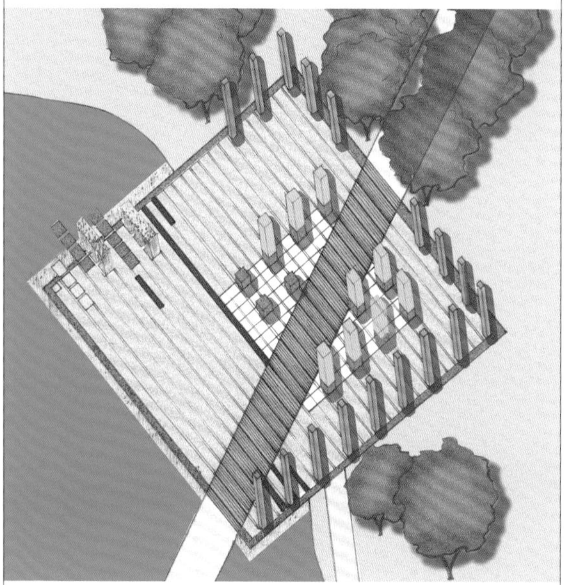

1.71 **Axonometric projections showing details of the Green Dragon Park in Shanghai, China. Turenscape.** These parallel projections show details of the park from different angles on the ground plan, displaying each situation from the best possible view.

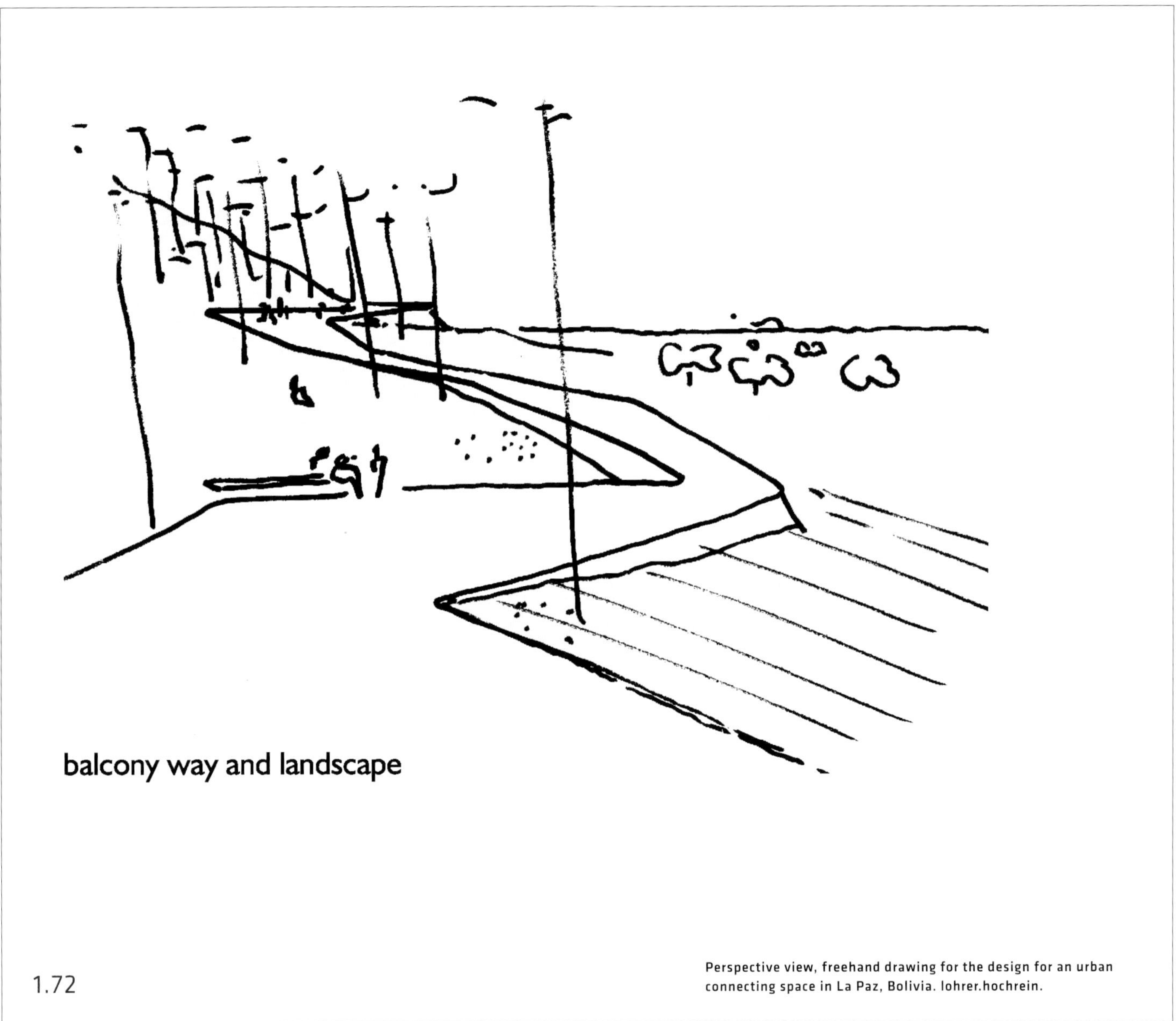


1.72

Perspective view, freehand drawing for the design for an urban connecting space in La Paz, Bolivia. lohrer.hochrein.

## Freehand drawings

This freehand perspective drawing (Ill. 1.72) presents the central design idea, the balcony way, using a single black line thickness, on a sloping area shown in green on an otherwise white surface. The balcony way is a walkway running along the slopes of the city of La Paz, 3,600 m above sea level. It is intended to combine various central facilities along the city's vivid topography, creating a new central park landscape and at the same time the city's longest square, even though it will not be a typical urban square. The drawings are utterly clear in what they convey, and interesting at the same time. The impression of perspective is created largely by the way the trees are depicted in the foreground, middle ground and background, and also by the tapering of the walkway in the distance. The vegetation in the background is not coloured, it is intended to convey depth and increasing distance. The urban character of this open space planning is not emphasized, there are none of the typical attributes of urban life such as vehicles, buildings and people. Keeping precisely to scale was no primary requirement here.

1.73

**Perspective view, freehand drawing for the design for Lohberg pit in Dinslaken, Germany. lohrer.hochrein.**
This freehand drawing for a former pit site illustrates the planned structure and use of space in clear lines and areas coloured mainly in green.

1.74

**Perspective view, freehand drawing for the design for a park in Chia, Columbia. Grupo Verde Ltda.**

1.75

**Perspective view, free-hand drawing for the design for the Parque Metropolitano el Indio in Bogotá, Colombia. Grupo Verde Ltda.**
The site is shown on a small, inserted ground plan with indication of the viewing direction, so that the perspective view can easily be located within the overall planning.

1.76

**Perspective view, freehand drawing for the design for the Parque Metropolitano. Grupo Verde Ltda.**
This perspective includes both a detail from the ground plan and a section of the situation.

1.77

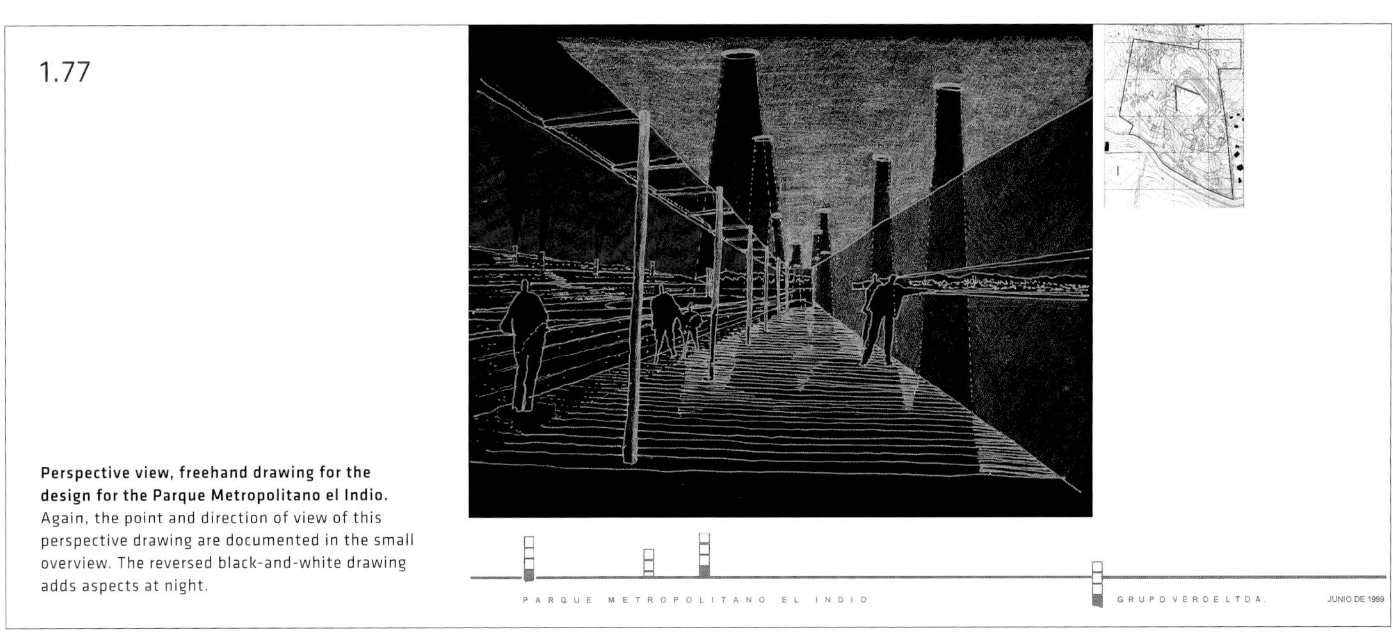


**Perspective view, freehand drawing for the design for the Parque Metropolitano el Indio.**
Again, the point and direction of view of this perspective drawing are documented in the small overview. The reversed black-and-white drawing adds aspects at night.

1.78

**Perspective view, freehand drawing for the Bärentorplatz – Rathausstraße – Rathausplatz area in the town of Leimen, Germany. lohrer.hochrein.**

1.79

**Perspective view, freehand drawing for Leimen.**
Some buildings are strongly emphasized, while human figures and trees are shown only in faint outline. They indicate the proportions in a very unobtrusive manner. Superimposition and the graphic, two-dimensional emphasis on the buildings create lively urban spaces. The grey background makes the drawing stand out and gives it a frame.

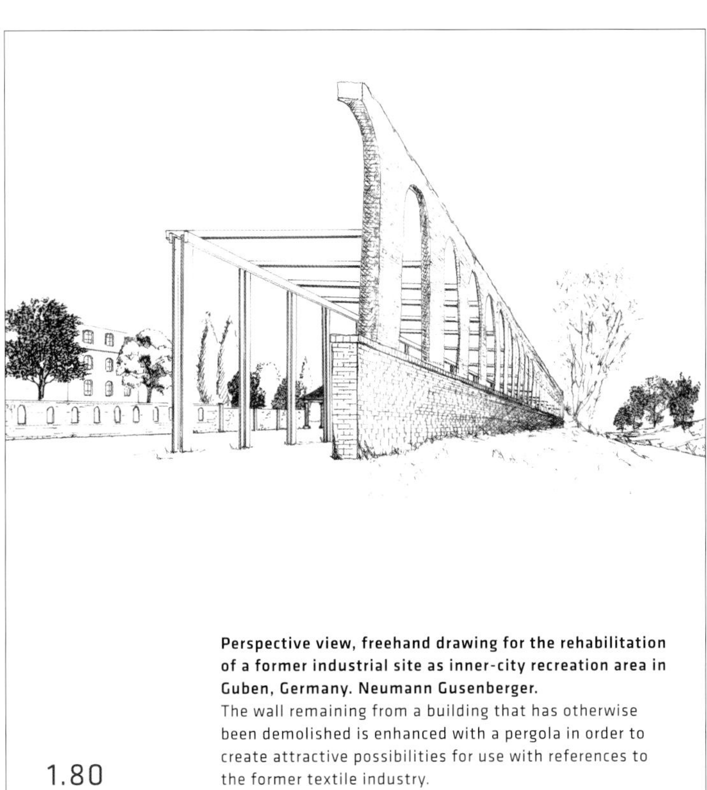

1.80

**Perspective view, freehand drawing for the rehabilitation of a former industrial site as inner-city recreation area in Guben, Germany. Neumann Gusenberger.**
The wall remaining from a building that has otherwise been demolished is enhanced with a pergola in order to create attractive possibilities for use with references to the former textile industry.

1.81

**Perspective view, freehand drawing for the design for the Green Dragon Park in Shanghai, China. Turenscape.**
This water-coloured ink drawing in near-natural colours shows possible uses by adding in appropriate human figures.

1.82

Collage of hand drawing, photography and digital elements for the open space planning in Cartagena de Indias, Colombia. By Grupo Verde Ltda.

1.83

Computer-generated perspective for the proposal of a terraced lawn on the banks of the Danube in Neu-Ulm, Germany. Plancontext.

## Computer-generated drawings

Computer-generated perspective representations also permit varying degrees of closeness to reality. The project areas may be represented in colour while the surroundings are shown in black and white, for instance, or human figures may be added, either taken from real-life photographs or as generic outlines. Realistically portrayed people will dominate the viewer's attention, while abstract human figures avoid detracting from the design.

1.91

**Computer-generated perspective for the design for an urban square in Ribnitz, Germany. Stefan Pulkenat.**

In this perspective (Ill. 1.91), the viewing point is set a little higher than human eye level, directing the eye towards the church and the newly designed urban square. This means that viewers are looking at the scene from close by, but are not involved in it themselves. They are not "standing" in the square, they are "floating" above it and see the square as a whole.

The church dominates the open space, while the square with the planned features takes up only about a third of the picture. Another quarter shows the buildings bordering and defining the square. The fact that the sky takes up almost half the picture, along with the dominance of the church and the calm activities of the human figures, creates an almost silent atmosphere. This impression is further reinforced by the choice of colour: the discreet grey-blue of the square with small inlaid lights in the complementary colour, as well as the yellow and grey of the rest of the picture. Time seems to stand still: it seems that the place would not change when people leave it, when they move or when other people come to use it. Even the time of day seems to play only a minor role: bright daylight is shown, but the sky seems overcast, there are few shadows with little emphasis on them, which calms the picture as a whole. Despite daylight, the lighting is shown as yellow, so the change to night would consist only of a darkening of the sky; no further changes seem to be intended.

1.92

Computer-generated perspective for the town centre of Göttingen, Germany. WES & Partner.

1.93

Computer-generated perspective for the Promenade on Governors Island in New York, USA. West 8.

The computer-generated perspective views shown here demonstrate the individual approaches the planners are taking and go beyond the factual, unambiguous presentation of the project. They are pictorial manifestations of the planning theory of the open, process-oriented design, thus opening this theory up to discussion as well. Landscape architecture is to become a source for aesthetic experiments (again). Formulating individual presentations is part of the planners' design concepts; visual presentations attract a great deal of attention and thus exercise considerable influence over today's landscape architecture.

1.84

**Computer-generated perspective view, artistic impression of the garden of the Grand Egyptian Museum in Cairo, Egypt. West 8.**
A special feature is the position of the vanishing point at the top edge of the picture towards which the palms are directed. This gives the image an unusual and appealing dynamic.

1.85

**Computer-generated central perspective for the design for a garden inside a residential area in Dubai Pearl. WES & Partner.**
The added human figures give a scale to the cramped space to be created. The planting in strong colours adds to the impression of a pleasant new recreation area.

1.86

**Computer-generated perspective, view for the design for the harbour and the Statue of Liberty of Governors Island in New York, USA. West 8.**
Children with their urge to be on the move and their gift for observing their surroundings precisely dominate this drawing, which with its birds and the plants shown in great detail in the foreground renders an everyday situation very realistically.

1.87

**Computer-generated perspective of the terracing in Potters Fields Park in London, Great Britain. GROSS.MAX.**
This is an interesting composition of coloured sections, essentially green, yellow and black-and-white; the children playing give the calm little park a light, appealing dynamic.

1.88

**Computer-generated perspective for the design for children's play hills on Governors Island in New York, USA. West 8.**
The figures of children demonstrate the wide range of activities for which the place is planned.

1.89

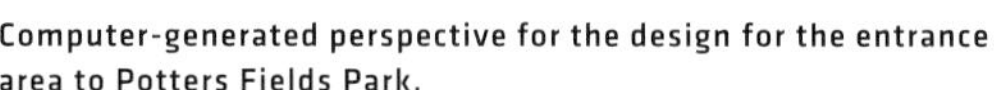

**Computer-generated perspective for the design for the entrance area to Potters Fields Park.**
The features emphasized are the entrance via the gate, whose striking ornaments are repeated by the shadows cast, the colourful herbaceous planting and the women entering the park.

1.90

**Computer-generated perspective for the open space outside the Festhalle in Frankfurt am Main, Germany. RMP.**
The emphasis is on garden design and vegetation; human figures feature as white bodies, enlivening the image but without adding colours that would distract from the message.

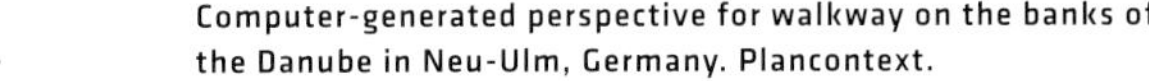

1.94 Computer-generated perspective for walkway on the banks of the Danube in Neu-Ulm, Germany. Plancontext.

1.95 Computer-generated perspective for the market place in Neubrandenburg, Germany. Noack.

1.96 Computer-generated perspective for the Dubai Pearl portal square, United Arab Emirates. WES & Partner.

1.97 Computer-generated perspective for the design and use of the Royal Plaza in Dubai Pearl at night.

1.98

Computer-generated perspective for the design for the Zuiderzee Museum in Enkhuizen, Netherlands. GROSS.MAX.

GROSS.MAX and Piet Oudolf have developed a proposal for the natural area surrounding the Zuiderzee Museum for the museum's 60th anniversary.

1.99

Computer-generated perspective for the design for the Zuiderzee Museum.

1.100

Computer-generated perspective for the design for the Zuiderzee Museum.

1.101

**Computer-generated perspective for the design for the 1001 Trees public park in north-west Copenhagen, Denmark. SLA.**
This collage of trees, with a child looking at the viewer and the apparently falling apples, presents an unreal situation in which dreaming has its place as well.

1.102

**Computer-generated perspective to explain the design intentions for the 1001 Trees public park.**
In this central perspective, the human figures on the hill give a sense of its height; the moon and the sky underline the special mood.

1.103

**Computer-generated perspective to explain the design intentions for the 1001 Trees public park.**
In this central perspective, the human figures on the hill give a sense of its height; the moon and the sky underline the special mood.

1.104

**Collage as a view inside the rotunda in Liverpool, Great Britain. GROSS.MAX.**
The light colouring and the many flowers and butterflies represent a calm and friendly atmosphere, which also seems attractive without people.

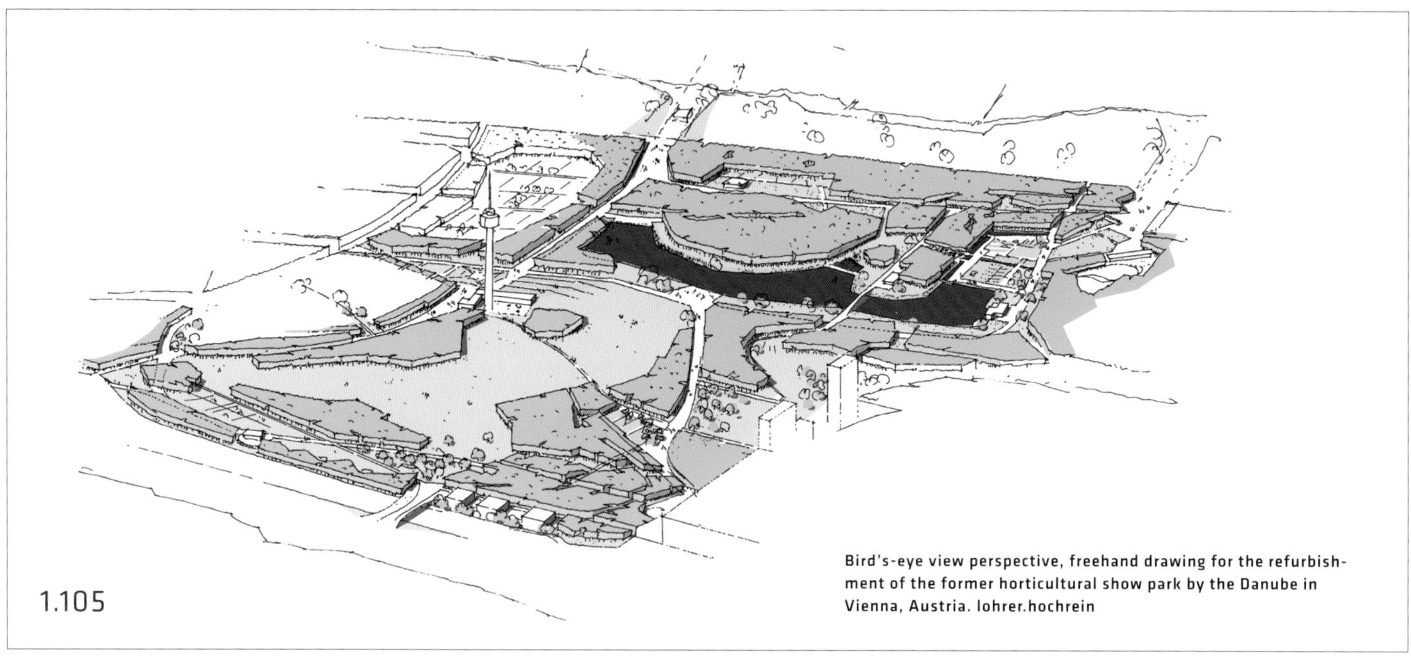

1.105

Bird's-eye view perspective, freehand drawing for the refurbishment of the former horticultural show park by the Danube in Vienna, Austria. lohrer.hochrein

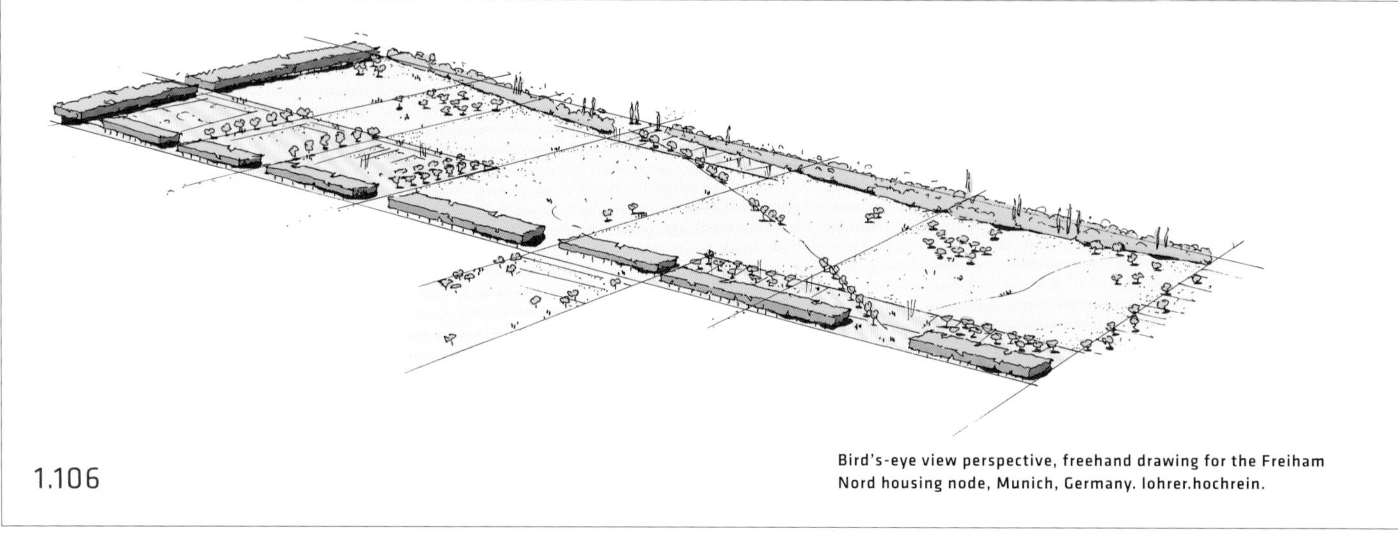

1.106

Bird's-eye view perspective, freehand drawing for the Freiham Nord housing node, Munich, Germany. lohrer.hochrein.

## Bird's-eye view perspectives
### Freehand drawings

If the view of the perspective runs from above to the ground level, the viewers' standpoints are placed outside the planning area. This makes it possible to convey an impression of a large part of the area or even the area as a whole. The spatial structure can be shown very clearly. Human figures can either be omitted altogether, or drawn in on a very small scale, but they cannot play a major role. The bird's-eye view perspectives shown here (Ills. 1.105-107) give a view of the whole project area. The viewer's position at a great distance and the chosen colour scheme make the area's borderlines stand out particularly clearly. The vegetation is divided up into open grassy spaces and more heavily planted areas. The television tower and the blue water (Ill. 1.105), the only other colour alongside the green of the vegetation areas, provide orientation points. Clearly discernible are also the connecting routes inside and outside the project area; adjacent buildings are indicated. Viewers are not stepping into the area, they remain observers from the outside.

1.107

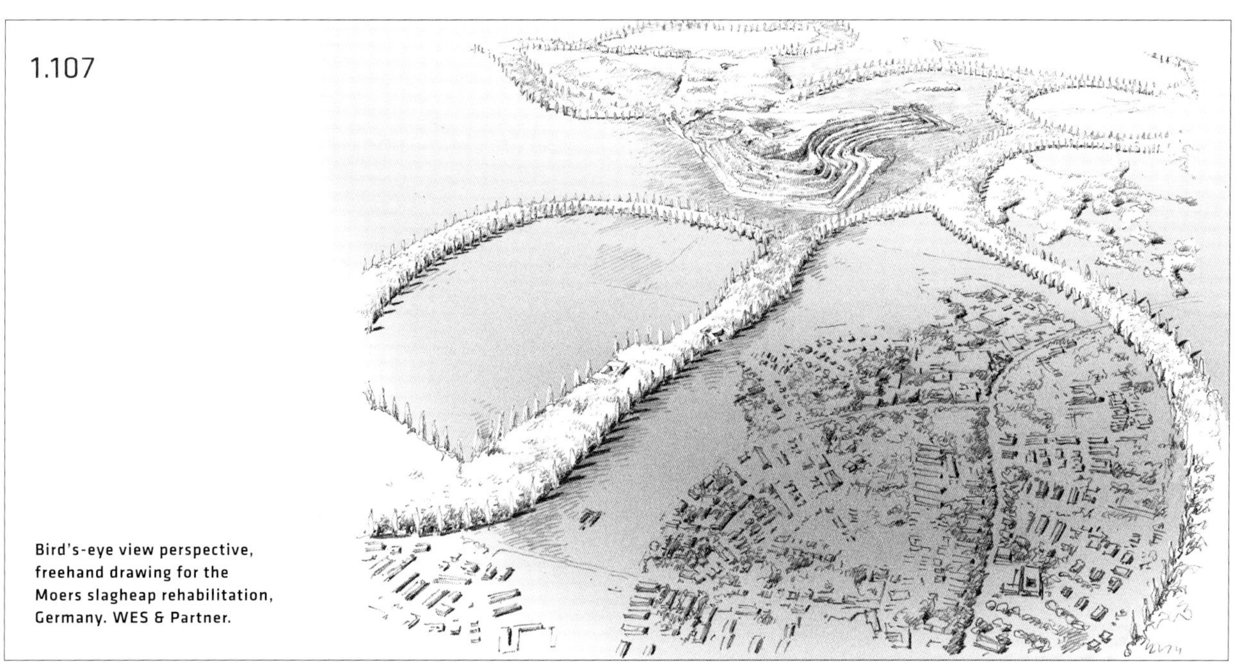

Bird's-eye view perspective, freehand drawing for the Moers slagheap rehabilitation, Germany. WES & Partner.

1.108

Bird's-eye view perspective, freehand drawing for the Moers slagheap rehabilitation.

This design for one of the largest slagheaps in the coal extraction area has "hill of silence" as its motto. This idea is impressively supported by the first perspective shown here, with the white-grey shading and the slagheap apparently in the middle of nowhere.

Similarly the viewpoint in the second perspective drawing (Ill. 1.108) is outside the area, at hilltop level, but now looking upwards, so that it is not the whole site that comes into view. The dimensions of the human figures are indicative of the distance taken, and so is the lack of detail in the vegetation in the foreground of the drawing.

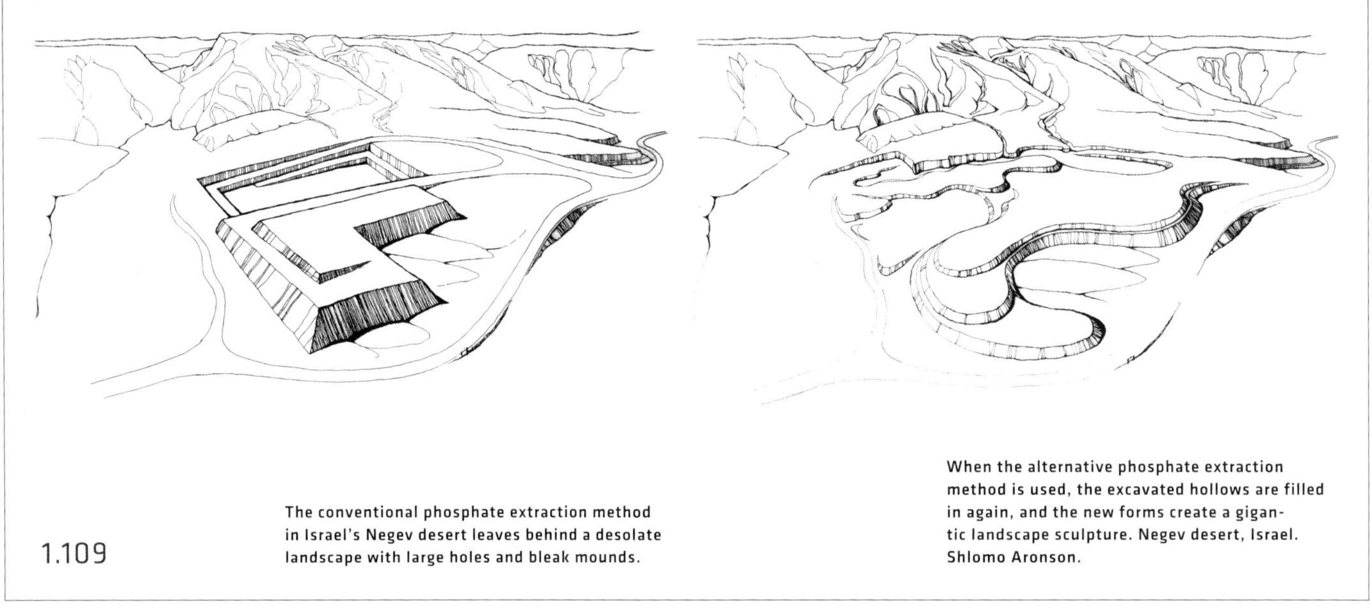

1.109

The conventional phosphate extraction method in Israel's Negev desert leaves behind a desolate landscape with large holes and bleak mounds.

When the alternative phosphate extraction method is used, the excavated hollows are filled in again, and the new forms create a gigantic landscape sculpture. Negev desert, Israel. Shlomo Aronson.

1.110

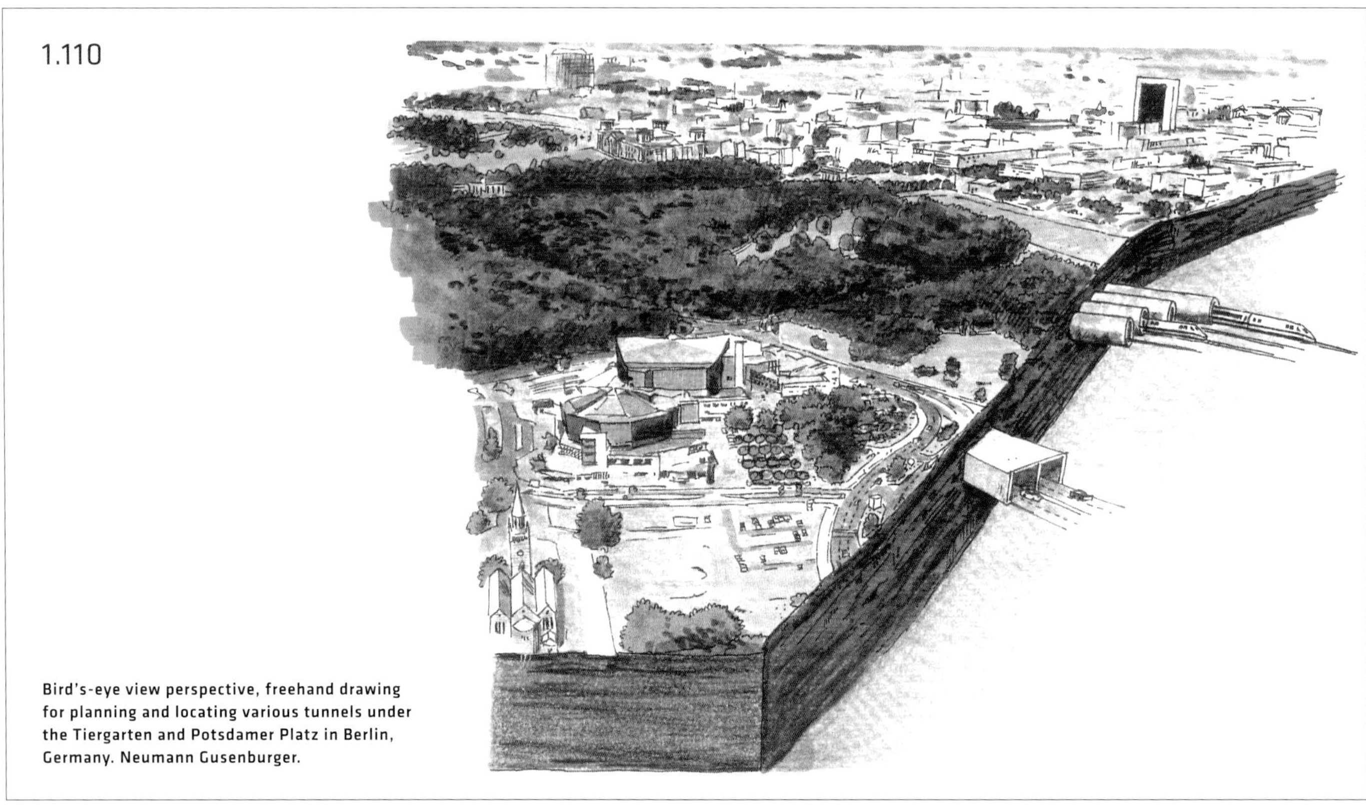

Bird's-eye view perspective, freehand drawing for planning and locating various tunnels under the Tiergarten and Potsdamer Platz in Berlin, Germany. Neumann Gusenburger.

This drawing for the tunnelling under the Tiergarten park in Berlin (Ill. 1.110) shows the developed urban area and the park on the left-hand side, and on the right-hand side the sub-surface area with the tunnels for the railway and the autobahn drawn in. Using a coloured hand drawing as a means of representation makes it easy to bring together uses above and below ground level. This is a good technique for illustrating highly complex, superimposed areas in cities in a clear way.

1.111

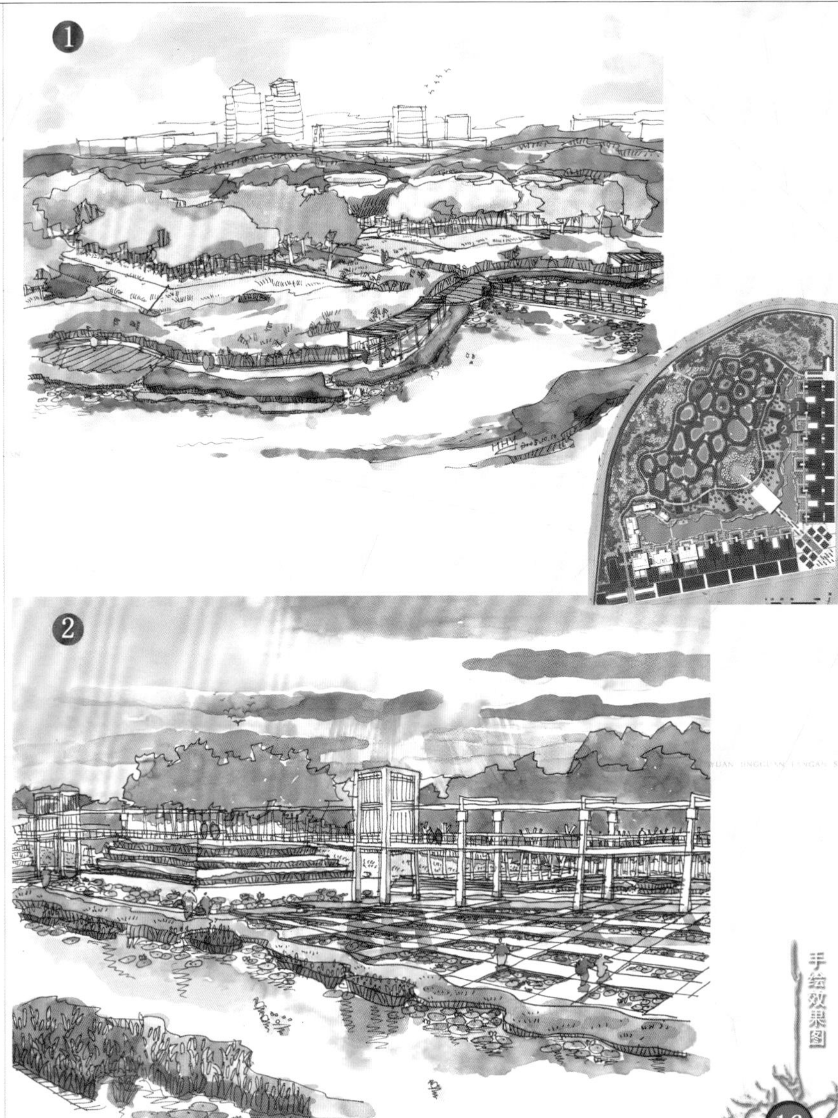

**Bird's-eye view perspectives, freehand drawings for the Qiaoyuan Park in Tianjin, China. Turenscape.**
Viewing points and lines of vision are drawn into the reduced ground plan, so that the perspectives can be located precisely.

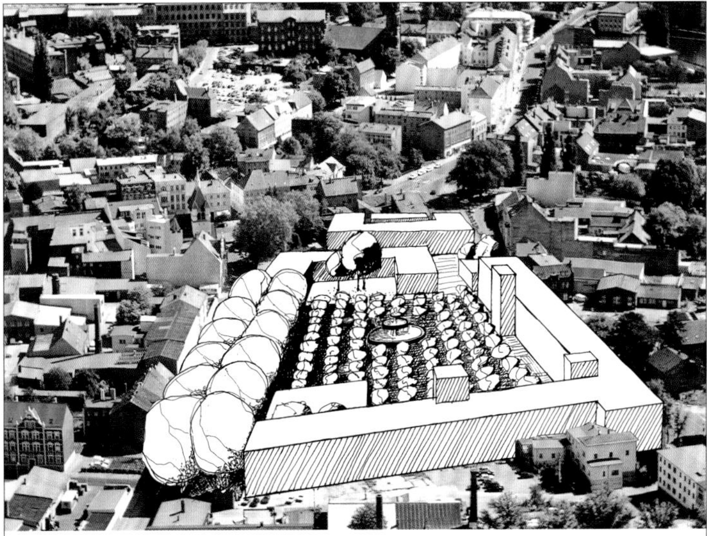

1.112

**Bird's-eye view perspective, freehand drawing over the existing urban structure in Guben, Germany, to illustrate the design. Neumann Gusenburger.**

1.113

**Bird's-eye view perspective, over-drawing on the existing urban structure by hand, showing the design idea for Guben.**

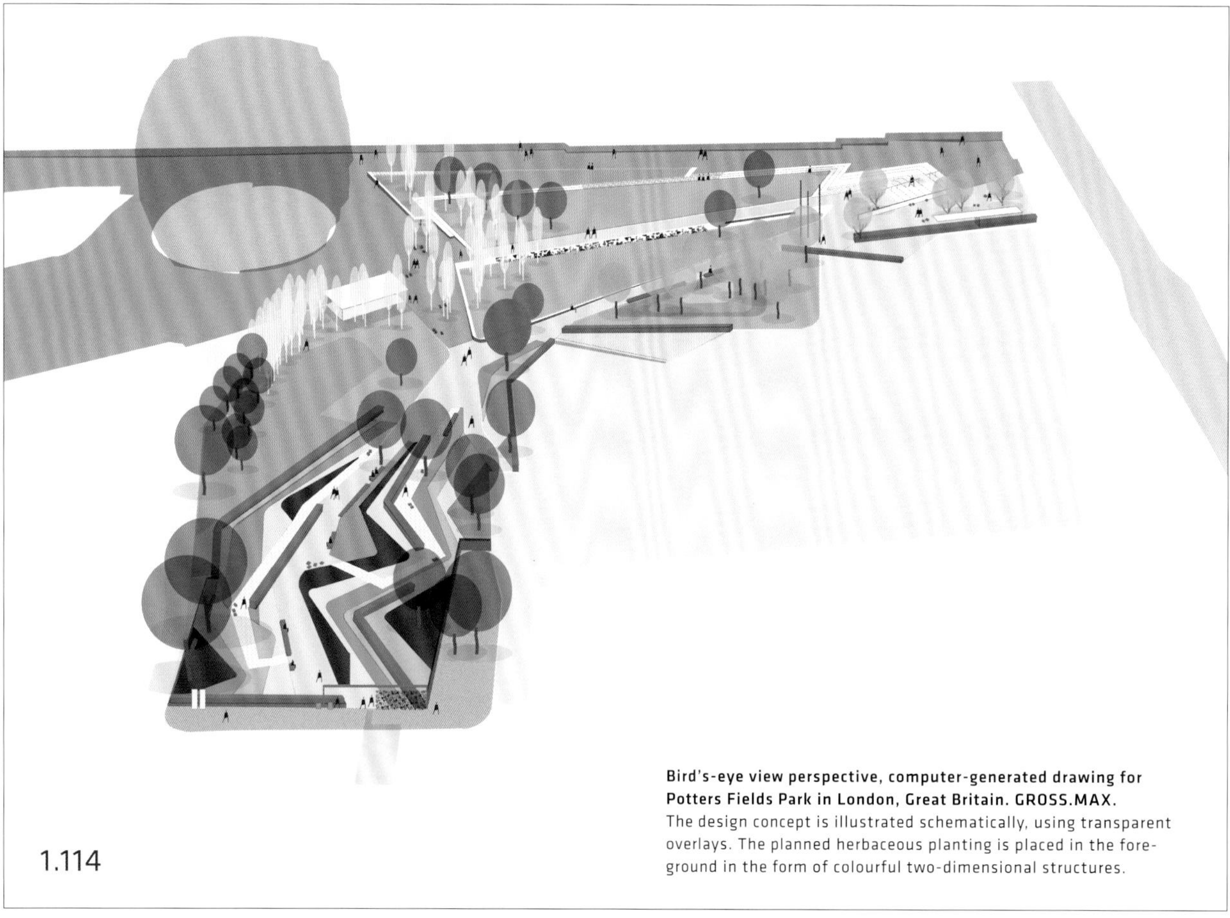

1.114

**Bird's-eye view perspective, computer-generated drawing for Potters Fields Park in London, Great Britain. GROSS.MAX.**
The design concept is illustrated schematically, using transparent overlays. The planned herbaceous planting is placed in the foreground in the form of colourful two-dimensional structures.

## Computer-generated drawings

The following perspective views are computer-generated, some of them combining digital and hand drawings. While hand drawings for presentation require some practice in freehand sketching, computer graphics can usually be created without this skill, thanks to the wide range of support offered by the various kinds of software. As design plans are mainly drawn by computer today, spatial representation suggests itself on an extended data base to include the third dimension. Another advantage is that computer material for a project will look more uniform even if generated by different people, whereas hand drawings always show individual approaches, and have their own expressive quality. Computer graphics are typically generated from the digital model's data stock, which also allows testing viewing angles and heights in advance. They are then frequently further manipulated by other programs or even hand drawing in order to emphasize the author's personal view and approach. This makes for an unlimited variety of results. Photographs of the site in its existing state are often used as a basis for representation of the planned changes, which makes it easier to recognize the place and understand the design ideas.

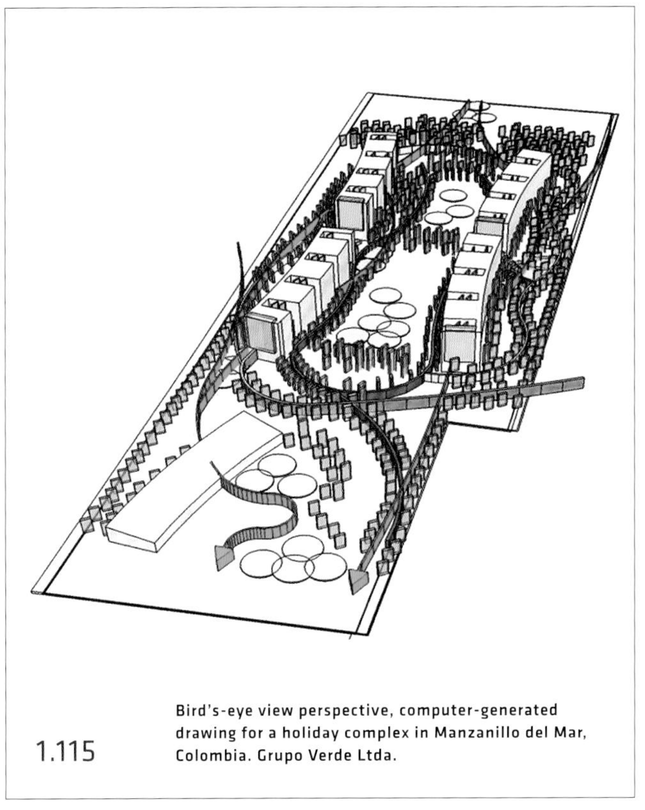

1.115 **Bird's-eye view perspective, computer-generated drawing for a holiday complex in Manzanillo del Mar, Colombia. Grupo Verde Ltda.**

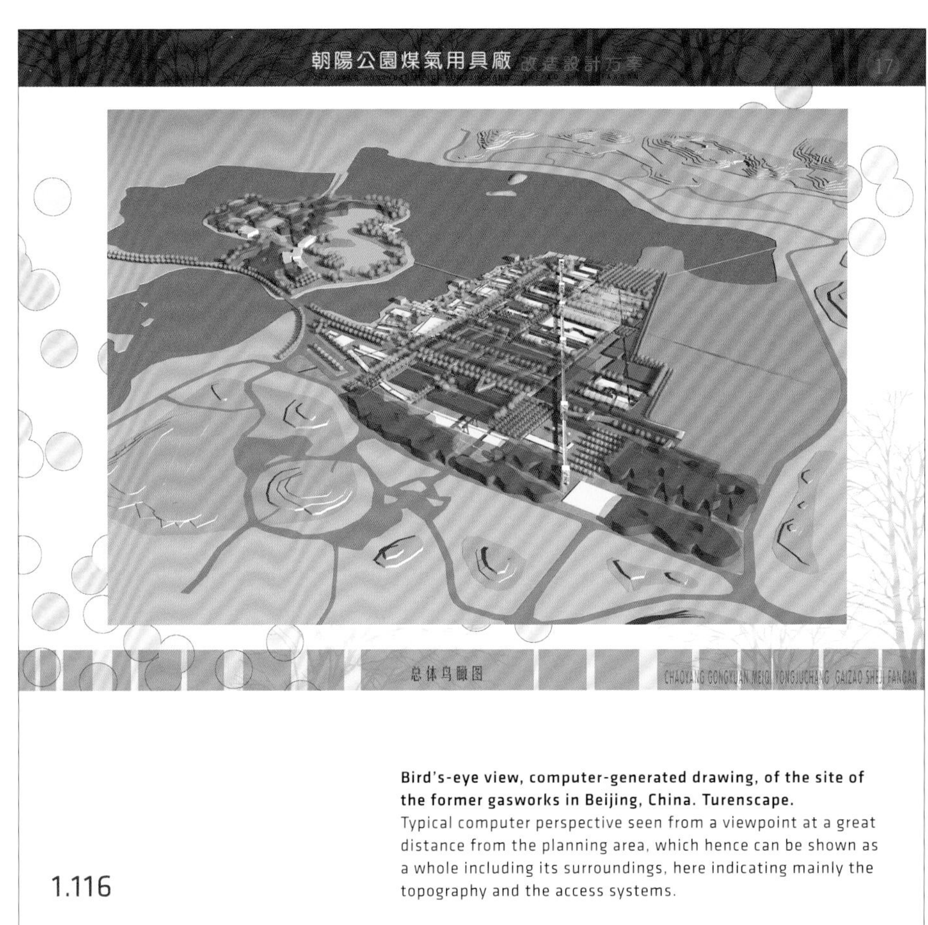


1.116 **Bird's-eye view, computer-generated drawing, of the site of the former gasworks in Beijing, China. Turenscape.**
Typical computer perspective seen from a viewpoint at a great distance from the planning area, which hence can be shown as a whole including its surroundings, here indicating mainly the topography and the access systems.

1.117 **Bird's-eye view perspective, computer-generated drawing showing part of the regional horticultural show in Neu-Ulm, Germany. Plancontext.**
This central perspective shows a general view of the location of the individual gardens and the boundary ditches to the left and right.

1.118 **Bird's-eye view perspective, computer-generated drawing for gardens on Singapore Bay. Gustafson Porter.**
The viewing point is so close to the area that human figures can be included; a sector of the project area is shown in a detailed view.

1.119

**Bird's-eye perspective view, computer-generated drawing of part of the Qiaoyuan Park in Tianjin, China. Turenscape.**
Detail view focusing on buildings and vegetation, with human figures indicated only schematically.

1.120

**Bird's-eye view perspective, computer-generated drawing for the Green Dragon Park in Shanghai, China. Turenscape.**
This collage of black-and-white and coloured areas and super-impositions shows a part of the overall plan; human figures are depicted only in outline, while the shadow cast by the bridge is executed very precisely.

1.121

**Bird's-eye view perspective, computer-generated drawing for the Green Dragon Park.**
This is a realistic depiction, the colour becomes paler towards the upper edge of the image to distinguish the selected sector from the remaining project area.

1.122

**Bird's-eye view perspective, computer-generated drawing for a roof garden for Dubai Pearl, United Arab Emirates. WES & Partner.**
The close distance to the planning area allows the depiction of recognizable human figures as well as relief and the furnishings for the planned roof garden.

1.123

**Bird's-eye view perspective, computer-generated drawing for Dubai Pearl.**

1.124

**Bird's-eye view perspective, computer-generated drawing for the Spa Hotel Aluna near Bogotá, Colombia. Grupo Verde Ltda.**

1.125

Bird's-eye view perspective, computer-generated drawing for the 1001 Trees public park in north-west Copenhagen, Denmark. SLA.

This perspective view shows the planned park in colour, the vegetation merging into white-transparent areas, while the existing development is partly outlined and presented in superimpositions.

1.126

Bird's-eye view perspective, computer-generated drawing with the viewing axis pointing almost vertically downwards, for the Vertical Garden in London, Great Britain. GROSS.MAX.

The extreme perspective in combination with the colour scheme and the luxuriant vegetation, and also the butterflies, some of them shown as transparent, create a surreal image that attracts particular attention.

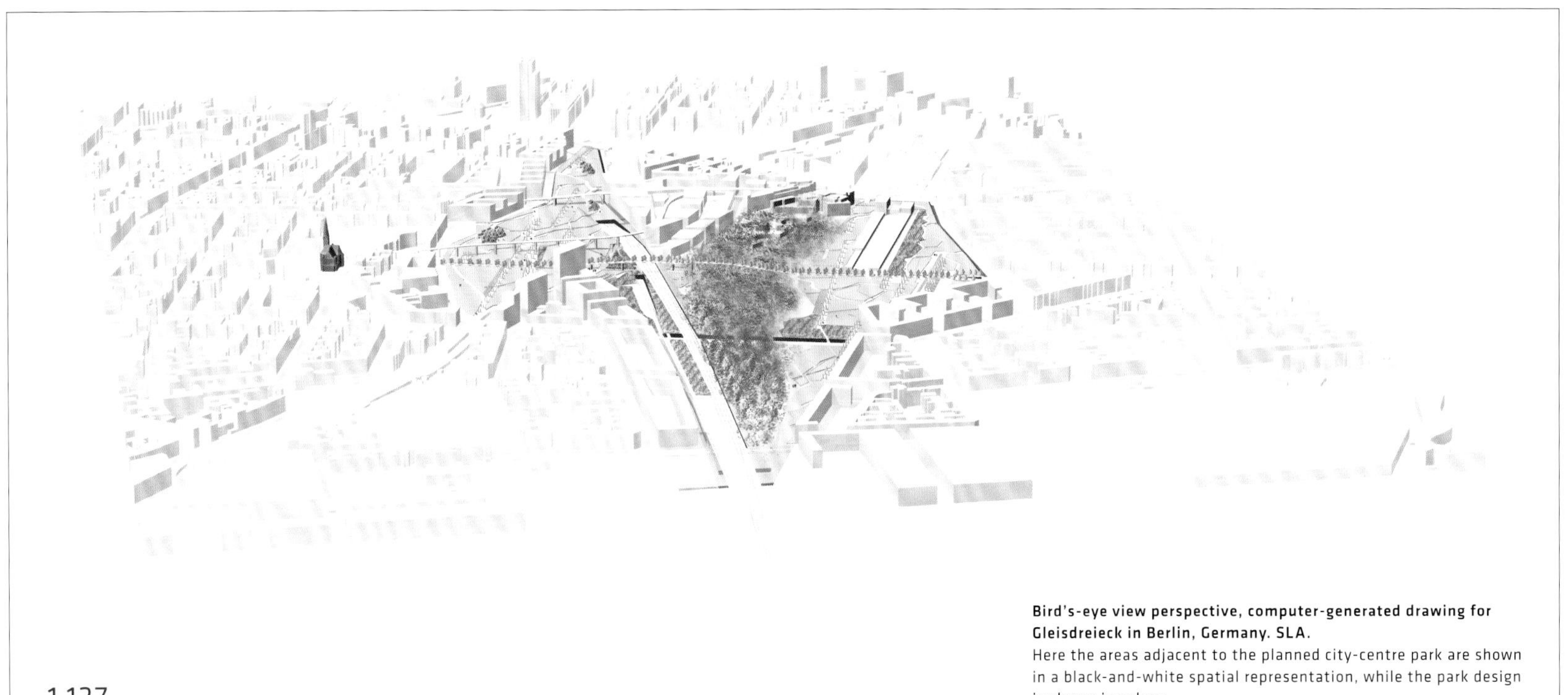

1.127

**Bird's-eye view perspective, computer-generated drawing for Gleisdreieck in Berlin, Germany. SLA.**
Here the areas adjacent to the planned city-centre park are shown in a black-and-white spatial representation, while the park design is shown in colour.

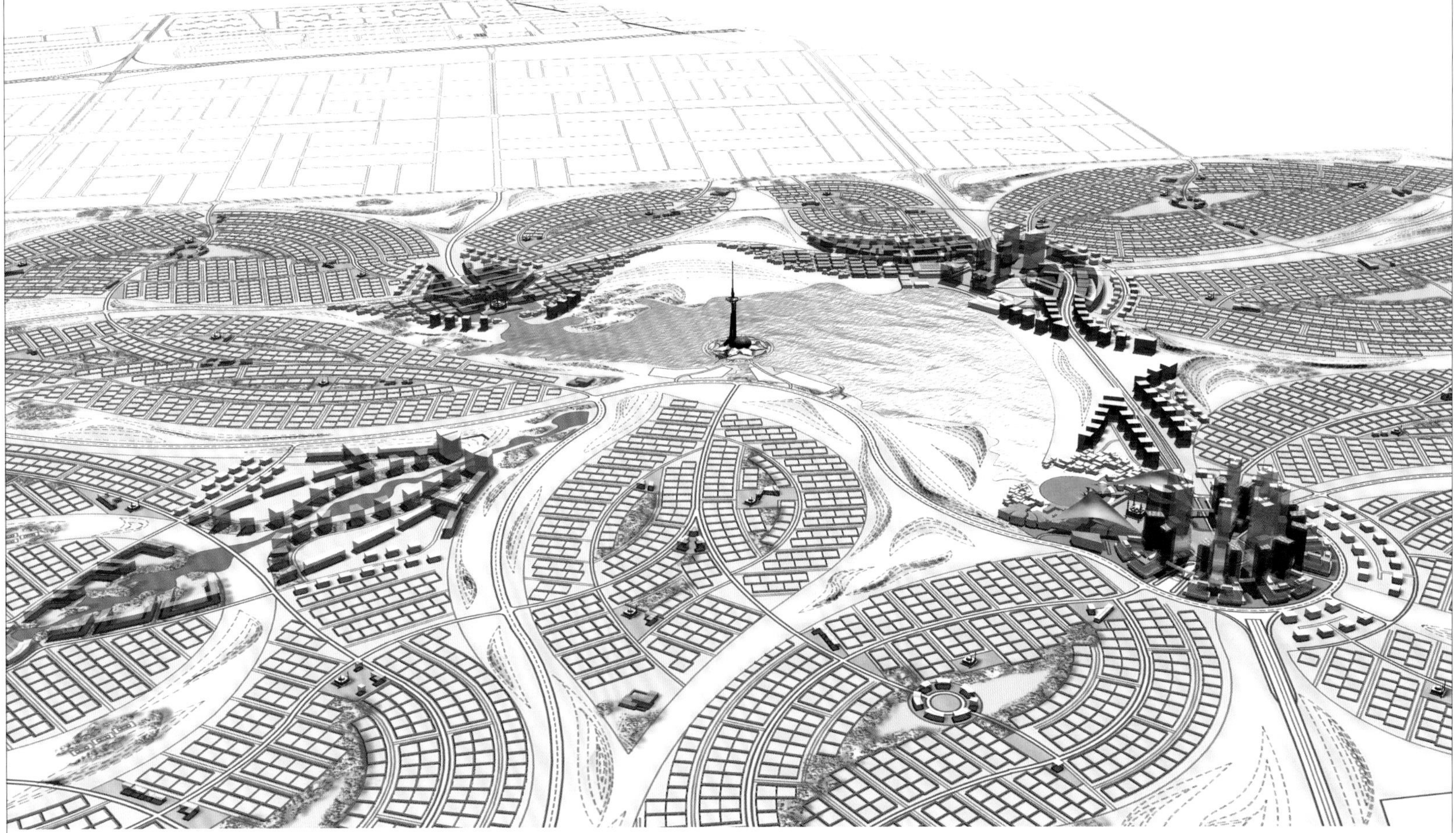

1.128

**Bird's-eye view, computer-generated drawing for the design for Khalifa City C, Abu Dhabi, United Arab Emirates. Neumann Gusenburger.**

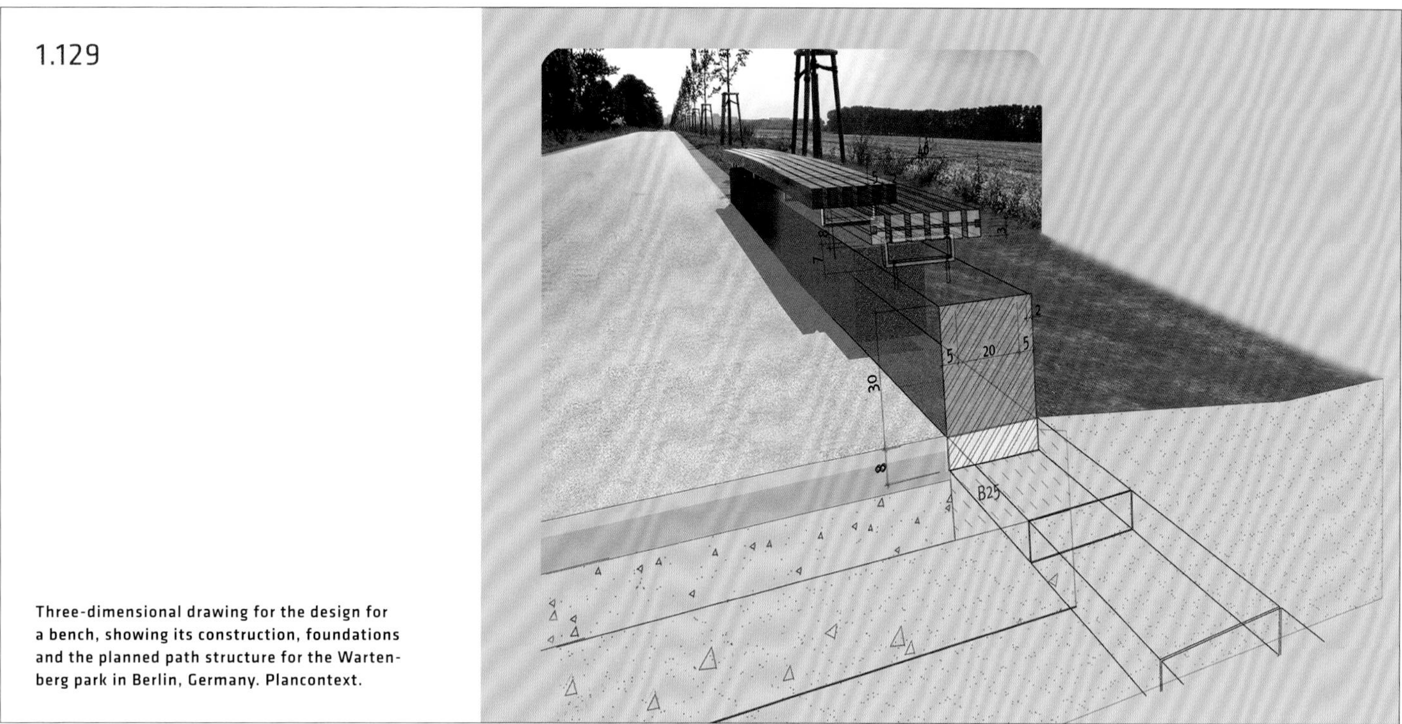


1.129

Three-dimensional drawing for the design for a bench, showing its construction, foundations and the planned path structure for the Wartenberg park in Berlin, Germany. Plancontext.

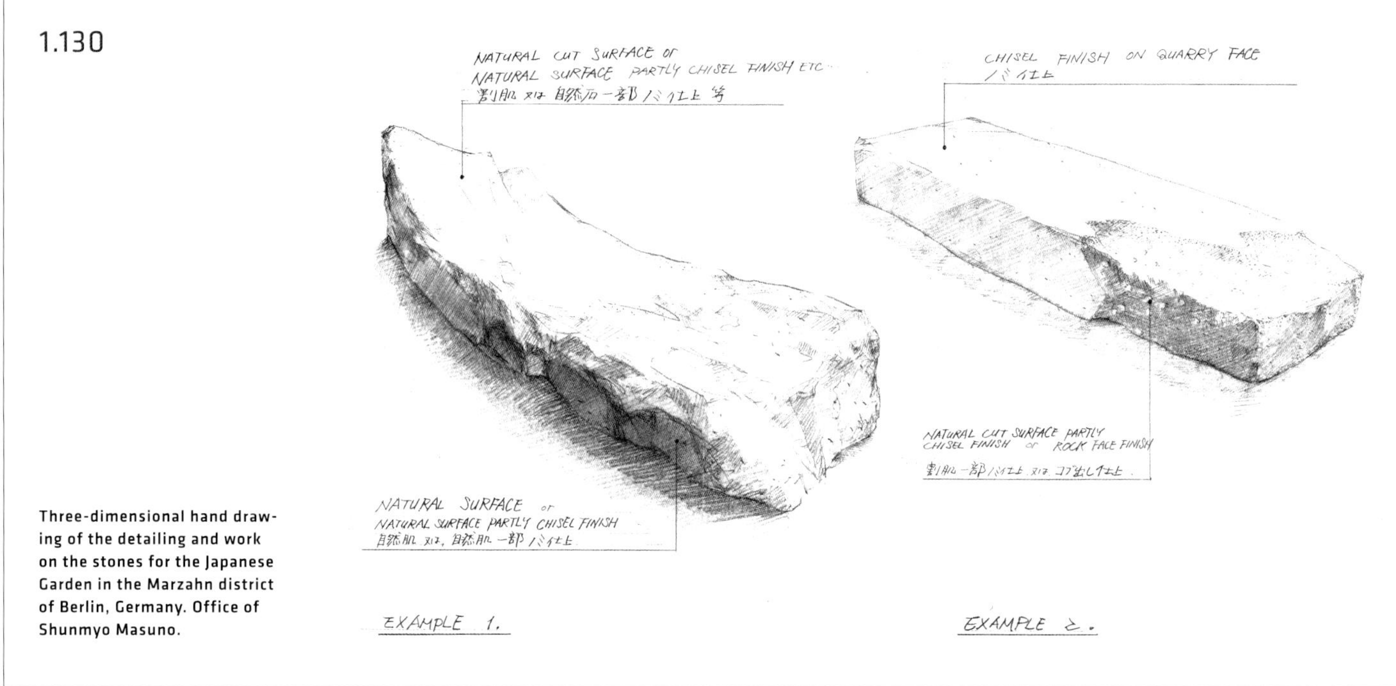


1.130

Three-dimensional hand drawing of the detailing and work on the stones for the Japanese Garden in the Marzahn district of Berlin, Germany. Office of Shunmyo Masuno.

## Spatial representations for working planning

Two-dimensional plans tend to be favoured in this design phase. Even though more time and effort are required than for the two-dimensional instructions, which are easy to dimension, spatial representations do help those carrying out the work to understand the concept. Of course, perspective drawings always have the disadvantage of convergence, and can be used only in selected cases. Three-dimensional hand drawings can express the designer's personal slant and at the same time convey instructions for the necessary craft work, for instance when special manufacturing is required, as in this example showing the stone to be cut (Ill. 1.130).

1.131 Physical model for the design of the gardens on Singapore Bay. Gustafson Porter.

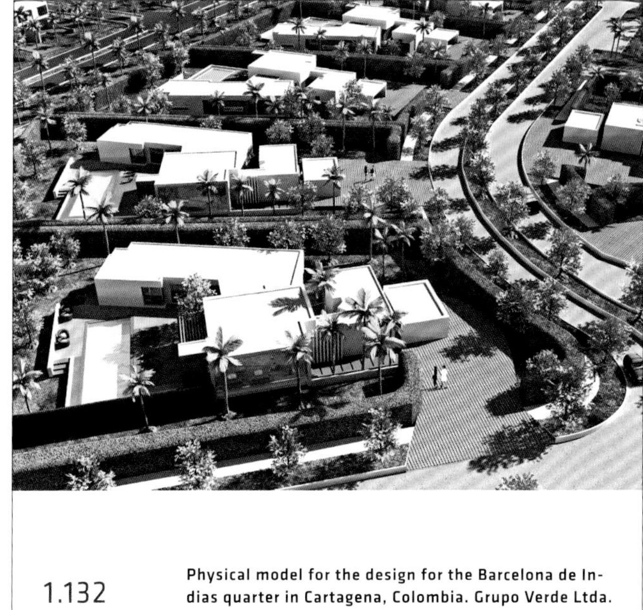

1.132 Physical model for the design for the Barcelona de Indias quarter in Cartagena, Colombia. Grupo Verde Ltda.

1.133 Physical model for the Marienhof competition in Munich, Germany. Plancontext.

## Physical and digital models

The models shown here, made by hand or generated digitally, support the design process or the presentation of the designs. The software generally used in planning practices makes it possible to construct simple digital models. Built models tend to be used more for large urban development or very prestigious projects. As the possibilities for reproduction in a book are confined to photographs of the models, the expressive force of these resources for design can be shown only approximately here.

1.134

Detail of the physical model for Khalifa City C, Abu Dhabi, United Arab Emirates. Neumann Gusenburger.

1.135

Physical model in wood and acrylic glass, simulation of nightscape for Khalifa City C.

1.136

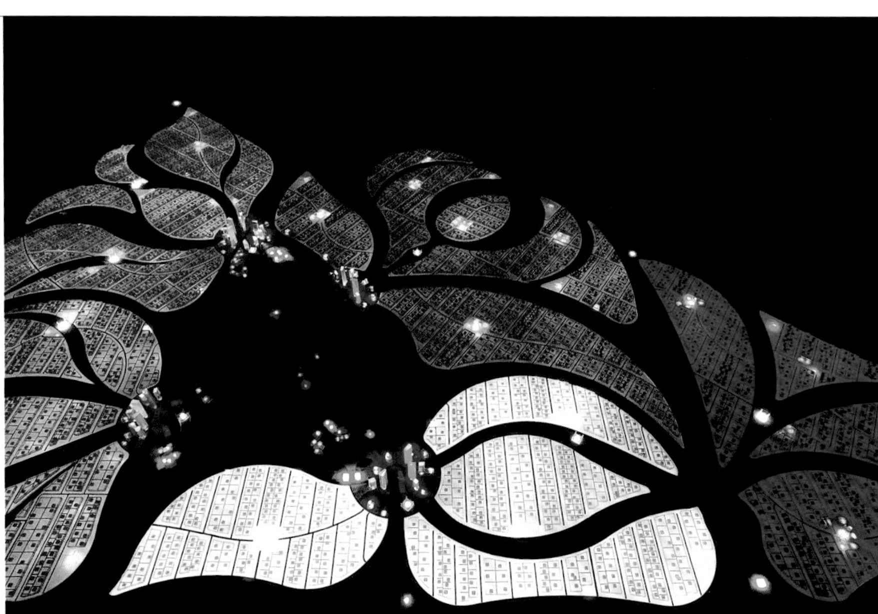

Photograph from above of the illuminated model for Khalifa City C.

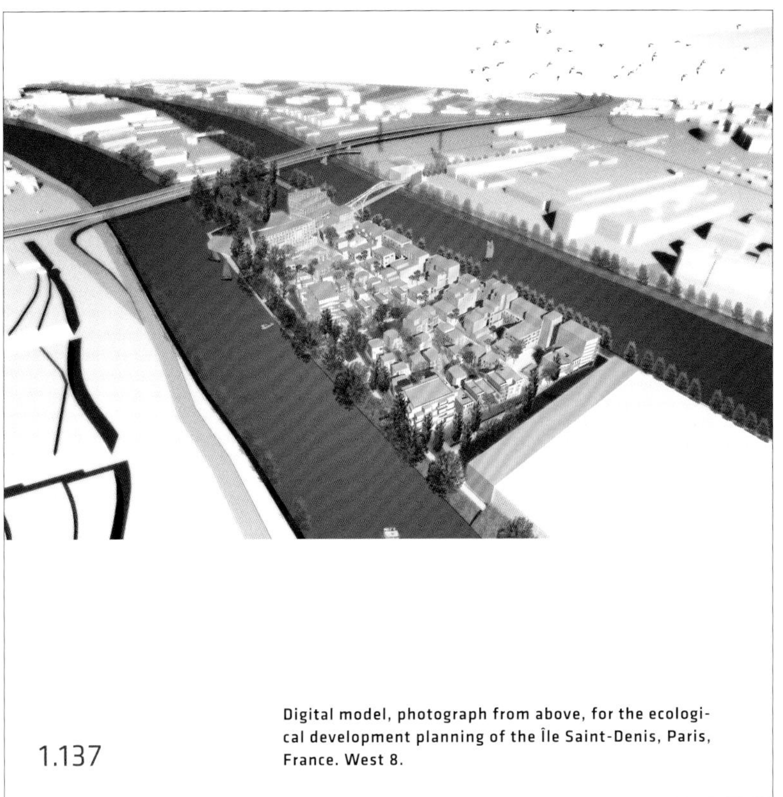

1.137 Digital model, photograph from above, for the ecological development planning of the Île Saint-Denis, Paris, France. West 8.

1.138 Physical working model for the design of the rotunda in Liverpool, Great Britain. GROSS.MAX.

1.139 **Physical model of the outdoor facilities for the Qatar National Museum in Doha. Michel Desvigne.**
This detail from the model shows very clearly the topography and its different shapes for a variety of uses.

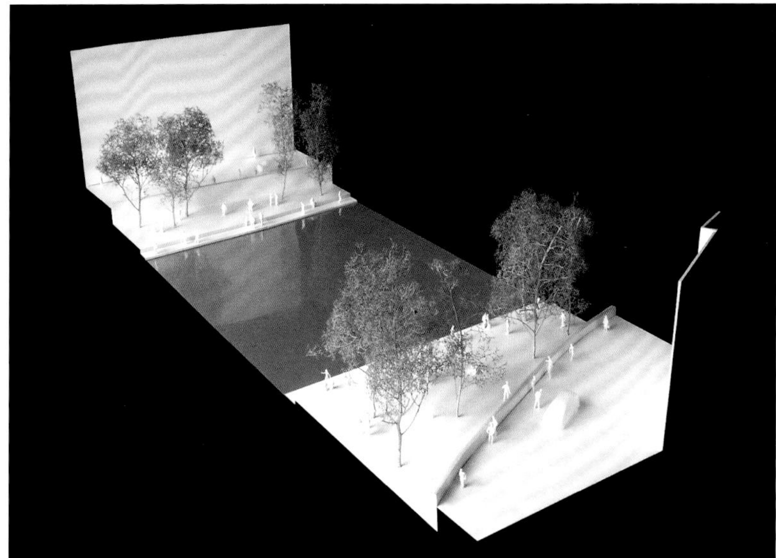

1.140 **Physical model for the "Oude Dokken" in Ghent, Belgium. Michel Desvigne.**
This model shows the principles, boundaries and possible uses for the newly designed embankment areas of the old docks.

# FUNCTIONS **TIME**

## Time as the fourth dimension

Time is a given medium for life, for the natural sciences it is a dimension of the universe as a fundamental measurable value. It has a very specific meaning for landscape architecture. The way open spaces are perceived, and their usefulness, do not depend on location, design and content alone, but to a large extent on time as well. Time is one basis on which the interface between man and nature is organized. The rhythms of days, weeks and years have a direct effect on open spaces. Planning is always directed at changes that lie ahead in time.

As a dimension that cannot be felt or seen directly, time is a way of saying that change is a given, things never stand still. Depending on the geographical location of a place the day will pass from light to dark, with differing degrees of twilight in between; spring, summer autumn and winter follow one another in the course of a year; rainy and dry periods alternate, coupled with fluctuating temperatures, precipitation and periods of daylight. These aspects are of vital importance for the uses of open space, and planning has to take the lighting conditions and climatic situation into account. The extent to which open spaces can be used is also highly dependent on time, the design and content of open spaces are guided by the use requirements referring to the course of the days and seasons.

### Change as a subject of design and presentation

Most visual presentations of open space planning show situations during the day. But as urban open spaces in particular are also used in the hours of darkness, and lighting is required to meet the need for safety, among others, drawings and other visualizations provide nightscapes. Lighting serves different purposes, dependent on the location, including safety, direction and orientation, and ecological purposes, but creative design is always involved as well.

Planning typically does not vary much with reference to daytime. Uses are mostly not planned differently for situations running through the 24 hours of a day. Yet planning could be more differentiated, the schemes for dealing with spaces more creative. For example, a given location could be a children's playground by day and a car park at night. Projects like this already exist, and developing this issue further would point to the future in urban open spaces.

As landscape architects are the experts in planning and designing open space for different uses, it should be essential to look at the possible and actual uses in the course of a day and a year. If users are shown in visualizations, in the form of human figures, these are young and active middle-aged adults as a rule, as well as young people playing sport and children playing. Older people tend to be shown as clichéd types rather than as actively involved in what is happening. This limited cross-section of society conveys a desire for youthfulness, independence and full capacities that certainly exists and that is reflected and in fact reinforced by visualizations.

The question remains whether desirable goals can actually be achieved by implementing this kind of planning, or whether the design should take account of those who will in fact use the open spaces, for example people who do not work in the daytime. With an increasing amount of effort and highly realistic, almost photographic methods, many illustrations show a section of society that probably can be found in the open spaces only on the rarest of occasions, perhaps on a summer Sunday afternoon, if the weather is good.

In the same vein, lighting conditions that change with the time of day and the season, which has a direct effect on possible and actual uses, are rarely taken into account in visual presentations. Neither is moderately good weather addressed. Open spaces are used differently at different times of the year; if temperatures are unduly hot or cold they are either avoided, visited for a short time only or sheltered areas are sought out. It is rare to see a visual representation of what an open space will look like in the course of a year; as a rule the best possible moment is chosen, with favourable climatic conditions. Statements about how long this situation will last or how frequently it will come about are usually omitted.

Another aspect of landscape architecture, for which time is particularly important and that is not as significant in any other discipline, is the way open spaces change because vegetation changes. Plants are entirely subject to the rhythm of the seasons, to a much greater extent than human activities in open spaces. Deciduous trees and shrubs look entirely different as the year progresses. As trees are typically used to shape space, these changes affect the open space directly. In design they mostly serve for creating and defining space, so that their changes affect open spaces directly. Shrubs and herbaceous plants all bloom at different times of the year, and this is often the time at which they are most attractive. But at other times as well each plant has its own characteristic appearance, and this influences open spaces in various ways. Projects are planned for a long period after completion, and as visualizations of open space design show the project at a specific moment, special attention needs to be paid to the development of vegetation over the years. As a rule, plants grow bigger with age: some tend to get higher, others wider, and others multiply. Not all plants develop at the same rate, and ageing processes in plants differ as well. In central Europe bedding plants will live for a few months, herbaceous plants for some years, and woody plants will last from a decade to over 1000 years. These natural laws are taken into account for the foreseeable future in every planning operation, but representing the concurrent changes visually is both a great challenge and something that clients rarely ask for.

Open spaces are largely created in areas that are in use and have been designed previously. Even though planning and design relate to new uses and to development from the present into the future, it is necessary to look back into the past at the start of every project. Often new design ideas will result from such research. For projects on historically significant open spaces, the past should be made visible and laid open to experience in the future development. With a survey of the existing development at the start of a project, historical sources and photographs, excavations or aerial photographs in which overgrown structures can be seen, or other resources are used to show a former condition. In historically significant places in particular, creative work can relate to existing design or design that existed in the past, as a rule by reinterpreting history. Visualizations must show, in detail and comprehensibly, how the place changed over time, identifying the respective points in time so that the new design can be seen to be linked with the past.

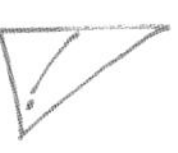

The acceptance of a proposal often depends to a considerable extent on the presentation of research and studies about the history of a place. It is important to present changes carefully and with as few gaps as possible, thus also providing documentation for subsequent generations. Visualizations can meet both these requirements, and they are irreplaceable for this work.

We also need time to look at and understand drawings, but even more we need time to approach and use the open spaces themselves. Time determines how much and what can be perceived and enjoyed of a landscape or an open space. Open spaces are experienced with differing degrees of "speed", on foot, in a vehicle, a bicycle, car or bus, for example, and certainly most rarely from the air. The different periods that are needed or available to experience and use a place, and the sequence of changing impressions when moving through future open space cannot be directly represented in images that remain static in time. Moving pictures, videos, films and the like, can take up and present all three aspects of duration in time that have been mentioned – the future development of the "finished" project, the way the project combines past, present and future, and also the temporal aspects of experiencing a place.

## Survey

The past is always part of the development of open spaces in time. It is included in both the design process and the presentation, so that conclusions can be drawn about future design. Recording and analysing the existing situation also includes development to the present day and possibly reasons for changes that occurred in the past. Situations of past moments in time are linked graphically with each other or with the present conditions. The ensuing visual document provides indications for reconstruction or for design approaches that may be effective.

In this presentation of the existing situation for monument preservation (Ill. 1.141 a), the result of the current survey is superimposed as a line drawing in black over the coloured historical plan, to show correspondences and deviations. This is a way to simultaneously show the condition as designed and implemented in the past, along with the current state of affairs. A revealing superimposition of this kind, complemented with details about the height of the land and the walls, makes it possible to move towards restoration according to the regulations of monument preservation.

Ill. 1.141 b shows which parts of the historic complex were identified in current archaeological excavations. In this example, the length of time between survey and excavation work was much smaller than in the previous one, and the degree of correspondence between the two methods applied is significantly greater.

When photographs and drawings (Ills. 1.142-145) are prepared so that they can be superimposed directly on the computer screen, the situation as planned can be recognized directly from the existing situation. In the example shown, the design practice presents the superimposed drawings on its website. New open spaces are thus generated from photographs of the existing fabric, using structures and materials that are available on the site.

1.141 a-b

Superimposing historic planning dating from 1869 on a 1996 survey to establish the historical substance present in the castle garden in Schwerin, Germany. Stefan Pulkenat.

Superimposing documentation of the archaeological excavations in 2006 and the 1996 survey in the castle garden.

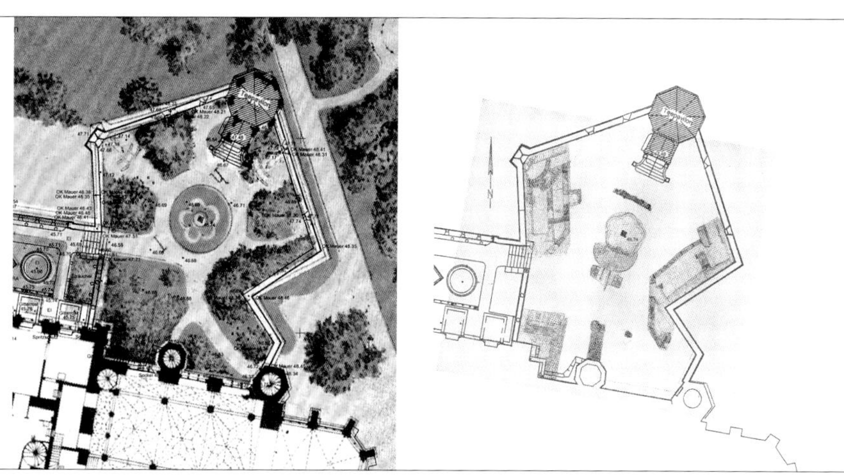

1.142-143

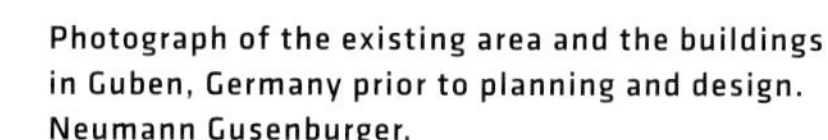

Photograph of the existing area and the buildings in Guben, Germany prior to planning and design. Neumann Gusenburger.

Design drawing for the open space in Guben.

1.144-145

Photograph of the existing wall of the building in Guben prior to planning and design.

Drawing of the redesigned open space in Guben, including the changes to the existing situation.

1.146

View for the open space design for the festival hall in Frankfurt am Main, Germany, in the daytime. RMP.

1.147

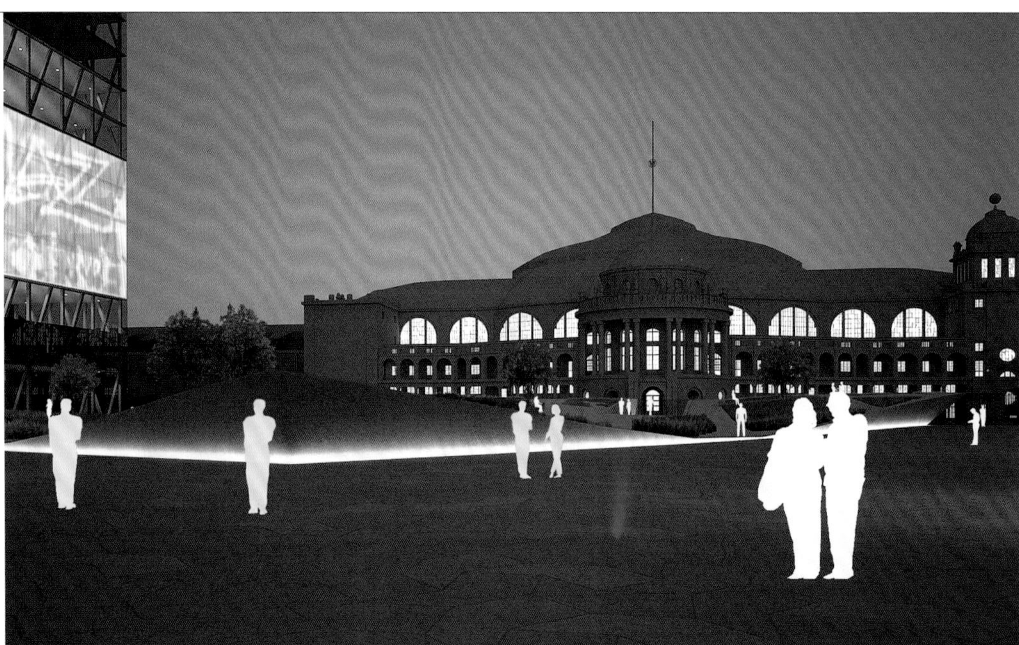

View for the open space design for the festival hall at night.

## Times of day

Places change their appearance in the course of the day, and sometimes the way they are used as well. These examples (Ills. 1.146 - 147) exhibit visual impressions of the same view in daylight and darkness. In the design for the festival hall the significance of lighting as a design tool is emphasized to make the garden a stronger presence as a sculpture in front of the hall. This sculptural garden is structured by light at night-time: its edges are lit from below, so that the shape of the complex makes an impact, without taking attention away from the hall as the central feature.

1.148

View for the design for the market place in Neubrandenburg, Germany, in the daytime. Noack.

1.149

View for the design for the market place at night.

In the design for the market place the perspective view (Ill. 1.148) shows the intention to create a square for various activities like games and sport, and for people of different ages. Choosing a viewpoint at about the viewer's eye level gives the impression that that he or she is part of the scene. The square's surface covering is presented in great detail, just as it would be seen from the chosen viewpoint in the area. The proposed fountains are mainly perceived as a centre of activity of the people playing by and in them, while the buildings dominate the background as a conclusion to the square. The people's clothing, the blue sky, the short shadows and the brightness of the picture suggest a summer's day, and the depicted activities, adults playing with children, skating, playing by and in the water, show an aspect of leisure and relaxation. Viewers would like to be involved in this scene.

1.150

Visualization of the "Fibre Optic Marsh", a project for reconstructing and stabilizing an aquatic ecosystem in Field's Point, Rhode Island, USA. Abigail Feldman.

The contrasting view at twilight with lighting (Ill. 1.149) shows the various effects in the open space. It is not just the use that changes, the way the space is perceived is different. The building in the background becomes more important at night, also as a result of the lighting, which gives a sense of security, an aspect of planning that should not be underestimated. What we see here is a square that appeals to people, a visualization essentially characterized by the season chosen and the weather, and also by the relaxed way in which the square is used.

Fibreglass rods are positioned in the water in an attempt to restore a damaged sea-grass marsh (Ill. 1.150) in a badly polluted coastal area. Epiphytes cling to the rods, breaking down the unduly high nutrient levels in the water. This in turn improves the quality of the water, and the natural vegetation can develop again. The glowing fibreglass supports the ecological development of the biotope, and at the same time serves as a measurement and indicator system for the condition of this stretch of coast. The changing colours of the light make a special impression, particularly at night, as illustrated here (bottom). These visualizations demonstrate how ecological demands can be met creatively and presented accordingly.

This presentation sheet for a square in Hamburg (Ill. 1.151) contains among other iullustrations two perspective views of the proposal in the daytime and at night. The two views show the planned square from the same viewpoint with very slight differences. Comparison of the images in the daytime and at night shows the different uses of this open space, and ways of experiencing it. By day, the proposal is for a straightforward, modern inner-city square. Vegetation forms the border of the square on the right-hand side, while the buildings are less important as spatial borders. Then at night the square seems bright, the lights from the surrounding streets,

1.151

**Presentation of the design for Spielbudenplatz in Hamburg, Germany. Plancontext.**

1.152

**Photograph of the model for Spielbudenplatz.**

buildings and advertisements are reflected in the gleaming, polished asphalt surface. Because of their lighting and the neon advertising, the buildings around the square make a stronger impression than by day, but the vegetation makes less of an impact. The choice of colour suggests that the designers intended a wide variety of uses at night, while keeping the square more reticent in the daytime. This reversal of the normal weighting gives the design an accent that the visualization emphasizes accordingly. The model (Ill. 1.152) complements the presentation sheet with an imposing and impressively reproduced representation of the buildings around the square, thus also providing proportions and dimensions. The various possible uses and different times of the day are not addressed in the model. Both the neutral attitude towards uses of the model and the diversity of uses shown in the perspective views underline the designers' view that successful public spaces must offer the possibility of unpredictable moments, surprises, variable and multiple meanings and uses, diversity and ambivalence.

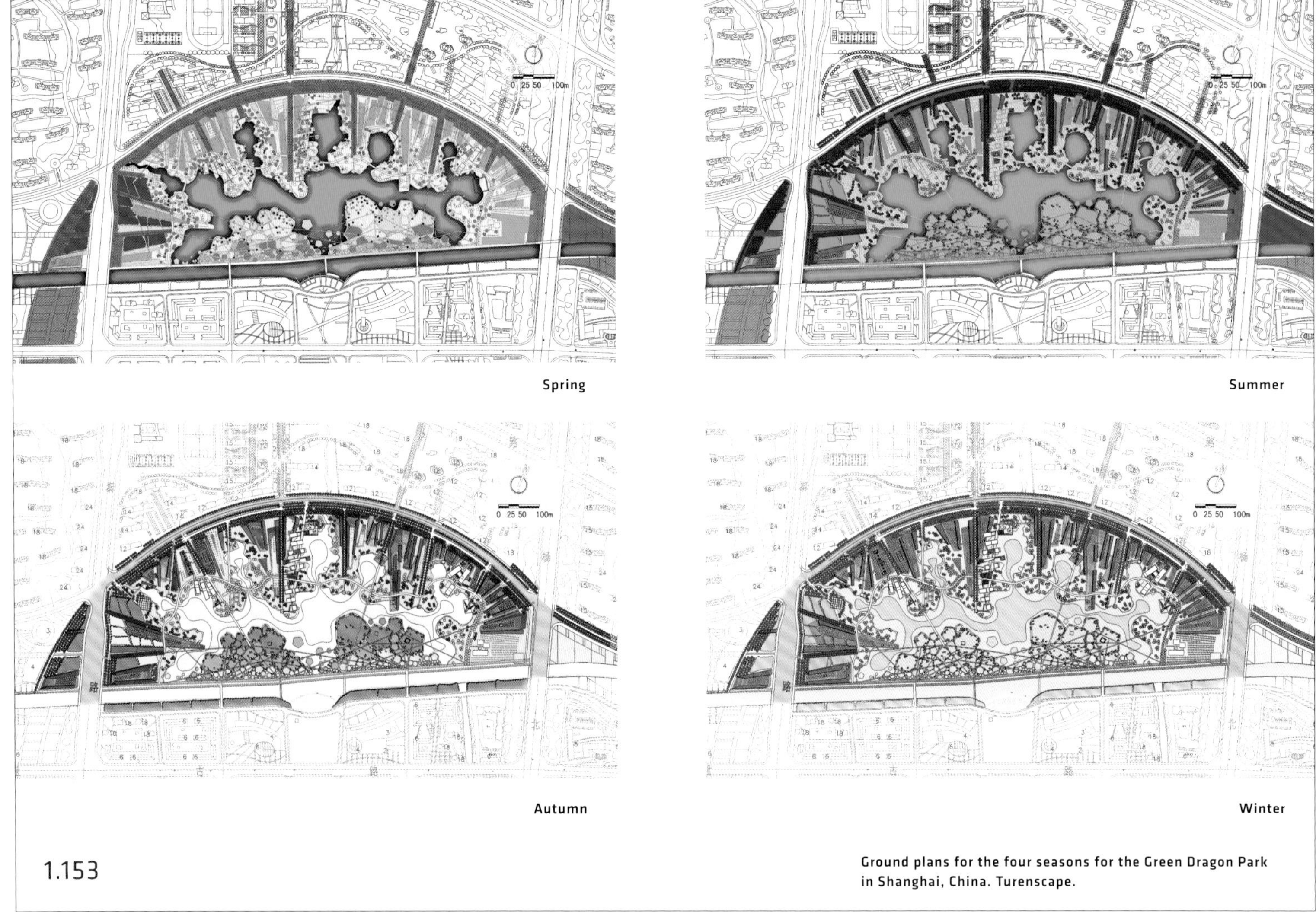


1.153

Ground plans for the four seasons for the Green Dragon Park in Shanghai, China. Turenscape.

## Seasons

Changing times of the year, according to the climate zone from summer to winter and back to summer, or alternating dry and rainy seasons, determine the appearance of open spaces and their possible uses. Trees that are green in summer are more transparent in winter, when they do not create so much shade and make their effect by growth and habit alone. Herbaceous plants as a rule make no effect in winter, and constantly change a planted area for short periods, while annual bedding plants create an image that may stay the same for months. Visualizing different activities according to the seasons supports the aim of continuous use for the planned open space throughout the year. Snow is often employed to suggest the winter aspect, even though snow does not fall throughout the winter in many European countries. Lighting such a scene has to match the more diffuse lighting circumstances.

Different seasons are not often shown, especially in ground plans. Views of winter scenes can set a special accent.

In these hand drawings (Ills. 1.154 -155), the different areas, each standing out in colour, represent the outstanding blossom aspects of a tall herb meadow in a design close to nature. This simple presentation shows a possibility of marking different blossom aspects on one and the same drawing, in an attempt to convey the changing impressions of herbaceous plantings.

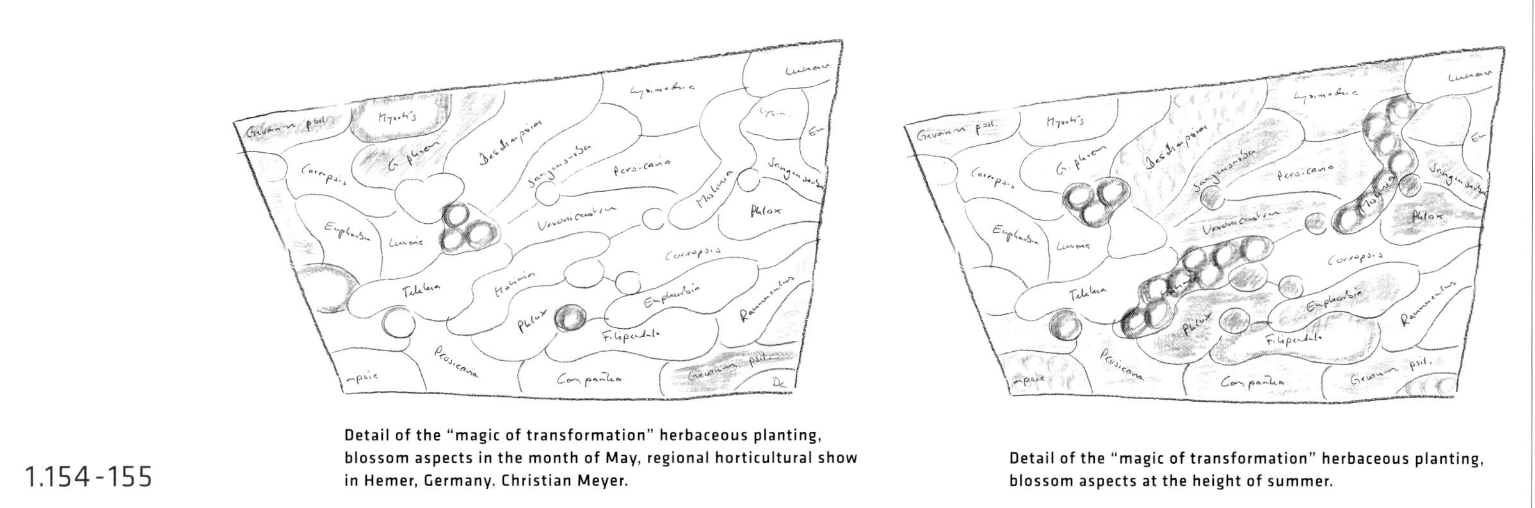

1.154-155

Detail of the "magic of transformation" herbaceous planting, blossom aspects in the month of May, regional horticultural show in Hemer, Germany. Christian Meyer.

Detail of the "magic of transformation" herbaceous planting, blossom aspects at the height of summer.

1.156-157

Scenario for experimental forestry: a Nelder plantation on the former open-cast mine in Welzow (Lausitz), Germany. Lenné 3D.

1.158

Winter view for the design for Schillerplatz in Schweinfurt, Germany. Dirk Stendel.

## The passage of time

The development and change of open space over several years is astonishingly rarely worked out and presented graphically. Typical design representations relate to a point in time about 20 years after planting; solitaire trees have been replanted three times by then and are at least thirty years old, and the majority of trees show the habit typical of their species or variety at that age. However, this kind of presentation shows an open space only in a static state, dependent on the growth and changing appearance of the plants, and in a condition that can only come about a long time after they are planted.

Immediately after they are set up, open spaces with a great deal of vegetation do not usually correspond with the ideas evoked by visual presentations. Large trees in particular, which contribute a great deal to creating space, cannot completely fulfil their function because of their delayed development. Therefore, often an attempt is made to use plants that are already older, larger and further developed, so that the desired image and ability to function can be achieved, and the plants' different stages and speeds of development can be better combined with each other. But this approach also distorts the natural development of a planted area, for example when very old trees are combined with young ground cover or shrubs, which often happens. It is technically possible to transplant old trees, but it can take years of preparation and involves breaking up the root ball, and this often stops or greatly inhibits the plant's further development. Therefore, this intensive planting method is used only if few trees are involved, or for a single tree in a key position.

As a result the open space changes its appearance significantly less in subsequent years and looks more rapidly and more enduringly like the picture as presented. Whether it makes sense to use trees in this way has to be decided for each case. Developing ecological equilibrium in consideration for the animals that are present or will move in, and securing habitats, depend on appropriate choices of plant species as much as on their development potential.

As landscape architects, with their knowledge of plants and experience of plant development under different growing conditions, have expertise in changes that open spaces undergo in the passage of time, this skill should be demonstrated and demanded. The current tendency to shorten development periods rather than waiting for them to happen often leads to decisions that make new landscaping necessary at ever shorter intervals than was the case in earlier decades. Many existing parks are so popular because they had a long time to develop, and were tended appropriately.

The different development of plant types, from annual summer flowers via herbaceous plants, ground cover and shrubs to large and small trees has to be considered even at the design stage, and translated into a cultivation plan. Gardening and landscaping firms or the local authorities involved provide cultivation plans for measures that go beyond annually recurring tasks such as mowing grass, or weeding and trimming woody plants, and that lead only gradually to achieving development aims, but landscape architects often do not present these in graphic form. It would make sense to visualize a variety of alternative development aims, linked with appropriate measures such as planting a greater number of shrubs to structure spaces and replanting or removing some of these plants after a development period.

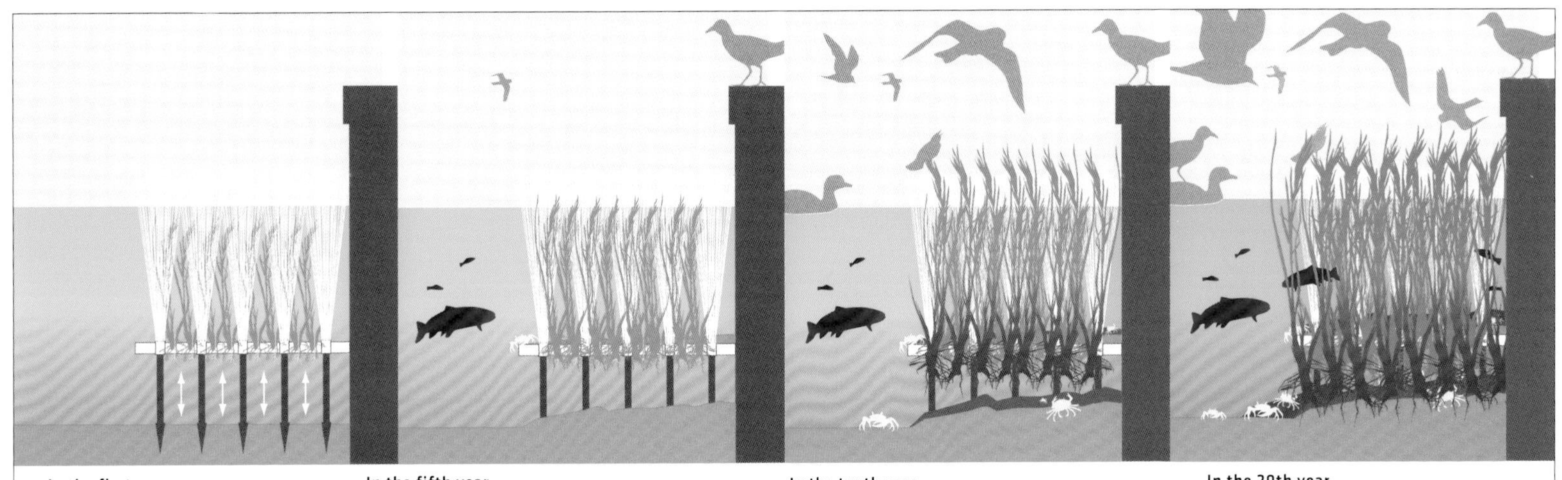


1.159

The development of the "Fibre Optic Marsh" in Field's Point, Rhode Island, USA. Abigail Feldman.

In domestic gardens, people often wish to see a completed picture almost as soon as the garden is laid out. As soil improvement and fertilization can often create very favourable conditions in small gardens, plants tend to crowd each other out, and make the garden look cluttered. Design, cultivation and further development are very closely linked here. The demand for drawings and visualizations, showing the development of a garden over a period of ten to 50 years and giving hints about the best time for particular interventions, would surely be there if such images were available. Potential uses would have to be shown as well as the development of vegetation, but as a rule, visualizations tend to be static in this respect as well. Even when the vegetation is shown in a state that will not come about until the distant future, the activities, fashions and leisure occupations illustrated are those of the present. In this way images communicate design intentions comprehensibly, but the conditions as depicted will become reality only in rare cases. Of course it is scarcely possible to predict how climate change will affect future habits, demands and possibilities. All in all, visual representations remain the best way for representing the design and further development of open spaces, but it is never possible to take every possible influence into account.

This schematic image shows the planned progressive development of plant growth in an experimental project, the "Fibre Optic Marsh" (Ill. 1.159). Plant growth starts as the fibreglass rods are introduced and spreads to the surrounding land over the years. The increasing number and species diversity of animals with time indicates the anticipated period for stabilization of the eco-system. The visualization does not show a final condition, but a process that the project intends to initiate. These images can show the way for an innovative project of this kind without similar precedents.

## Example: Transformations of an urban landscape: Bordeaux

Most large inner-urban projects involve altering existing structures or uses. Neighbourhoods typically evolve over a period of about 30 years, changing constantly. The initial plan should therefore allow for changes, integrating in its concept a methodical assessment of how locations can be expected to change in the long term. Alongside creating a desirable future situation, planning is to include the creation and management of a solid road map through the development phases.

For this kind of project, a prototypical planning method may be developed which can then be repeated for different locations. The method for this type of planning is similar to the method of scientific experimentation: departing from a given situation, the idea of a possible transformation arises. When this transformation has been translated into reality, the parts of the idea which have been proved to work are defined as rules which are then applied on a larger scale and over a longer period of time.

In the case of the city of Bordeaux, landscape architect Michel Desvigne envisaged planting trees to create an urban forest. This forest's envisaged texture and density relates and interacts in a complex way with the existing ownership situation. On the right bank of the Garonne river, a series of measures were planned for the existing urban space, the industrial area and parks and paths no longer needed by the city today. Three chronologically consecutive situations are represented here, as the area is gradually acquired by the city and planted with trees. This makes the ongoing transformation of the urban landscape visible and understandable. The size of the planted areas varies from plot to plot. The visualization shows the development of individual plantings at different points in time and in different stages of growth, with a map used as the basis. A top view presents the progressive increase in development and density, while abstract images present individual areas, each with a different appearance.

After the city had given the go-ahead for the project, building land was redesignated as park land and designs were commissioned for adjoining residential areas. It is rare for such a large park to be created within a city centre. The implementation of this project will continue for several decades.

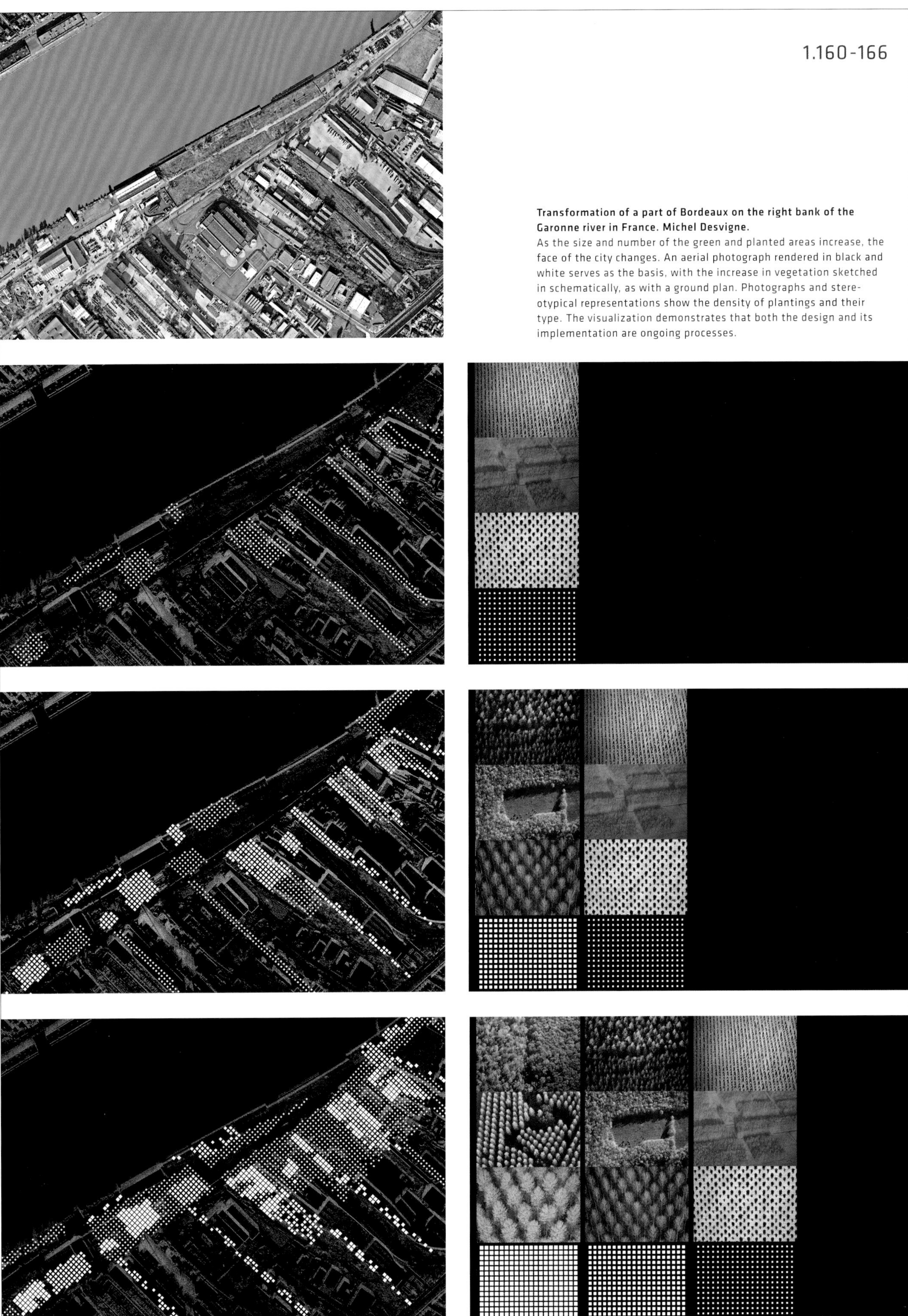

1.160-166

**Transformation of a part of Bordeaux on the right bank of the Garonne river in France. Michel Desvigne.**
As the size and number of the green and planted areas increase, the face of the city changes. An aerial photograph rendered in black and white serves as the basis, with the increase in vegetation sketched in schematically, as with a ground plan. Photographs and stereotypical representations show the density of plantings and their type. The visualization demonstrates that both the design and its implementation are ongoing processes.

## Films

Essentially there are two possible ways for making films – a term used here to designate videos, as well – to present design ideas: firstly by using software for visualizing the design in three dimensions and simulating movement around or across the project area. Another possibility is to arrange drawings and visual graphic presentations in a sequence of images to create a narrative that can be enriched with other means like explanations, music, photographs or small excerpts from films, showing details that have been devised here and have already been realized in other places, or conveying the desired atmosphere. Spoken words in particular offer an excellent opportunity for relieving the burden on the eye in a film, whose explanatory texts have to be read by the viewers themselves. If a narrative is professionally designed it can be easier to absorb, as the spoken word can make the context more readily accessible. Film also offers the opportunity of arranging and commenting on the images in such a way that viewers can be introduced to the design in a logical, pre-determined sequence of all essential aspects. The latter is particularly important if a proposal is to be presented without the presence of the designer. The order in which issues are considered and also the time allotted to the individual aspects are laid down, and can be matched to the priorities. As a rule, conveying ideas through the medium of film in this way requires less time than by other graphic techniques, while on the other hand making a film means a considerable challenge.

Films considerably increase the possible range of visual presentation. As a rule, books and prints are not a suitable medium for reproducing moving pictures, even though video stills have their own aesthetic and fascination. Hence the examples relating to this theme are to be found on the DVD accompanying the book.

Aerial traverse forwards 1

Aerial traverse backwards

Traverse at ground level

Aerial traverse forwards 2

## Museumsplatz in Vienna, Austria. Norbert Brandstätter and Stefan Raab

These short films by Stefan Raab and Norbert Brandstätter on their proposal for Museumsplatz in Vienna show the potentials of a digital three-dimensional simulation of walking through or flying over the square. The great advantage demonstrated by these films is that the speed of the camera movement can be matched to the type of movement that is being simulated: from realistic sequences to fast motion or slow motion. Movement can be directed both forwards and backwards. It becomes clear from looking at the films how many and what impressions will make a particular impact in the open space shown. Passages with background music convey a good impression of the difference from a silent film.

Typical features

Structure and function of the landscape

## Green Dragon Park, Shanghai, China. Turenscape

Two films were produced for this park design. The first brings out the particular features of the design, with cinematic resources similar to those used for the Khalifa City C development. First a speaker explains the idea, then the situation is shown, emphasizing the site as a glowing red area on maps of differing scales. Perspective drawings are explained by the speaker, and so is a shot of the model in a tracking shot complemented by pictures of the present state of the site. Drawings and shots usually move from right to left, like the script that is introduced at the beginning. Here, too, movement is created by changing the distance of the camera from the film. Drawings of various garden areas are shown, enlarged one at a time and explained. Photographs show the sources of inspiration for the design ideas, which are presented in visualizations subsequently.

The second film for this project explains the structure and function of the park spaces as the basics of the design. The film is broken down into sections, each of which presents an aspect and an area of the park. At the beginning of each section the subject is identified and located on the overall design plan by a flashing effect. The design ideas are then introduced mainly by details from drawings, visualizations and photographs, linked with explanations by the speaker, or just by the spoken work accompanied by highlights on the plan. The film makes it possible to show drawings in more varied ways than static images can: here for example using axonometric diagrams opening like pages of a book. This film's priority is conveying information rather than its entertainment values or artistic aspects.

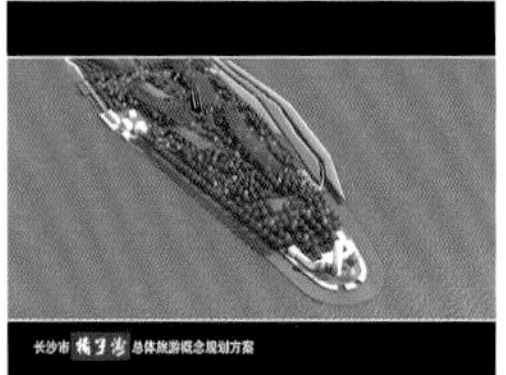

## Orange Island, Changsha, China. Turenscape

This is another design explained in a film complementing the drawings and visual presentations. Orange Island is located in the city of Changsha in Hunan province in southern China. The island is very important for tourism, which the planned project aims to develop.

The film begins by emphasizing the great length of the project area, by shooting the models in an aerial view, starting from the south. Here the analogue, built model is superimposed by digital models, accompanied the speaker's explanations and followed by visual presentations, these too accompanied by background music. Black-and-white illustrations have coloured ones superimposed on them, complemented by photographs and views showing the future use of the buildings. The plan moves slowly past viewers, before the film concludes by showing the same scenes as at the beginning, in aerial view, this time flying backwards over the digital model. The speaker is heard only in the first quarter of the running time of a little over five minutes, while for the rest of the time the sequence of images is accompanied by impressive music.

## Biomass in future landscapes, a virtual landscape journey. Lenné3D

This film was produced completely digitally, and shows changes in the image of the landscape when different plants are introduced for biomass production. It is an impressive example of the possibility of using visualizations to convey an idea of the effects of land use of this kind. Examples of different cultures are given in a variety of sequences, as aerial or normal views, with agricultural vehicles and human figures used for indicating dimensions. The background music appropriately gives way to the sound of helicopters flying over; sometimes birdsong can be heard, supporting the impression of closeness to nature and recreation. Textual explanations fade in on the bottom edge of the picture, changes of subject are announced by turning pages as in a book, and a dynamic is created by superimposition and camera tracking or panning.

## Experimental videos on the perception of landscape. Swiss Federal Institute of Technology, Zurich, Professor Christophe Girot

These two short videos were made in the real environment. They do not relate to planning, but use the resources of this medium to show special aspects of landscape and the way people perceive it. The intention is to give fresh impetus to landscape development and to suggest an appropriate resource for communication and presentation for students. Analysis of the visual environment forms the basis for the precise presentation of proposals and designs. The camera can be made into a design tool. The examples also demonstrate that the perception, analyses and interpretation of landscape, as well as the subsequent planning steps, reflect highly individual attitudes.

### Shortcut

This fast-motion video by students Hegnauer and Koch runs in a straight line through a landscape and any obstacles that it presents, even passing right through a building. Normally we perceive landscape in the same way as we are able to move through it, but here the emphasis is deliberately shifted, creating an unusual access to familiar surroundings. The speeding-up effect makes the sequence amusing and dramatic. Viewers can only cope with this speed and assimilate the meaning of the images in this video because it lasts for such a short time.

### Affoltern_Encircled

This video by students Pestalozzi and Leibacher was shot with a hand-held camera, shaking with any movement. It shows different scenes from the landscape surrounding objects that were selected as the centre of a circle, filmed from the point of view of a pedestrian at a constant distance. In the first sequence the central point is a tree in a landscape of fields with an adjacent wood, which the camera also passes through. The second sequence centres on a play apparatus in a playground. Other open spaces are shown as the video proceeds, with the camera moving faster and faster, so that at the end the movement itself becomes the key feature, while the significance and attributes of the spaces shown shift into the background.

# PART 2 CONCEPTS

This section presents concepts for using sequences of images in planning processes. Unlike the previous part, this section will put the emphasis on how to convey the message of the planning as a whole. Two projects will be presented as examples in the first chapter, with selected drawings, model photographs and simulations. On first sight, it seems that the role of any individual image is relatively small, but it becomes ultimately clear that every visual representation has a part to play in the overall scheme. Each visualization changes, fleshes out and shapes the process to some extent.

Presenting image sequences in an easily readable, comprehensible and convincing way is crucial to any planning concept. One very important skill is the presentation of comprehensive concepts for competitions, which typically require handing in design concepts, primarily in visual form, at an agreed time. This means that visual material has to be produced within a very short time. A competitive environment calls for consistency and conciseness, as entries have to make a good impression as quickly as possible.

Gabriele Holst, Collage, Unframed.

# CONCEPTS
# PLANNING PROCESS

## Visual presentations over the course of the planning process

In the previous chapters, visual presentations were primarily introduced individually and considered according to their different functions and their ability to represent a design in two, three or four dimensions. Every drawing, simulation or model, however, is part of a series of presentations accompanying the design process, in which each of these contributes to the solution for the assigned task. Together, the images and drawings present the ideas behind the design – and sometimes some of them cannot be fully understood without referring to others. This chapter deals with sequences of images and drawings from selected design projects. They demonstrate the role of visual presentations in the different stages of the design process, with an emphasis on the ways in which different forms of presentation relate to each other.

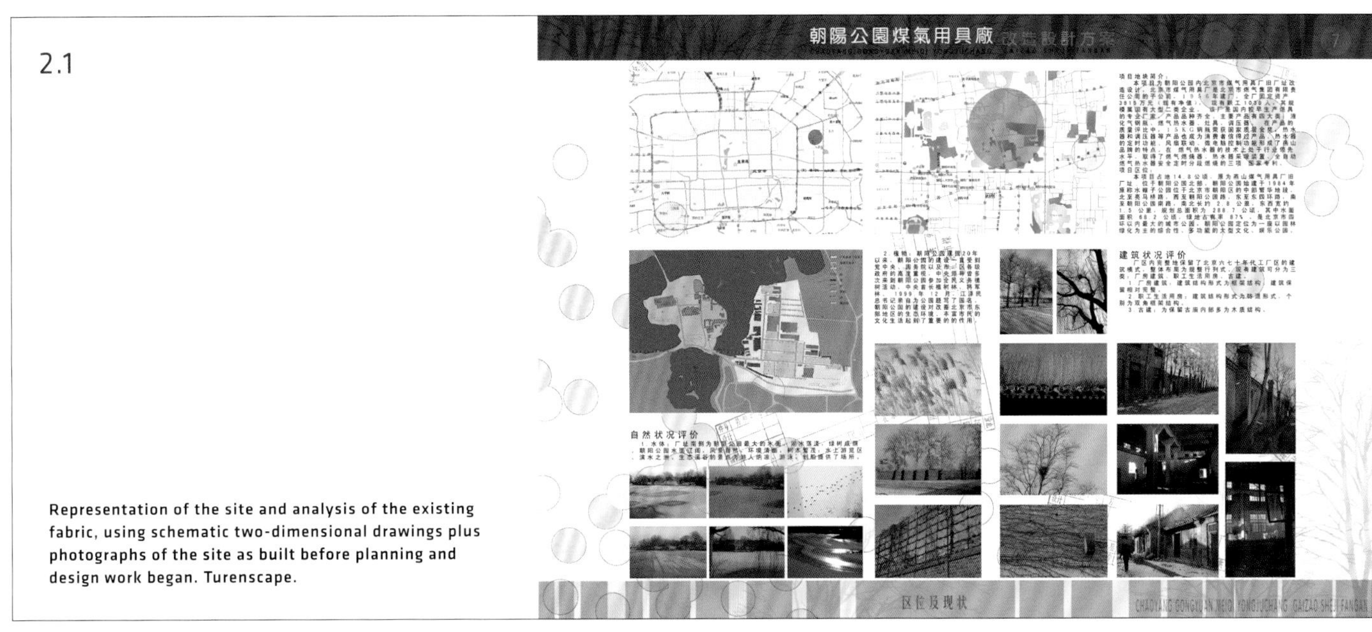


2.1

Representation of the site and analysis of the existing fabric, using schematic two-dimensional drawings plus photographs of the site as built before planning and design work began. Turenscape.

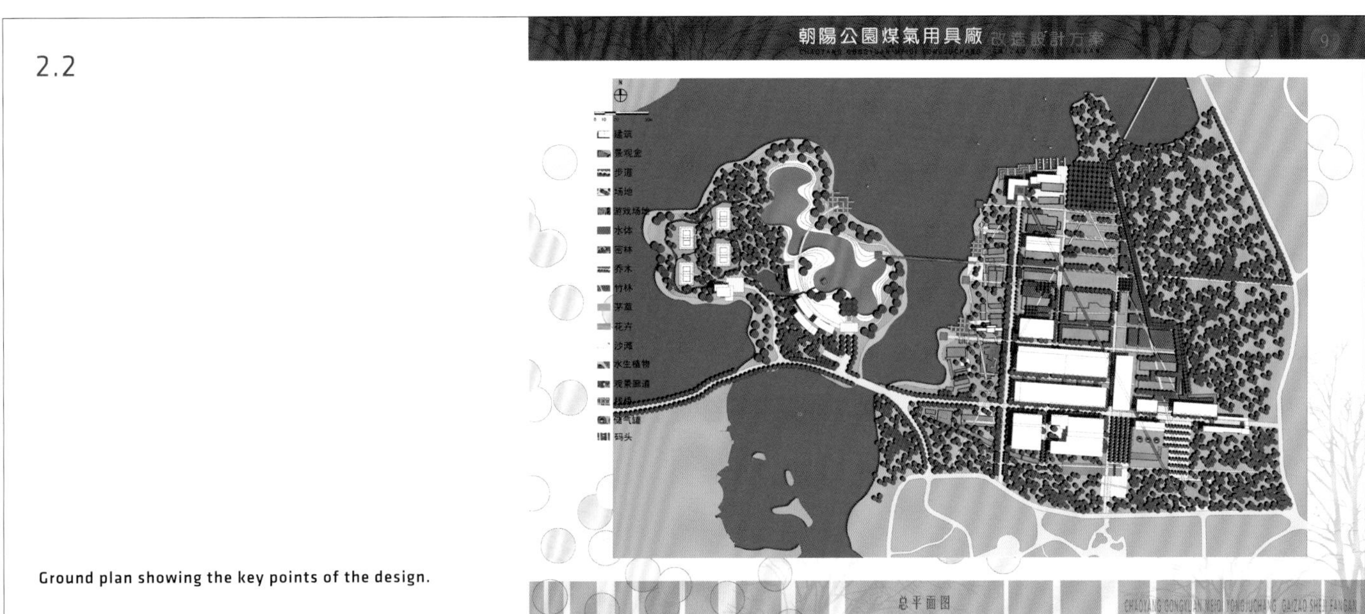


2.2

Ground plan showing the key points of the design.

## Example 1: Beijing Yanshan Gas Implements Factory Park

The Turenscape practice is planning an urban park for the site of a 1950s gas factory in Beijing, 15 ha in size. In this project, the site's nostalgic atmosphere, recalling the 1960s and 1970s China of the socialist revolution, it taken up and transformed, while the red brick factory, existing structures and vegetation are retained. Within this setting, the design creates a modern park landscape in which the site's existing elements and materials are reused or recycled. Spaces for entertainment, shopping, living and working are created in the existing buildings, and materials from the old walls are reused for the walls for a series of gardens and courtyards. The project also creates spaces within the existing fabric for indigenous plants, while the added connecting buildings offer views onto the newly created park.

A variety of visual presentations were produced in the course of the design process, ranging from analyses of the existing fabric to design drawings for individual areas within the site and detail solutions. Various techniques and modes of representation interact to convey the design ideas. The images were arranged as pages of a coherent presentation, with a uniform layout and framing; the images reproduced here are a selection of pages from this presentation. They give an impression of the range of different presentational techniques.

朝陽公園煤氣用具廠
景观功能分析图
CHAOYANG GONGYUAN MEIQI YONGJUCHANG GAIZAO SHEJI FANGAN

朝陽公園煤氣用具廠
景观结构分析图
CHAOYANG GONGYUAN MEIQI YONGJUCHANG GAIZAO SHEJI FANGAN

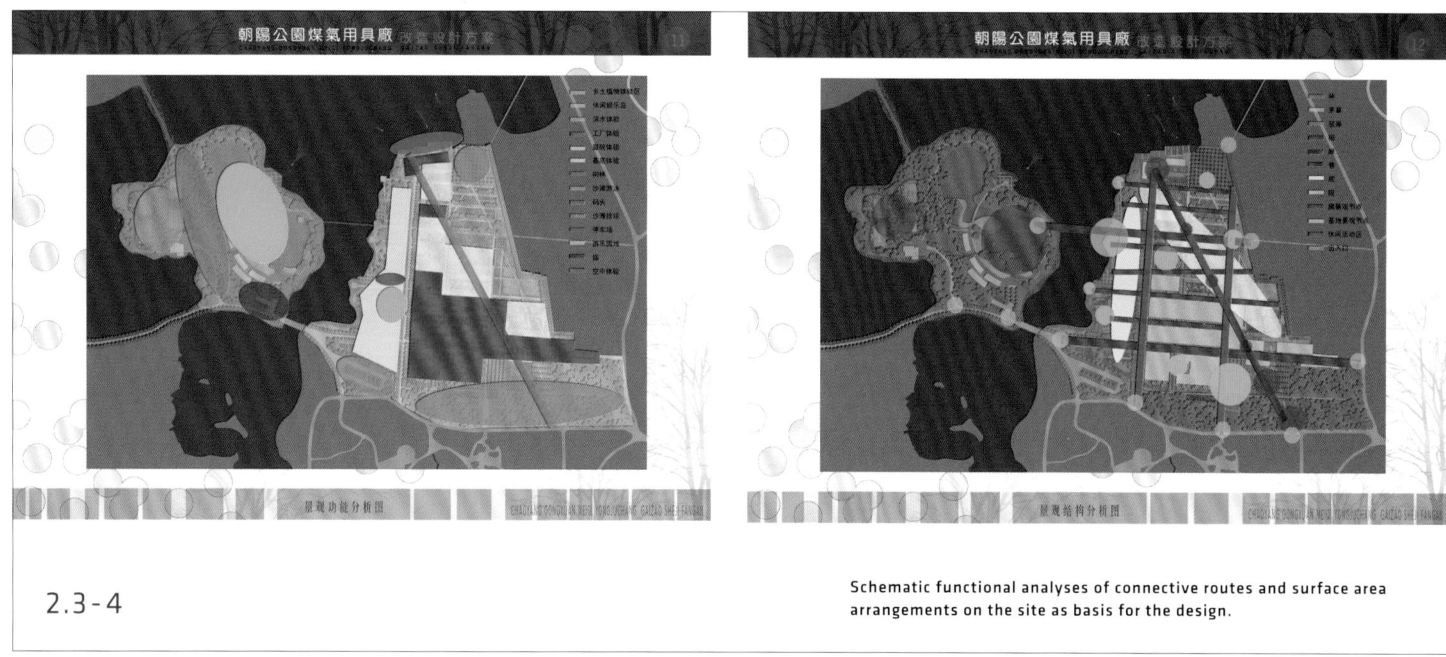

2.3-4

Schematic functional analyses of connective routes and surface area arrangements on the site as basis for the design.

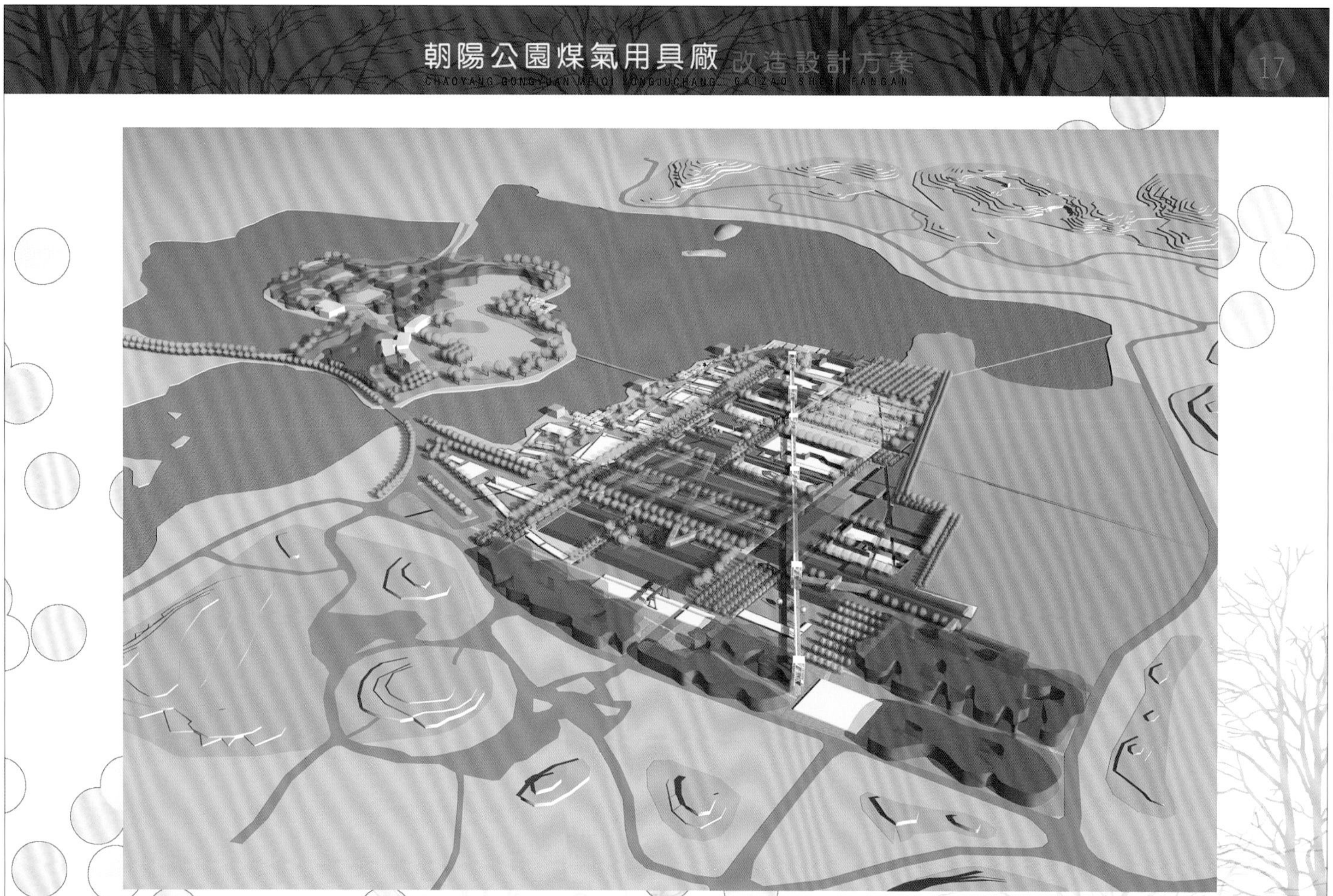

朝陽公園煤氣用具廠 改造設計方案
CHAOYANG GONGYUAN MEIQI YONGJUCHANG GAIZAO SHEJI FANGAN
17
总体鸟瞰图
CHAOYANG GONGYUAN MEIQI YONGJUCHANG GAIZAO SHEJI FANGAN

2.5

Digital model of the design, presented as a bird's-eye view of the entire site.

2.6-8

**Sectional elevations showing the site's typical relief of the ground.**
The position of each section line is marked on a scaled-down floor plan. These hand drawings on different scales and in different degrees of detail highlight key areas. Due to the dimensions, several drawings are needed to convey the design.

2.9-12

**Design for individual areas presented in hand drawings and computer-generated images.**

Black-and-white illustrations taken from photographs of the existing structures serve as a basis for the planned interventions.

2.13

**Design for individual areas: a water garden.**

2.14

**Design for individual areas: use of a former building as a garden, shown in ground plans, perspective views and photographs of the existing fabric.**

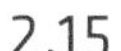

2.15

Design for individual areas: a garden incorporating a greenhouse, illustrated on the ground plan of a former building.

2.16

Design for individual areas: a garden on the theme of "steel", recalling the site's former use, shown in ground plans and perspective views.

2.17

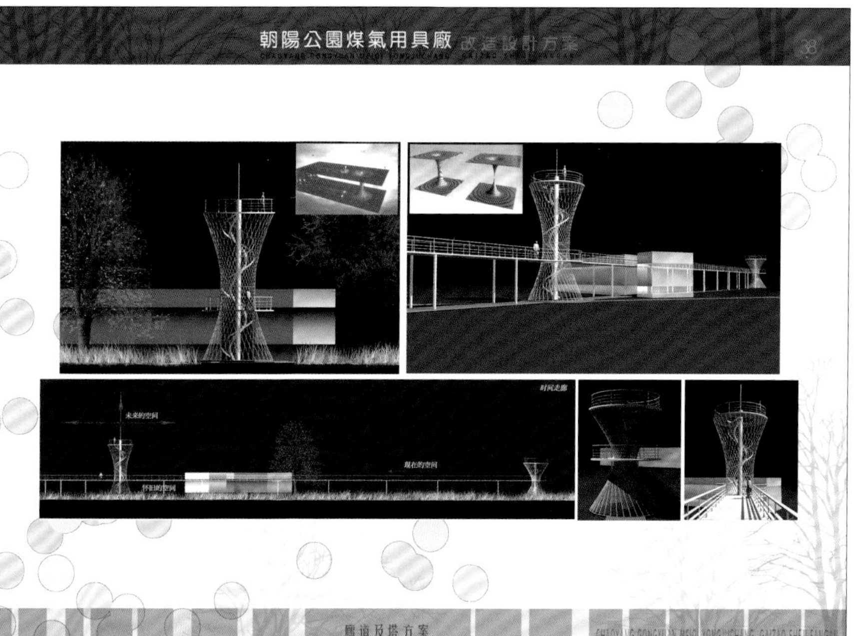


Design for individual areas: connective walkway with access stair structures, which also serve as viewing towers.

2.18

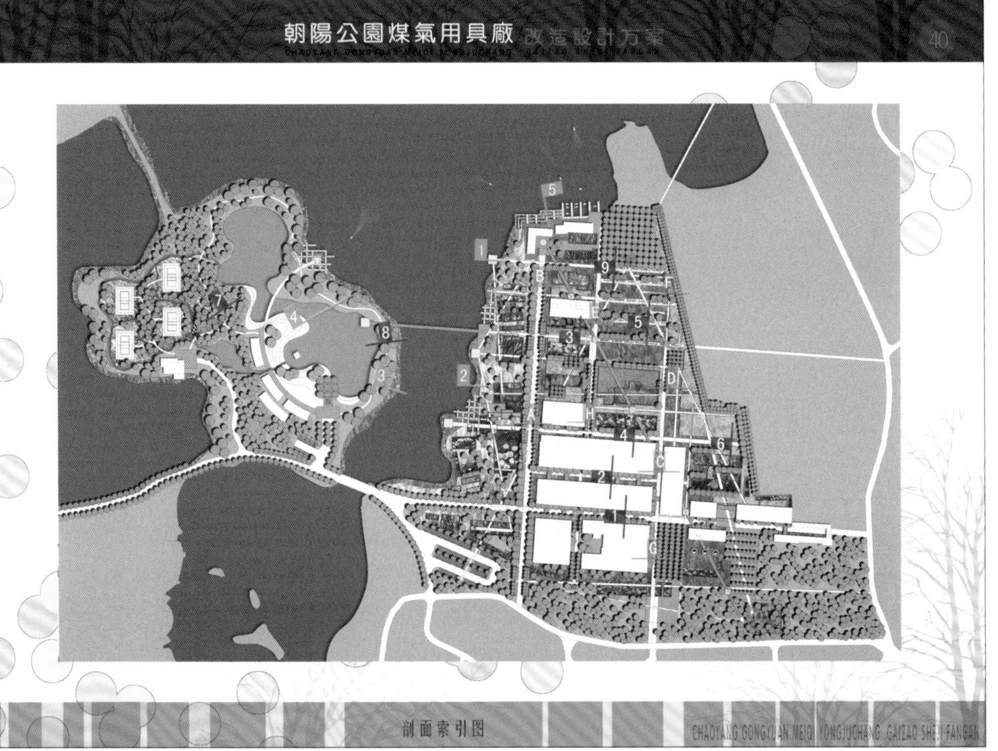


**This drawing locates the following topographical section drawings for important locations in the ground plan.**
The degree of detail anticipates implementation planning.

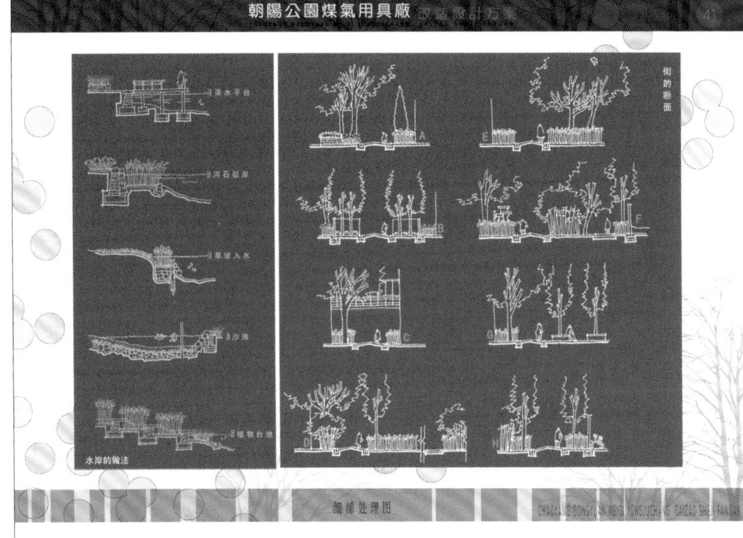

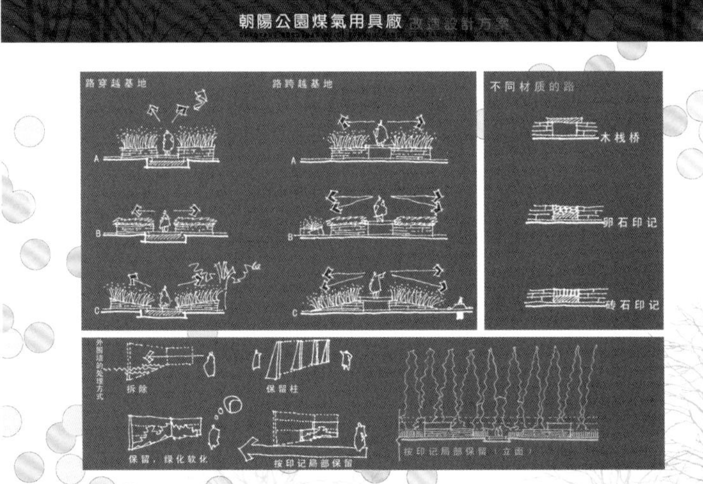


2.19 - 21

**Hand-drawn sections.**

2.22

Compilation of photographs of the planned vegetation, which is based on the site's existing vegetation.

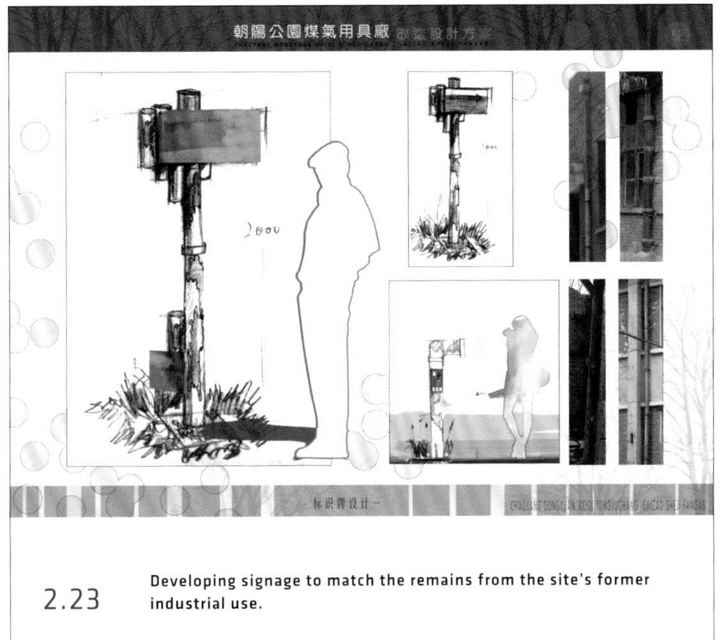


2.23 Developing signage to match the remains from the site's former industrial use.

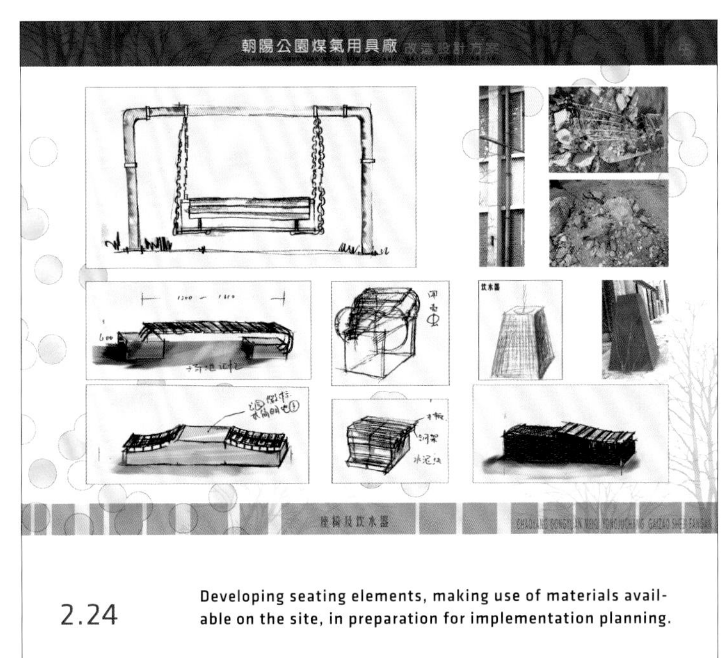


2.24 Developing seating elements, making use of materials available on the site, in preparation for implementation planning.

2.25

Presentation drawing for new uses of, and connections between, the existing buildings.

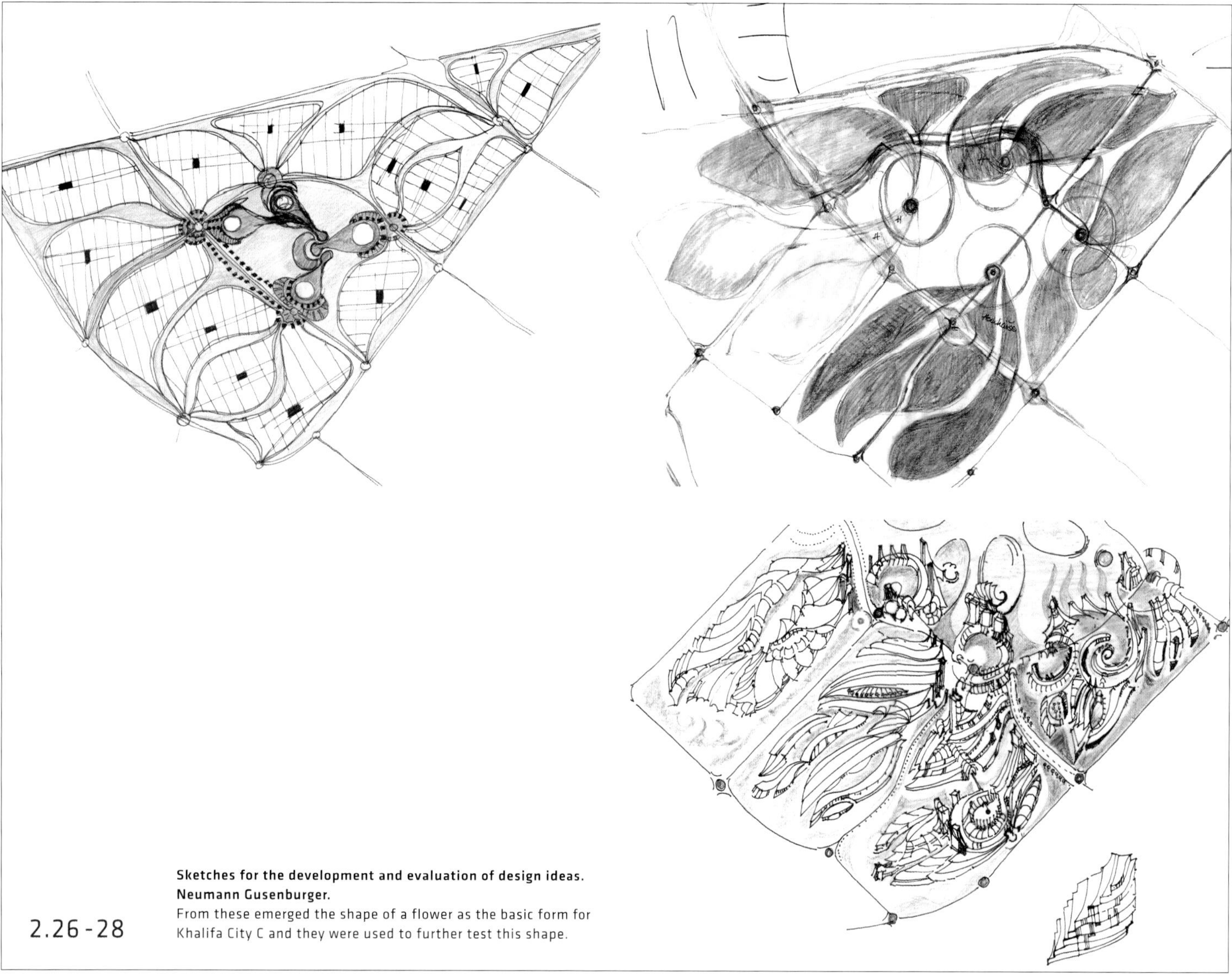

2.26-28 **Sketches for the development and evaluation of design ideas. Neumann Gusenburger.**
From these emerged the shape of a flower as the basic form for Khalifa City C and they were used to further test this shape.

## Example 2: Khalifa City C

Khalifa City A and C are new districts in Abu Dhabi, which has developed at a very rapid pace in recent decades. While Khalifa City A retains a strict orthogonal plan, Khalifa City C is laid out in a pattern based on flowers, symbolizing organically grown shapes. The open space design by the firm Neumann Gusenburger, including public green spaces and squares as well as street and road space, emerged from a comprehensive assignment, which was elaborated in series of very different visual presentations.

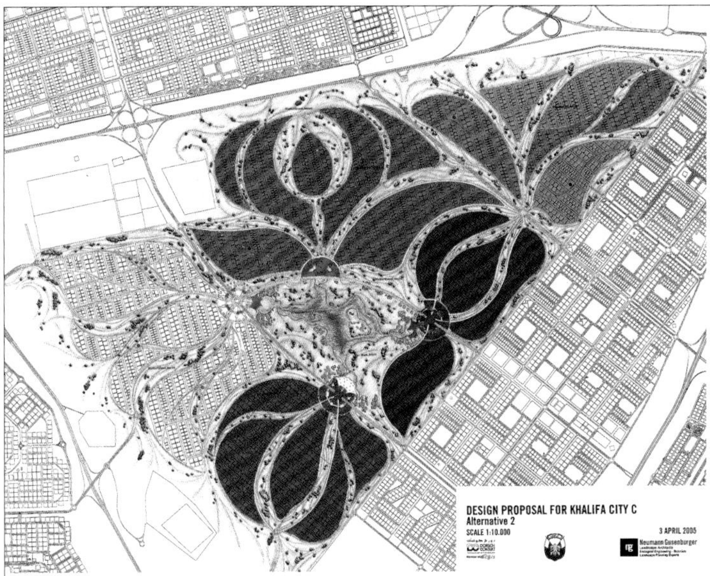

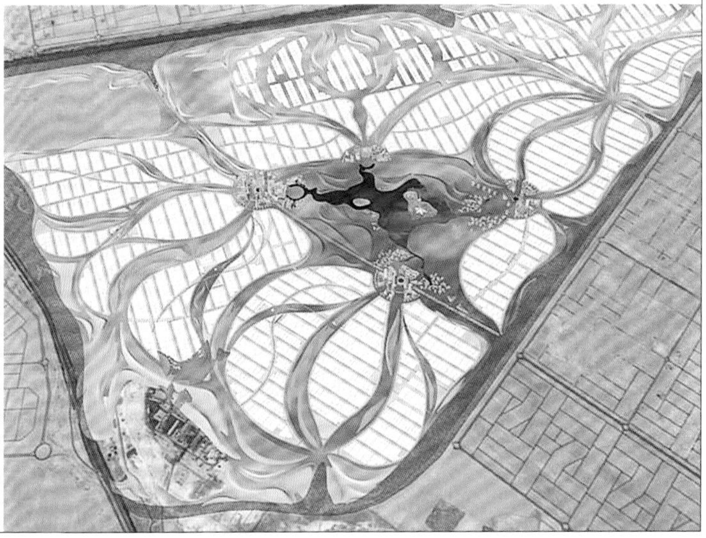

2.29 - 31 **Design drawings.**
The design was developed from the sketches, producing a number of colour presentations focusing on various aspects.

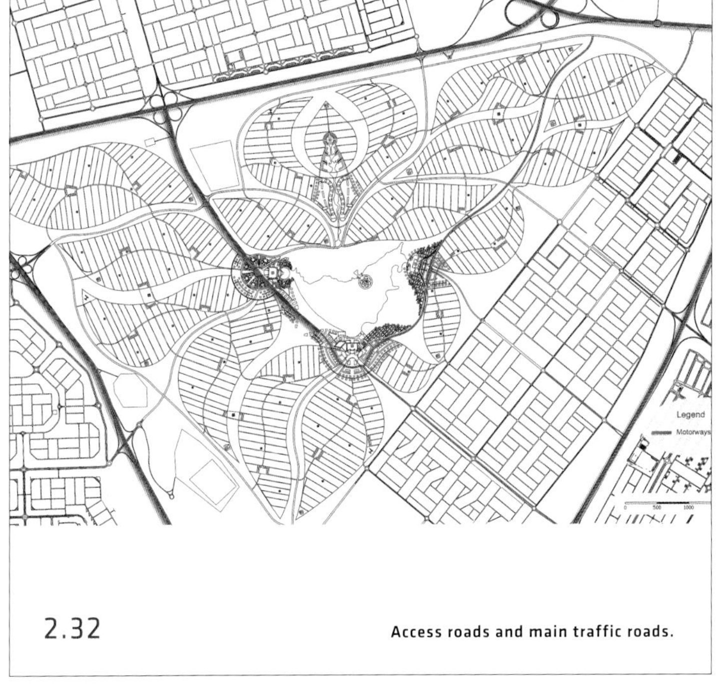


2.32 **Access roads and main traffic roads.**

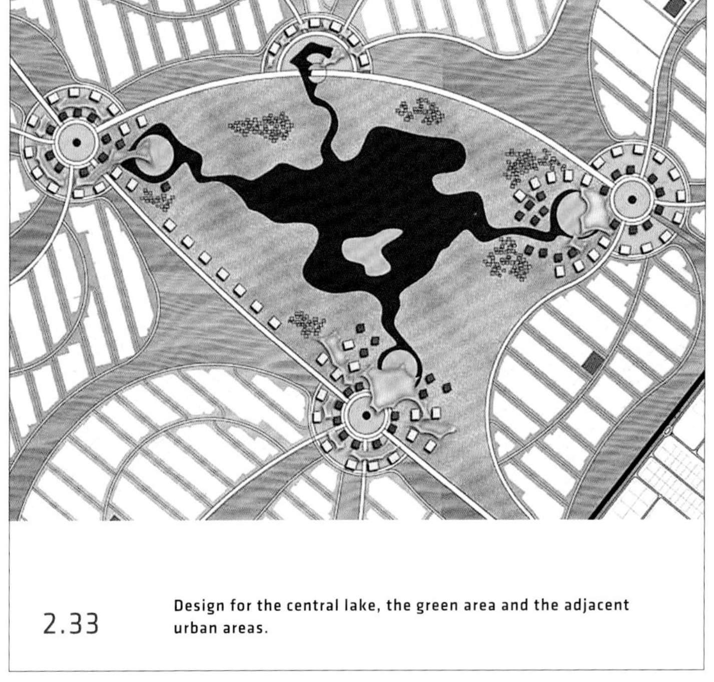

2.33 **Design for the central lake, the green area and the adjacent urban areas.**

2.34

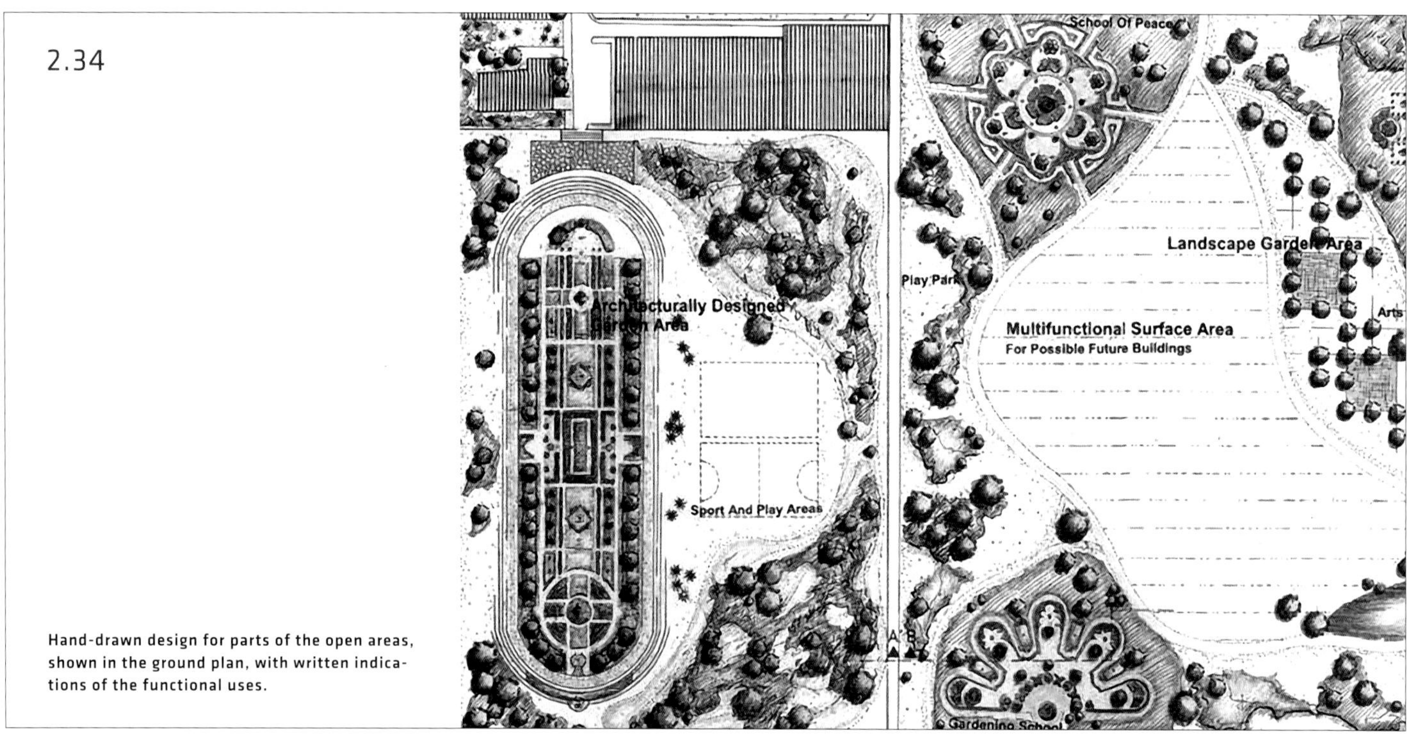


Hand-drawn design for parts of the open areas, shown in the ground plan, with written indications of the functional uses.

2.35

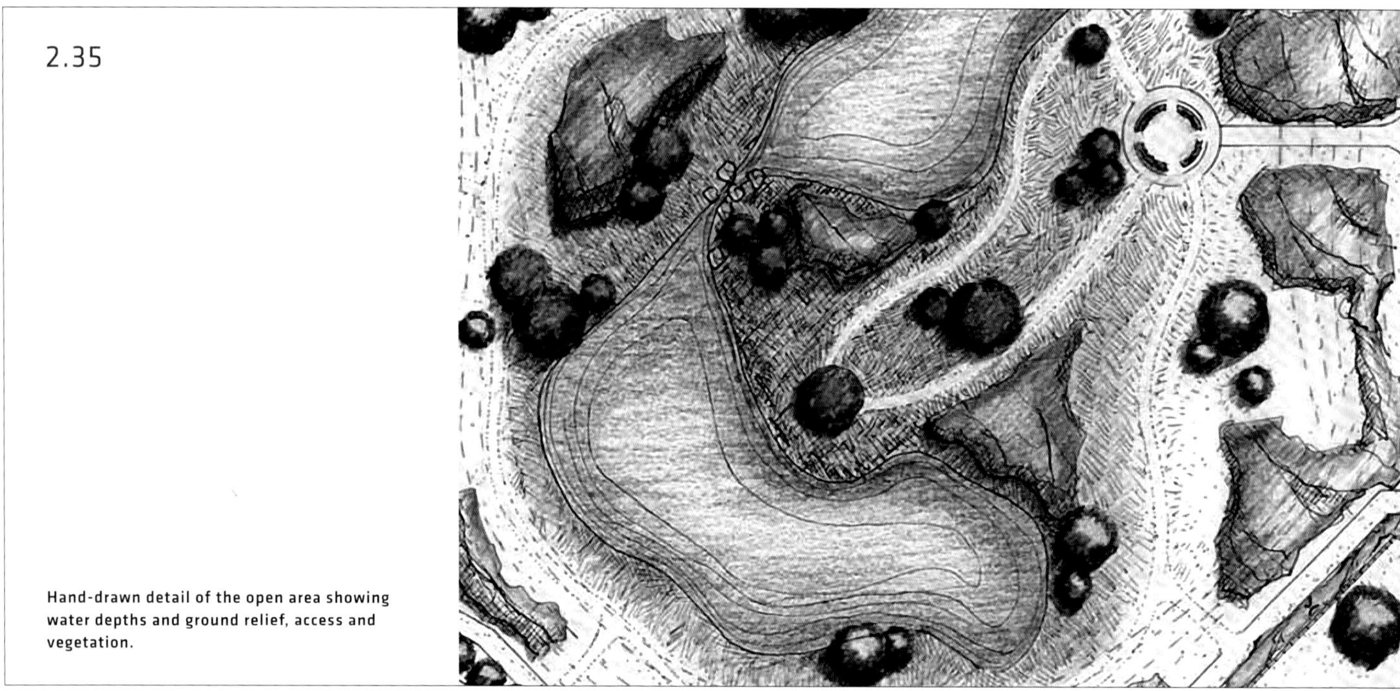

Hand-drawn detail of the open area showing water depths and ground relief, access and vegetation.

2.36

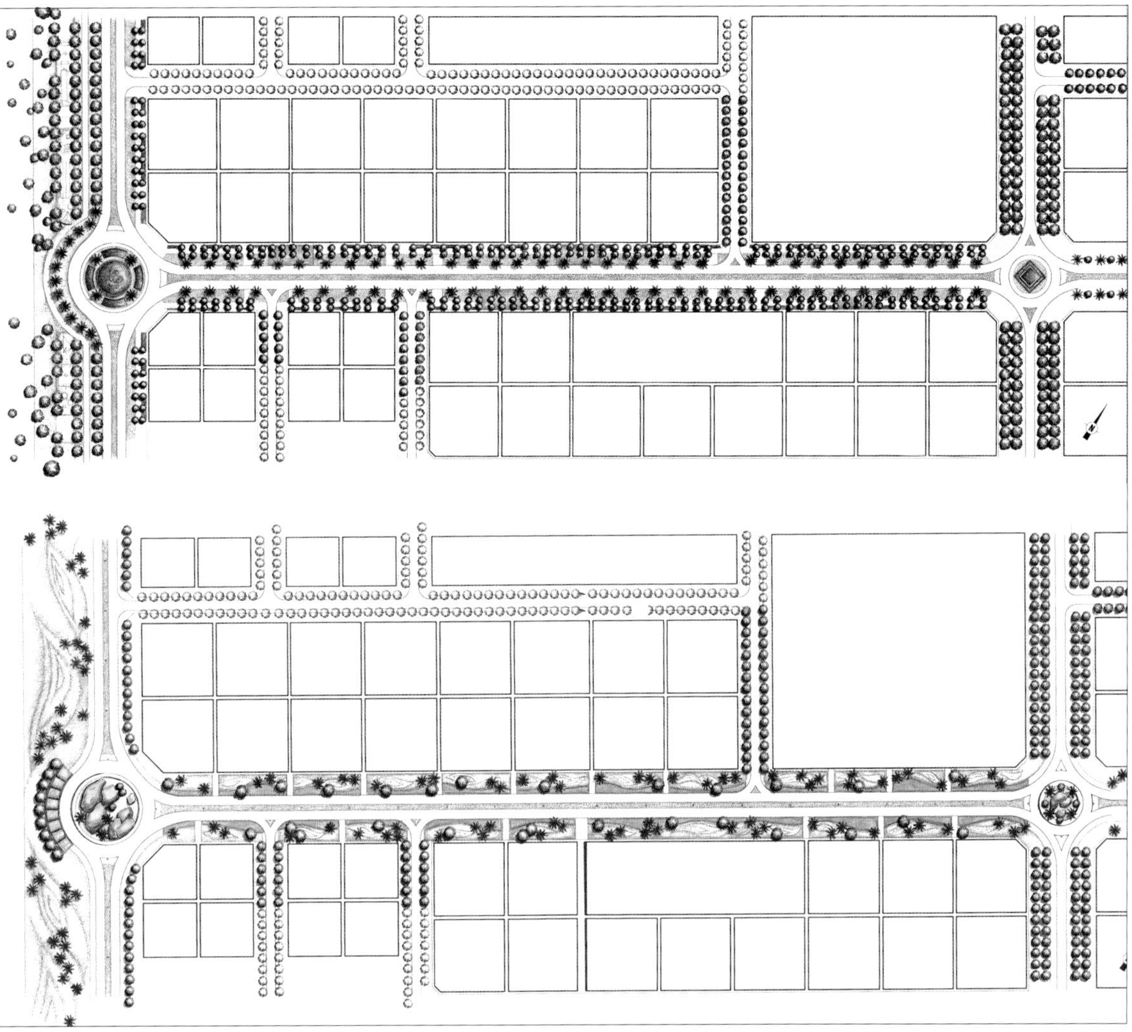

Hand drawing of alternative planting in a street space.

2.37

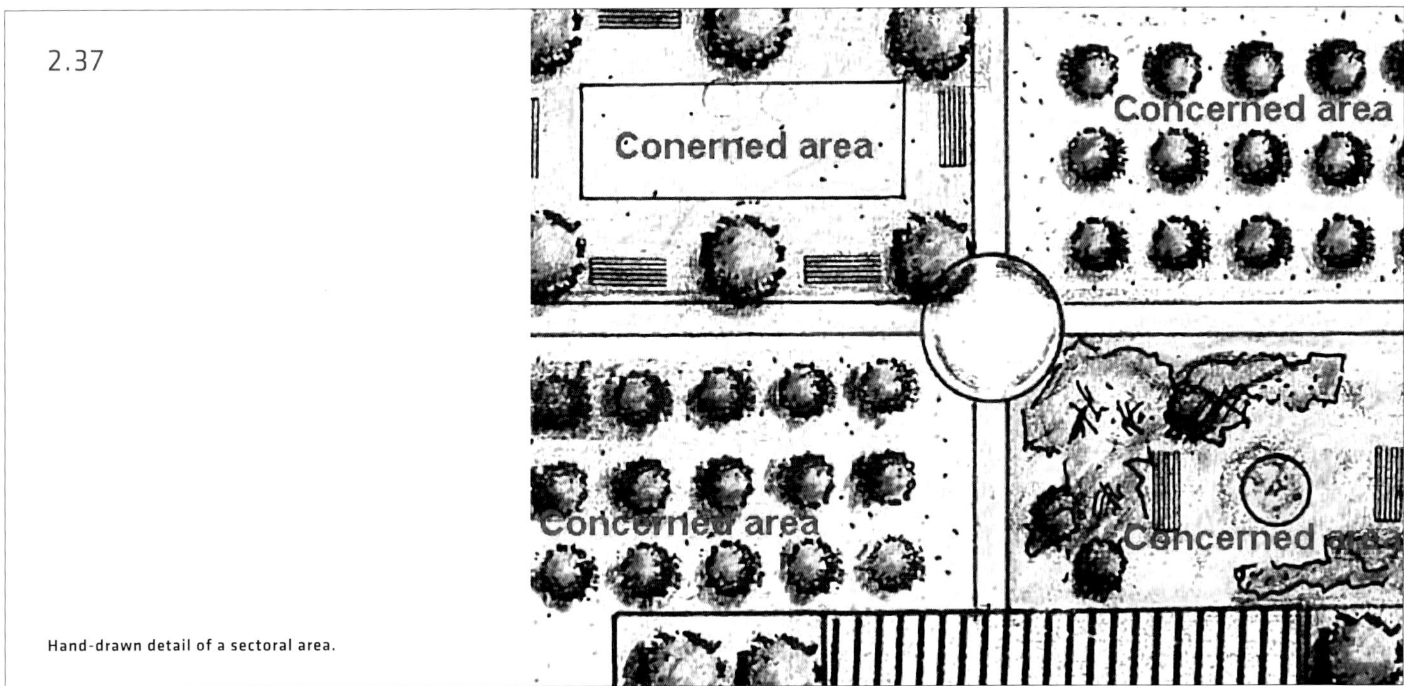


Hand-drawn detail of a sectoral area.

2.38

Hand-drawn detail of a sectoral area.

9,0 m | 7,3 m | 7,3 m | 9,0 m

Service reservation

Walkways and Activities with Low Maintenance, DroughtTolerant, Extensive Planting

Walkways and Activities with Low Maintenance, DroughtTolerant, Extensive Planting

Service reservation

Khalifa Town "A"

Distributor Road / II. Category, First Phase Landscaping

Main Avenue / II. Category, First Phase Landscaping

White light MEETING

Yellow light FUNCTION

White light MEETING

9,0 m | 7,3 m | 7,3 m | 9,0 m

Service reservation

Walkways and Activities with Low Maintenance, DroughtTolerant, Extensive Planting

Service reservation

Khalifa Town "A"

2.39

Computer-generated sectional views of various road spaces at different times of day.

2.40

Hand-drawn perspective view at eye level of a square in a footpath area of the road.

2.41

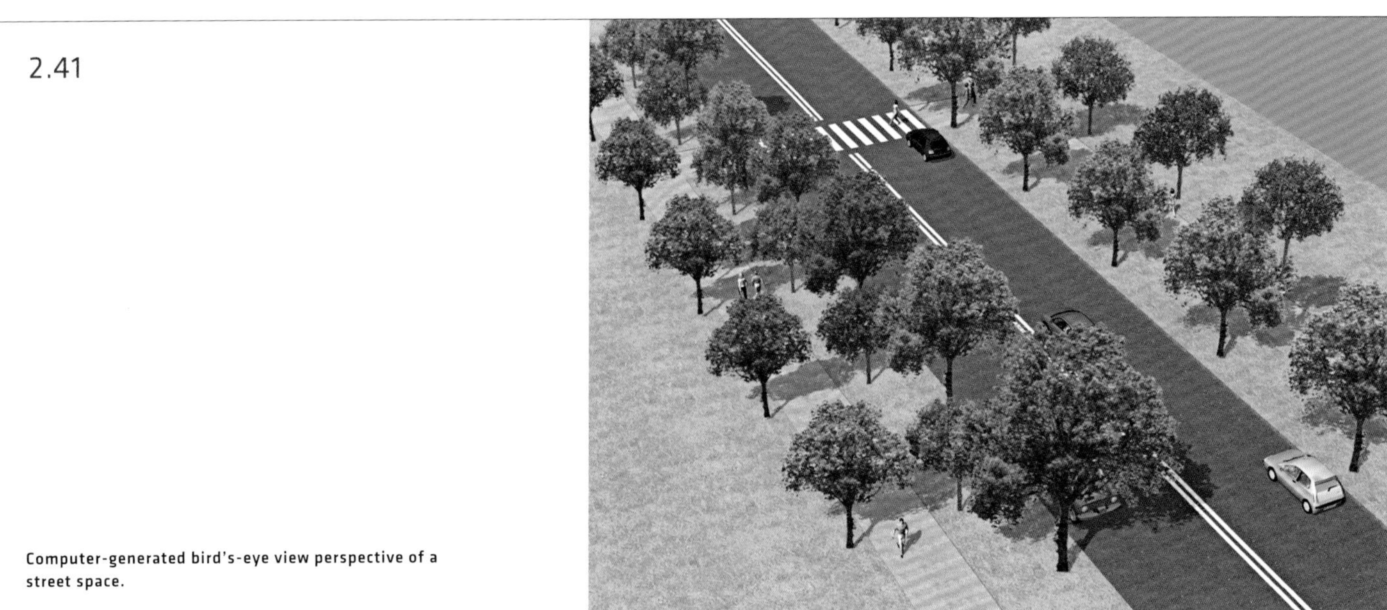

Computer-generated bird's-eye view perspective of a street space.

2.42-44

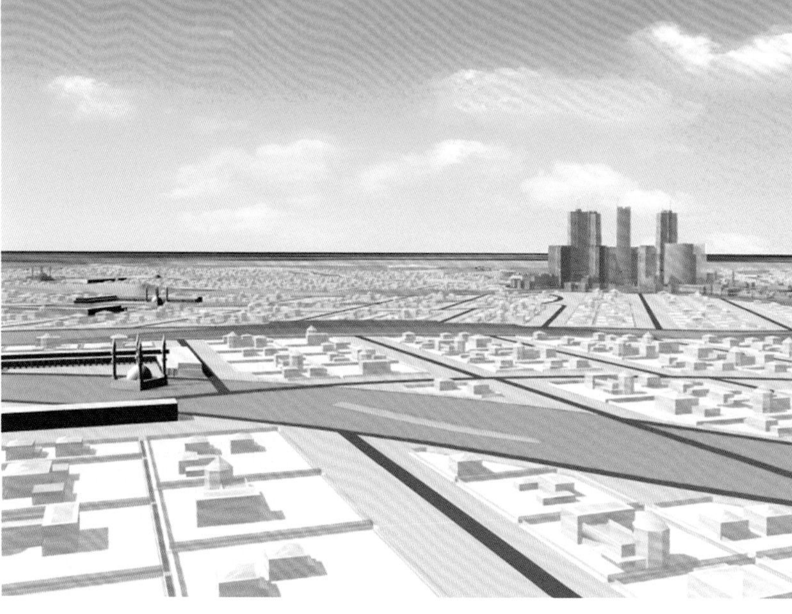

Digital models in simplified presentation, used for testing design variants.

2.45-47

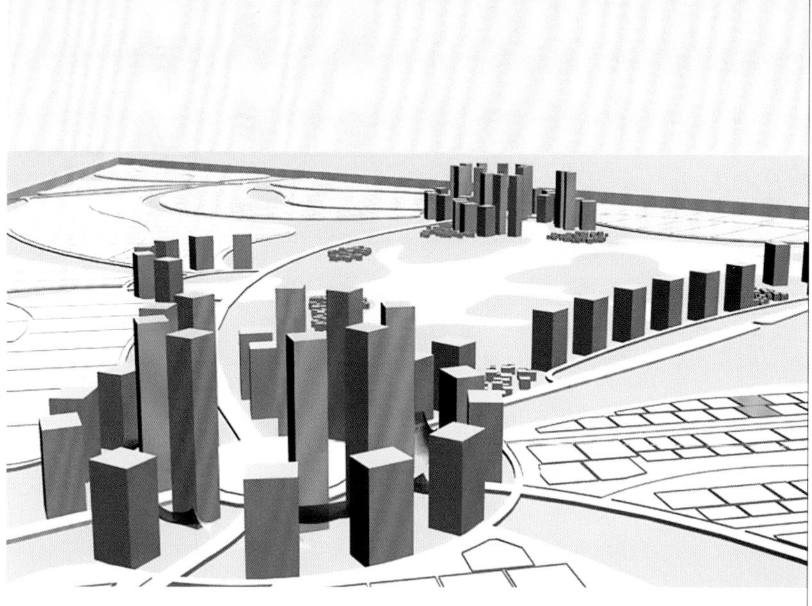

**Digital models presenting the design with varying degrees of detail and information.**
Models are a particularly good way of visualizing the dimensions, proportions and aspects of large planning areas.

# CONCEPTS
# COMPETITIONS

## Visual presentations for competitions

Competitions are held in order to find the best solutions. This is one way of responding to the varied and exacting demands a given project has to satisfy, which may be functional, social, ecological, economic or technological, relating to urban planning or construction issues as well. As design results are not definable, in the sense that they cannot be judged solely by means of a price competition, a more complex decision-making process, in the form of a performance competition, is needed: a competition between several planners' intellectual performances. Only the task is defined before submission, while the concept and the elements of the solution cannot be defined clearly and exhaustively at this stage. A performance competition is an appropriate way of choosing both a design concept and a design firm. It compares the intrinsic quality of the proposals, not their respective costs: while the cost of implementing any given design may be one of the selection criteria, the intellectual achievements of all the firms taking part are evaluated on an equal basis of objective guidelines. The client who commissions the design is buying the designer's ideas and the designer's competence.

Another reason why performance competitions are a good way of choosing landscape architecture solutions is that much work in this field is non-standardized and highly complex. For large and pioneering projects in particular, a competition process is a good way to find the best possible solution. Often competitions are open to other disciplines as well; this promotes high-quality economic and innovative solutions. Competitions can also help in bringing debates and issues in landscape architecture out into the open and advocating for high-quality open spaces. Last not least, a democratic competition process is in principle more widely acceptable than the direct awarding of a contract. For planners, this democratic approach increases the importance of communicating ideas or proposals to an audience effectively.

Competitions generally have submission guidelines. These cover, for instance, the number and format of the panels to be submitted, as well as the scale and hence the size of the respective plans (consequently also the size of the presentation), making it easier to compare the submitted entries. The main elements of a competition entry are drawings, other visual material and a – generally quite brief – explanatory text. Sometimes models are also requested. Apart from the time limit, the greatest challenge faced by entrant firms is how to present their plans – all the individual plans and images must be arranged on the specified number of panels, the layouts of individual panels must go together well, and the entry must appear as a harmonious, unified whole. Entries must impress readily and quickly in order to be successful, particularly where there are a large number of firms taking part. This is achieved first and foremost by the quality of the drawings and images. Firms are increasingly calling for the submission process to be made more flexible and to permit new submission media, such as films.

Three competition entries that won a first prize are discussed in the following pages. It is, of course, also worth perusing other entries to these and other competitions; the winners were chosen here because a future comparison of the visual presentations with the completed projects can help to evaluate the employed methods of representation.

## Example 1: Landscape planning competition for the realization of the International Garden Show 2013 at Hamburg-Wilhelmsburg

This single-stage, two-phase anonymous building competition was advertised internationally in 2005. 48 firms took part in the first phase of the open process, and nine were selected to further develop their submissions for the second phase. The task was to create a concept and detailed design for the 2013 Hamburg International Garden Show on the development of open spaces and the green structure for the Wilhelmsburg district. Here more comprehensive urban development and landscape planning aims, looking beyond the design of the open spaces, had to be taken into account. Key points were: innovative social urban development, enhancing the unique natural conditions of Wilhelmsburg as an island in the Elbe (including its industrial monuments, its water areas and its historical cultural landscape as a growing area for fruit, ornamental plants and vegetables). The Garden Show is to be central to the city of Hamburg's urban development policy for the next ten years. All firms taking part in the competition were required to remain within the specified budget.

The first phase of the competition involved creating a whole-area concept for the Garden Show site that incorporated its green connections with the Elbe banks, and working out a preliminary landscape architecture design for the exhibition site. This meant evolving proposals for its design and use in the framework of a spatial concept, with the main focus on the central area of the Garden Show park and the indoor exhibition areas, which are approximately 55 ha in size. The spatial division and arrangement of exhibits for this area had to be resolved; this applied particularly to designing and linking the areas for the horticultural exhibition with the parks, which were to remain after the event.

For the second phase, the selected firms were to undertake a more detailed version of their proposal, with particular emphasis on submitting an itemized estimate of costs. From the sending out of documents on the 22nd of April 2005 to the meeting of the prize jury to discuss the second phase on the 28th of November 2005, the whole process lasted only seven months. As a result, the city received a proposal on which to base its further plans and decisions.

For the first phase, two pages in vertical DIN A-0 format and two pages in horizontal DIN A-2 format were requested: a structural plan with a scale of 1:5,000, a site plan for the central area with a scale of 1:2,500, a partial site plan for the entrance area with a scale of 1:500 with sections and elevations on a scale of 1:200 and a non-defined panel, plus an explanatory report, surface area calculations and a rough overview of costs. For the second phase, an overall plan for the central area and a partial site plan for the entrance area were required, reworked from the phase one plans. A partial site plan for the flower exhibition halls with sketched views and design details was required, as well as partial plans of exemplary areas, a further costs estimate, a surface area calculation and the explanatory report.

The winner of this competition was the firm RMP Stephan Lenzen, in collaboration with the firm Fischer Architekten, Professor Peter Schmitz and Seeberger Friedl und Partner as specialist planners. The motto for their design was: "Around the world in 80 gardens – the visitor as voyager and the garden as a journey". Journeys are the central theme, inspired by the spatial structure of the area and the history of Wilhelmsburg as the embarkation point for journeys to America. On the occasion of the International Garden Show, these journeys become the conceptual basis for the intensive exhibition areas. A circular route beginning at the two main entrances combines the individual journeys within the full day's program into an intensive park. The design's interpretation of gardens as journeys, loosely based on Jules Verne's "Around the World in 80 Days", puts the visitor in the position of a voyager. Each voyage has a legendary journey as its theme – from Paris to Peking on the Orient Express, for instance, or following in the footsteps of famous travelers such as James Cook, Marco Polo, Odysseus and Goethe. The landscape architecture design for each journey has its own individual theme.

A concept was to be developed for re-use after the conclusion of the Garden Show. Taking "journeys" as a central theme made it possible both to reduce the areas devoted to the passages and to reactivate them at a later point in time. Their decentralized position and relatively small scale was intended to allow use and maintenance to subsequently be taken over by neighbouring interest groups.

In the second-phase version, this competition entry consists of five DIN A-0 (841 x1189 mm) panels. The overall site plan for the central area, shown as a ground plan (Ill. 2.48), takes up its own single panel. The upper sections of the panels that follow (Ills. 2.49 -51) show perspective drawings of different views and clarify the "journey" theme, while their central fields show further ground plans of various sectors of the site on a small scale, with section drawings arranged below on two panels. The final panel (Ill. 2.52) deals with structural schemes and shows the overall layout, the individual areas and the parts of the site important to the design as a ground plan and in several smaller schematic drawings. The explanatory text is a single column positioned at the side of this panel. Overall, the amount of text is very low in relation to the number of drawings, with the drawn plans containing all the design's significant content. The colour and style of all the panels are similar, and their layouts match, creating an overall impression of a unified and competent plan.

The design has been consistently developed from a general overview into the more detailed plans. Ground plans on different scales, section drawings and schematic representations as means of two-dimensional representation are supplemented by three-dimensional perspective views. On the ground plans with a scale of 1:500, shaded areas indicate plan components with a vertical presence, such as trees and buildings. Striking light-green tones dominate both the plans and the views and appear prominently on all the panels. This choice of colour scheme is surely one of the things that make this contribution as a whole stand out from the other entries.

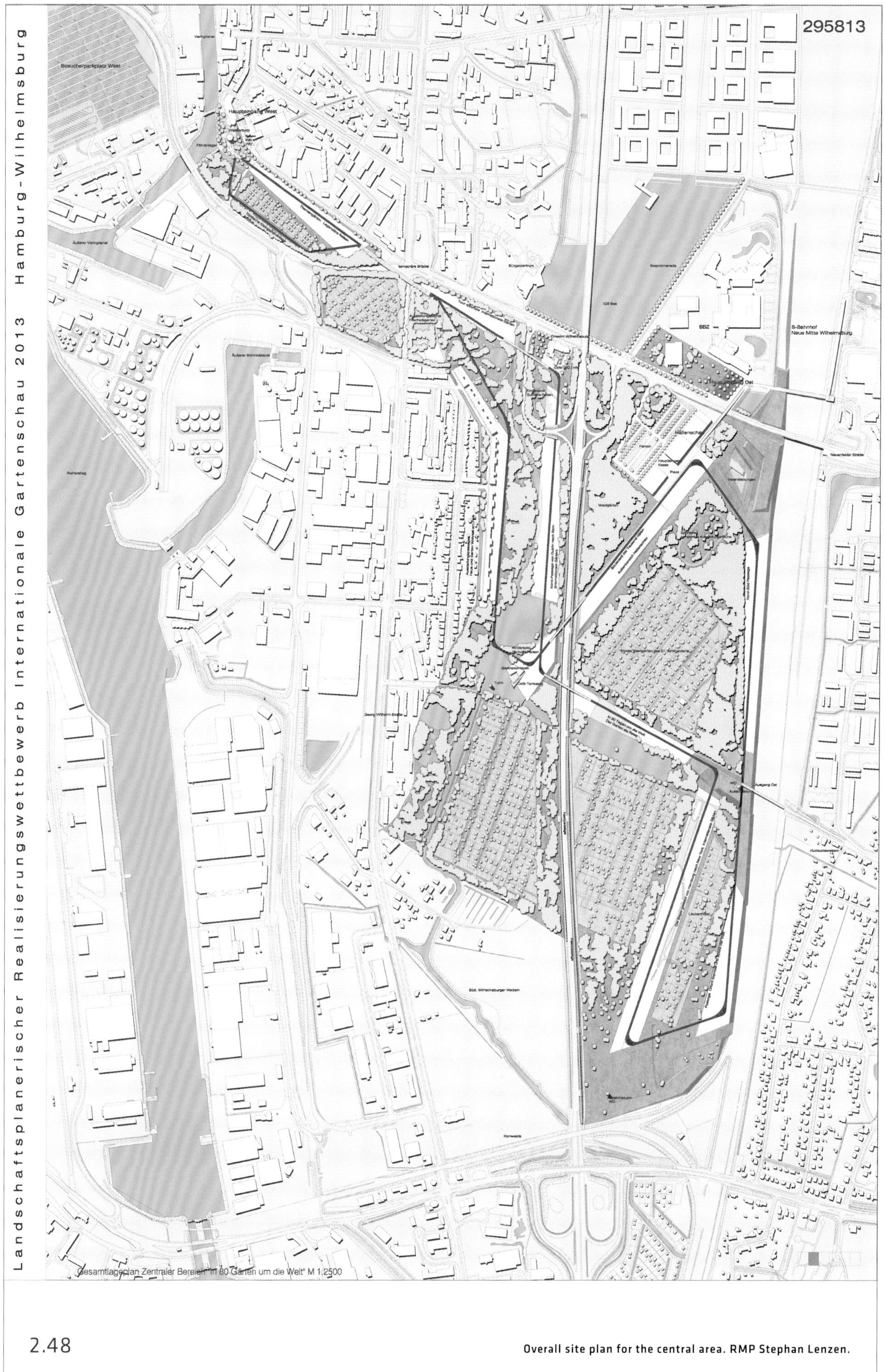


2.48 Overall site plan for the central area. RMP Stephan Lenzen.

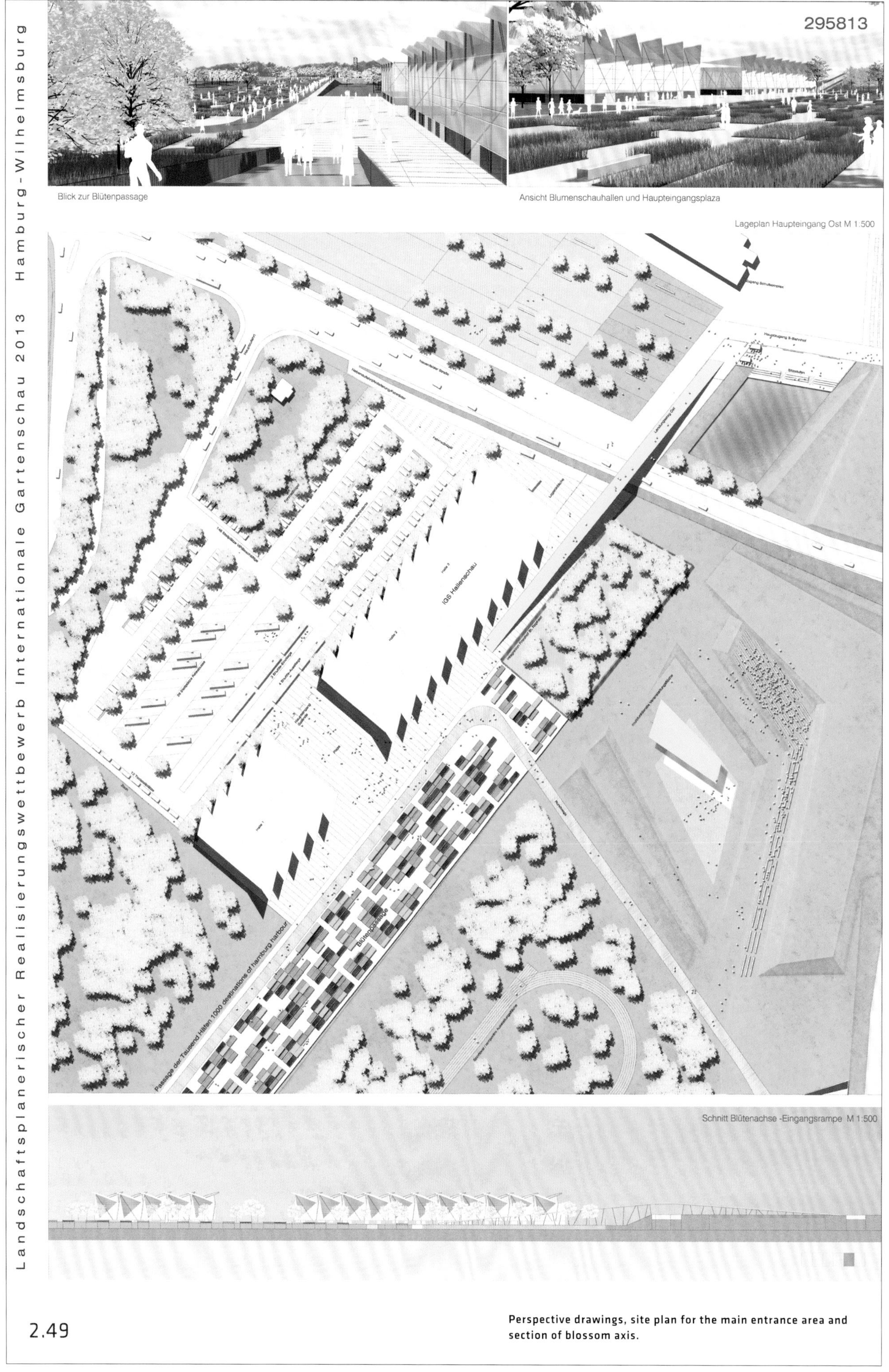


2.49

Perspective drawings, site plan for the main entrance area and section of blossom axis.

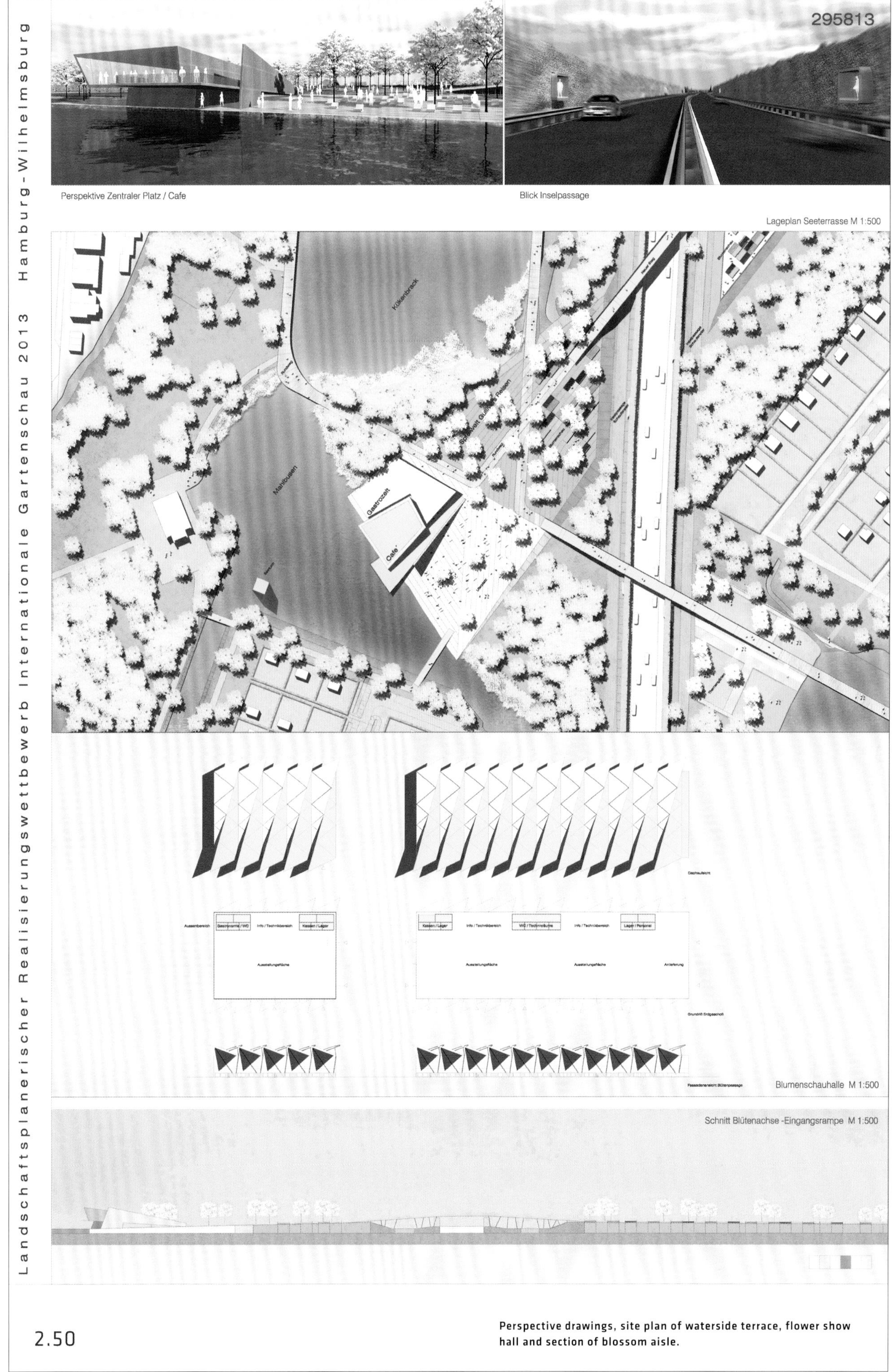


2.50

Perspective drawings, site plan of waterside terrace, flower show hall and section of blossom aisle.

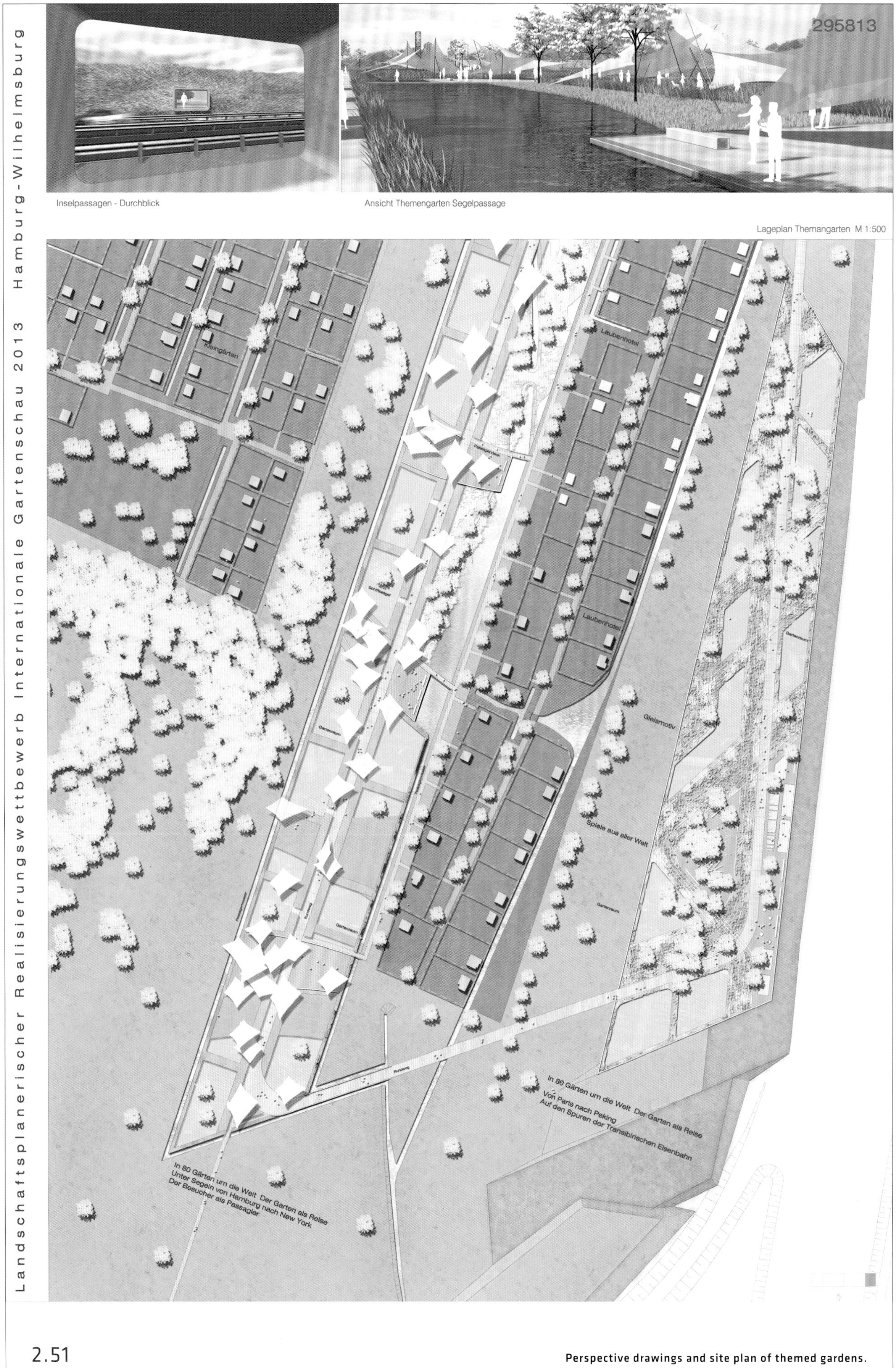


2.51 **Perspective drawings and site plan of themed gardens.**

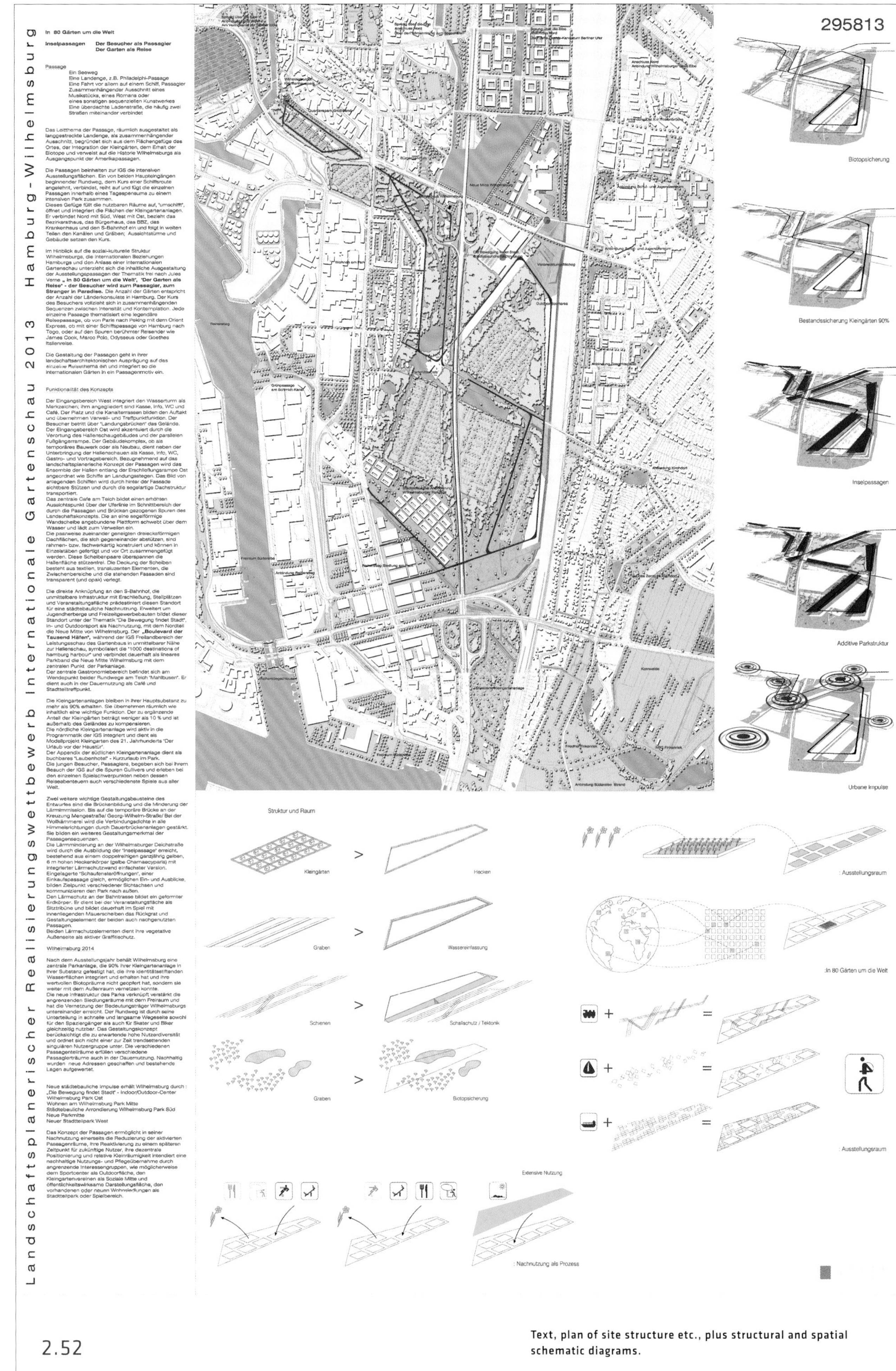


2.52

Text, plan of site structure etc., plus structural and spatial schematic diagrams.

## Example 2: Toronto Waterfront competition

In 2006, a competition was announced to create a design for the 3.5 km waterfront area on the bank of Lake Ontario. Out of the 38 teams who applied (including experts of many disciplines), the jury chose five project teams to take part. The task was to make the area accessible to the public by water and to develop a new identity for Queen's Quay, a historic boulevard that lies along the waterfront. The city of Toronto's official plan for the central waterfront area (entitled "Making Waves") identifies creating unrestricted access to the banks and to the water and developing the area between the water and Queen's Quay as its top priorities, with the planning area encompassing the whole Queen's Quay area. The selection criteria included: developing uninterrupted public promenades; extending and further developing the Martin Goodman Trail for cyclists, joggers, walkers and inline skaters; creating designs for the areas where the quays meet the Queen's Quay; implementing unified standards for surfaces and furnishing features and sustainably improving the area as a living space, together with its water quality. The development time was a period of six weeks from March to May of 2006. After being submitted, the entries were on public display for ten days, giving citizens the opportunity to cast their votes. Only then was the prize for the best design solution awarded.

The project group that won the competition, under the overall direction of the firm West 8 Urban Design & Landscape Architecture from Rotterdam, included also du Toit Allsopp Hillier, Schollen & Company, Diamond + Schmitt Architects, Halsall Associates, David Dennis Designs from Toronto and Arup from New York. They envisioned a continuous public promenade running along the edge of the water and the Queen's Quay as a connecting boulevard at the place where "the city kisses the lake". 18 m wide, this promenade, with its wooden walkway or boardwalk, is supplemented by floating piers shaped like fingers and a double row of large trees of indigenous species. A row of bridges connects the boardwalk with the ends of the quay, which provides the public with direct access to the lake. In addition to the pedestrian and cycle paths, new open squares were created along Queen's Quay, which is also now lined with trees. Sustainability is well served by a storm surge management system and floating pontoons for the piers, which improve fish habitat and water quality.

The jury decided unanimously in favour of this design, taking into account public opinion (canvassed, for instance, by means of a public forum and public reactions recorded in writing from the six exhibitions) as well as their own expertise and the votes of the institutions concerned.

The design is presented on six 120 x 85 cm panels. The first three (Ills. 2.53 - 55) present the main ideas and basic outlines of the proposal, while the design itself takes up the final three panels (Ill. 2.56). Texts on the first panel briefly summarize the issues and ideas involved. Most of this panel, as with all the other panels, is taken up by various representations with minimal explanatory text. Axonometric representations show the designers' ideas for prominent areas, the design for the 18 m wide waterfront route, the pontoons shaped like maple leaves that can be walked on and the areas of Queen's Quay Boulevard where the water-filled basin and the road come together. Schematic diagrams demonstrate the fundamental idea, section drawings clarify the plan and views convey the atmosphere the design seeks to achieve.

The third panel shows the desired connection between the inner city and the waterfront area in ground plans, photographs and visual presentations. The required lighting plan is also inser-

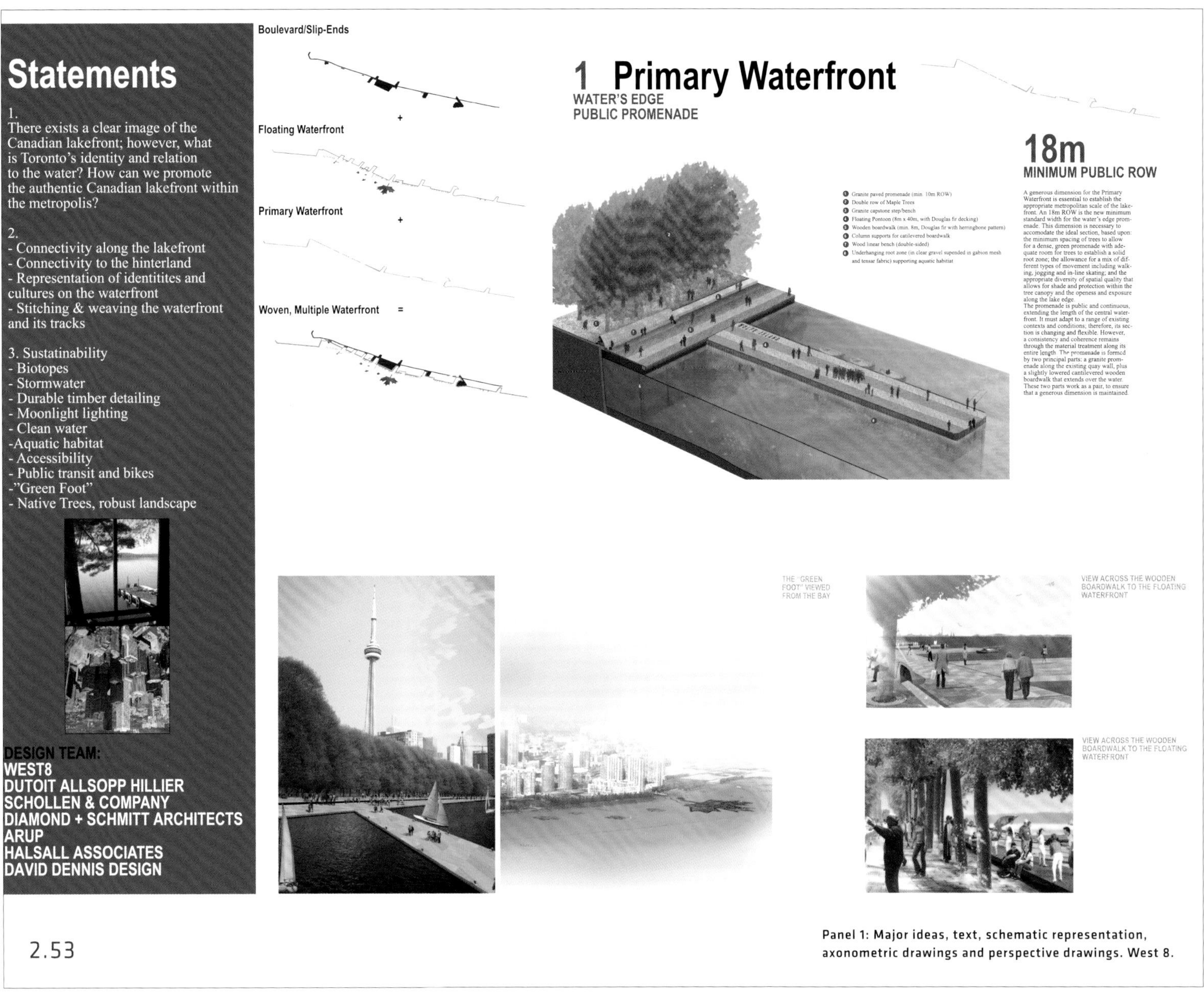


2.53

**Panel 1: Major ideas, text, schematic representation, axonometric drawings and perspective drawings. West 8.**

ted here. Panels four, five and six show the whole design as a ground plan based on an aerial photograph. In the upper field, it has been traced over and is still visible, while in the design area field it has been entirely redrawn.

This entry reverses the usual rule of the ground plan serving as a basis for more detailed planning and development of individual areas. The parts of the plan that initially stand out are the three-dimensional axonometric drawings and perspective drawings. Text is added to the images primarily as keywords or captions, making them easily readable. Another striking thing about this plan is the large number of detail and technical elements. Rather than providing an initial overview, the plan demonstrates the uniqueness of the site, and emphasizes possibilities for its use and technical solutions for problem areas. A ground plan drawn across three consecutive panels with some realistic representation impressively conveys the size of the area, the positioning of individual critical planning areas and the way the whole project area fits together.

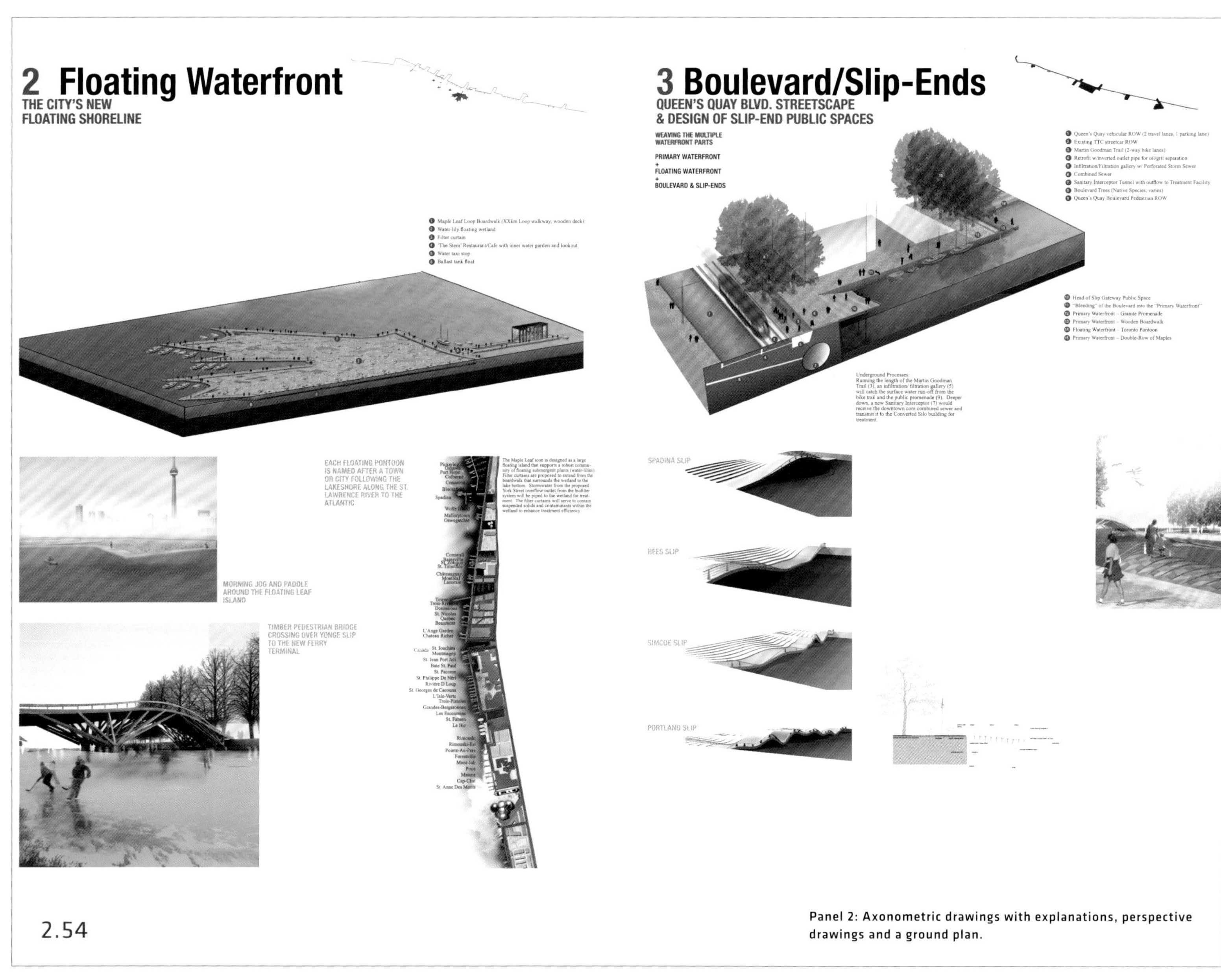


Panel 2: Axonometric drawings with explanations, perspective drawings and a ground plan.

# 4 Culture from the City

LINES OF CULTURE FROM THE HINTERLAND
CLAIM AN ADDRESS WITHIN THE WATERFRONT

VIEW FROM UNDER THE BOULEVARD TREES

VIEW EAST ALONG QUEEN'S QUAY BLVD. AT THE MUSIC GARDEN

VIEW OVER THE SLIP HEAD AT INTERFACE WITH THE BOULEVAR

SPADINA SLIP AT NIGHT

LIGHT PROJEC - TIONS FROM THE SLIP-ENDS AT NIGHT

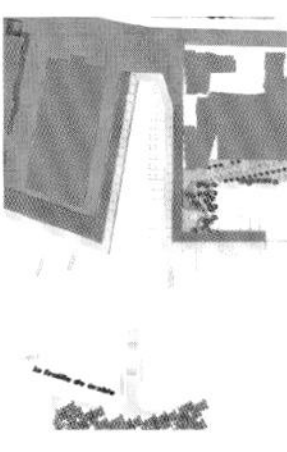

**UNIVERSITY AVENUE/YORK STREET**
The city's avenue of civic representation is articulated with the national symbol: the maple leaf. The new park also features a wooden column with a statue of Simcoe.

**YONGE STREET**
The longest street in the world ends at the new ferry terminal and market building, reconstructing the historic Yonge Wharf structures.

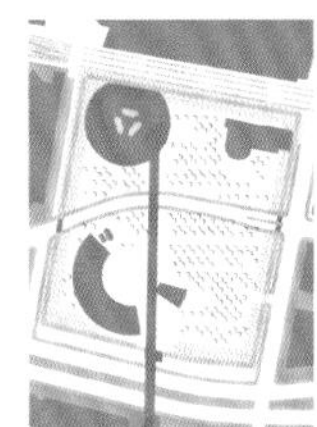

**CN TOWER TO THE WATER!**
The new park with its stair makes a monumental decsent from the CN Tower to the lake, embedding the previousely "footless" landmark into the city and the waterfront.

**REES SLIP**
An ideal Canadian Shield shoreline and the canoe and kayak basin will reflect a more distant past...

**HARBOUR DISTRICT**
At the foot of the downtown the Harbour District introduces a smaller grain of urban tissue.

**SPADINA**
Reflecting in the water, the archway, pier and floating restaurant suggest an extension of the Chinatown out into the lake. A sign of the city's multiple cultures...

**JARVIS STREET**
Landmark Institution as the eastern "bookend" for the Central Waterfront.

**PORTLAND DISTRICT**
The iconic Canada Malting Silos are retrofitted as a water filtration plant where the ecological processes are made publicly visible.

2.55

Panel 3: Perspective drawings, lighting plan, ground plans and visual presentations of individual areas.

CN Tower Park
The Round House
Monumental Stairs
Tower Steps
Relocated Nautical Centre
Queen's Quay Boulevard
Spadina Slip-Head
Rees Slip-Head
Simcoe Slip-Head
Music Garden
Future Trudeau
Memorial Park
Children's Playground &
HTO Original
HTO Urban Beach
Canoe / Kayak Launch
Simcoe Slip
Festival Square
Harbourfront Centre
Relocated TFC Waiting
arts and crafts)
Queen's Quay Terminal
The Power Plant
41.6m carved wood
column
Little Norway Park
Silo-Filter
Water Filtration
Plant & Nightclub
Portland Slip
Spadina Slip
Peter Slip
Rees Slip
Hydraulic Bridge
Timber Boardwalk
Lift Bridge
Lions
Floating Chinatown
"O" Arch
Tower Pier
HTO West/Little
Norway Park
Extension
Western Channel

2.56

**Panels 4, 5, 6: The design for the whole planning area was presented on three large panels, with an overall length of 3.6 m, based on a correspondingly large aerial photograph.**
The individual panels are juxtaposed very precisely.

## Example 3: The High Line competition

The High Line is a former railway line in West New York that was built between 1929 and 1934 so that freight train traffic could be separated from street traffic to improve safety. It covers 22 blocks, from 34th Street to Gansevoort Street, is 2.3 km long, 10 to 20 m wide and lies 6 to 10 m above street level. In total, it covers an area of 2.7 ha. Its construction is mainly steel and reinforced concrete, made to take the weight of two fully loaded freight trains.

In 2003, the Friends of the High Line, seeking proposals for the design and use of a new High Line inner-city park, launched an international open ideas competition. Ideas were not excluded for lacking feasibility or uneconomic cost. The competition resulted in 720 entries from 36 countries. In 2004, a competition open to project teams consisting of landscape architects, architects, urban planners, engineers, horticultural engineers and other disciplines was staged jointly by the Friends of the High Line and the city of New York. Out of 52 submitted applications, seven interdisciplinary teams were chosen to submit, as a first step, a detailed version of their proposals, based on which the deliberation process selected four firms, whose proposals were to be elaborated in a way that it could be put on public display. The purpose of this step-by-step process was to choose the project team who would ultimately create the design; at this point, the actual design for implementation was not under discussion. Only afterwards, when a committee of city representatives and Friends of the High Line had chosen the team who would create the design, did they ask the winning team to create specific material dealing particularly with accessibility, the High Line's relationship to neighbouring buildings, the treatment of the construction's underside and its appearance when seen from the street.

The competition was ultimately won by a project team directed by James Corner Field Operations and including Diller Scofidio + Renfro, Olafur Eliasson, Piet Oudolf and Buro Happold. They took the question: "What will grow here?" as the central theme of their entry. Their chosen strategy was summed up by the term "Agri-Tecture", a concept combining organic and inorganic materials and surfaces. In bringing together agriculture and architecture, the surface of the High Line was divided into individual sections with paving and planted areas, in different degrees ranging from completely paved and sealed ground to open soil. Specially created concrete planks with open joints allowed opportunistic vegetation to take root. These long planks with tapered ends are laid out within the planted areas in a comb shape, creating a landscape with no fixed paths within which people can move freely. The result is the revival of a post-industrial site as a place for recreation, life and growth. The "agrarian architecture" strategy sets the rules for the relationship between plant growth and use, creating a synthesis of changing proportions containing places for wildness, cultivation, the familiar and social space. The idea behind the design was that the space would remain unfinished, with constant growth and changes taking place over time.

The competition entry consists of six 90 x 70 cm panels. The first two of these present the individual ideas, along with the central text, dealing with the significance of agrarian architecture, methods of defining different habitats and places to linger, the development of vegetation over time, and the development of ecological richness and diversity of species (Ills. 2.57-58). Ground plans, axonometric drawings, schematics and section drawings clarify ideas and present different possibilities for development. The third and fourth panels show a ground plan of the High Line, supplemented with section drawings for individual areas and axonometric presentations of particular sectoral areas (Ills. 2.59-60). The final two panels contain perspective views representing areas of the High Line and their relationship to their surroundings (Ills. 2.61-62).

# WHAT WILL GROW HERE ?

Inspired by the melancholic, unruly beauty of the High Line where nature has reclaimed a once vital piece of urban infrastructure, the team retools this industrial conveyance into a postindustrial instrument of leisure, life and growth. By changing the rules of engagement between plant life and pedestrians, our strategy of **AGRI-TECTURE** combines organic and building materials into gradients of changing proportions that accommodate the wild, the cultivated, the intimate, and the hyper-social. In stark contrast to the speed of Hudson River Park, this parallel linear experience is marked by slowness, distraction and an other-worldliness that preserves the strange character of the High Line. Providing flexibility and responsiveness to the changing needs, opportunities, and desires of the dynamic context, our proposal is designed to remain perpetually unfinished, sustaining emergent growth and change over time.

## 1 AGRI-TECTURE: A FLEXIBLE, RESPONSIVE SYSTEM OF MATERIAL ORGANIZATION WHERE DIVERSE ECOLOGIES MAY GROW.

The striated surface transitions from high intensity areas (100% hard) to richly vegetated biotopes (100% soft), with a variety of experiential gradients in-between.

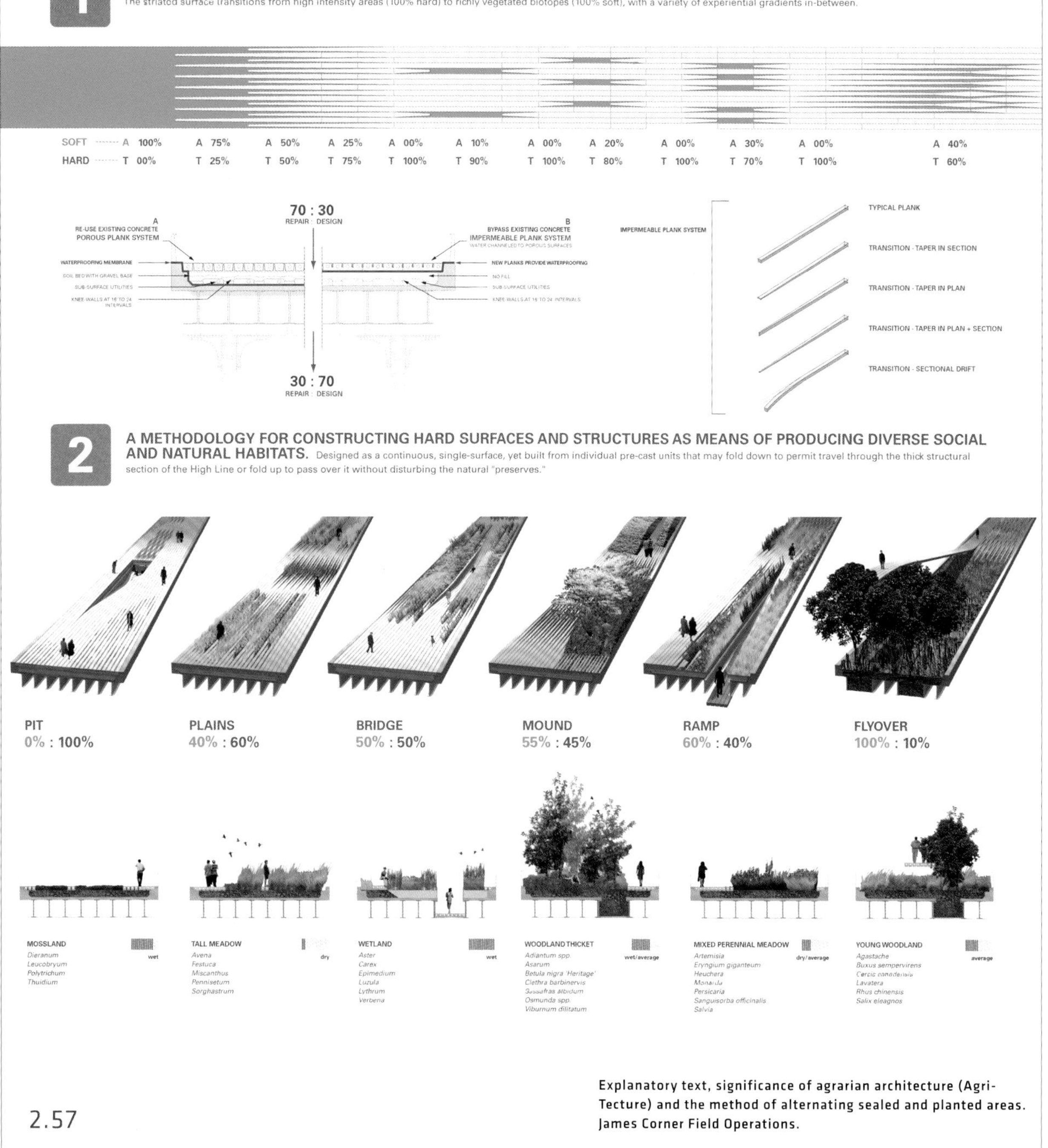


2.57

Explanatory text, significance of agrarian architecture (Agri-Tecture) and the method of alternating sealed and planted areas. James Corner Field Operations.

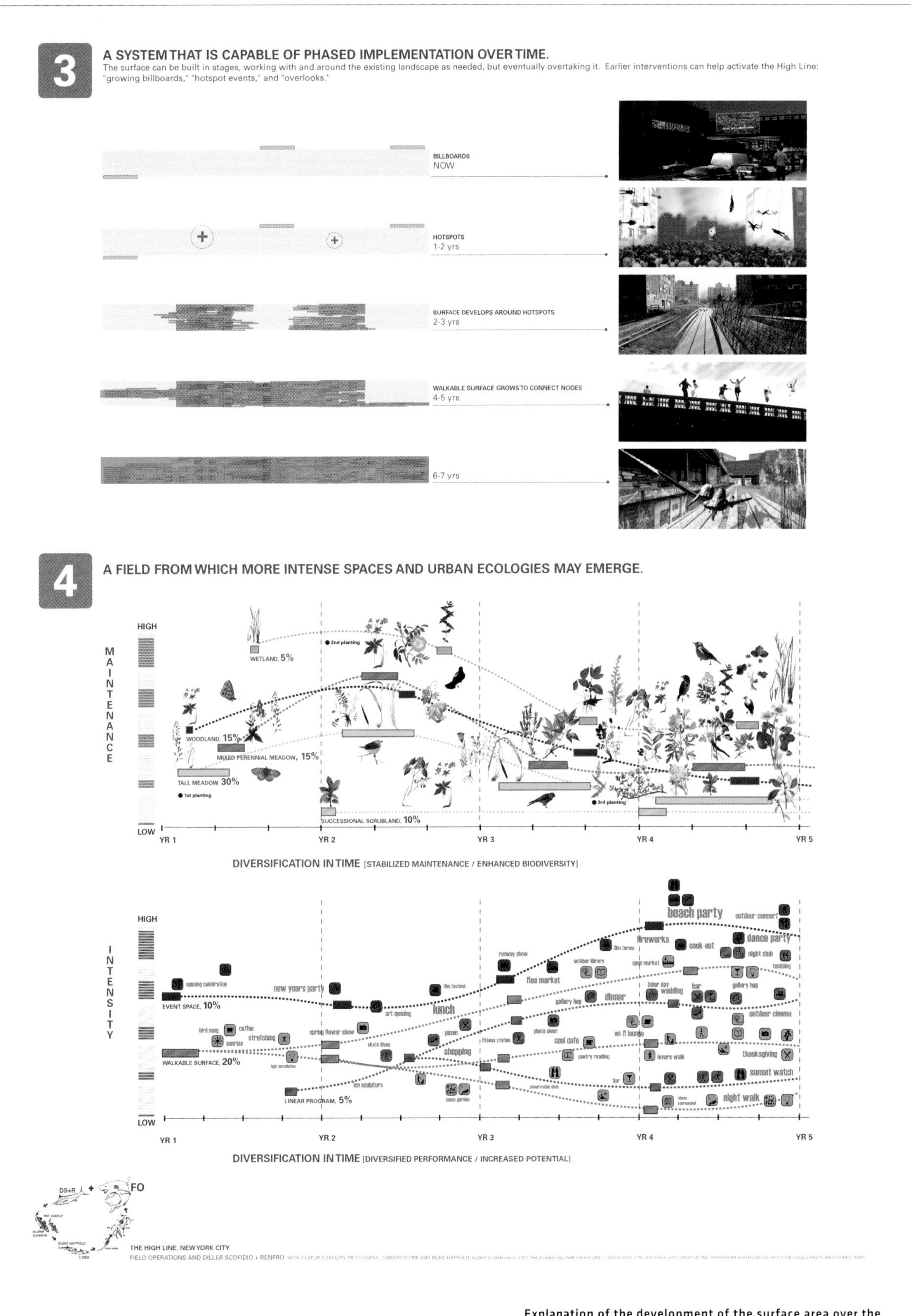


Explanation of the development of the surface area over the course of the first seven years and development of ecological diversity as well as the use over the first five years.

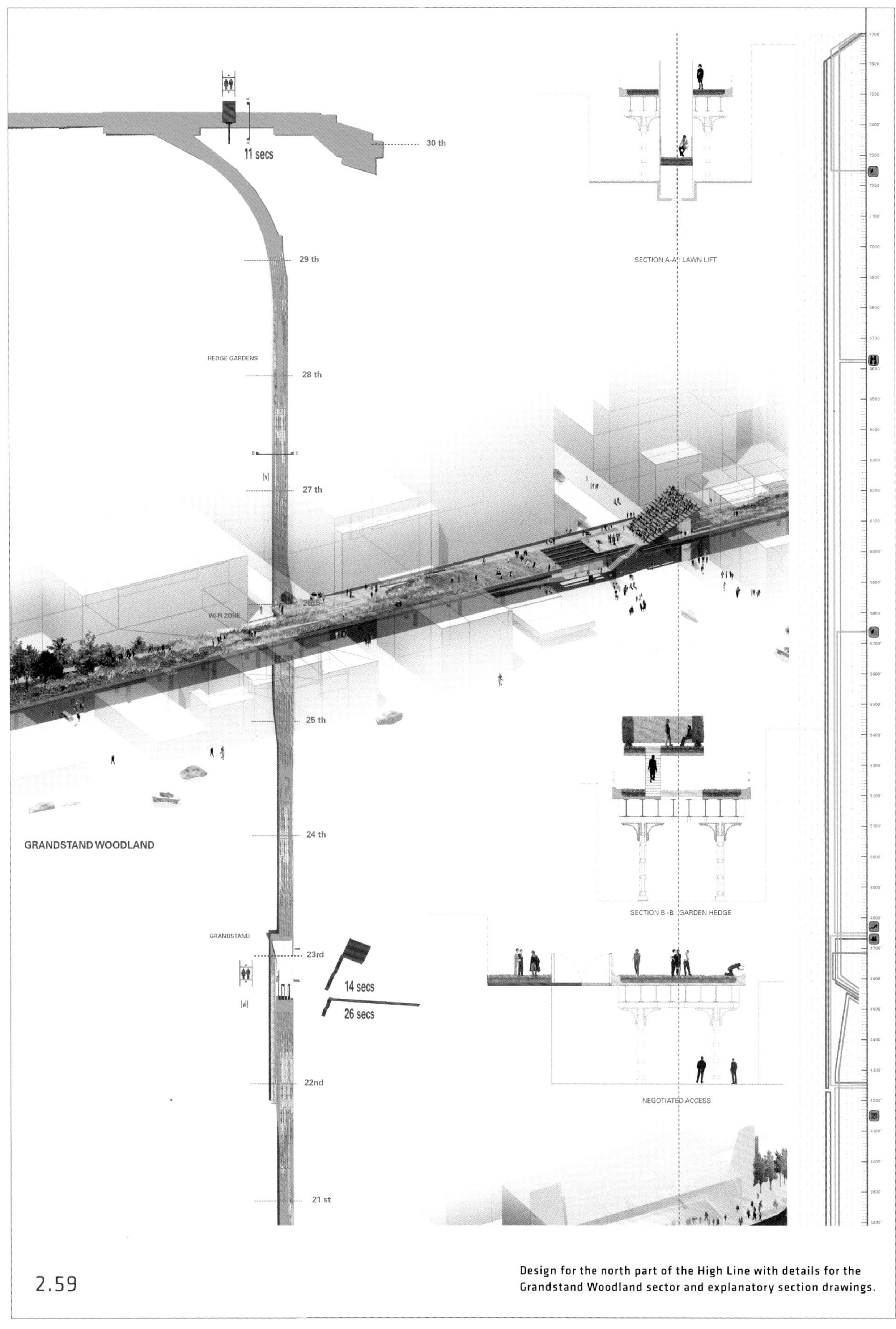


2.59

Design for the north part of the High Line with details for the Grandstand Woodland sector and explanatory section drawings.

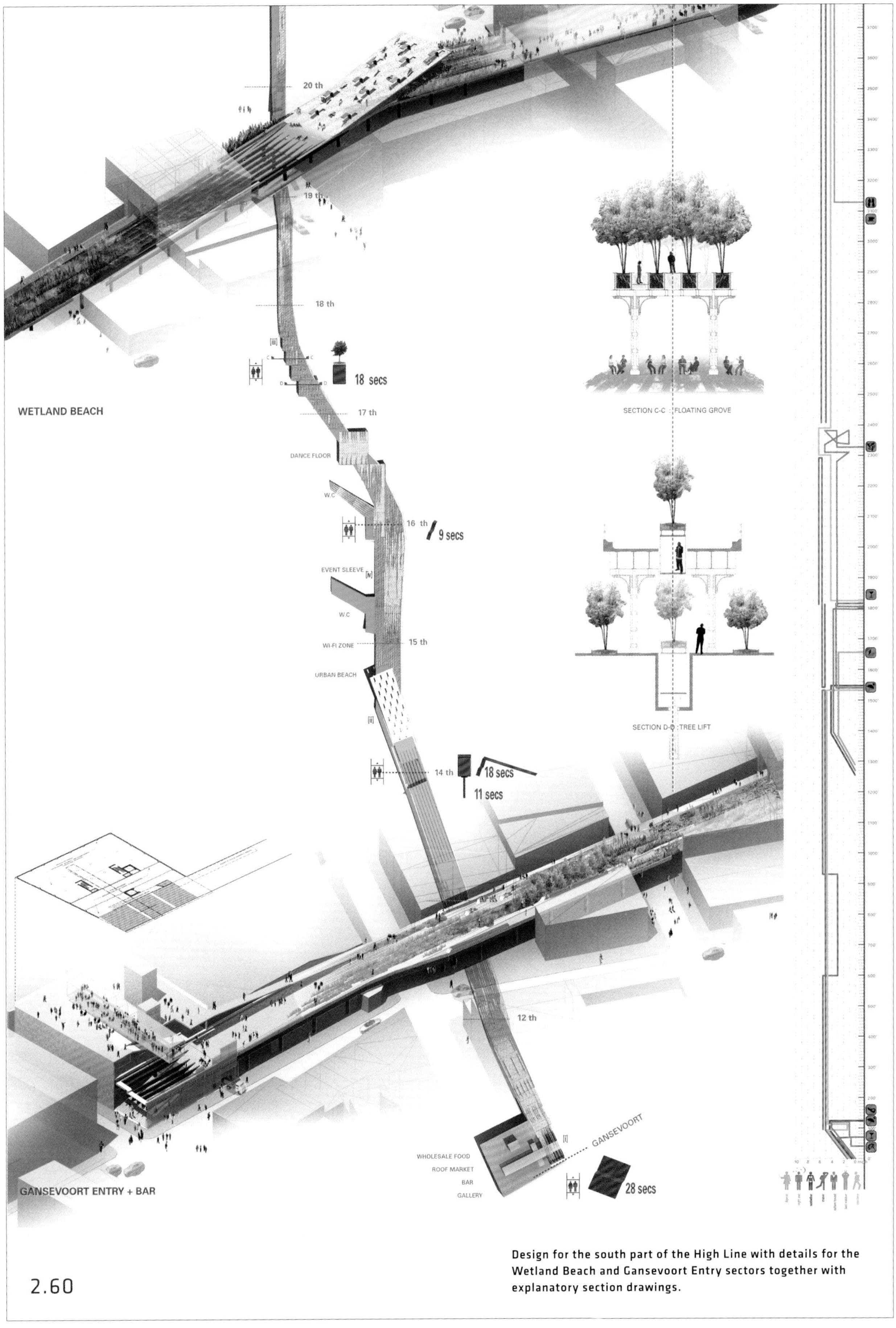


Design for the south part of the High Line with details for the Wetland Beach and Gansevoort Entry sectors together with explanatory section drawings.

2.60

2.61-62

**Perspective drawings.**

This entry is unusual in that it begins with a question: What will grow here? The diverse two- and three-dimensional representations or schematics of sectoral areas on the first two panels (Ills. 2.57-58) aim to answer this question, rather than presenting design solutions for specific places. Instead, these are represented on the third and fourth panels (Ills. 2.59-60) – on too small a scale for detailed design – with added perspective drawings and section drawings (Ills. 2.61-62). Put together, the images create a complex picture of the design. The two final panels, with their coloured perspective visualizations arranged immediately next to each other with no gap in between, are eye-catching because they speak an entirely different language to the precise drawings that come before them. The changes to the open space over the course of time (an important aspect) are represented in a ground plan and as a schematic drawing.

# PART 3 STRATEGIES

Looking beyond concrete planning and design for individual sites, landscape architects have always been involved with the comprehensive development of wider areas. This creates a need for strategies for the visualization of complex projects and scenarios. Both past experience and the ecological challenges of the present time indicate the need for global planning, both for the open landscape and especially for cities, where most of the population presently live. For regional planning, large-scale contexts in terms of spatial and temporal dimensions must be taken into account. This involves changes in the planning process and also in planning culture. Again, the time aspect and the different dynamics of planning processes and implementations are vital here.

For the purpose of reducing the negative consequences of climate change through spatial planning, and to address the need for compatible, forward-looking urban growth, the following pages present ways of applying scenario-generating techniques to landscape architecture and of presenting the results visually. Scenarios are a good way of dealing with complex planning contexts, and a good basis for discussions involving several groups of interested parties. This involves the creation of visual presentations of the consequences of realistic or extreme estimates, and of possible models for development. The varying consequences of developments whose conditions are influenced by human activity can be compared. Communicating information through illustrations also allows laypeople – a category that often includes the key decision-makers – to relate to it. Planning can thus gain currency and allow citizens to take part in designing the future in a responsible way. The importance of this procedural method to landscape architecture can be expected to increase in the future.

Gabriele Holst, Vertical Collage II.

# STRATEGIES
# LANDSCAPE PLANNING

## Urbanization: a challenge for sustainable landscape planning

In 2008 – for the first time in history – there were more people living in the world's cities than in its rural areas. By 2030, the UN estimates that the proportion of city-dwellers to country-dwellers will have shifted even further in the same direction, with the number of people living in rural areas expected to remain the same or decline slightly while the overall population increases. Population growth in the cities of Asia and Africa is particularly strong, but Europe and the USA, whose populations are expected to remain relatively constant, can also expect major challenges in this area. The per capita living space in cities, another significant factor in urban expansion, is also rising. As these trends progress, infrastructural innovations will take place in and between cities rather than in rural areas. Organizing the movement of goods and people between cities will become a challenge, as will ensuring sufficient quantity and quality of well-designed open spaces for recreation and preserving ecological functions in growth regions.

China is an example of an extremely rapid urbanization process, with an approximate annual urbanization increase of 1%. At present, less than 40 % of China's 1.3 billion citizens live in cities, but this figure will increase to more than 70 % over the next 15 to 20 years. Reconciling preservation of open spaces for ecological purposes with the march of urbanization is therefore a key question facing China. A landscape must be developed that not only protects natural habitats and provides recreation areas but also gives settlements maximum protection from natural forces such as flooding, storms and earthquakes and recognizes their importance as part of a cultural landscape and as home to many individuals. Land must also be reserved for agricultural production: China has only 7 % of the world's cultivated land with which to feed 20 % of the world's population.

In a conventional urban growth process, the first stage is to plan the supply systems and essential functions and to construct the necessary infrastructure. The need to preserve natural resources is often not taken into account early enough in the planning process, leading to valuable habitats being eradicated and settled areas being threatened – by flooding, for instance. On China's booming east coast in particular, urban green spaces now play a greater role in the urban development process, and the number of urban parks is increasing. This, however, does not go far enough. If crucial natural resources are to be protected, fostered and utilized, urban development planning must be integrated with the wider context, and this requires a more strategic planning methodology, as exemplified by planning firm Turenscape's model for the city of Taizhou. The radically different nature of this method has led the firm to use the term "negative planning". It involves urban development scenarios on various scales and a combination of ecological and sociocultural development planning with economic and urban planning requirements.

## Example: Ecological Infrastructure as the basis for "negative planning" for Taizhou, China

Turenscape's ecological infrastructure planning method is demonstrated here by the city of Taizhou. The development is represented on three different levels, ranging from representations of the wider regional context to representations of individual urban structures. Flood protection, conservation of biological diversity, cultural heritage preservation and the open landscape are all examined at on the wider scale – for an area of more than 100 km² – to reveal the city plan's underlying circumstances. These aspects are then collated to give a picture of the region's ecological infrastructure. How the ecological infrastructure fits into the region's urban developments in terms of spatial pattern is analyzed and adapted on a medium level (on a scale of 10 to 100 km²). Regional ecological functions are integrated into the city's structure and form the basis for land use designations. This is represented on the microscopic level (areas of less than 10 km² in size).

Taizhou is situated in the province of Zhejiang on China's south-east coast. Originally a rural and agricultural area, this is now one of the fastest-growing regions in China thanks to the rapid expansion of privately owned small businesses. Taizhou has 9,411 km² of land, 80,000 km² of water and a population of approximately 5.5 million people. The inner city's population (presently 0.7 million) is expected to increase to 0.9 million by 2010, 1.3 million by 2020 and 1.5 million by 2030. A network of channels covers the landscape. By integrating with the natural water system and its 700-plus rivers and streams, this network has effectively protected agriculture from climate-induced flooding for thousands of years. Wetlands and ditches, bridges, dikes and dams characterize the cultural landscape. Modern Taizhou is also among the most famous fruit-growing areas in China. Citrus fruits and strawberries, rice, tea and cauliflowers are its most important crops. The fishing industry is also vital for Taizhou's productivity.

This landscape is now facing destruction at the hands of the rapid urbanization process that first set in during the early 1990s. Wetlands have been drained, rivers have been straightened and turned into canals, parts of the region's cultural heritage not protected under law have been destroyed, and the scenic and recreational properties of the landscape have been ignored entirely. This has disrupted the region's water balance and led to the pollution and destruction of wetlands. Habitats and species diversity are threatening to disappear, while the risk of floods, epidemics and drought is increasing, and the landscape's cultural identity is in danger of being lost. Crucially, China's southeast coast lies within the subtropical climate zone, which is subject to monsoons and often produces typhoons which number among the most severe natural catastrophes in the northwest Pacific. Severe damage is caused not only by the high wind speeds but also by very heavy rain falling within a short period of time, as this can cause flooding and landslides.

Traditionally, urban development planners include green belts to protect the landscape from urban sprawl. These, however, usually remain unimplemented – mainly because most are planned as artificially and arbitrarily as the urban developments themselves. They are barriers to development rather than structures that positively support the local ecology. New and more effective instruments must therefore be identified to ensure an intelligent and sustainable approach for the urban extension that is to be restricted.

The planners developed an Ecological Infrastructure (EI) to guide and contain urban expansion. The EI is a structural network within the landscape consisting of the threatened landscape elements and of areas with a specific strategic importance. The goals of the EI are to preserve the integrity and identity of the natural and cultural landscape, to maintain a sustainable, functioning ecosystem, to protect cultural treasures and to provide recreational opportunities. Rather than being planned at odds to or with total disregard for ecological conditions and ecological needs, the city's development should be planned with these factors in mind. Just as the urban infrastructure provides social and economic services, the EI protects areas of ecological significance as well as cultural treasures and answers the need for recreation.

Three kinds of processes are specifically protected by the EI:

• abiotic ecological processes, with particular attention given to flood protection and rainwater management;
• biotic ecological processes, including protecting native species and preserving biological diversity;
• cultural processes, including protecting cultural treasures and catering for leisure and recreational needs.

With the aid of a Geographical Information System (GIS), data on the area's ecological balance and cultural landscape, as well as socio-economic data, were collated in map form. The maps were then overlaid on each other for analysis. Planning the regional EI meant identifying strategically important landscape structures. Working with models and suitability analyses allowed every aspect of development to be controlled. In order to identify hazard potentials, three hazard levels were established: low, medium and high. With the help of the superimposed sets of data, the security levels that applied to each individual process were combined within the plan and alternative EI options were developed for the region. These were also classified using three quality levels: low, medium and high.

Scenarios for urban growth were simulated based on three alternative EI framework structures: the Adjusted Sprawl Scenario, the Aggregated Scenario and the Scattered Scenario. A planning committee made up of various decision-makers and concerned parties compared each scenario and its implications. Finally, the decision-makers chose the most suitable scenario – which was, as expected, the Aggregated Scenario based on the medium quality level, judged to be the most balanced option and the easiest to implement. In addition, "green lines" were

3.1

Urbanization and urban sprawl in the region surrounding the city of Taizhou which is under threat of losing its present character.

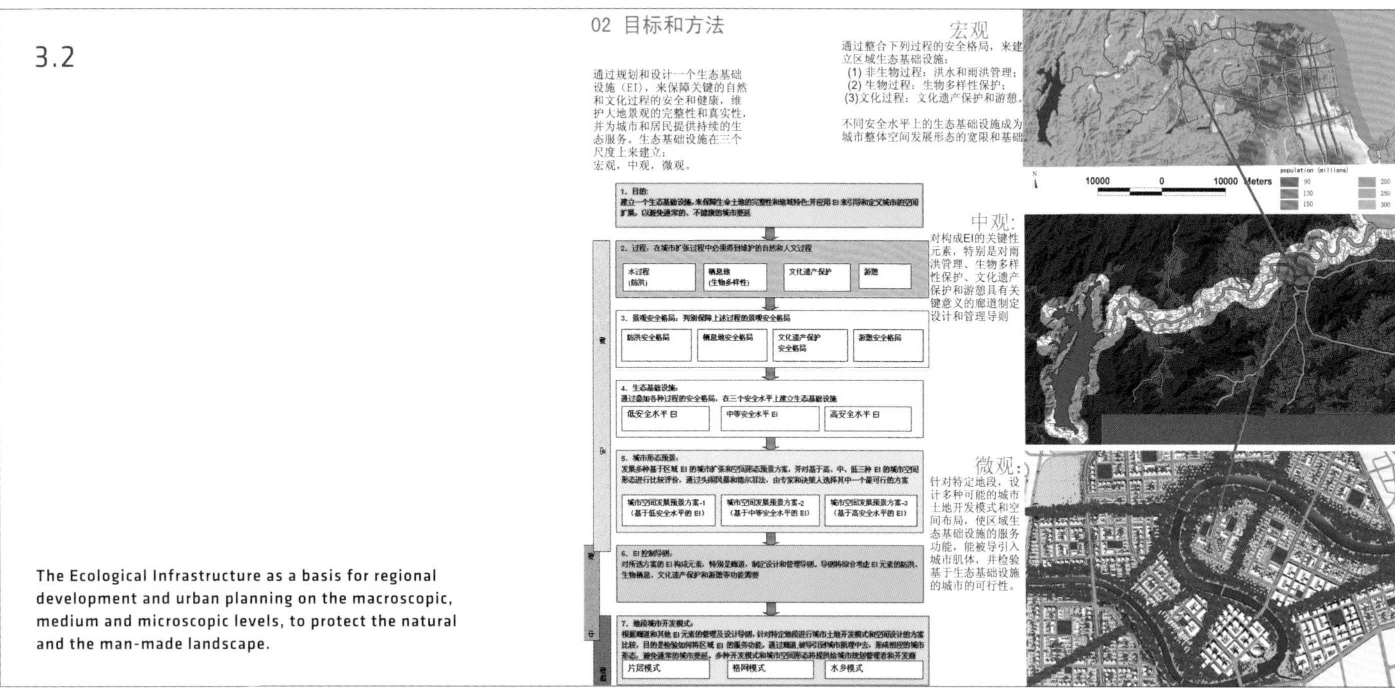


3.2

The Ecological Infrastructure as a basis for regional development and urban planning on the macroscopic, medium and microscopic levels, to protect the natural and the man-made landscape.

enshrined in municipal law as the first legal ruling protecting the regional ecological infrastructure. Guiding principles for the development of the EI were evolved based on the selected growth scenario and the green lines. These were primarily concerned with green connections, which are particularly important to water management and biological diversity, as well as cultural heritage sites and recreational facilities.

Alternative urban development models based on the EI's guidelines were elatorated for a selected area 10 km² in size, with the aim being to conceive a city based on an EI. These models integrate ecosystem services into the city's structure, excluding the threat of urban sprawl in favour of ecologically and economically balanced sustainable development.

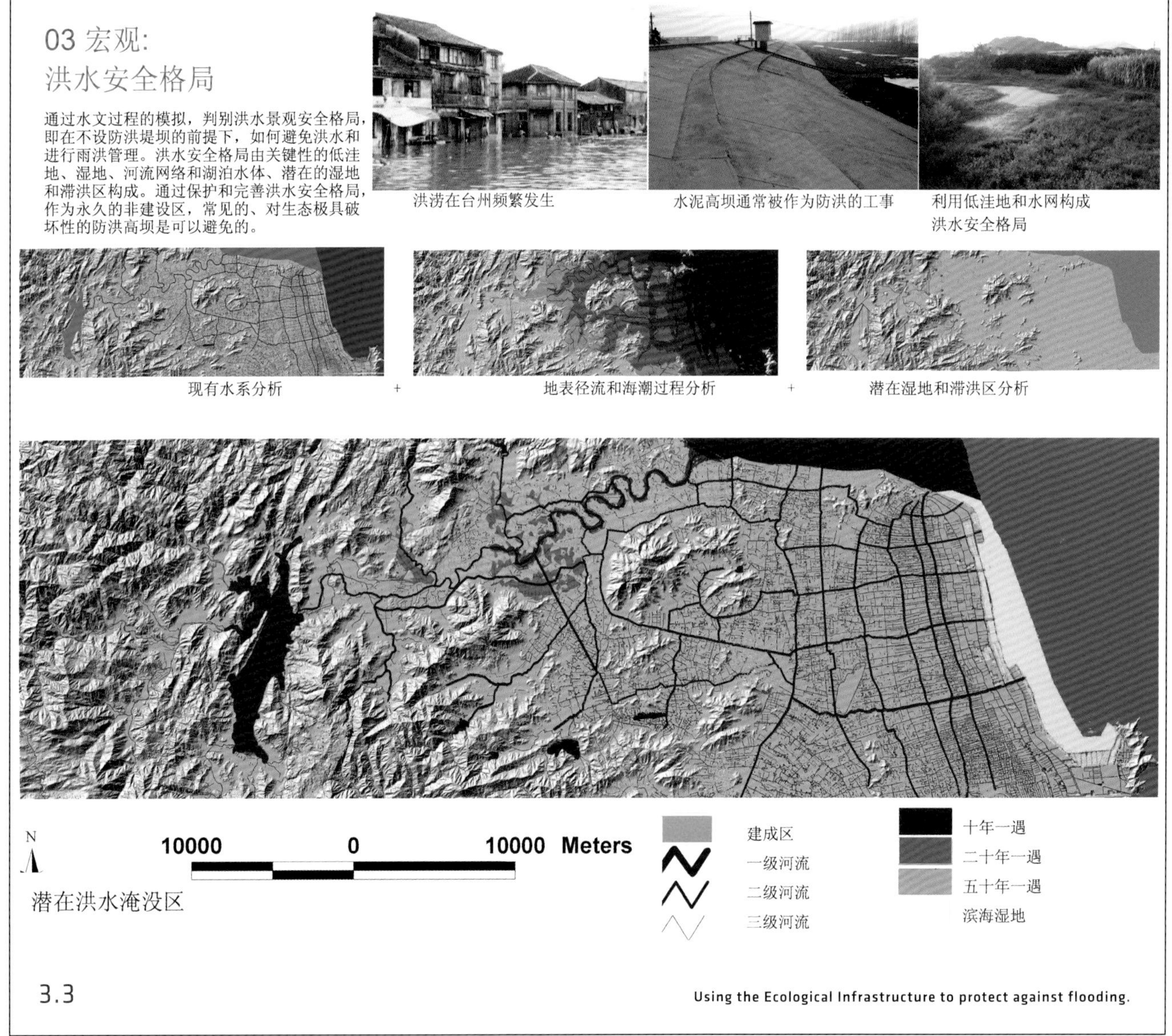


3.3 Using the Ecological Infrastructure to protect against flooding.

The initial situation for this project is represented by photographs and drawings (Ill. 3.1). The photos in the upper row show canalized waterways, unstructured open spaces and unauthorized dumping of rubbish. A photo shows an example of urban sprawl on the plain, while a map excerpt represents the region's population density. This is contrasted with the EI approach in a visual scheme with explanatory text showing the EI's phases of development as well as the three different scale levels as floor plans.

These images are followed by four planning goals, shown individually and superimposed to create a unified picture (Ill. 3.2). All these maps have a similar graphic structure. This makes the data they contain readily comprehensible, easy to compare with each other and enhances the coherence of the statements made.

One major concern is to prevent flooding (Ill. 3.3). Photographs show a flooded urban area, an artificially created reservoir and a natural wetland area. Digital maps simulate scenarios for different levels of flood protection, with particular emphasis on the region's topography. Together the wetlands, rivers and lakes form a network that maintains the area's water balance. Protecting the native animal and plant profile and preserving biological diversity is another

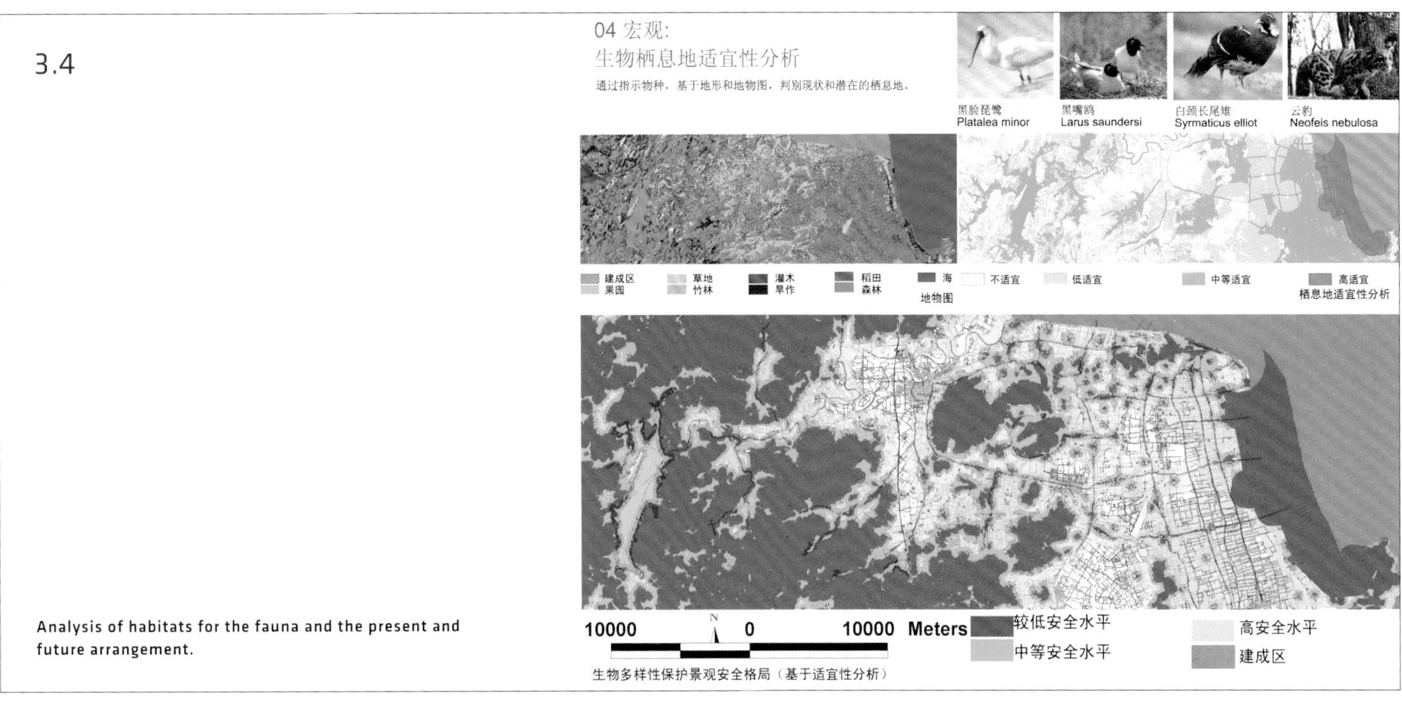


3.4

**Analysis of habitats for the fauna and the present and future arrangement.**

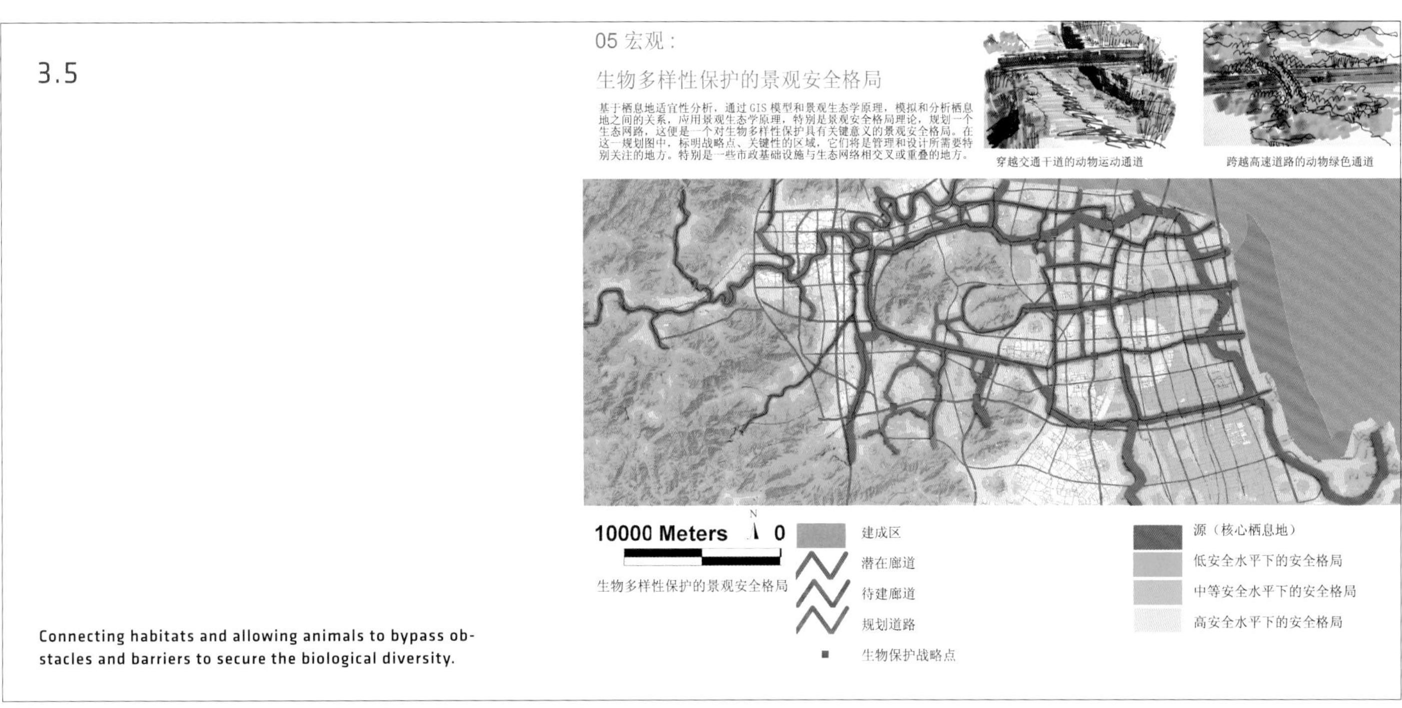


3.5

**Connecting habitats and allowing animals to bypass obstacles and barriers to secure the biological diversity.**

important goal, and the suitability of the area as a potential habitat is therefore represented here (Ill. 3.4), based on a range of indicator species.

The creation of connections between habitats and ways of bypassing barriers represent the highest development level. Protection for the area's cultural heritage is organized in the same way: protection of separate areas represents the minimum level, the medium level is given where individual areas are both protected and connected together, and the highest level is achieved where individual locations are protected, connected together and surrounded by a properly maintained buffer zone where protection is required. When it comes to the protection of wetlands, woods and cultural landscapes as venues for leisure activities, the suitability and accessibility of individual landscape elements are evaluated in the same way.

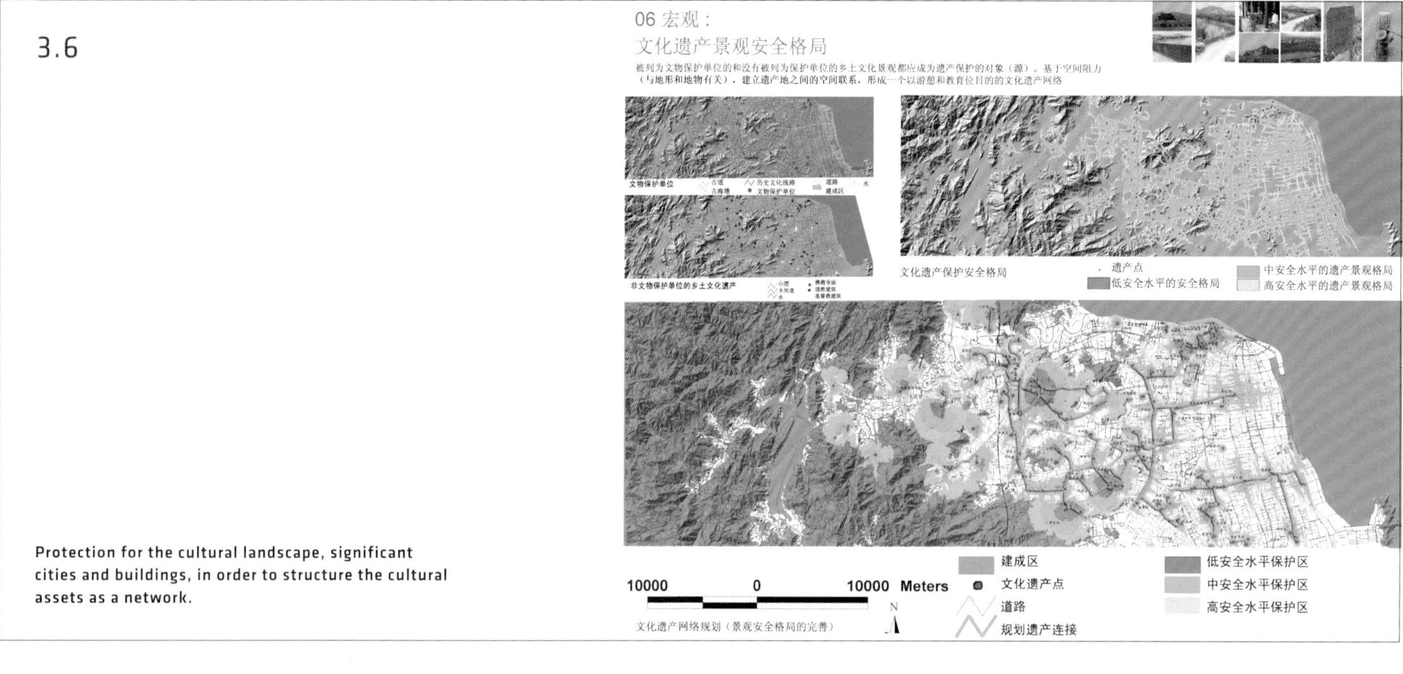


## 3.6

Protection for the cultural landscape, significant cities and buildings, in order to structure the cultural assets as a network.

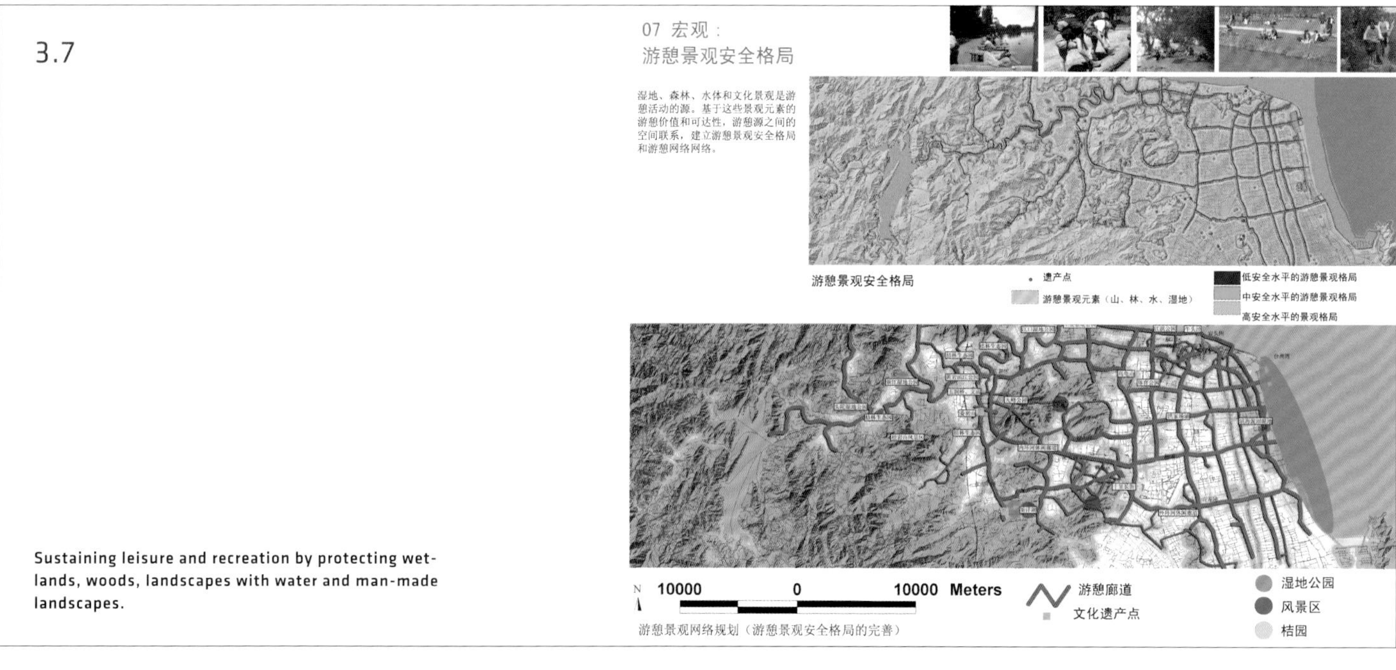


## 3.7

Sustaining leisure and recreation by protecting wetlands, woods, landscapes with water and man-made landscapes.

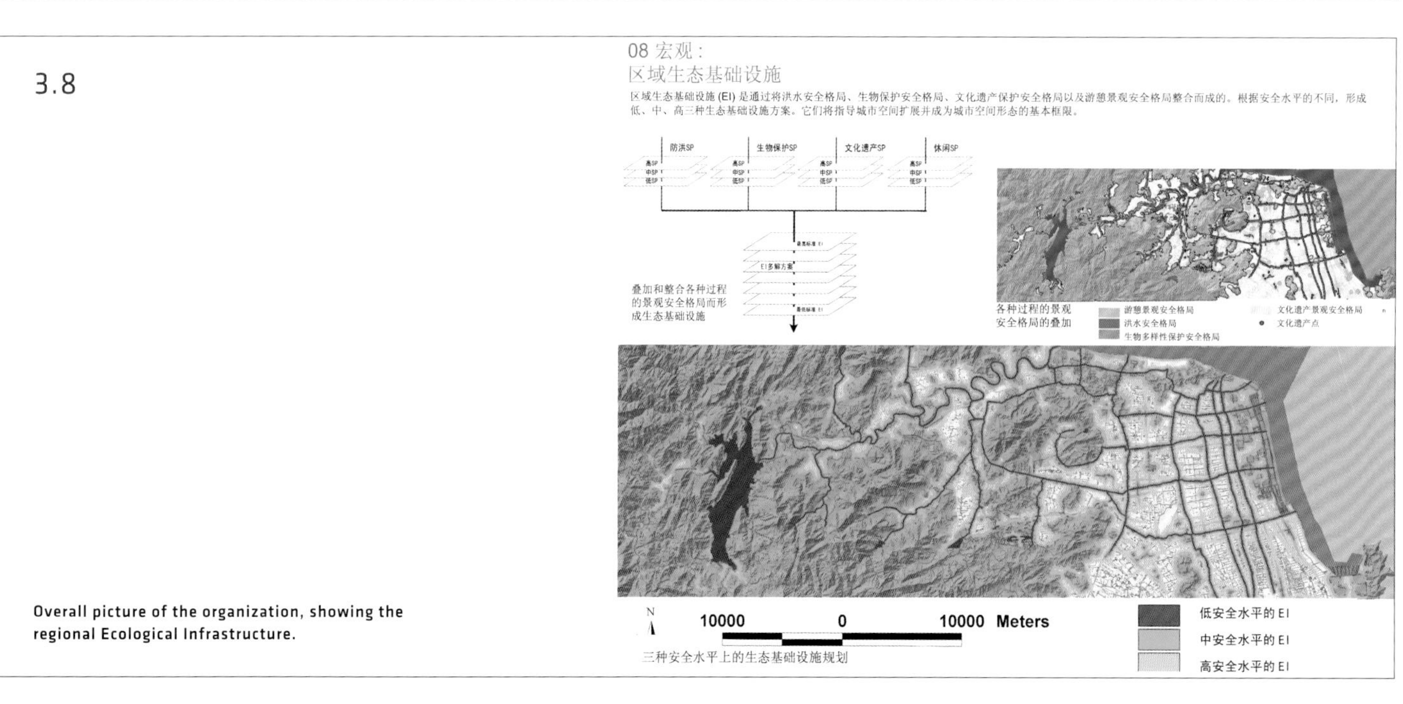


## 3.8

Overall picture of the organization, showing the regional Ecological Infrastructure.

## 3.9

09 城市扩张预景：蔓延改良式
基于低安全水平 EI 的城市格局



Scenario for the city's growth in the context
of the Ecological Infrastructure's lowest level.

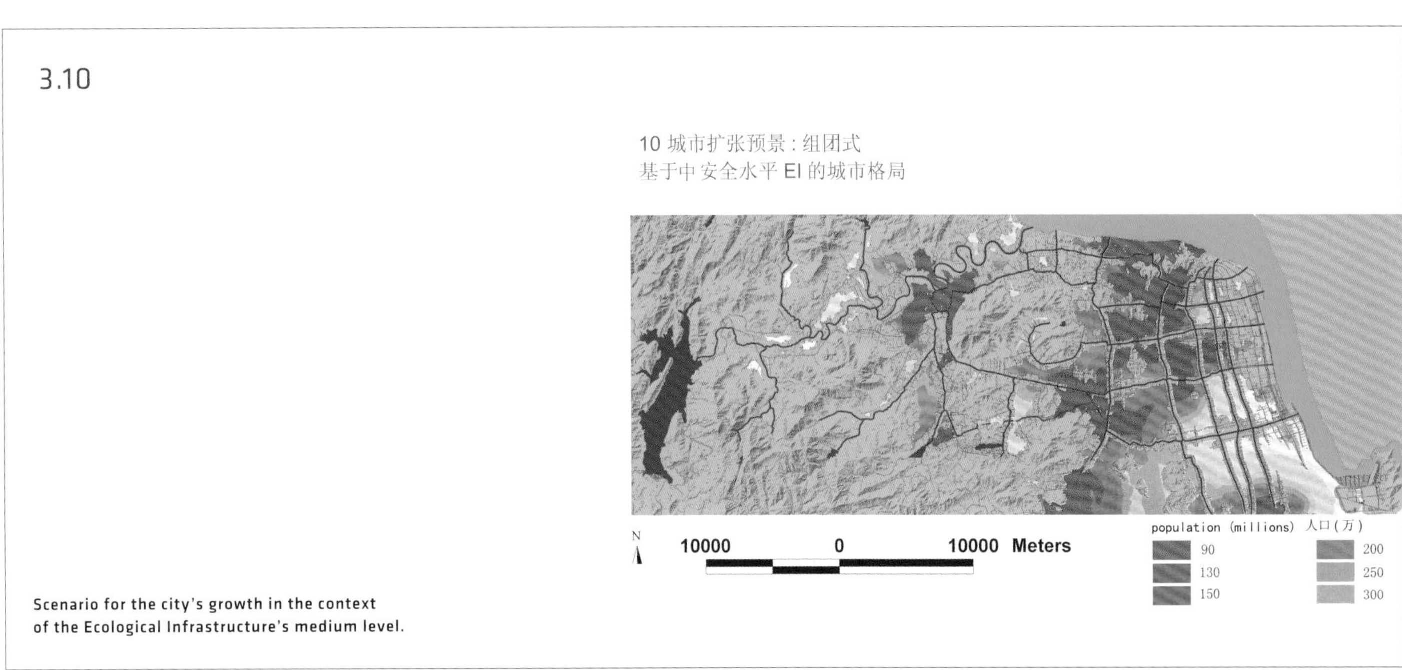

## 3.10

10 城市扩张预景：组团式
基于中安全水平 EI 的城市格局



Scenario for the city's growth in the context
of the Ecological Infrastructure's medium level.

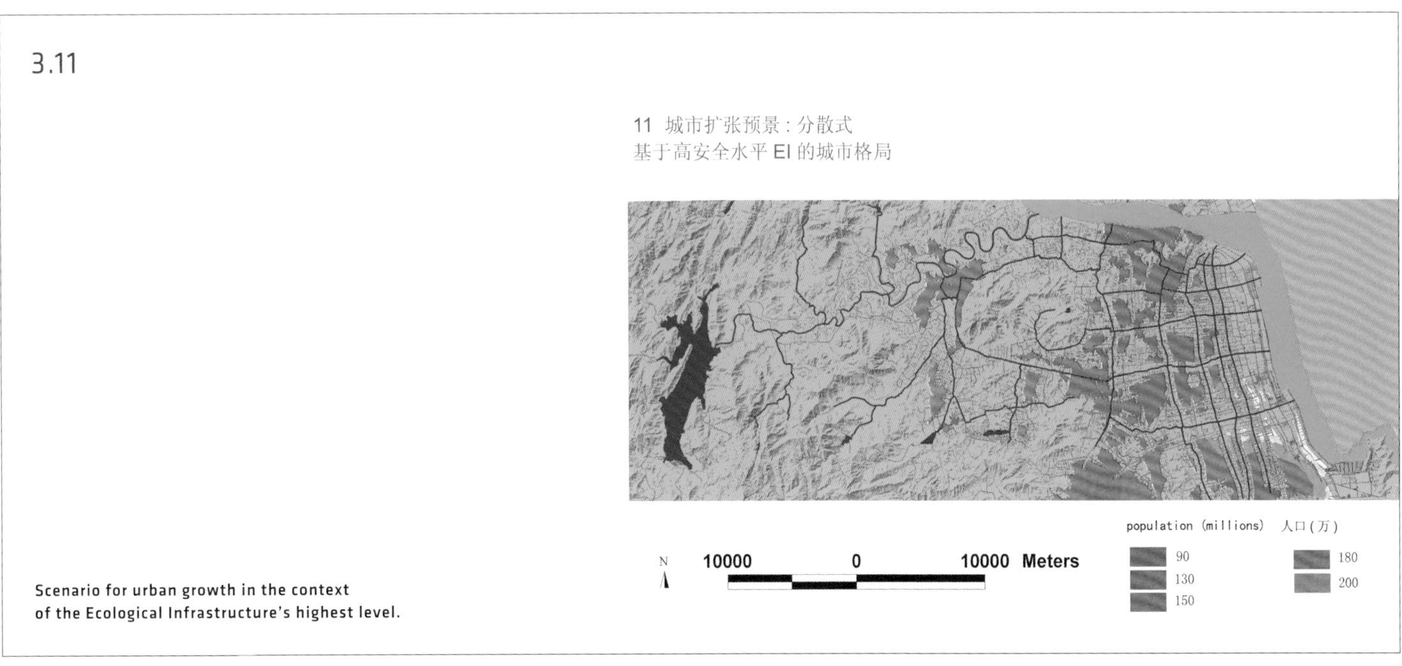

## 3.11

11 城市扩张预景：分散式
基于高安全水平 EI 的城市格局



Scenario for urban growth in the context
of the Ecological Infrastructure's highest level.

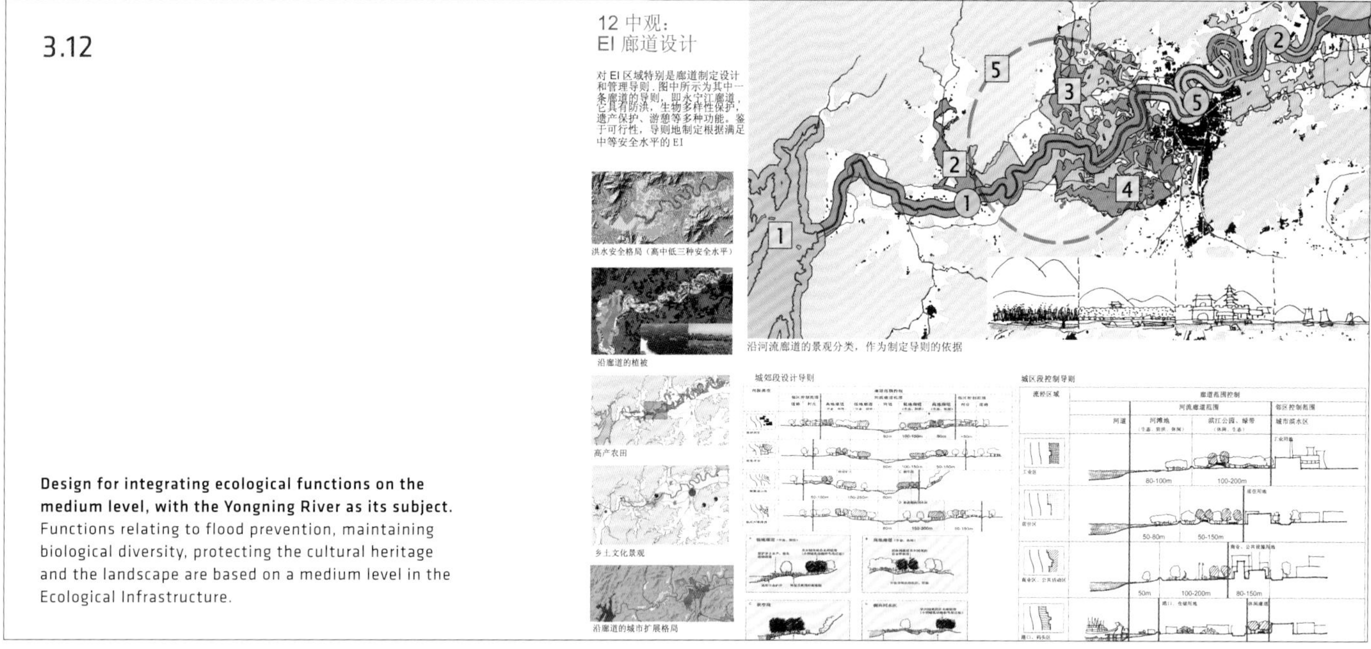


3.12

**Design for integrating ecological functions on the medium level, with the Yongning River as its subject.** Functions relating to flood prevention, maintaining biological diversity, protecting the cultural heritage and the landscape are based on a medium level in the Ecological Infrastructure.

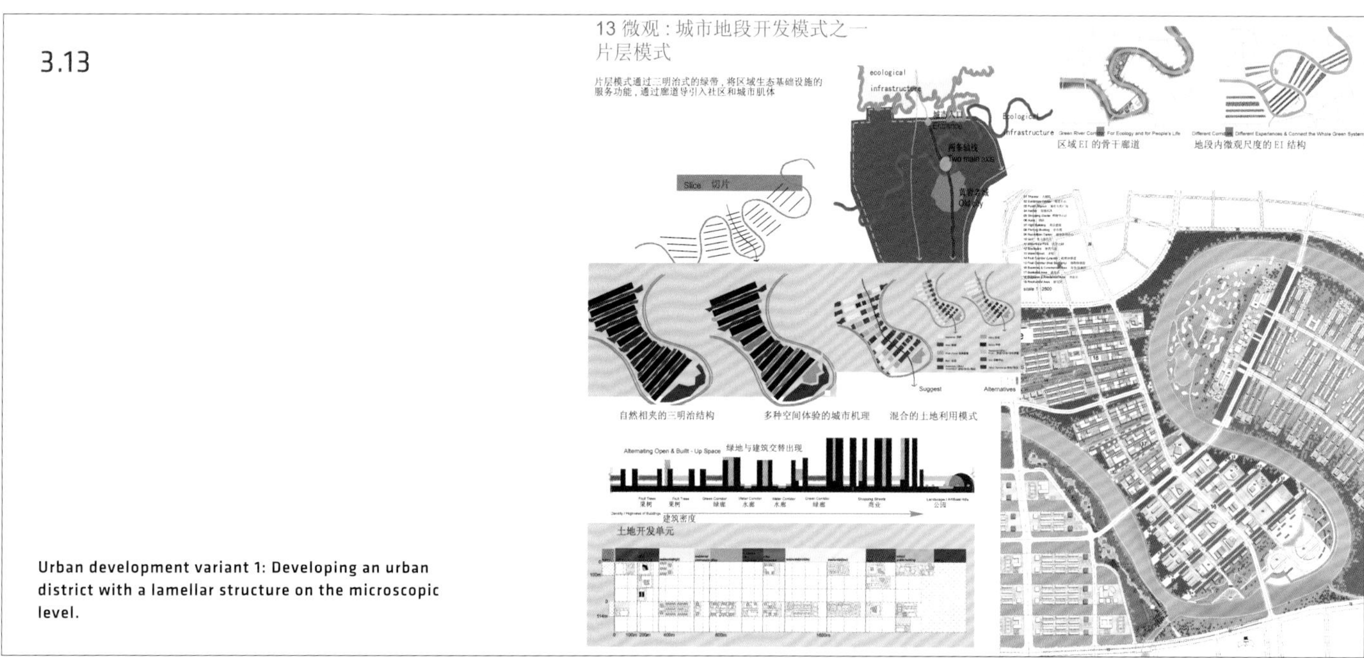


3.13

**Urban development variant 1: Developing an urban district with a lamellar structure on the microscopic level.**

The EI map (Ill. 3.8) was developed by superimposing the individual maps representing flood protection, conservation of biological diversity, the cultural landscape and leisure and recreation opportunities. Put together, the different protection levels for each individual parameter create three EI levels. These represent a context for limiting urban development, at the same time creating a basis for the further planning shown in the representations that follow. These pages also share a uniform pattern.

The smaller-scale, detailed plans are based on the macroscopic-level plans for the region as a whole. The plan for the vital ecological corridor functions of the Yongning River is an example of medium-level planning (Ill. 3.12). The microscopic level (Ill. 3.13) was used for three different urban planning scenarios: the lamellar structure, the grid structure and the water city development pattern. The parallel sequence of ecological corridors and urban functions that was ultimately chosen creates a harmonious, unified profile. This system is easy to develop, and is also dynamic and progressive.

3.14

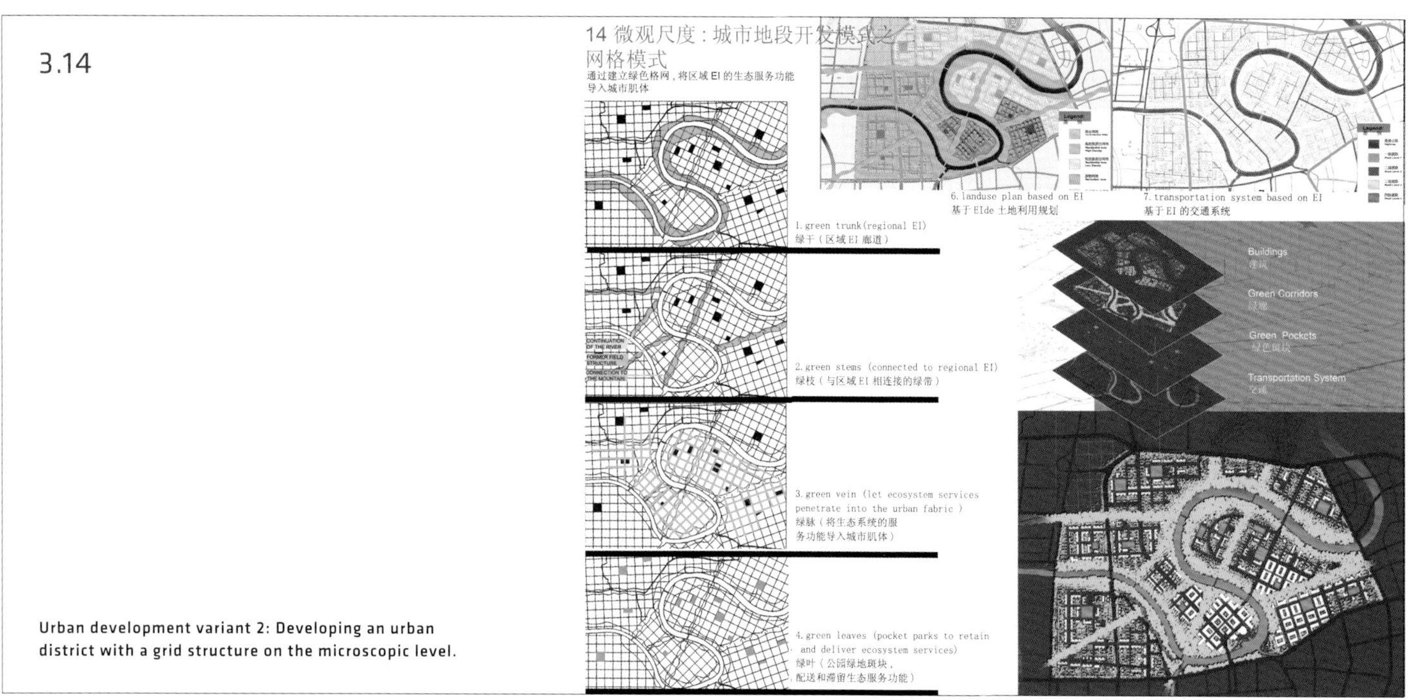


**Urban development variant 2: Developing an urban district with a grid structure on the microscopic level.**

3.15

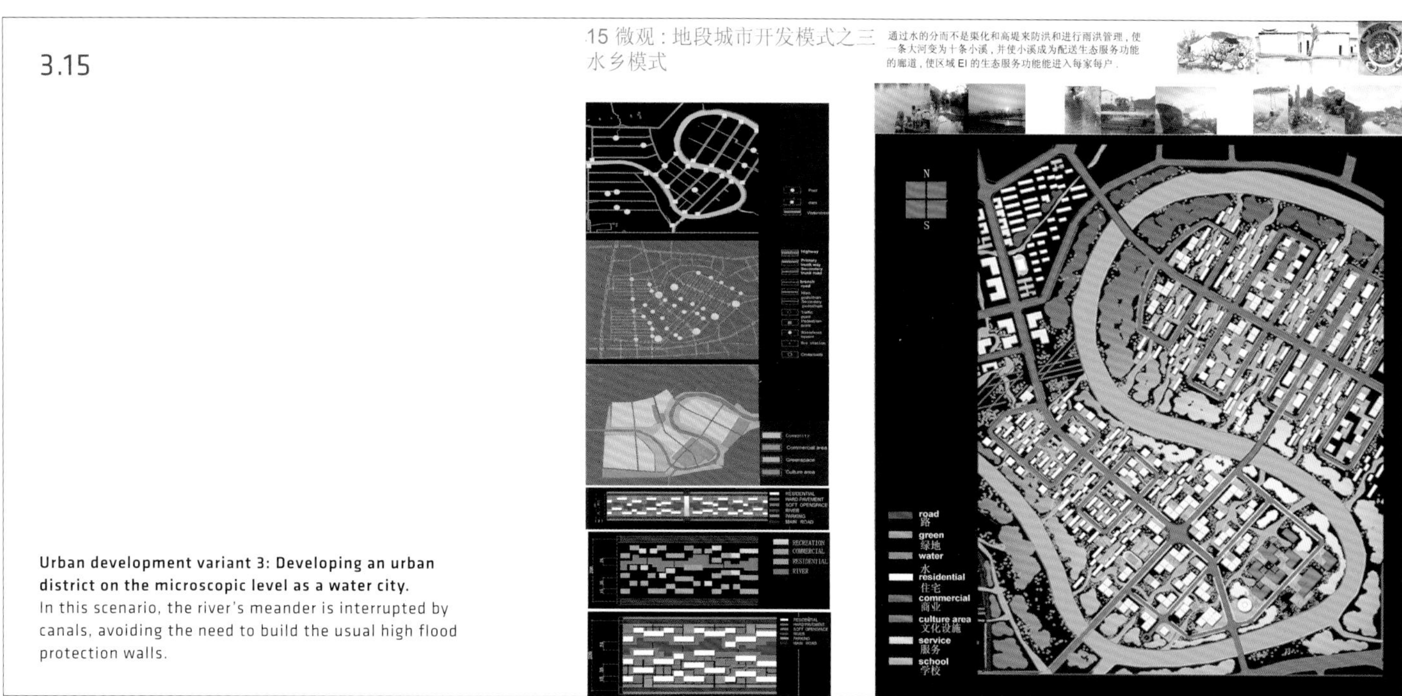


**Urban development variant 3: Developing an urban district on the microscopic level as a water city.**
In this scenario, the river's meander is interrupted by canals, avoiding the need to build the usual high flood protection walls.

The reversed urban and regional planning priorities of "negative planning" are primarily a response to rapid urbanization and the unpredictable impact of this kind of development on natural resources. The graphic tools used are mainly traditional: photographs showing the existing situation and maps as representation of the ground plan. The choice of colours is also conventional and familiar, as is the use of a Geographical Information System to compile the plans and the overlaying of individual maps. This makes the images readily comprehensible to professional planners. The special features of planning based on ecological parameters stand out clearly.

# STRATEGIES
# CLIMATE CHANGE

## Planning with climate change

In 1988, after global climate change was first foreseen, the World Meteorological Organization (WMO) and the United Nations Environment Programme (UNEP) founded a global climate advisory body: the Intergovernmental Panel on Climate Change (IPCC). The results of climate researchers' scientific investigations and models are usually represented in tables, diagrams or large-scale maps, which often represent the entire world. Climate models and energy-use scenarios are used to create projections for the next 100 years identifying trends and probable climatic developments – but it is impossible to apply the resulting information on the scale of a single city or city district without undertaking detailed analysis first. Such climate analyses, therefore, do not provide specific planning information; rather, they are a form of stocktaking, with the Earth's atmosphere as the subject. The reductions in greenhouse gas emissions that the governments of many countries have committed to must be implemented by specific adaptation on a local level.

For designers, this means focusing on both avoiding (or "mitigating") additional greenhouse gas emissions and on adapting to the foreseen climate changes ("adaptation"). Integrating options for reducing greenhouse gas emissions into local planning is the greatest challenge currently facing urban planning, with all innovations depending first and foremost on the commitment of those responsible and on the support of the wider public. Visual presentations are helpful in juxtaposing strategies for avoiding additional greenhouse gases with strategies for adapting to the consequences of climate change. To achieve this purpose, scientific insights must be represented in a generally comprehensible and non-distorted way, reduced to key statements. It is important to present the impact climate change will have within a human lifetime. The impact of the pictorial directness of visual presentations makes it particularly important to clearly state all preliminary assumptions and underlying scientific information; as these representations are prognoses rather than design projects, the basis for the predicted situation should always be provided in full.

### Example 1: Retreat of the snow line

The projected consequences of climate change include the retreat of the snowline. In the research project "VisuLands", new computer-assisted visual presentation tools were created to represent changes to Entlebuch, a UNESCO biosphere reserve in Switzerland. One goal of this project was to promote public participation in the landscape change debate. Both scenically and with regard to its animal and plant life, the Entlebuch cultural landscape has unique features

3.16 - 18

**Top left: The present-day snow-covered area: the starting point of alterations to snow line in Sörenberg, Switzerland, brought by climate change.**
The blue fields represent areas that already receive artificial snow. The black lines represent ski lifts and cable cars, and the blue lines represent ski slopes.

**Top right: The year 2100. The snow line has risen to 1,500 m.**
This scenario suggests that it is very unlikely that skiing tourism will continue to be economically feasible below the green line, which represents the snowline.

**Bottom right: The "worst case scenario". The snow line has risen to 1,800 m.**

**Visualizations: Olaf Schroth.**

of national and international significance, and it is also a significant region for tourism and agriculture. Created by investigating and representing the interactions between the visual and functional qualities of landscapes, the visual presentations are intended to help both designers and the public assess the implications of different landscape planning strategies.

For this project, Olaf Schroth develops scenarios for the retreat of the snowline. He compares their consequences for the Swiss community of Sörenberg (1,500 m above sea level) in the year 2100 and, in another case study, the consequences of the different scenarios at 1,800 m above sea level (Ills. 3.16 -18). By itself the underlying data is insufficient to convey a picture of the implications of the retreating snowline. It takes the visual presentations to reveal the inevitable changes snowline retreat would bring to the use of the mountain landscape in winter.

The three-dimensional perspective drawings are based on a digitally created landscape model. Once a correct model has been created, the various changes in the snow line are easy to represent. It is important to use objective prognoses – particularly for the step-by-step application of the global or (at best) regional model to local circumstances.

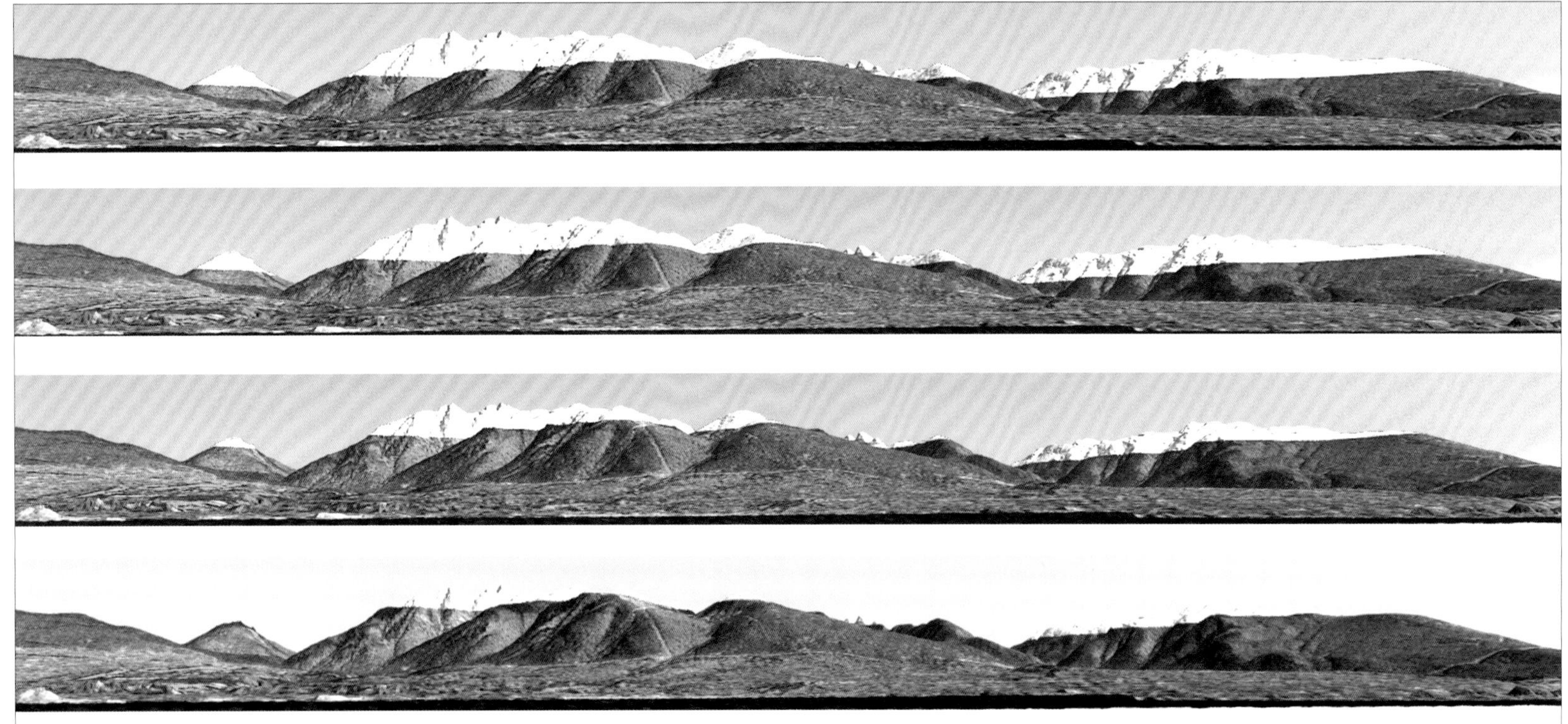

3.19-22

From top to bottom:

Average snow line for the Northshore Mountains, Canada, in the year 2000: at approximately 759 m.

Predicted average snow line for the year 2020: at approximately 789 m.

Predicted average snow line for the year 2050: at approximately 920 m.

Predicted average snow line for the year 2100: at approximately 1074 m.

Visualizations: David Flanders and Stephen Sheppard.

3.23-26

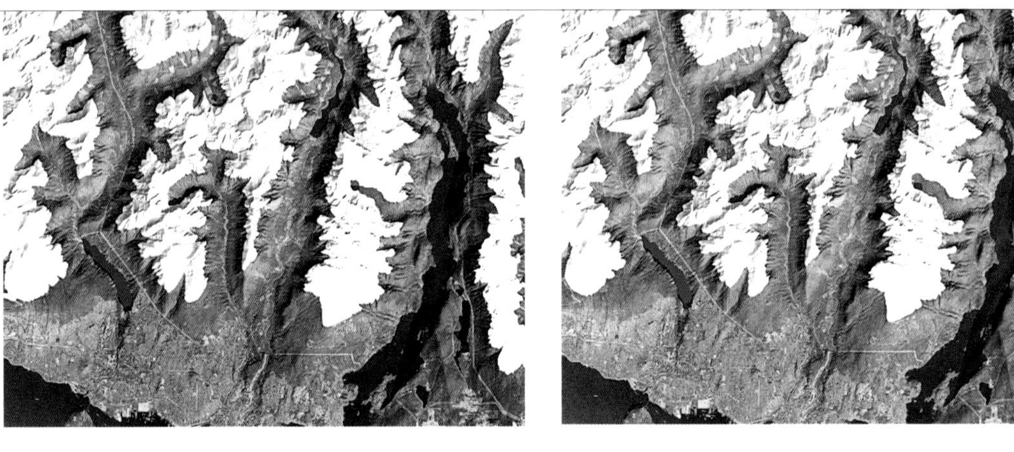

Top left: Average snow line for the Northshore Mountains in the year 2000: at approximately 759 m.

Top right: Predicted average snow line for the year 2020: at approximately 789 m.

Bottom left: Predicted average snow line for the year 2050: at approximately 920 m.

Bottom right: Predicted average snow line for the year 2100: at approximately 1074 m.

Visualizations: David Flanders and Stephen Sheppard.

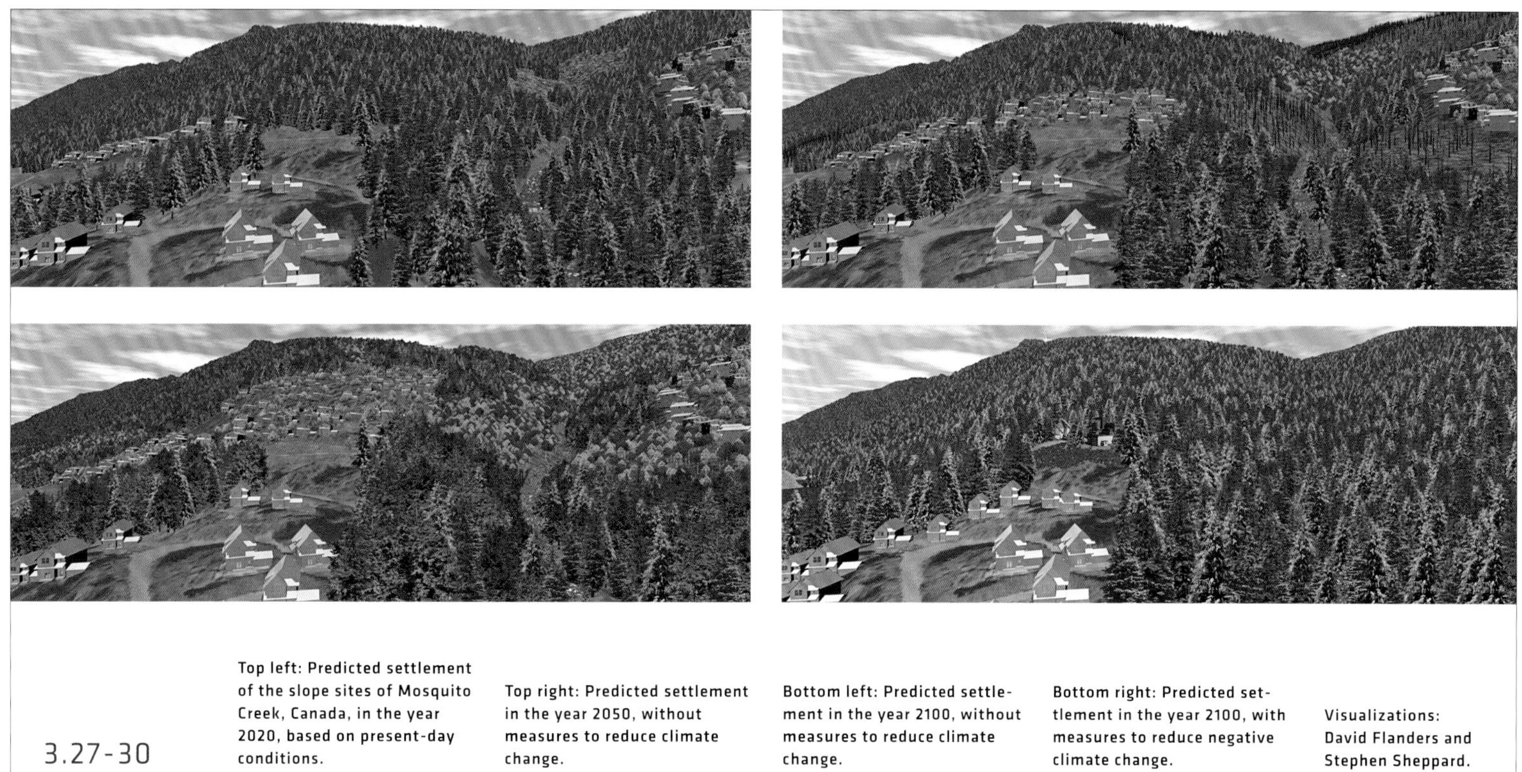

3.27-30

Top left: Predicted settlement of the slope sites of Mosquito Creek, Canada, in the year 2020, based on present-day conditions.

Top right: Predicted settlement in the year 2050, without measures to reduce climate change.

Bottom left: Predicted settlement in the year 2100, without measures to reduce climate change.

Bottom right: Predicted settlement in the year 2100, with measures to reduce negative climate change.

Visualizations: David Flanders and Stephen Sheppard.

The Collaborative for Advanced Landscape Planning (CALP) is an informal group of researchers from a variety of disciplines at the University of British Columbia in Canada, specializing in visual presentation of landscapes, human perception of the environment, managing of public open spaces and sustainable landscapes. To visually represent localized climate change for interactive participation processes involving citizens and decision-makers, this group creates impressive, engaging and easy-to-understand scenarios. Landscape architects David Flanders and Stephen Sheppard have created various projects both for landscapes and for urban areas.

The predicted snowline retreat in the Northshore Mountains in Vancouver as a result of climate change was visually presented for various years between 2000 and 2100, both from the perspective of a person on foot at a distance and from a bird's-eye view (Ills. 3.19-22 and 3.23-26).

## Example 2: Sprawl landscape

Images were created representing various scenarios for the Mosquito Creek area (Ills. 3.27-30) on the slopes of the Northshore Mountains in North Vancouver. These correspond to the IPCC scenario groups A1, A2, B1 and B2. First, a normal development extrapolated from events in many other locations is displayed, beginning with urban sprawl and increased development of slope regions leading to deforestation, creation of open spaces and construction of roads (by the year 2020). By 2050, urban sprawl expands into wooded areas; the representations include the first forest fires which are caused, among other things, by climate change. With no change in the trend, development would bring more urban sprawl by 2100, impairing ecosystem function, damaging forests and changing the slope's water balance. Where suitable measures are taken, on the other hand, the visual presentation of the area in the same year shows a largely intact landscape with sustainably managed forests and streams, high-density, concentrated building development and land used for biomass production.

## Example 3: Urban growth: Delta and Beach Grove

For the Greater Vancouver Regional District ("Metro Vancouver"), the Collaborative for Advanced Landscape Planning (CALP) developed a method of translating the challenges of global climate change into possible actions on the local level. They used visual presentations based on digital landscape models, applying several alternative climate scenarios. The climate scenarios are derived from the hypotheses of the IPCC's third assessment report on climate change in 2001. Essentially, there are four different scenarios, with different amounts of $CO_2$ in the atmosphere. The optimal variant assumes a reduction in $CO_2$ emissions, while the pessimistic variant is a "business as usual" scenario and the two additional variants are located somewhere between the two. Once again, it was Flanders and Sheppard who conducted studies based on these scenarios, this time for the community of Delta, and created visual presentations of the results. 85 % of Delta's inhabitants work in other locations, making commuter traffic a major cause of high $CO_2$ emissions.

The visual presentation starts with a bird's-eye view of the urban waterside location and its surrounding landscape in the year 2000 (Ill. 3.31), a view familiar to the town's inhabitants from aerial photographs. Assuming that the global population continues to grow rapidly, economic growth continues as well and $CO_2$ emissions triple, average temperatures would increase by 3.75 °C and the sea level would rise by 58 cm. If development were to continue unchecked, the town would expand into the flood plain area by the year 2100, necessitating a high dike wall to protect the new development from flooding (Ill. 3.33).

A city plan optimally adapted to the necessities of climate change would combine living and working space, thereby reducing commuter traffic (Ill. 3.35). Decentralized biogas and biomass power plants on agricultural sites could produce $CO_2$-neutral energy. This would change the face of the city as well as its surroundings, its space management policy and its recreational facilities.

Visual presentations have to be continually refined and compared with results from up-to-date climate research; the results of the most recent research, for instance, suggest that the sea level may rise even more than expected. Nevertheless, the images impressively demonstrate that a plan to prevent climate change influences from damaging the city is both necessary and potentially effective.

3.31

The city of Delta near Vancouver, Canada in the year 2000.

Visualizations: David Flanders and Stephen Sheppard.

3.32

Flooding in the event of a burst dike, assuming unchecked development.

3.33

Development by the year 2100, assuming unchecked growth and continuing high $CO_2$ emissions.

3.34

Reduced urban sprawl and greater concentration in the inner city, with appropriate urban density.

3.35

Development with increased concentration of the inner city and reduced $CO_2$ emissions, showing commercial and residential areas, integrated in a mixed-use plan, as well as biogas and biomass power plants.

3.36 - 39 Top left: The community of Beach Grove today.

Top right: Projected impact of climate change in the event of a storm surge in 2100, if growth and the behavior of the population do not change for the better and $CO_2$ emissions continue to rise.

Bottom left: Development in 2100, with mitigated climate change conditions.In an urban planning response to climate change, the row of houses nearest the water is replaced with an open space planted with flood-resistant trees.

Bottom right: Development with low-energy houses, local wind energy plants and local food production.

Visualizations: David Flanders and Stephen Sheppard.

Part of the Beach Grove community, situated on Delta's coast, was visually represented by Flanders and Sheppard, both under present conditions and in light of different future climate scenarios (Ills. 3.36 - 39). Due to their large scale, these pictures are much more detailed. The bird's-eye views clearly show their character as digitally produced images, but they are specific enough to allow people involved with the area to identify the locations they are familiar with. They represent the implications of the different variants in a way that is easily comprehensible and allows comparison. These pictures are also intended to make both the wider public and those responsible in the worlds of politics and planning aware of the opportunities and options inherent in urban planning and architectural design when climate change is taken into consideration.

3.40 - 41

Photograph of the high street in the community of Burnaby in Vancouver, Canada, documenting the present-day situation.

Representation of what the city would look like after interventions to reduce $CO_2$ emissions.

3.42 - 43

Photograph of a typical suburb on a sloping site.

Representation of possible changes to the suburb by the year 2050 if the government of British Columbia keeps to its goals of reducing $CO_2$ emissions.

Visualizations: David Flanders and Stephen Sheppard.

## Example 4: Developments in the cityscape

Even more effective than series of representations showing change over time are Flanders and Sheppard's juxtapositions of the present and future state of cityscapes. If the goals for the reduction of $CO_2$ emissions are retained and implemented, that would deeply influence the changes to be expected. In these scenarios (Ills. 3.40 - 41), the issues include low-emission public transport, creation of footpaths and cycle paths, higher-density construction, decentralized, local energy production and local food production to avoid high food-miles counts and overuse of valuable open spaces. This friendly, harmonious presentation method is an effective way of promoting the envisioned change to the city's development.

The proposed planning changes are not necessarily spectacular, as is demonstrated by the simulation of a typical suburban scene (Ills. 3.42 - 43). By 2050, photovoltaic plants and electrically powered vehicles, more local shopping and use of available green spaces for growing vegetables could be helping to reduce $CO_2$ emissions. The visual presentation emphasizes the importance of changing lifestyles as well as the city plan. This is a theme which is likely to be unpopular if phrased as a decree, or presented as a renunciation of the consumer lifestyle, but the image represents the changes in a more friendly way.

The images created for this purpose are not necessarily "beautiful" or perfect, as they can only show the level of detail provided by geodata and model-based assumptions. They do not show a perfect situation that could be reached through short-term building interventions, nor are they a dramatic way of representing climate change; instead, they are a way of conveying its implications and presenting possible (or indispensable) strategies to counteract it.

Unlike plans and visual presentations for specific design projects, the main challenge in creating these visual presentations was to translate scientific information based on a wider picture into concrete suggestions and represent it on a scale appropriate to a human community.

The suggestions and contrasts presented in the images must be specific enough to reveal the advantages and disadvantages of different alternatives, while the visualizations must remain recognizable as what they are – images of a possible situation, rather than a reality.

# STRATEGIES **SCENARIOS**

## Scenarios as a basis for guiding and designing the growth of major cities

Where a city is predicted to grow substantially over future decades, those concerned must consider whether development can continue along the same lines as in the past or whether the priorities should change. As a rule, the built-up area actually grows more quickly than the city's population, as the demands made on residential and working space are increasing. The siting of workplaces and residential complexes in the transition zones between town and open countryside accelerates urbanization. Globalization exacerbates this process by favoring large industrial and trade building complexes which take up a lot of space. These transition zones are heavily affected by the negative consequences of urban growth, and they remain vital to the provision of food, energy, water and construction materials for the city. This urbanization process calls for land-use planning that promotes the positive potentials and shapes the sustainable development of cities over the long term.

This is a task unprecedented in its dimension, which assigns to landscape architecture a unique role in urban development, as it is capable of bringing together diverse needs and creating an integrated plan for the future. Megacities with more than 10 million inhabitants may be impressive due to their population size not achieved until the 1950s, but urban growth can be expected to take place mainly in comparatively small cities. The former view that urban growth is inevitably a bad thing is today set against the advantages of a high population density. Although cities cause environmental problems, they also hold the greatest potential for a sustainable future – if problems are recognized and overcome. As a general rule, smaller cities can solve the typical problems of urbanization more easily, but as yet few of them have actually addressed them. For these challenges to be addressed in a creative way as well as overcome in administrative terms, a unified and long-term vision tailored to the needs of the individual city is requested. This vision should cover the issues of how urban space should be used for building, open space, infrastructure and services; how built structures and open spaces should be designed; what sources of energy and materials should be used and what distances should be covered by which forms of transport.

Becoming involved in possible creative solutions, also by way of visualizations, allows a large percentage of the population to take an active part in designing the future of their city. Images of the implications of planning principles reach more of those concerned than administrative initiatives or political discussions. Citizens are generally very interested in the future of their city, when they are properly informed about the relevant processes and involved in the proceedings. Municipal authorities must present the visual presentations for discussion in an appropriate participation process.

## Example: Scenarios of development for the city of Perth

This project for the Australian city of Perth creatively represents ways to achieve a highly developed synthesis of city and landscape in the course of urban growth. The criteria taken into account were the "urban ecological footprint", water provision for the population, ground quality as well as climate change management and the positive effects of globalization (in making use of a global range of techniques and gains).

Perth's current population of 1.5 million is predicted to double by the year 2050, due to a booming economy and a mass influx of new inhabitants. Not only does this mean that the number of homes and other buildings will roughly double, it also means that the whole of the city's infrastructure will have to increase its capacity to 200 %. The development of the past 179 years will have to repeat itself within the next 41 years.

Present-day Perth is 100,000 ha in size and 170 km long, making it one of the most spread-out cities in the world. 88 % of its surface area serves as living space, with most of the inhabitants living in detached houses in suburban districts. One consequence of this is that the "urban ecological footprint" for Perth – the surface area needed to support an individual's lifestyle and standard of living given present production conditions – is one of the largest of the world. The city government has endorsed a strategic framework plan for the city's development until 2032 known as "Network City", intended to limit urban sprawl, meet the challenges of climate change and curb the consumption of water, mineral oil and other scarce resources. This plan sets out a series of principles and goals, but from the point of view of landscape architect Richard Weller it also has a number of shortcomings. Its proposals do not extend far enough into the future, its guidelines are based on a surface area use increased by urban sprawl and no alternative development options are identified. The lack of plans or visual presentations to support this vision for the development is a particular issue of criticism. For this reason, the framework plan was unable to attract the necessary attention, with both insiders and the public at large puzzled as to how its verbal descriptions would be translated into forms and shapes.

This was the starting point for Richard Weller and his team for elaborating city development scenarios with clear targets and creating appropriate visual presentations of these that can be used to promote a public discussion. They use tried-and-tested landscape planning methods combined with creative landscape architecture solutions and advanced urban planning. Their alternative scenarios represent the city in 2050, with a wider timeframe than that of the city framework plan.

In an initial comprehensive analysis of the relevant landscape conditions, the authors identified 118,000 ha of land as suitable for urban development from a landscape-ecological perspective. This was land that was neither too steep nor subject to flooding, had already been cleared and was of low quality, while not including swamp areas, waterside zones, areas with natural vegetation or areas vital to groundwater recharge. Most of this surface area presently sees little or no agricultural use. If this land were to be developed to a moderate density of 12 houses per hectare, with 2.3 people living in each unit, the city would easily have enough space to cope with the predicted doubling of its population. However, extending up to 120 km from the inner city, this scenario would result in an increase in private automobile traffic. Without further planning, the probable result would be the total overdevelopment of the Perth area. The following scenarios suggest alternatives to this.

Out of seven scenarios, four deal with urban expansion in the landscape beyond the city boundaries, while the other three illustrate possible developments within today's urban areas. Their guiding principles are elaborated partly by taking theoretical urban development models from the past and factoring in modern-day needs and the preferences of Australian citizens, and partly by evolving new possibilities.

The first group are scenarios permitting expansion of settled areas beyond the present built-up area.

"Food City" is a scenario based on Frank Lloyd Wright's Broadacre City plan (1932 to 1958), an American urban planning utopia. The low construction density and dependence on automobile traffic appear problematic, but the interspersing of residential and industrial areas with agricultural land would reduce the city's ecological footprint, particularly if most essential foodstuffs were produced within the city itself. Assuming a similar level of productivity to that of European agriculture, food for 3 million people could be grown on 60,000 ha of land. Out of the available 118,000 ha of land, 58,000 ha would then remain for 1.5 million people to live on, requiring a moderate construction density of 15 houses per hectare – still significantly more than for the Broadacre City concept, and three times more than the average Perth suburb of today. This scenario also includes plans for public transport lines, which would also serve already existing suburbs.

In the bird's-eye perspective (Ill. 3.44), the viewer is joined by a man in a hat; a likeness of Frank Lloyd Wright, who inspired this scenario. This marks the picture as a visionary model, while the word "scape" on the horizon draws our attention to the fact that a landscape is considered here in terms of design. Various touches accompanying this visualization of ideas state clearly that it would be neither possible nor desirable to implement the represented scenario on a 1:1 basis.

"Garden City" applies the ideas of Ebenezer Howard, which were published for the first time in 1898. Howard envisioned small, compact urban units surrounded by agricultural green belts (Ill. 3.45). In this plan, each garden city would have a designated size of 404 ha, and would be surrounded by 2020 ha of agricultural land. 32,000 inhabitants would live in each of these cities, which would have a building density of 40 houses per hectare. To accommodate the predicted growth, Perth would need 48 garden cities; these would be connected to each other and with the existing city by a rail link. The garden cities could be positioned on the most favourable

3.44

"Food City" a scenario for integrating agricultural, industrial and residential landscapes. Richard Weller.

3.45

"Garden Cities" arranged around the city's present-day built-up area.

sites within the available 118,000 ha of land; they would need 19,392 ha of land, while the remaining land could be used for parks, agricultural land and forest planting to offset the city's carbon footprint, as well as the creation of ecological habitats.

In a bird's-eye perspective, the proposed garden cities are laid out on the area earmarked for settlement as varied circular forms. They appear as new independent and coherent settlements. The inserted figure – a honey-bee – is less conspicuous than in the first scenario, and seems in terms of scale to correspond better with the viewer's perspective. Once again, it emphasizes that the image serves as an example of an extreme scenario, rather than a fully developed and finely detailed proposal.

The proposed individual identity for each garden city is demonstrated as clearly as the constant number of inhabitants and surface area (Ill. 3.46). The circular form used for the schematic representations is a rather atypical shape for a district or individual city, but it fits well with the ideal of the garden city. In all the patterns, built-up areas and the course of roads can be made out – with the exception of one field shown beneath a magnifying glass, which invites the viewer to take a closer look. It shows an ancient Roman master builder with the archetypal tool of his trade. He is in the process of founding a new city. Only when the image is reproduced at a sufficient magnification and looked at very carefully does the difference between this circle and the other fields become apparant.

The "Sea Change City" scenario envisions the city expanding along the line of the coast, with its 1.5 million new inhabitants living in single-family homes close to the sea – the dream of many people. A 2 km wide strip development along the coast is shown (Ills. 3.47-48). Residents would not be more than 25 minutes from the water. Applying the usual low construction density of 12 houses per hectare, the city would expand by 600 km. This development would be supplied by trains and hydrofoil craft, while water would be provided by wind-powered desalination plants. Such a development should be situated high up, to prevent future rises in sea level from endangering the houses. The development has a form based on the existing topographical contour line.

The bird's-eye view emphasizes the city's extreme expansion. Coast, sea and sky are realistically represented. A figure of a flying pelican in the first image extends beyond the picture's boundaries, thereby creating a certain dynamic. The second image shows the urban development from closer by, represented in a much more schematic way and very uniformly illustrated. It shows the infrastructure, supply lines, centres, wind-powered desalination plants and routes for the hydrofoil craft. A zeppelin has been added, appearing to overfly the city district at a great height. Whether it also plays a role in the function of the city is unclear. In any case, the figure helps to clarify the scale and the viewer's distance from the represented city.

3.46

"Garden City", scenario with 48 garden cities, each with 32,000 inhabitants.

3.47

"Sea Change City", city development along the coast.

3.48

"Sea Change City".

"Tree Change City": This scenario takes into account the possibility that not all citizens will wish to live along the coast. A series of villages would be situated in a recultivated area of 1.2 million hectares within the bend of the Avon River: the area necessary to offset the city of Perth's $CO_2$ emissions. It would also contain a "solar forest": 100 km² of land with solar arrays, envisioned as providing the city of Perth with energy in 2050. The images (Ills. 3.49 - 50) are a cartographic representation of the situation and spread of the city plus the size and spread of the recultivated area. Additionally, the bird's-eye view shows the expansion of the city into the interior, the position of the districts, the recultivated areas and the areas for solar arrays. In this picture, we clearly see the dimensions of the areas required for the first time.

In the first four scenarios, the city is permitted to expand beyond its present boundaries, but without creating unplanned urban sprawl. The second group of scenarios shows possible ways to develop the city within its existing boundaries. At present, 23,000 ha of land on the edge of town are earmarked for residential developments. If the average low building density of 12 houses per hectare is maintained, there will be enough space for 634,800 additional residents, while creating further residential units would mean increasing the density. These scenarios assume that living space will still be needed for an additional 865,200 people after the available 23,000 ha have been built on.

Three scenarios entitled "Sky City", "River City" and "Surf City" were developed corresponding to three favoured residential locations: near the coast, on the river and in the inner city. All three envision local developments that would increase the city's density. As increasing urban density is generally regarded with disfavour, these plans also represent a move to make the citizens aware of this probable necessity.

"Sky City": In this scenario, increased density and high-rise development are permitted, but are coupled with favourable locations. Rather than showing designs for individual buildings, the images represent the density involved: 250 living units per hectare. Three such cities are proposed, all located in desirable environments within the landscape and housing a total of 450,000 residents in 20-storey developments. The high-rise buildings envisaged for the inner city are represented schematically as identical stelae, which are "flown in" in the bird's-eye view (Ill. 3.52). In Ill. 3.51, the three selected city districts are shown using the ground plan as a basis for an urban model. Le Corbusier is shown at the top right, apparently building the city on his worktable. Le Corbusier's 1933 publication *La Ville radieuse* propounded the principle of the "radiant city", on which this scenario is based. In a symbolic way, the period desk lamp emphasizes this connection. As with the other scenarios, the inserted figure on an unusual scale serves to characterize the represented developments as virtual.

In "River City", the higher-density city districts are arranged along the river, in a good residential area. In the first of the two variants represented (Ills. 3.53 - 54), the development runs along two roads which are parallel to the river but are situated some distance away from it. This would give residents good access to the traffic network and a good view of the river. With a density of 250 living units per hectare, such a development could provide living space for 500,000 people.

On the planimetric map of the city this strip city type is represented by a red area, while the water surface of the river is highlighted in dark blue. Landing stages, jetties and bridges are marked in along the water. In the bird's-eye view, the highly developed, compacted city areas

3.49 "Tree Change City", development of a recultivated area of sufficient surface for balancing the carbon emissions of Perth.

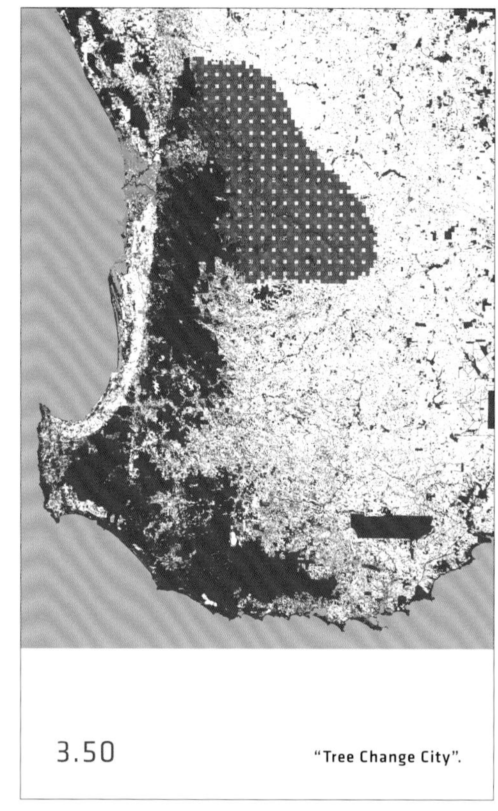

3.50 "Tree Change City".

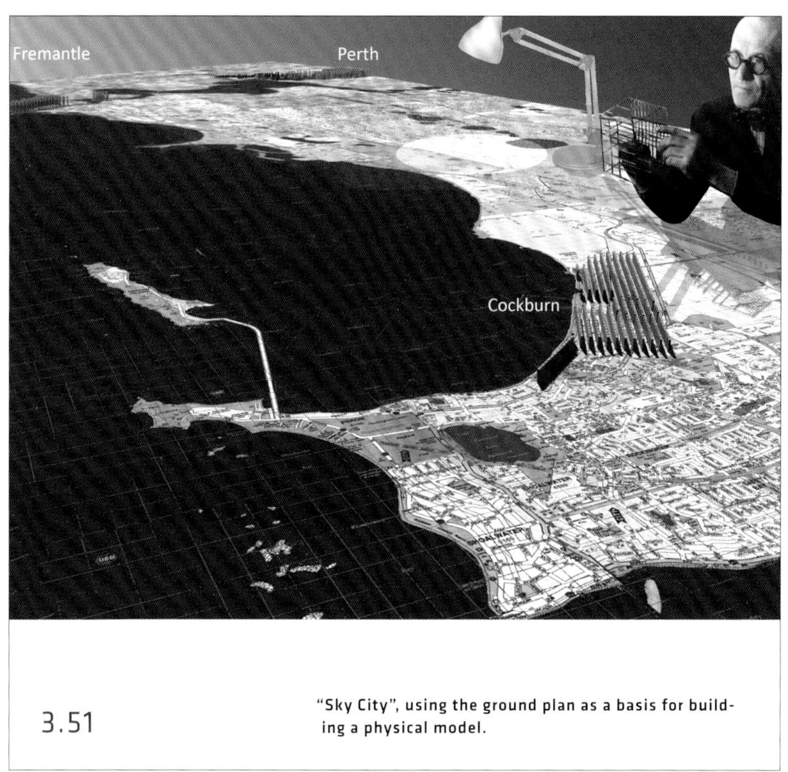


3.51 "Sky City", using the ground plan as a basis for building a physical model.

3.52 "Sky City", bird's-eye view perspective with a strong effect of convergence.

3.53 "River City", scenario with high-density city districts along the river. Two-dimensional ground plan.

3.54 "River City", bird's-eye view perspective.

3.55 "River City", variant with development directly on the Swan River and with "living bridges" over the river.

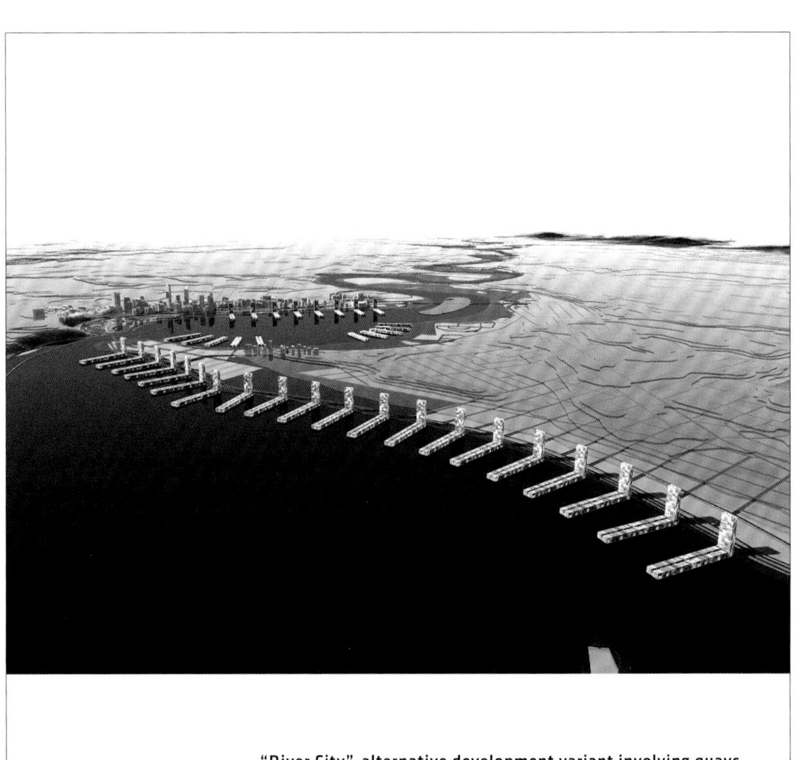

3.56 "River City", alternative development variant involving quays along the river.

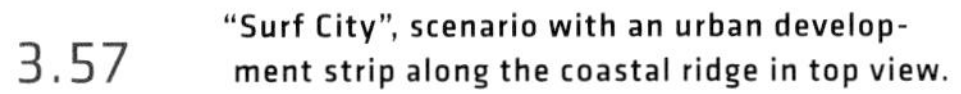

3.57 "Surf City", scenario with an urban development strip along the coastal ridge in top view.

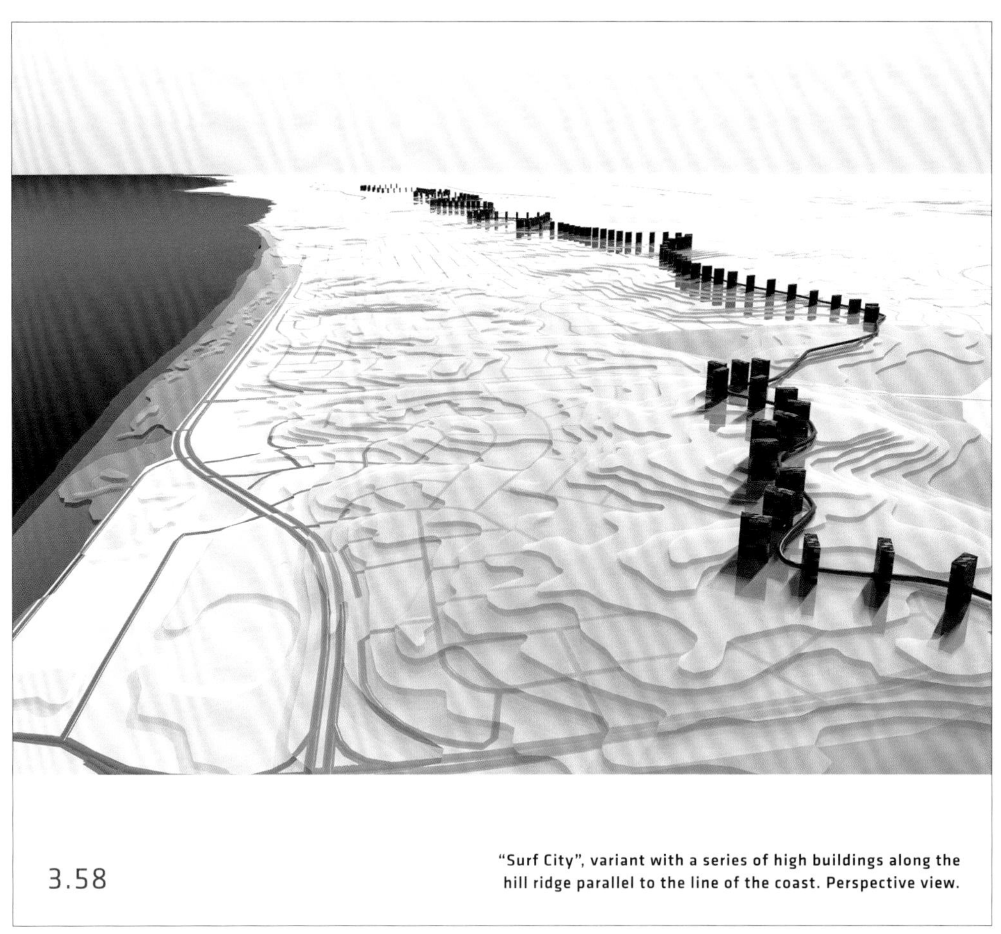

3.58 "Surf City", variant with a series of high buildings along the hill ridge parallel to the line of the coast. Perspective view.

are also represented in red. The houses are grouped together in blocks, the recreational areas along the coast and the river are marked in green and the city is overlaid on a representation of its topography, with the existing urban districts visibly marked.

A variant on the "River City" scenario involves placing developments on quays and bridges over the river (Ill. 3.55). This plan would reinforce the city's connection to the river and revitalize it, but could only create accommodation for 50,000 people. The bird's-eye view for this design (Ill. 3.56) shows it from a moderate distance, with the blocks of buildings and bridges displayed schematically on the city plan as white structures and leaning to one side at the edges of the picture due to the perspective chosen. The quay-type residential developments at regular intervals along the river banks are shown from a greater distance.

The "Surf City" scenario involves developing Perth's coast, which is approximately 160 km long and has previously not been heavily developed. The coast is represented as a red line on a city map. As high-density development of areas near the water is expected to be unpopular, a variant strip-city type development on a less sensitive tract of land, on the foremost hill ridge along the coast, was also envisioned (Ills. 3.57-58).

As well as environmental conditions, water resources etc., the scenarios presented here also take into account the options offered by today's construction industry and aim to enhance the local culture and economy. They present extremes in order to give a clear picture of the consequences. Detailed planning and a more human perspective will be needed before their social, ecological and economic implications can be fully understood. In the meantime, however, they help to stimulate the public debate on the city's future; they are frequently displayed and meeting with a great deal of interest. This design work on a large scale shows landscape architecture taking a leading role in solving the major urban development challenges of the future.

## Illustration credits

**Cover** SLA, Copenhagen, Denmark

**Page 8** Dr. Gabriele Holst, landscape architect, Berlin, Germany

**0.1-5** akg-images

**0.6** Stiftung Preußische Schlösser und Gärten Berlin. Brandenburg, Planslg. 3674

**0.7** Stiftung Preußische Schlösser und Gärten Berlin. Brandenburg, Planslg. 3705

**0.8** Architekturmuseum TU Berlin, inv. no. 19296

**0.9** Architekturmuseum TU Berlin, inv. no. MK 10-008

**0.10** Architekturmuseum TU Berlin, inv. no. MK 10-011,1

**0.11** Architekturmuseum TU Berlin, inv. no. 40421

**0.12** Architekturmuseum TU Berlin, inv. no. 27294

**0.13** Architekturmuseum TU Berlin, inv. no. 27290

**0.14** Kamel Louafi, Landschaftsarchitektur, Landschaftskunst, Berlin, Germany

**0.15** Adelheid Rosenkranz, Landschaftsplanung und Geo-Allchemy, Miltenberg, Germany

**0.16-18** Inga Schröder, Dipl.-Ing. Landschaftsarchitektur, Zurich, Switzerland; from: „Erarbeitung eines Freiraumkonzeptes für eine neu entstehende Wohnbebauung in Horgen am Zürichsee", PhD thesis, Hochschule Neubrandenburg, 2008

**0.19-24** Turenscape, Beijing, China

**0.25** Neumann Gusenburger, Berlin, Germany

**0.26-28** CBCL Limited, Halifax, Canada

**0.29** Gustafson Porter, London, Great Britain

**0.30-31** Heavy Meadow, Principal: Abigail Feldman, New Orleans, Louisiana, USA

**0.32** Abigail Feldman

**0.33-34** SLA

**Page 30** Gabriele Holst

**Pages 33, 35** Jan and Jens Steinberg, Landschaftsplanung, Grafik und Malerei, Berlin, Germany

**1.1** Landschaftsarchitekturbüro Stefan Pulkenat, Gielow, Germany

**1.2-3** Turenscape

**1.4** Stefan Pulkenat

**1.5** Catherine Mosbach, Paris, France; © Kazuyo Sejima + Ryue Nishizawa/SANAA/Imrey Culbert/Catherine Mosbach

**1.6** Stefan Pulkenat

**1.7-8** Neumann Gusenburger

**1.9** Stefan Pulkenat

**1.10** Shunmyo Masuno + Japan Landscape Consultants, Yokohama, Japan

**1.11-12** Turenscape

**1.13** Stefan Pulkenat

**1.14** Gustafson Porter

**1.15-16** Neumann Gusenburger

**1.17** Lutz Mertens, Mertens & Mertens, Berlin, Germany

**1.18-19** Turenscape

**1.20** GROSS.MAX, Edinburgh, Great Britain

**1.21** Gustafson Porter

**1.22** Grupo Verde Ltda., Cundinamarca, Colombia; Martha Fajardo, Noboru Kawashima, Douglas Franco

**1.23** SLA

**1.24** GROSS.MAX

**1.25** Gustafson Porter

**1.26-29** plancontext landschaftsarchitektur, Berlin, Germany

**1.30-31** GROSS.MAX

**1.32-33** West 8 Urban Design & Landscape Architecture bv, Rotterdam, Netherlands

**1.34-35** Stefan Pulkenat

**1.36-37** GROSS.MAX

**1.38** Shlomo Aronson, Landscape Architects, Town Planners and Architects, Jerusalem, Israel

**1.39** Neumann Gusenburger

**1.40-41** West 8

**1.42** GROSS.MAX; Mark Dion

**1.43-45** Stefan Pulkenat

**1.46-49** WES & Partner Schatz Betz Kaschke Wehberg-Krafft Landschaftsarchitekten, Hamburg, Germany

**1.50** Judy.Green.Landscape.Architecture, Jerusalem, Israel; in co-operation with the Lawrence Halprin practice, San Francisco, USA

**1.51-52** Stefan Pulkenat

**1.53** Gustafson Porter

**1.54** Turenscape

**1.55** SLA

**1.56** Catherine Mosbach

**1.57** Turenscape

**1.58** Neumann Gusenburger

**1.59** plancontext with Peter von Klitzing Architekten, Berlin

**1.60** plancontext

**1.61-62** Stefan Pulkenat

**1.63** GROSS.MAX

**1.64** Abigail Feldman

**1.65** Neumann Gusenburger

**1.66** Stefan Pulkenat

**1.67** Lenné3D GmbH, Berlin, Germany; "Strawberry Fields Forever" with Jan Walter Schliep commissioned by the Leibniz-Zentrum für Agrarlandschaftsforschung

**1.68** Dirk Stendel, Landschaftsvisualisierung, Berlin, Germany

**Pages 71 (2), 72 (3)** Jan and Jens Steinberg

**1.69-70** CBCL Limited

**1.71** Turenscape

**1.72** lohrer.hochrein landschaftsarchitekten, Munich, Germany; in co-operation with UIA Paris

**1.73** lohrer.hochrein; in co-operation with stegepartner Architektur und Stadtplanung, Dortmund, und ambrosius blanke verkehr.infrastruktur, Bochum

**1.74** Grupo Verde Ltda.; Martha Fajardo, Noboru Kawashima, Douglas Franco

**1.75-77** Grupo Verde Ltda.; Martha Fajardo, Noboru Kawashima, Chen Yingfang

**1.78-79** lohrer.hochrein; in co-operation with ambrosius blanke verkehr.infrastruktur, Bochum

**1.80** Neumann Gusenburger

**1.81** Turenscape

**1.82** Grupo Verde Ltda.; Martha Fajardo, Noboru Kawashima, Chen Yingfang

**1.83** plancontext

**1.84** West 8

**1.85** WES & Partner; with Schweger Associated Architects

**1.86** West 8

**1.87** GROSS.MAX

**1.88** West 8

**1.89** GROSS.MAX

**1.90** RMP Stephan Lenzen Landschaftsarchitekten, Bonn, Germany; with bloomimages, Hamburg

**1.91** Stefan Pulkenat

**1.92** WES & Partner; with Hans-Herman Krafft, Berlin

**1.93** West 8

**1.94** plancontext

**1.95** Noack Landschaftsarchitekten, Dresden, Germany; with virtual-architects, Dipl.-Ing. Damian Idanoff

**1.96-97** WES & Partner; with Schweger Associated Architects

**1.98-100** GROSS.MAX

**1.101-103** SLA

**1.104** GROSS.MAX

**1.105** lohrer.hochrein

**1.106** lohrer.hochrein in co-operation with stegepartner Architektur & Stadtplanung, Dortmund

**1.107-108** WES & Partner with Observatorium group of artists, Rotterdam

**1.109** Shlomo Aronson

**1.110** Neumann Gusenburger

**1.111** Turenscape

**1.112-113** Neumann Gusenburger

**1.114** GROSS.MAX

**1.115** Grupo Verde Ltda.; Martha Fajardo, Noboru Kawashima, Chen Yingfang

**1.116** Turenscape

**1.117** plancontext

**1.118** Gustafson Porter

**1.119-121** Turenscape

**1.122-123** WES & Partner; with Schweger Associated Architects

**1.124** Grupo Verde Ltda.; Martha Fajardo, Noboru Kawashima, Chen Yingfang

**1.125** SLA

**1.126** GROSS.MAX

**1.127** SLA

**1.128** Neumann Gusenburger

**1.129** plancontext

**1.130** Shunmyo Masuno + Japan Landscape Consultants

**1.131** Gustafson Porter

**1.132** Grupo Verde Ltda; Martha Fajardo, Noboru Kawashima, Chen Yingfang

**1.133** plancontext; with karl+probst Architekten, Munich

**1.134-136** Neumann Gusenburger

**1.137** West 8

**1.138** GROSS.MAX

**1.139-140** Michel Desvigne, Paris, France

**1.141a/b** Stefan Pulkenat

**1.142-145** Neumann Gusenburger

**1.146-147** RMP Stephan Lenzen with bloomimages, Hamburg

**1.148-149** Noack; with virtual-architects, Dipl.Ing. Damian Idanoff

**1.150** Abigail Feldman

**1.151-152** plancontext; with Peter von Klitzing Architekten, Berlin

**1.153** Turenscape

**1.154-155** Christian Meyer, Garten- und Bepflanzungsplanung, Berlin, Germany

**1.156-1.157** Lenné3D

**1.158** Dirk Stendel

**1.159** Abigail Feldman

**1.160-166** Michel Desvigne

**Page 120** Gabriele Holst

**2.1-25** Turenscape

**2.26-47** Neumann Gusenburger

**2.48-52** RMP Stephan Lenzen

**2.53-56** West 8

**2.57-62** James Corner Field Operations, New York, USA; with Diller Scofidio + Renfro, Piet Oudolf

**Page 158** Gabriele Holst

**3.1-15** Turenscape

**3.16-18** Olaf Schroth, Institut für Raum- und Landschaftsentwicklung, ETH Zurich; from: EU-project VisuLands with Prof. Willy A. Schmid, Prof. Eckart Lange, Dr. Ulrike Wissen (all Swiss Federal Institute of Technology ETH, Zurich), Canton of Lucerne, UNESCO Biosphere Entlebuch

**3.19-26** David Flanders, Stephen Sheppard, University of British Columbia, Canada, Collaborative for Advanced Landscape Planning CALP

**3.27-43** David Flanders and Stephen Sheppard

**3.44-58** Richard Weller, University of Western Australia, Faculty of Architecture, Landscape and Visual Arts, Crawley, Australia; project funded by the Australian Research Council and conducted by Richard Weller in collaboration with Professor David Hedgcock, Head of the School of Built Environment, Art & Design, Curtin University of Technology; the research team includes Research Associates Donna Broun and Karl Kullmann with assistance from Julia Robinson and Phivo Georgiou.

## Film credits

**Museumsplatz Wien, 3D rendering clip**
Stefan Raab, Norbert Brandstätter,
interactive 3D open space design visualization of the new Museumsplatz in Vienna, diploma project for the Vienna University of Technology/University of Natural Resources and Applied Life Sciences, Vienna, 2001.

**Green Dragon Park, Shanghai, special features; Green Dragon Park, Shanghai, landscape structure and function; Orange Island, Changsha**
Turenscape, Beijing, China.

**Biomass in future landscapes, a virtual landscape exploration in pictures**
Lenné3D GmbH, Berlin, Germany,
commissioned by the Deutsches BiomasseForschungs-Zentrum, supported financially by the Ministry of Transport, Building and Urban Development (BMVBS), 2009.

**Shortcut**
Janine Koch, Philipp Hegnauer, 2006
**Affoltern eingekreist**
Luca Pestalozzi, Peter Leibacher, 2008
Swiss Federal Institute of Technology, Zurich, Institute of Landscape Architecture,
Professor Christophe Girot,
Assistance:
Susanne Hofer, Pascal Werner, Fred Truniger
Experimental videos on the perception of landscape.

## About the author

Dr.-Ing. Elke Mertens is a landscape architect and member of the Federation of German Landscape Architects (bdla). After training as a landscape gardener she studied at the Technical University of Berlin where she worked subsequently as an academic assistant, gaining her doctorate with a thesis on the climate of urban building structures in 1997. After a period of free-lance work she was appointed, in 1998, to the garden architecture department at the Hochschule Neubrandenburg, University of Applied Sciences, where she teaches presentation technology and design, which is her major teaching area, with some subsidiary aspects.

As professor, Elke Mertens represents the Hochschule Neubrandenburg's Landscape architecture and environmental planning section at the European Council of Landscape Architecture Schools (ECLAS) and has been a member of the Executive Committee there since 2006. She is a member of the Steering Committee for the European "LE:NOTRE" network, which was established by ECLAS.

## Subject index on visualization in landscape architecture

## Index of practices and projects

Dirk Stendel, Landschaftsvisualisierung,
Berlin, Germany
www.3d-landschaften.de

Schematic representation and example of the lenticular screen technology
1.68

Schillerplatz, Schweinfurt, Germany
1.158

Turenscape, Beijing, China
www.turenscape.com

Qiaoyuan Park, Tianjin, China
0.19, 1.2, 1.18-19, 1.54, 1.111, 1.119

Green Dragon Park, Shanghai, China
0.20–24, 1.11-12, 1.57, 1.71, 1.81, 1.120-121, 1.153

Orange Island, Juzizhou, Changsha, China
1.3

Yanshan Gas Implements Factory Park, Beijing, China
1.116, 2.1-25

Ecological planning for Taizhou and surroundings, China
3.1-15

Richard Weller, University of Western Australia, Faculty of Architecture, Landscape and Visual Arts, Crawley, Australia

Scenarios for the possible growth of Perth and its ecological, urban, and free-space planning aspects
3.44-58

WES & Partner, Schatz Betz Kaschke Wehberg-Krafft Landschaftsarchitekten, Hamburg, Germany

Slagheap in Moers, Germany
1.46-49, 1.107-108

Dubai Pearl, United Arab Emirates
1.85, 1.96-97, 1.122-123

City centre, Göttingen, Germany
1.92

West 8 Urban Design & Landscape Architecture bv, Rotterdam, Netherlands
www.west8.nl

Grand Egyptian Museum, Cairo, Egypt
1.32-33, 1.84

Île Saint-Denis, Paris, France
1.40-41, 1.137

Governors Island, New York, USA
1.86, 1.88, 1.93

Competition for Toronto Waterfront, Canada
2.53-56

## Historical projects

Vasily Ivanowich Bajenov
Adam Fountain in the park of Peterhof Palace, 1796
0.5

Erwin Barth
Garden plan for a villa in Potsdam, c. 1901
0.11

Joan Blaeu
Tycho Brahe's Uranienbaum castle on the island of Hveen, 1663
0.2

Charles Cameron
Pavlovsk Palace, c. 1780
0.4

Herta Hammerbacher, Hermann Mattern

National Horticultural Show of the Federal Republic of Germany in Kassel, general plan, 1955
0.12

National Horticultural Show of the Federal Republic of Germany in Kassel, bird's-eye view of the entire show site
0.13

Peter Joseph Lenné

Plan of Charlottenhof or Siam, 1839
0.7

Plan of Sanssouci and surroundings including the project of introducing flowing waters and fountains and of embellishing the promenade ways, 1816
0.6

Tiergarten near Berlin, 1840
0.8

Gabriel Perelle
Park of the Palace of Versailles, Bassin d'Apollon, c. 1670
0.3

Ippolito Rosellini
Garden on the Nile, 1832
0.1

Gotthilf Ludwig (Louis) Runge
Plan of a villa with gardens, 1835
0.9

Ernst Steudener
Plan of a villa with gardens, 1835
0.10

## Bibliography


Andrews, Jonathan. *Architectural Visions. Contemporary Sketches, Perspectives, Drawings.* Berlin: Verlagshaus Braun, 2009

Bendfeldt, Jens, Klaus-Dieter Bendfeldt. *Zeichnen und Darstellen in der Freiraumplanung. Von der Skizze zum Entwurf.* Stuttgart: Eugen Ulmer Verlag, 2002

Bertauski, Tony. *Plan Graphics for the Landscape Designer. With Section-Elevation and Computer Graphics.* Upper Saddle River, New Jersey: Pearson Prentice Hall, 2002

Bielefeld, Bert, Sebastian El Khouli. *Basics Design Ideas.* Basel, Boston, Berlin: Birkhäuser, 2007

Buhmann, Erich, Christina von Haaren, William R. Miller (Eds). *Trends in Online Landscape Architecture. Proceedings at Anhalt University of Applied Sciences.* Heidelberg: Herbert Wichmann Verlag, 2004

Buhmann, Erich, Matthias Pietsch, Marcel Heinz (Eds). *Digital Design in Landscape Architecture 2008. Proceedings at Anhalt University of Applied Sciences.* Heidelberg: Herbert Wichmann Verlag, 2008

Cejka, Jan. *Darstellungstechniken in der Architektur.* Stuttgart: W. Kohlhammer Verlag, 1999

"Darstellung". Thematic volume of *Garten + Landschaft*, 3/2008.

Davis, David A., Theodore D. Walker. *Plan Graphics.* Hoboken, New Jersey et al.: John Wiley & Sons, 1990

De Jong, Eric, Michel Lafaille, Christian Bertram: *Landschappen van verbeelding. Vormgeven aan de Europese traditie van de tuin- en landschapsarchitectuur 1600-2000.* Rotterdam: NAi Uitgevers, 2008

Doyle, Michael E. *Color Drawing. Design Drawing Skills and Techniques for Architects, Landscape Architects and Interior Designers.* Hoboken, New Jersey et al.: John Wiley & Sons, 2006

Garmory, Nicola, Clare Winsch, Rachel Tennant. *Professional Practice for Landscape Architects.* Oxford et al.: Architectural Press by Elsevier, 2007

Griffin, Anthony W., Victor Alvarez-Brunicardi. *Introduction to Architectural Presentation Graphics.* Upper Saddle River, New Jersey: Pearson Prentice Hall, 1998

Henz, Thomas. *Gestaltung städtischer Freiräume.* Berlin, Hanover: Patzer Verlag, 1984

Holder, Eberhard, Martin Peukert. *Darstellung und Präsentation. Freihand und mit Computerwerkzeugen gestalten. Ein Handbuch für Architekten, Innenarchitekten und Gestalter.* Stuttgart, Munich: DVA, 2002

Holst, Gabriele. *Der Weg des Kreativen am Beispiel des Kritzels. Bedeutung und Analyse von Empfindungsbildern als eine Vorstufe des landschaftsarchitektonischen Entwerfens.* Saarbrücken: Vdm Verlag Dr. Müller, 2008

Leonard J. Hopper. *Landscape Architectural Graphic Standards.* Hoboken, New Jersey et al.: John Wiley & Sons, 2007

Knauer, Roland. *Entwerfen und Darstellen. Die Zeichnung als Mittel des architektonischen Entwurfs.* Berlin: Ernst & Sohn Verlag für Architektur und technische Wissenschaften, 2002

Knauer, Roland. *Transformation. Basic Principles and Methodology of Design.* Basel, Boston, Berlin: Birkhäuser, 2008

Loidl, Hans, Stefan Bernard. *Open(ing) Spaces. Design as Landscape Architecture.* Basel, Boston, Berlin: Birkhäuser, 2003

Paar, Philip: *3D-Visualisierung als Bestandteil der Landschaftsplanung.* Contribution for the International Academy for Nature Conservation, October 2004

Pavord, Anna. *Gärten gestalten mit Pflanzplänen.* Munich: Christian Verlag, 2001

Porter, Tom, Sue Goodman, Bob Greenstreet. *Manual of Graphic Techniques for Architects, Graphic Designers, and Artists.* New York: Scribner, 1980

Prinz, Dieter. *Städtebau. Vol. 1: Städtebauliches Entwerfen.* Stuttgart: W. Kohlhammer Verlag, 1999

Prinz, Dieter. *Städtebau. Vol. 2: Städtebauliches Gestalten.* Stuttgart: W. Kohlhammer Verlag, 1997

Reid, Grant W. *Landscape Graphics.* New York: Watson-Guptill, 2002

Richter, Gerhard. *Handbuch Stadtgrün. Landschaftsarchitektur im städtischen Freiraum.* Munich: BLV Verlag, 1981

Schroth, Olaf. *From Information to Participation. Interactive Landscape Visualization as a Tool for Collaborative Planning.* PhD Thesis, Swiss Federal Institute of Technology, Zurich 2007

Sheppard, Stephen R. J. *Visual Simulation. A User's Guide for Architects, Engineers and Planners.* New York: Van Nostrand Reinhold, 1989

Stankowski, Anton, Karl Duschek (Eds). *Visuelle Kommunikation. Ein Design-Handbuch.* Berlin: Reimer Verlag, 1994

Steenbergen, Clemens. *Composing Landscapes. Analysis, Typology and Experiments for Design.* Basel, Boston, Berlin: Birkhäuser, 2008

Wang, Thomas C. *Plan and Section Drawing.* Hoboken, New Jersey et al.: John Wiley & Sons, 1996

Wöhrle, Regine Ellen, Wöhrle, Hans-Jörg. *Basics Designing with Plants.* Basel, Boston, Berlin: Birkhäuser, 2008

Layout and cover design: Oliver Kleinschmidt, Berlin

Translation from German: Michael Robinson with Alison Kirkland, London

Lithography: Licht & Tiefe, Berlin

Printing: Medialis, Berlin

Cover: Perspective view for the design for Gleisdreieck, Berlin, Germany. SLA.

This book is also available in German (ISBN 978-3-7643-8788-4).

Library of Congress Control Number: 2009935406

Bibliographic information published by Die Deutsche Bibliothek
Die Deutsche Bibliothek lists this publication in the Deutsche Nationalbibliografie; detailed bibliographic data is available in the Internet at <http://dnb.ddb.de>.


P.O.Box 133, CH-4010 Basel, Switzerland
Part of Springer Science + Business Media

Printed on acid-free paper produced from chlorine-free pulp. TCF ∞
Printed in Germany
ISBN 978-3-7643-8789-1

9 8 7 6 5 4 3 2 1

www.birkhauser.ch